# COMMAND OR CONTROL?

## Command, Training and Tactics in the British and German Armies, 1888–1918

MARTIN SAMUELS

FRANK CASS
LONDON

*First published in 1995 in Great Britain by*
FRANK CASS PUBLISHERS
Crown House, 47 Chase Side
Southgate, London N14 5BP

*and in the United States of America by*
FRANK CASS PUBLISHERS
ISBS, 5824 N.E. Hassalo Street
Portland, Oregon 97213-3644

*Website:* www.frankcass.com


Reprinted 2003

British Library of Cataloguing in Publication Data

Samuels, Martin
Command or Control?: Command, Training and Tactics in the British and German Armies, 1888–1918
I. Title
355.5

ISBN 0-7146-4570-2 (cloth)
ISBN 0-7146-4214-2 (paper)

Library of Congress Cataloging-in-Publication Data

Samuels, Martin.
Command or control?: command, training, and tactics in the British and German armies, 1888–1918 / Martin Samuels.
p. cm.
Includes bibliographical references and index.
ISBN 0-7146-4570-2 (cloth); 0-7146-4214-2 (paper)
1. Military doctrine-Great Britain-History-19th century.
2. Military doctrine-Great Britain-History-20th century.
3. Military doctrine-Germany-History-19th century. 4. Military doctrine-Germany-History-20th century. 5. Great Britain. Army-Organization. 6. Germany. Heer-Organization. 7. Great Britain. Army-Drill and tactics. 8. Germany. Heer-Drill and tactics.
I. Title.
UA647.S182 1995
355′.033541-dc20 95-7053
CIP



Typset in 10½pt/12pt Ehrhardt
by Vitaset, Paddock Wood, Kent
Reprinted in Great Britain
Anthony Rowe, Eastbourne, Sussex

# Contents

# Maps

# Foreword

For three-quarters of a century, from its victory in the Franco-Prussian war of 1870–71 until its defeat in the *Götterdämmerung* of 1945, the German army stood out from all its rivals by virtue of the sheer excellence of its fighting power. Other armies incorporated within their ranks specialised units which could demonstrate high levels of tactical virtuosity, and larger formations could – and did – perform outstandingly on individual battlefields. But for consistent excellence in combat performance the German army set a standard which none of its rivals could match. Indeed, Germany's defeats in the two world wars are now often ascribed to a degree of strategic ineptness, and a proclivity to make the same major mistakes twice, which seem in retrospect quite astonishing but which leave the German soldier still the undisputed master of his craft – although in neither war was he ultimately master of the field.

The First World War tested the German army as much as it tested all other combatants. Machine guns, barbed-wire, concrete bunkers, gas and high explosive shell combined to create an entirely new kind of battlefield. To survive and to succeed required that the pre-war rules of attack and defence be fundamentally rethought and reformulated, and that the new doctrines which resulted from this process then be effectively put into action.

In the pages that follow, Martin Samuels shows both why and how the German and British armies adopted quite different postures in the face of the new twentieth-century battlefield. The extent to which the German army succeeded in its task is evident in the contrast between the operational rigidity of the Schlieffen plan as executed by the German field army in August and September 1914, and the flexibility and fluidity which characterised the 'Michael' offensive which Ludendorff unleashed on 21 March 1918.

In adjusting to the new operational landscape, the German army had one important advantage over its British rival. Ever since 1806, German practice had incorporated a system of directive military command which devolved the control of battle to subordinate commanders. When, at quite an early stage in the war, senior German soldiers recognised that traditional pre-war infantry doctrines, which rested upon linear formations of infantry attacking with fixed bayonets, were quite unsuited to trench warfare, it was therefore possible to accommodate new methods of attack which empowered lower-level commanders to achieve their objectives through the use of dispersed formations and new combat techniques. In terms of both attack and defence – and in contradiction to a popular stereotype which still portrays the Great War as a continuous and unvariegated blood-letting – the speed with which the German army identified and analysed the new problems of attack and defence and evolved effective answers to them is quite remarkable. However, a command structure characterised by flexibility and a readiness to listen to creative criticism from relatively junior officers could show occasional signs of bureaucratic rigidity: despite its efforts, the German General Staff could not get the artillery expert Colonel Bruchmüller promoted to the rank of permanent colonel.

In contrast to Germany, Great Britain lacked both an established General Staff and an intellectual tradition to accompany it. A very different pattern of British generalship had developed by 1914 and persisted during the war – one which combined rigidity and inflexibility in planning with a marked reluctance on the part of senior commanders to interfere with any aspect of their subordinates' handling of divisions or corps. In the British army, disdain for – or incomprehension of – the kind of staff work which was characteristic of the German command system was both deep-rooted and long-lived: as late as 1941, discarding strategic and operational skills, Field Marshal Lord Wavell opined that administration was 'the real crux of generalship'.

It is perhaps scarcely surprising, then, to learn that the British GHQ possessed no equivalent to the German sections which developed and tested new tactical doctrines. Even the best Corps instructional schools such as Maxse's XVIII Corps School, set up in 1917, had no authority to enforce their methods on lower commanders. An even more telling observation which Martin Samuels draws from his analysis is that the British Army would probably have been unable to implement German doctrines even if they had properly understood them, as they required skills and practices which were beyond the capabilities of most British officers and men.

By juxtaposing the German and British armies as models for historical analysis, and by contrasting structural and functional differences between them as they went about their business of fighting one another between 1914 and 1918, Martin Samuels makes an important contribution to the literature of military effectiveness. The result is a genuinely comparative military history which, by contrasting two very different military institutions, matched against one another for four bloody years of continuous campaign, highlights the vital ingredients of German combat excellence. After critically re-examining them during the inter-war years, the *Reichswehr* would apply the doctrines devised by its predecessor to the campaigns of 1939–41. Thus, the Imperial German Army can fairly claim to have invented modern warfare during the Great War.

JOHN GOOCH

# Acknowledgements

The writing of this book was aided by the support of a number of people. The British Academy awarded me the financial assistance necessary for the research to be undertaken. The staff of the following establishments gave me invaluable help in gathering material: the departments of Printed Books and Documents at the Imperial War Museum; the Tactical Doctrine Retrieval Cell and the library of the Staff College, Camberley; the Liddell Hart Centre for Military Archives at King's College, London; the British Library; and the Public Record Office, Kew. Particular thanks are owed to the Trustees of the Liddell Hart Centre for Military Archives for permission to use and to quote from archives in their care. My thesis supervisor, Michael Elliott-Bateman, of the Department of Military Studies, University of Manchester, spent many hours discussing my ideas and provided constructive criticism of the manuscript. My wife, Helen, drew the maps and gave me support throughout. All translations from sources given in German in the bibliography are mine. Any errors or omissions are my own.

*Note*: In numbering military units, I have adopted the following conventions: First Army, I Corps, 1st Division, 1st Brigade. British battalions are denoted, for example, 1/Border. German battalions are given as I/175 and companies as 1/175.

# Introduction

> It may well be that my history will seem less easy to read because of the absence in it of a romantic element. It will be enough for me, however, if these words of mine are judged useful by those who want to understand clearly the events which happened in the past and which (human nature being what it is) will, at some time or other and in much the same ways, be repeated in the future.
>
> Thucydides

'Is the British Army 50 years out of date as a fighting force?'[1] asked Captain Graeme C. Wynne in 1957, arguing that the army was indeed out of date, owing to a failure to develop its tactical ideas beyond the sterile practices employed on the Somme and the retention of the concept that '*l'artillerie conquiert, l'infanterie occupe*'. Over the previous 20 years, Wynne had consistently pointed to differences between the methods used by the British and German armies and had contrasted the results achieved. Unlike many military theorists, Wynne based his arguments upon an unrivalled knowledge of the evidence. As a member of the Historical Section of the Committee of Imperial Defence from 1918 to 1956, he had played a major role in the production of the official history of the First World War on the Western Front. Although his name appeared on only one volume,[2] he was largely responsible for the two 1915 volumes, the first 1916 volume and the 1917 volumes on Vimy and Passchendaele. In short, the historical core, although not the editorial line, of the official history of the central part of the war was his work.[3] His knowledge of events on the British side was matched by his research concerning 'the other side of the hill'. His footnotes indicate that he examined hundreds of German regimental histories, as well as numerous personal accounts, and kept abreast of German analysis of the war.

Despite Wynne's unique knowledge and understanding of British and German military theory and practice, his conclusions were vigorously denounced.[4] In 1938, an editorial in the *Canadian Defence Quarterly* stated: 'In our opinion Captain Wynne's criticisms [of the British Army] are anything but reasonable and almost certainly are not founded upon fact.' It urged its readers to dismiss his ideas, claiming that he had completely misunderstood the modern British tactical doctrine, which was in any case, it argued, little different from German practice.[5] Although the Germans achieved a number of stunning successes at the beginning of the Second World War, their eventual defeat was widely seen as confirming the apparent superiority of British arms shown by the result of the First World War. Despite the accuracy of many of his predictions, Wynne was once again ignored and no reputable publisher was willing to touch his controversial material.[6]

The orthodoxy that the British Army had proved itself more effective than the German Army remained largely unshaken until 1977. In that year, a book was published which claimed to prove statistically that in fact the Germans had been over 20 per cent more effective, man for man, than the British in both world wars. The author of these astonishing claims, retired US Army Colonel Trevor Dupuy, based his assertions upon the results of a mathematical model of combat which he had developed, using data from the Italian campaign of 1943–44. Having taken every material factor into account and having adjusted for attack and defence, Dupuy found that he could match the historical outcomes of battles only by heavily weighting the German score.[7] The conclusions were startling:

> On the average, a force of 100 Germans was the combat equivalent of 120 American or 120 British troops. Further refinements in the model began to reveal that in terms of casualties the differential was even greater, with the German soldiers on the average inflicting three casualties on the Allies for every two they incurred . . . A less detailed analysis of World War I battles suggested that during that war the Germans had enjoyed a similar 20 per cent combat effectiveness superiority over the Western Allies, and also the same 3-to-2 casualty-inflicting superiority.[8]

Dupuy argued that the German superiority could not be dismissed as being due merely to circumstances or to particular skill at one form of combat. The Germans enjoyed a similar level of superiority 'when they were attacking and when they were defending, when they had local numerical superiority and when, as was usually the case, they were outnumbered, when they had air superiority and when they did not, when they won and when they lost'.[9] While Dupuy's figures are not without their difficulties, his basic contention, that the German Army was considerably more combat-effective than the British Army, is now generally accepted.

Although Dupuy's work is of great value in demonstrating the extent of German combat superiority, his analysis of the causes of this superiority is disappointing. Having rightly dismissed the idea of inherent militarism. Dupuy claimed the General Staff was the key to the 'institutionalising of excellence'[10] in the German Army. Although the General Staff was indeed a vital aspect of German combat effectiveness, to argue that this body alone was the cause of that effectiveness appears too one-dimensional an explanation.

Far more promising in this regard is Martin Van Creveld's *Fighting Power.*[11] In this wide-ranging work, Van Creveld contrasted German and US Army practices in areas such as officer selection, personnel management and training during the Second World War. Owing to the very multidimensional nature of his study, Van Creveld was able to do little more than demonstrate that the German and US armies operated different philosophies, there being insufficient space to examine these in detail or their effect in combat.

The aim of the present study is to adopt a middle way between the narrow focus of Dupuy's work and the broad focus employed by Van Creveld. The basic method is comparative analysis of the German and British armies between 1888 and 1918. As Van Creveld has shown, this method can produce a more rounded picture than if attention is focused on a single army in isolation.

The direction of the analysis is guided by a number of hypotheses. The first and most basic is that this study is not concerned with absolutes of effectiveness but with comparatives of effectiveness. The argument is not that the German Army was effective and the British Army was ineffective. It is that, in the given circumstances, the German Army's combat effectiveness was greater than that of the British Army. In war, it is often the army which is the least ineffective that achieves victory. In short, German combat superiority should be explained as much by British performance as by German performance. Study of the German Army in isolation can give only half the picture.

The second hypothesis is that the differences in effectiveness resulted in large part from different philosophies of combat. It is suggested that the German philosophy saw combat as inherently chaotic. The key to success was seen as being the ability to operate effectively in this uncertain environment. The British philosophy was that combat was essentially structured. Effectiveness was seen as being achieved through the maintenance of order.

The importance of the dialectic between the philosophy of chaos and that of structure may be illustrated by an examination of the concept of 'tempo'. When used in the military context, tempo has been defined as 'the actuality of total domination of the "being" of the enemy; that is, of his physical, mental and spiritual existence'.[12]

The essential concept of tempo is that the enemy force is so dominated by the actions of the force with tempo that it becomes unable to respond in any co-ordinated or effective fashion. Count Alfred von Schlieffen taught that 'the enemy, surprised by the suddenness of the attack must become more or less confused, thus following up his rash decisions with a hasty execution'.[13] As the actions of the enemy force become increasingly ineffectual, it enters a state of 'high stress', rendering clear thought all but impossible. If overwhelming pressure is maintained by the force with tempo, the enemy's 'central nervous system' collapses, the organisational equivalent of a nervous breakdown. Once this has occurred, the enemy force becomes largely unresponsive and may be annihilated with comparatively little further effort.

Briefly, the goal of inflicting a nervous breakdown is achieved through four stages. The first stage is marked by a sudden and violent action, intended to 'dislocate' one part of the enemy structure. 'Dislocation' has been defined as 'the displacement and disarrangement of parts causing a disordered state throughout the organism containing those parts'.[14] The second stage is the enemy's reaction to the initial dislocation. The third stage involves a second violent action at another point. The enemy, having committed his reserves, cannot react effectively to this new threat. The final stage involves further actions to maintain the pressure and so prevent the enemy regaining his balance. This allows the force with tempo to take full advantage of the enemy's confusion.

Essential to the question of tempo is 'rhythm'. It is rhythm that governs the pauses and timings essential if pressure is to be put on the enemy while confusion of the dominating force avoided. In this context, rhythm has been compared with a jazz improvisation session,

> where the whole band works to one broad harmonic framework or direction, but each individual player improvises upon it harmonically, melodically and rhythmically, introducing new shades of colour and new tensions and resolutions to intensify – or relax – the sense of pace over the underlying progression. It is the adaptability of individual initiative to emergent opportunities that makes the jazz session an evolutionary rather than a static process. Each player is sensitive to any change of direction, either from the lead instrumentalist or from something good arising out of the developing music, to which he then makes his own response, enhancing and exploiting it in accordance with his own skill and imagination.[15]

An essential feature of tempo is that the pressure of actions is maintained, giving the enemy no opportunity to recover his balance and analyse the situation, in accordance with the teaching of Clausewitz:

> It is one of the most important and effective principles of strategy: *a success gained somewhere must be exploited on the spot as far as the circumstances permit it*; for all efforts made whilst the enemy is involved in that crisis have a much greater effect and it is a bad economy of force to let this opportunity slip away.[16]

As more recent authors have written, effective and rapid exploitation

> involves the utilisation of a wide variety of opportunities created by the almost random fluidity of . . . warfare. These opportunities usually appear and disappear suddenly. Therefore, a tactical system that utilises decentralised decision-making, rapid movement, small-unit initiative, and imagination are basic if a military organisation is to convert these fleeting advantages into battlefield success. By contrast, tactical systems that stress set-piece battles, rigid schedules for reaching objectives, and tight central control do not create the conditions necessary for timely exploitation.[17]

The need to exploit fleeting opportunities was an essential part of the German philosophy of combat as being inherently chaotic. Von Schlieffen considered that the history of war presented but a catalogue of generals' mistakes. This led him to state that the aim of a commander should be to identify and exploit to the full the inevitable errors committed by the enemy.[18] General von Freytag-Loringhoven wrote: 'A mind that adheres rigidly and unalterably to original plans will never succeed in war, for success goes only to the flexible mind which can conform at the proper moment to a changing situation.'[19] Such a perception is entirely alien to the philosophy of combat as structured, where the emphasis is on steady progress based on centralised planning. The seizure of fleeting opportunities, which would inevitably disrupt this process, is therefore rejected. The incompatibility of this philosophy with the effective seizure of tempo is clear.

The third hypothesis is that these differing philosophies of combat were expressed most clearly in the command systems employed by the two armies. It is argued that the German system was largely one of 'directive command', while the British system was based on 'restrictive control' and 'umpiring'. Directive command is a command system in which decision-making is decentralised. Commanders at every level are assigned general tasks, allocated resources and then allowed to complete their tasks by means of their own initiative, within the context of the whole. Key characteristics are flexibility, independence and initiative. Restrictive control is based upon the centralisation of decision-making. Commanders are assigned detailed missions, which they must carry out exactly as prescribed. Key characteristics are rigidity, conformity and a reliance on exact orders.

The fourth and final hypothesis is that an army's philosophy of combat, and thus the command system which it employs, has a great effect upon the system of training and of tactics which it uses. The philosophy of chaos results in a demand for a very high level of training of both individuals and units and that the tactics used emphasise adaptability to circumstances and rapidity of response. The philosophy of structure has a far lesser emphasis on training, except on the development of rigid obedience, and the resulting tactics are characterised by standard solutions and detailed advanced planning.

In short, the difference in combat effectiveness between the German Army and the British Army may be best understood as a consequence of different philosophies of combat, as expressed in the command, training and tactical systems of the two armies.

An essential part of the argument is that it is the philosophy rather than the form of a system which is the key to its performance. On several occasions, the British sought to adopt the mechanics of certain parts of the German system, such as its system of elastic defence-in-depth in the winter of 1917–18. In each case, there was little understanding of the underlying philosophy. The result of such attempts to graft alien techniques onto a radically different philosophy was invariably a gross distortion of the system supposedly copied. The resulting hybrid possessed the advantages of neither philosophy and the disadvantages of both.

Finally, it should be noted that although the German command system was largely based upon the concepts of directive command, it would be incorrect to equate the two. Directive command is a theoretical system and as such it is a pure extreme. The German command system was a reality, employed by an organisation of millions of men. As such, it was a compromise between directive command and restrictive control, with individuals varying as to which system they favoured. It would therefore be erroneous to argue that the German command system represented directive command pure and simple. One can state only that the German command system was largely based upon the concepts of directive command and that this was the dominant, though not exclusive, philosophy. The same care must be taken with the relationship of the British command system with restrictive control.

# 1
# Directive Command and the German General Staff

> In issuing orders, detailed instructions should be especially avoided in cases where circumstances may have changed before the order can be carried out . . . The general views of the commander for the conduct of the intended operation should be given, but the method of execution must be left open. An order thus issued assumes the nature of a *directive*.
>
> *Felddienst Ordnung* 1908

> A superior should never prescribe from a distance, what a subordinate on the spot is in a better position to determine for himself.
>
> Colmar von der Goltz

A constant thread running throughout German military history has been the need to achieve rapid and decisive victories in the face of potentially overwhelming odds. With a strategy of attrition therefore ruled out, victory had to be sought through qualitative superiority. Such superiority may be achieved by a variety of means. In 1870, the superior technology of the Krupp steel breech-loading cannon gave the Prussians a decisive advantage against the French bronze muzzle-loading guns, but all the Continental powers rapidly adopted the new technology. Indeed, German field guns were inferior in design to the French 75 mm cannon throughout the First World War. Von der Goltz considered that any technological advance would soon be copied. Superiority must therefore be sought in intangibles, primarily training and command.[1]

Training has long been recognised as a combat multiplier, but it must be geared to the circumstances of battle to be truly effective. A training system designed for an imperial garrison is unlikely to be appropriate for a Continental war. Further, advances in technology affect tactics, which in turn affect training. To rely upon achieving a superior level of training would therefore appear to be a dangerous policy, justified only for a long-service regular army facing a short-service conscript army. Since after 1870 Continental armies could swamp any regular army by sheer weight of numbers, such a policy was out of the question for Germany.

If qualitative superiority could not be guaranteed by technology or training, much could be achieved through an effective command system. If the individual soldier could not be decisively superior to the enemy, better direction of his actions could be. The essence of qualitative superiority through command is to employ the combat power of individual units at the decisive point and to multiply that combat power through the effective co-ordination of all the units involved. Central to this process is the *Schwerpunkt*.

## *Schwerpunkt*

As with many German military terms, it is difficult to translate *Schwerpunkt* into English adequately. The term was first applied to war by Clausewitz, who borrowed it from physics,[2] where the *Schwerpunkt* is the 'centre of gravity'. In a military context, it is usually translated as 'point of main effort', but this misses the full meaning of the term. We therefore suggest that a better translation might be 'focus of energy'.

Although apparently first defined in a military context by the *Reichsheer* in the 1920s, the *Schwerpunkt* was central to German military thought by the 1870s.[3] It was based on Clausewitz's maxim, 'The forces available must be employed with such skill that even in the absence of absolute superiority, relative superiority is attained at the decisive point.'[4] The concept of the *Schwerpunkt* was that this decisive point must be identified and all available energy focused upon it: victory at the decisive point rendered reverses elsewhere unimportant, whereas 'economy of force' at the decisive point might result in defeat, rendering victories at other points meaningless. Martin Van Creveld has shown that the *Schwerpunkt* applied not only to combat operations, but pervaded the entire approach to war of the German Army:

> The German Army . . . develop[ed] a single-minded concentration on the operational aspects of war [which it considered the decisive point] to the detriment, not to say neglect, of everything else. A fighting force first and foremost, the army's doctrine, training, and organisation were all geared to fighting in the narrower sense. In striking a balance between function-related and output-related tasks, it spent comparatively few resources – sometimes, perhaps, too few – on logistics, administration, or management. It systematically and consistently sent its best men forward to the front, consciously and deliberately weakening the rear. In matters of pay, promotion, decorations, and so on, its organisation was designed to produce and reward fighting men. It went for quality, and quality was what it got. In this, without doubt, lay the secret of its fighting power.[5]

The importance of the concept is evident from Hindenburg's maxim, 'An attack without a *Schwerpunkt* is like a man without character'.[6]

The *Schwerpunkt* applied equally to both attack and defence. In defence, it might be either ground of decisive importance, or an enemy force. An example of a ground-related *Schwerpunkt* occurred during the first day of the Somme, 1 July 1916. The 36th (Ulster) Division's initial attack seized the Schwaben Redoubt, which lay on the crest of a ridge and enjoyed excellent observation in all directions. The local German commander realised that possession of the redoubt was the key to the entire defensive system in that area: his *Schwerpunkt* was therefore its recapture. Six battalions were assigned from the reserve for a counterthrust.[7] An enemy-related *Schwerpunkt* was used at Neuve Chapelle, on 10 March 1915. An attack by four British divisions had breached a wide gap in the German defences. The commander of the only reserve immediately available, Jäger Bataillon 11, decided that the greatest danger was not a penetration deeper into the German defences, but any attempt to widen the gap already made. His *Schwerpunkt* was therefore the flanks of the British break-in. Accordingly, the four infantry companies of Jäger Bn 11 were sent to reinforce the defenders at those points. Only the machine-gun and cyclist companies held the head of the gap, against 48 British battalions.[8]

The *Schwerpunkt* was equally essential in attack, where the need was to penetrate rapidly through the entire depth of the enemy defensive system. Any partial penetration was of little value, as enemy reserves could soon restore the depth of the position, leaving the attacker in a dangerous salient. Deep penetrations were required, not broad linear advances. This could be achieved only through the identification of critical points in the defensive system, such as areas of weakness or positions whose capture would unravel the whole of the defence of a particular area, which became the attackers' *Schwerpunkte*. The unit attacking such a point became the *Schwerpunkt* of its formation and the efforts of all the other units in the formation were directed towards assisting it achieve its objective. On 21 March 1918, one German regiment, the *Schwerpunkt* of its division, was supported by a number of elite storm troopers, with their own infantry guns and flamethrowers, one company of elite machine-gunners, a unit of specialist mountain machine-gunners, the divisional mortar company, a battery of field guns, a battery of infantry guns, and half a platoon of *Pioniere* (combat engineers). If the regiment's own integral weapons are included, this unit was supported by 75 heavy weapons, for an attack on a 500-metre frontage.[9] Despite this concentration of forces, the location of a *Schwerpunkt* was not static. If greater success or opportunities were encountered elsewhere, the *Schwerpunkt* would be shifted: 'Put in reserves at the points where the enemy is giving way, *not* at the point where he is holding out.'[10]

A central feature of the *Schwerpunkt* was the *Absicht* (higher intent). To understand how this operated, it is necessary to examine briefly the mechanics of the German command system:

> The German army used mission statements . . . in the form of the commander's intent [*Absicht*] . . . The commander then assigned tasks (*Aufträge*) to subordinate units to carry out his and his superior's intent. The subordinate commander decided upon a specific course of action which became his resolution (*Entschluss*). The German army, therefore, did not build the commander's intent into a particular mission or vice versa . . . A subordinate commander could change or abandon his task within the framework of the higher commander's overall intent.[11]

Each part of the directive had a different priority, from the subordinate's own task, through his commander's intent, up to the intent of his commander's superior. While the situation remained as expected, the subordinate could follow his own task, sure in the knowledge that this was the best means of achieving the higher intents. Should the situation change, as it often would in combat, rendering his task no longer appropriate or offering greater opportunities elsewhere, the subordinate could relate his actions to his commander's intent, or even to the intent of his commander's superior. A vital necessity was for officers to be able to understand how their actions fitted in to the picture 'two-up'.

The *Schwerpunkt* concept meant that an officer was trained to identify the decisive element of a confused situation and focus his energies upon it. This involved two fundamental requirements. First, an order was not immutable, demanding absolute submission to its every letter. Orders, in the form of *Direktiven*, were guides to enable the commander on the ground to identify the decisive element. The second requirement was a common body of thought, a doctrine, which would ensure commanders agreed on the decisive element in a given situation and on the most effective response.

## Directive Command

The command system in which officers were guided by directives rather than orders was called *Führung nach Direktive* (directive command). A further dimension of this concept may be understood by reference to the current Bundeswehr term, *Innere Führung* (self-motivation or command from within). *Führung nach Direktive* required officers to act from their own motivation and be guided, rather than driven, by their superiors. Although the key development of this concept was made by Helmuth von Moltke,

Chief of the General Staff (CGS) from 1857 to 1888, its origins appear to lie in the Napoleonic Wars.

Directive command first entered official German usage in the Prussian *Exerzier-Reglement* of 1806.[12] The commander of an army was required, if possible, to show the ground to be fought over to his divisional commanders and to explain to them his general intent. The details of exactly what each division was to do were to be left to its commander. The rationale was that, even at this early date, the overall commander could not keep detailed control over all the actions of his army, due to the sheer size and fluidity of the battle. He therefore had to concentrate upon keeping an accurate overall picture in his mind, so that he might use his reserves to the greatest effect.

This system was extended in 1813. Owing to the large number of different national contingents, grouped into several separate armies, strict central control proved to be impossible. Instead, the army commanders were given general directives and allowed to act independently within these. The main factor in the adoption of this system of command appears to have been the number of different national forces, rather than questions of time and space, since Napoleon continued to employ a more centralised command system, often with considerable success.[13]

The principle of decentralised command had become firmly rooted by the mid-nineteenth century. In an essay, dated 1860, Prince Frederick Charles of Prussia stated:

> [It] seems to me to lead to the conclusion that in the Prussian corps of officers nowadays *there is a stronger desire for independence from above and for taking responsibility upon one's self than in any other army . . . This habit of thought has undeniably had an influence on our battle tactics.* Prussian officers object to being hemmed in by rules and regulations, like officers in . . . England. With officers like ours you cannot fight a formal defensive action of the kind that Wellington introduced, whereby every individual is bound by rules and procedures. We look at the way things tend to go and leave the individual more freedom to use initiative; we ride him on a looser rein, back up each separate success even if it had run counter to the intentions of a commander-in-chief such as Wellington, who used to insist on having full control over every unit at all times. But that you cannot have if subordinate commanders, without the knowledge or instructions of their seniors, go off into action on their own, exploiting each and every advantage, as they do with us.[14]

It was, however, during Moltke's 30 years as CGS that the system of directive command was established as a coherent theory, adapted to the prevailing circumstances, and enforced as official doctrine. Moltke's use of directive command appears to have been driven by both practical and theoretical factors. In practical terms, it became increasingly clear that centralised control over the ever-growing armies of Moltke's day was impossible. Difficulties of central command were increased by many senior commanders being princes appointed for dynastic rather than military reasons. Some of these princes were too confident of their own abilities and were not amenable to receiving orders from men of a lower social standing. As regards theory, Moltke believed that best use could be made of the abilities of subordinates if they were allowed to fight their own battles, guided by general directives, rather than being restricted by detailed orders.

Moltke's practical experience was gained between 1864 and 1871 in the Wars of Unification, as Prussia asserted her dominance over Germany against Denmark, Austria and France.

In 1864, the Prussian General Staff was a minor advisory body, with little influence and no power of command. Indeed, Field Marshal Wrangel, who was appointed to the field command against Denmark, 'declared that a General Staff was wholly unnecessary and that it was a shame and a disgrace for a Royal Prussian Field Marshal to have a lot of "damned clerking" put on him'.[15] In Berlin, Moltke knew that the field commanders were incompetent, but he had no access to official reports nor power of command. He solved these problems by the expedient of private correspondence with a number of General Staff officers in the field. On the basis of the information he was given, Moltke drew up operational plans, which he advised commanders to follow. Although it may be presumed that his General Staff contacts did their best to persuade their commanders to accept Moltke's advice, the execution of the plans was poor.[16] The war was going badly and Moltke was appointed to replace Wrangel's chief of staff, General Vogel von Falckenstein. Wrangel himself was soon succeeded by Prince Frederick Charles, whose views on the independent spirit of the Prussian officer we have already noted. Victory soon followed and Moltke's reputation was made.

The important factor for the development of directive command was that Moltke's plans in the first stage of the war had been compiled far from the theatre of hostilities, in Berlin, and had been purely advisory. These plans, therefore, had to be more general and give commanders on the spot more room for individual initiative than under the 1806 regulations.

General Patton, arguably America's finest combat general in the Second World War, said that command is only ten per cent about giving orders, but 90 per cent about seeing that they were carried out. Viewed from this perspective, Moltke's position was weak indeed. Although he was granted the right to issue orders in the name of the king on 2 June 1866,[17] a month before the victory over Austria at Königgrätz, Moltke's authority was by no means unquestioned. The right to issue orders only came into operation upon mobilisation. In peace, the CGS had no powers of inspection or command over any part of the German Army except the General Staff itself,[18] nor did he have any decisive influence over the appointment of senior commanders.[19] Although he was the de facto commander-in-chief in war, therefore, the CGS had no official power to enforce his views upon the army in peacetime. The result was seen in 1870, when commanders repeatedly came near to upsetting Moltke's plans by ignoring his directives.[20]

The theoretical factor in Moltke's use of directive command was the greater geographical spread of combat in his day, a result of reliance upon a limited rail network by mass armies. The commander of such a dispersed army who insisted on centralisation could either attempt to lay down the course of a campaign in advance, or he could try to control his forces by telegraphed orders. Moltke rejected both solutions as being unsuited to the development of maximum fighting power. He declared that it was impossible to lay down actions in advance, because 'no plan of operations survives the first collision with the main enemy body'.[21]

Moltke equally rejected the idea of telegraphed orders. Given a force of over one million men, as in 1870, moving as several separate armies spread over a previously-unheard-of front, it was impossible for Moltke to rely on a system of close control and yet still take advantage of fleeting opportunities offered by enemy mistakes. The sheer scale of the problem meant that, even if he were able to identify such opportunities (itself highly unlikely), any detailed orders he might give would long since be out of date by the time they came to be implemented:

> The advantage which a commander thinks he can attain through personal intervention is largely illusory. By engaging in it he assumes a task which really belongs to others, whose effectiveness he thus destroys. He also multiplies his own tasks to a point where he can no longer fulfil the whole of them.[22]

It was necessary to decentralise the command system. This may be illustrated by reference to the 'Boyd Loop', a concept developed by Colonel Boyd of the US Air Force from his analysis of aerial combat.[23] According to Boyd, participants in combat, be they fighter pilots or whole armies, go through a series of loops, each of four stages: observation, orientation, decision, action. In the first stage, the participant observes the current situation, noting the strength and location of his own and the enemy's forces. This data is then analysed in the second stage, in order to understand the situation. The third stage is marked by the participant deciding upon a particular course of action, the carrying out of which marks the fourth stage.

According to Boyd, victory will tend to go to the side which goes through the loop faster and more effectively. This is because the slower opponent will still be reacting to one action when the faster side has already begun another action which makes the opponent's original reaction inappropriate. As the combat continues, the slower side's actions become increasingly inappropriate, causing extreme stress to its commanders. Boyd's approach fits closely into the concept of tempo. The usefulness of the Boyd Loop is that it highlights the need to decentralise decision making in order to speed reaction times, because the referral of decisions to higher authority is always a time-consuming process. Moltke's command system was designed precisely to reduce these delays in the cycle.

In 1870, the range and rate of fire of artillery and small arms still allowed armies to fight in relatively compact bodies. While national armies had increased enormously, such that they needed to be sub-divided into several 'armies', it was still possible for an 'army' of several corps to be involved in a single battle on a relatively small frontage. While individual army or corps commanders could still be on the field of battle, able to see events for themselves and react rapidly to them, this was no longer possible for the commander-in-chief, concerned as he was with several separate armies.

The difference between 1806 and 1870 was that, whereas the commander in 1806 had been able to show his subordinates their missions on the ground and to co-ordinate them personally, in 1870 Moltke was in the rear, unable to see the ground or to keep track of events in 'real time'. His solution to this problem was to cut himself out of the Boyd Loop, as far as tactical decisions were concerned:

> Moltke refrained from issuing any but the most essential orders. 'An order shall contain everything that a commander cannot do by himself, but nothing else.' This meant that the commander-in-chief should hardly ever interfere with tactical arrangements. But Moltke went beyond this. He was ready to condone deviations from his plan of operations if the subordinate general could gain important tactical successes, for, as he expressed it, 'in the case of tactical victory, strategy submits'.[24]

An excellent description of directive command in operation is given by Bradley Meyer:

> In practice, it meant that higher headquarters would do two things. The first was to let subordinates in on the thinking of the high command by describing the overall intentions of the high command. The second was to issue directives and (usually general) orders to the subordinate units. Then, in theory, the local commander could combine his knowledge of the overall intentions of the high command

> with his detailed and up-to-date knowledge of the local situation. He would then execute the orders and directives of the higher command, exercising initiative to the fullest in the process. Hopefully the resulting operational decisions would be quicker and better adapted to local realities in a fluid situation.[25]

The system of directive command extended down as far as division level,[26] as in the 1806 system. This was also the lowest formation to which an officer of the General Staff was permanently assigned.[27]

## Directive Command and the General Staff

Having determined that only a decentralised system of command was consistent with the development of maximum fighting power, it was necessary for Moltke to create a common doctrine. This was essential if a commander was to have confidence that his subordinates would use the freedom given to them appropriately.

The traditional solution to this problem was for independent forces to be commanded by close associates of the supreme commander, who, as a result of long years of close contact, would come to know automatically what each would do in any particular situation. Given the size of the Imperial German Army, such a system was insufficient. Reliance on a few elite units being able to act independently was also inadequate: since an opportunity for independent action might occur at any part of the line, all units had to be capable of responding appropriately.[28] The solution chosen was to expand the General Staff from a small body primarily concerned with intelligence and planning[29] and make it into a corps of like-minded officers through which he could impose his doctrine on to the army as a whole. A key element in the General Staff's involvement in directive command was the attachment of its members to combat formations.

In 1914, the general staffs of the German armies totalled 625 officers. Only 352 of these (295 Prussian) were permanent members of the corps, a mere 2.14 per cent of the active officer corps. Of the rest, 113 were assigned to the *Grosser Generalstab* (Great General Staff) in Berlin.[30] The large majority, though still only 239 individuals, were available for service in the headquarters of field formations, the *Truppen-Generalstab* (General Staff with the Troops). The experience and skills of these officers were therefore of as much influence on the ethos of the General Staff as were those of their colleagues in the railroad section in Berlin. However, since the German Army of 1914 consisted of 50 active infantry divisions organised into 25 corps,[31] in addition to a large number of cavalry, fortress and reserve formations, it is clear that the officers of the *Truppen-Generalstab* were spread very thinly indeed.

This sparse allocation of staff officers was part of a deliberate policy. General Bronsart von Schellendorf wrote:

> There cannot be the slightest doubt that the addition of every individual not absolutely required on a Staff, is in itself an evil. In the first place, it unnecessarily weakens the strength of a regiment from which an officer is taken. Again, it increases the difficulty of providing the Staff with quarters, which tells on the troops that may happen to be quartered in the same place . . . Finally, it should be remembered . . . that *idleness is at the root of all mischief.* An unnecessarily numerous Staff . . . cannot always find work and occupation essential for its mental and physical welfare, and its superfluous energies soon make themselves felt in every conceivable kind of objectionable way. Experience, at any rate, shows that whenever a Staff is unnecessarily numerous, the ambitious before long take to intrigue, the litigious soon produce general friction, and the vain are never satisfied . . . Besides, the numbers of a Staff being few, there is all the greater choice in the selection of the men who are to fill posts on it.[32]

Von Schellendorf could have added that idle staffs tend to create work for themselves by demanding unnecessary reports from the formations under their command, according to the well-known principle that 'work expands to fill the time available'.

The distribution of General Staff officers in key positions in each of the army's formations was vital for the success of directive command. One of the main problems facing the CGS was ensuring that his orders were carried out. This difficulty was overcome by making commanders dependent in operational mattters upon the advice of their General Staff chiefs of staff, advice which would conform to the intent of the CGS.

Each division had only a single General Staff officer assigned, usually a senior captain or a junior major, who was in charge of operations, including planning for manoeuvres and mobilisation.[33] While not officially head of the divisional staff, he was usually the divisional commander's right-hand man. For him to be senior in rank to the other, non-General Staff, staff officers was considered to be an advantage,[34] but this was rarely the case. Each corps headquarters included three General Staff officers: a colonel, a major and a captain. A second captain was added on mobilisation. The colonel was chief of the entire headquarters staff and acted as the sole link between the commander and the staff, all messages for the commander having to pass him first. In the commander's absence, the chief of staff could issue orders in his own right, if the need was urgent. The remaining General Staff officers were grouped into a separate section, which controlled operations, peace-time manoeuvres and intelligence.[35] The system at army level was similar.

Although few in number, the General Staff officers in each formation filled the key posts: they controlled operations planning and manoeuvres and commanded the staff as a whole and so were able to ensure that operations received absolute priority. They were therefore the only source to which a commander might turn for advice on operations. Even given this monopoly on the giving of advice, commanders might have been tempted to ignore their chiefs of staff, particularly as these were very much junior in rank to themselves. This danger was avoided by the concept of dual command:

> The essence of this system lies in the fact that under it the chief of the staff officers attached to a commander is his commander's 'junior partner' and not a mere subordinate in the direction of operations. The ultimate decisions remain in the hands of the commander himself, but his chief of staff is not relieved thereby of his full share in the responsibility for the results. If his advice is disregarded on a major issue, he may insist on having his opinion to the contrary recorded, and, if his views persistently clash with those of his chief, he can resign; but . . . normally the relationship between the commander and his chief of staff is expected to conform to that prevailing in a happy marriage. The two men are expected to form a unity rather than two distinct personalities, supplementing each other, composing any differences that may arise without distinguishing the share which each of them contributes to the common good.[36]

The General Staff Officer could therefore not rely purely on technical knowledge but must display strength of character and leadership. The commander had good reason to accept the advice given, when his chief of staff could complain to more senior General Staff officers through the *Generalstabsdienstweg* (General Staff channels). Nor could a commander harm the career of a General Staff officer under his command by writing him a poor annual report, for officers of the *Truppen-Generalstab* received reports both from their commander and from the CGS, whose views naturally carried greater weight.[37] On the other hand, chiefs of staff were unlikely to give advice lightly, since they bore equal responsibility for the results.

> He [the General Staff officer] knows the general's views and intentions and can therefore see with the general's eyes. He is familiar with the methods and ideas of the army headquarters, for he has been trained in great general staff at Berlin under the personal influence of its chief. He is familiar with the working of the army corps, for he has held his post during years of peace before the war, and has been responsible for the arrangement of the corps manoeuvres. Thus his training and experience peculiarly qualify him to be the general's right-hand man.[38]

A vital factor in the German command system was the mutual trust of commanders and subordinates in each other's ability, a trust founded upon a common doctrine and a rigorous system of training. The officers of the General Staff were the cream of the German Army. Having passed through an exacting selection system to become members of the corps, General Staff officers continued their military education, under the direct tuition of the CGS. As von Moltke reported, the result was that in a given situation 99 out of 100 officers would react as he would himself.[39] Commanders could therefore be sure that the advice given by their chiefs of staff represented the views of the CGS, that is, the General Staff doctrine. This mutual confidence was further increased by the fact that many senior commanders had themselves served in the General Staff: of the eight army commanders in August 1914, von Kluck alone had no General Staff experience.[40]

Directive command was developed because of the need for rapid action appropriate to the situation, a demand incompatible with centralised control. The necessary decentralisation was prevented from degenerating into chaos by the assignment to every formation of an officer steeped in the way of thought of the CGS. As a result, senior commanders needed to give their subordinates only that information concerning the overall situation which they could not gather for themselves, outline their broad intentions and assign their subordinates their roles. No more was necessary, as senior commanders could be confident in the knowledge that their subordinates would act as they would do themselves, were they present.

Given such a loose rein, subordinates had to adapt to the local situation, exploiting each and every opportunity to the full, always seeking to further the overall intent to the best of their ability, but allowing their own initiative full scope, rather than merely implementing orders from above.

> In Moltke's view, a dogmatic enforcement of the plan of operations was a deadly sin and great care was taken to encourage initiative on the part of all commanders, high or low. Much in contrast to the vaunted Prussian discipline, a premium was placed upon independent judgement of all officers.[41]

## Selection and Training of General Staff Officers

An essential prerequisite for the successful employment of directive command was a body of officers, imbued with a common doctrine, holding the key posts in the army. Only given such a body could commanders be confident that the decentralisation of decision making inherent in directive command would result in greater responsiveness and thus higher combat power, rather than degenerating into utter confusion. The efforts required to create and maintain such a body are a vital aspect of directive command.

For most officers, the first step on the road to the General Staff was to attend the *Kriegsakademie* (War Academy). While it was in theory possible for an officer to be 'commandeered' to the General Staff without having passed through the War Academy, this became ever more unusual and ceased altogether under von Moltke II[42] (von Moltke II, CGS from 1906 to 1914, was the nephew of Helmuth von Moltke, CGS from 1857 to 1888).

### *Selection for the* Kriegsakademie

For the vast majority of officers, entry to the War Academy was by competitive examination. A small number of places were in the gift of senior commanders, but the nominated officers were required to sit the entrance examination at the end of the first year and were expelled if they failed.[43] As other avenues to the General Staff were closed off, competition for places at the War Academy grew. In the last years before the First World War, there were well over 1,000 applicants each year, for only 160 places.[44] All were officers with at least three years' service (before 1894 the minimum was five years) and with at least five years to go before promotion to captain.[45] No distinction was made between officers of the different arms.[46]

The examination consisted of eight papers: theoretical tactics; applied tactics; artillery and small arms; fortifications; topography; history; geography; and French or mathematics.[47] While there was a definite emphasis upon military subjects, Rosinski was perhaps over-stating the situation when he claimed that the examination 'dealt strictly with military matters, not, as in other countries, with the candidate's linguistic and scientific abilities'.[48]

The German Army appears to have been concerned to design a system of selection which did not exclude the officer with an irregular or original mind. For many years, Guards officers won a disproportionate number of places at the War Academy. Concerned that this might be due to favouritism, the CGS insisted that papers be marked anonymously, candidates being identified solely by a code number. The surprising result was an increase in the number of successful Guards officers.[49] This may in part have been because of the greater opportunities for instruction available to them in their garrisons around Berlin. Every applicant, however, was required to provide an autobiography in which he set out 'the course of his intellectual development' and had to state whether and for how long he had employed a 'crammer'.[50] The implication is that use of a 'crammer' would be penalised.

The second means by which selection was controlled was the choice of subjects for the initial examination. Five of the eight papers were on military subjects. These papers, while demanding, were not severe. Both von Schlieffen and von Seeckt claimed that most officers could reach the pass mark, 'if they only cared to exert themselves'.[51] By avoiding a direct linkage between selection and formal academic education, the German Army ensured that those successful in gaining places at the War Academy were, above all else, officers who had demonstrated their professional expertise. Had a direct linkage to academic education been made, middle-class officers would have been the main beneficiaries, for their education, involving study for the *Abitur* and at university, tended to be more academic than that of the aristocratic cadet academies.[52]

Schlieffen's comment that most officers should be able to pass the entrance examination ought not to be misunderstood. Places at the War Academy were not assigned on a simple pass or fail basis. The essence of the system was its competitiveness. Although there appears to be no surviving record of the scores, it may be suggested that a majority of applicants scored above the pass mark. Merely passing the examination was not enough. An officer had to be within top 20 per cent if he was to gain a place at the War Academy. While the standard of the examination was not severe, it was none the less necessary to score very highly in order to be successful.

> The object of the entrance examination is to ascertain whether the candidate possesses the degree of general education and the knowledge requisite for a profitable attendance at the lectures of the Academy. The examination is also to determine whether the candidates have the power of judgement, without which there could be no hope of their further progress .... The questions set are to be such as cannot be answered merely from knowledge stored up in the memory, and should test the capacity for clear, collected, and consistent expression .... The paper in applied tactics must be as simple as possible. It must consist of a problem for solution, so as to oblige the candidate to make a decision and give his reasons for it.[53]

It is evident that character and command ability were at least as important as intellect and technical knowledge. The selection process continued even after officers reached the War Academy. Although the course lasted for three years, students were appointed for only one year at a time: reappointment depended upon passing an examination. A further process of selection occurred upon completion of the course, officers being graded as fit for the General Staff, for a technical branch of the General Staff, for the *Adjutantur* (equivalent to the British Administrative Staff), for an instructor's post, or unfit.[54] Only 30 per cent were graded as fit for the General Staff,[55] perhaps five per cent of the original number of applicants. Nor was this the end of the selection process. Only a handful even of those graded as fit for the General Staff would don the coveted wine-red trouser stripes of the corps.

### *Training at the* Kriegsakademie

The War Academy was founded by Frederick the Great in 1765. Its purpose was to improve the quality of the Prussian officer corps after the heavy losses of the Seven Years' War and to add a new scientific element to the army. The new institution, initially called the *Academie des Nobles*, opened with a student body of 15 young nobles destined for the military and diplomatic services. Military officers were soon in the majority.[56] Although enlarged in 1804, the academy was closed down in the trauma of 1806.

The academy was reopened in a new form in 1810, largely at the instigation of von Scharnhorst, chief of the embryo General Staff and de facto Minister of War.[57] Renamed the *Allgemeine Kriegsschule* (General War School) or the *Allgemeine Militär Akademie* (General Military Academy),[58] the institution opened on 15 October 1810, the same day as the new University of Berlin.[59] Scharnhorst, who had lectured at the academy from 1801 to 1805, placed the emphasis of training upon the conduct of operations, rather than upon the technical details of staff work. The academy was intended to train officers for high rank and was closely connected to the General Staff.[60] It was placed under the direction of the Inspector-General of Military Education and Training in 1819, renamed the *Kriegsakademie* in 1859 and returned to General Staff control in 1872. As the army expanded, so did the academy, increasing from 40 students in each year in 1810 to 160 students in 1909.[61]

Spenser Wilkinson described the War Academy as a 'military university', but he highlighted an important difference between that institution and a civilian university:

> A university, strictly speaking, is a school of free thought, and should give to those who have lived its life and breathed its spirit a view of the world, of nature and of humanity, of which the characteristic is freedom, spontaneity, independence. The man who in this sense has had a liberal education may be reactionary or progressive in his sympathies, may be democratic or authoritative in his leanings, but in any case if the university has done its work he will choose his own way. He will take his bearings for himself, and his thought will be conditioned by no ordinances and limited by no authority. At this intellectual freedom the War Academy does not aim.[62]

For over 60 years after Scharnhorst, the academy provided a liberal education similar to a civilian university, but this approach underwent significant alteration after the General Staff took over the direction of the academy in 1872. From this time, it increasingly became a 'General Staff academy'.[63]

The shift in emphasis may be expressed as being from a broadening to a deepening process and parallels the development of the General Staff itself. In its early days, the officers of the General Staff were primarily intended as professional advisors to senior field commanders. Since armies were relatively small and compact, there was comparatively little scope for initiative by subordinate formations. The need was therefore for General Staff officers who could give clear and sound military advice. From von Moltke's day, the Prussian Army became ever larger and more dispersed in time of war. Formations were frequently out of immediate communication with higher headquarters, yet the need for separate formations to act in concert became ever more essential. To solve this problem, Moltke developed and extended the system of directive command, a system which depended upon a central core of key officers who would all react according to a common doctrine. Only in this way could united action be achieved. It was the inculcation of such a common General Staff doctrine which became the *Schwerpunkt* of the War Academy after 1872. This trend was reinforced by the growing importance of mobilisation planning and the technical skills associated with that complex process.

A common doctrine was in direct contradiction of the aims of a civilian university. A broad education of itself encourages a variety of opinions. The General Staff doctrine required its adherents to follow the same narrow approach, so that each could know what another member of the corps would do in any given situation, even if the two officers were personally unknown to each other.

From 1872, the control of the General Staff over the War Academy was total. The director, a General Staff lieutenant-general, was responsible directly to the CGS. In educational matters, the director was assisted by a studies committee. Apart from the director himself, its members were a lieutenant-general of engineers, an inspector of engineers, a major-general of artillery and three General Staff major-generals. The majority of the committee's members were therefore officers of the General Staff.[64]

The War Academy had a staff of only six full-time instructors: three officers and three civilians. The remaining 36 instructors worked part-time: 20 were officers of the General Staff with other postings in the Berlin area, while 16 were university professors.[65] Typical of the part-time military lecturers was von Hindenburg, who, as a major, taught tactics at the Academy for five years, in addition to his duties in the *Grosser Generalstab* and then as operations officer of III Corps.[66]

The system of part-time lecturers had both advantages and disadvantages. On the positive side, the instructors were fully integrated into the General Staff way of thought and so could inculcate their students into its doctrines. On the negative side, the system resulted in a definite narrowing of outlook from broader issues to more military technical questions. Since they already had demanding full-time jobs, the military instructors did not have the time to devise new courses. Instead they tended to teach what they knew best, which was the staff work that they performed every day.[67] The academic side of the training became increasingly subsidiary.

The formal supplanting of academic with purely military subjects began in 1888, when Moltke issued a new 'Order of Teaching' for the academy. This document laid down what was to be taught and how it was to be presented. It therefore provides an insight into the characteristics which Moltke considered necessary for the General Staff doctrine. The number of hours devoted to compulsory subjects was increased from 52 to 74 hours per week, spread over the three years of the course, leaving little time available for optional courses.[68] This marked a major step away from an academic education towards a more strictly military technical training. Since the majority of compulsory courses were military, while most academic courses were optional, the shift towards greater emphasis upon the military courses inevitably resulted in a narrowing of scope.

The 1888 'Order of Teaching' was revised in 1912.[69] In the new curriculum, the number of hours of instruction per week (over the three years of the course) were now set at:[70]

| *Subject* | *Hours* |
|---|---|
| Tactics and *Generalstabsdienst* (General Staff service) | 16 |
| War history | 12 |
| General military subjects | 11 |
| Academic subjects (for example, history and geography) | 13 |
| Mathematics or a foreign language | 15 or 18 |

Purely military subjects together filled almost 60 per cent of the time available, with the lion's share of this devoted to tactics, General Staff service and war history. The emphasis upon professional, as opposed to academic, subjects is clear.

That there was a definite narrowing of approach, even with regard to the military subjects themselves, is indicated by an officer who graduated from the *Kriegsakademie* in the eary years of this century:

> The Exercises at the Military Academy were most interesting, at times absolutely fascinating, but did not concern themselves in the least with the technique of the conduct of battles. No order that would have been given *in* combat was ever discussed, hardly even a real order *for* combat; it all turned around the 'operational element', around the question whether to move forward or backward or to the side, whether to envelop right or left (also whether one should execute an order or deviate from it). That in a division there occurred

> artillery orders, that with an army corps it was necessary to think of the 'means of communication', those were all technical details practically never touched upon at all.[71]

This emphasis on the operational level of war produced officers highly skilled in that area of the military profession, but at considerable cost. The administrative staffs, the *Adjutantur* (personnel) and *Intendantur* (supply), received only those graduates of the War Academy who were considered of insufficient ability to become members of the General Staff. As a consequence, most senior commanders, who had a General Staff background, were largely ignorant of logistics, while the officers of the administrative staffs had neither the status nor the ability to create an efficient logistic support service. This deficiency was revealed in the planning and execution of the Schlieffen Plan.

When Schlieffen formulated his plan for the invasion of France, the importance of logistics was largely disregarded and problems were passed over. Although the supply system coped remarkably well in 1914, largely owing to the motorisation of certain elements of the non-rail transport services, and cannot be blamed for the defeat on the Marne, it was stretched to the limits: Martin van Creveld concluded that further advance would have been impossible, even had that battle been won. The final judgement on the quality of the pre-war logistics service may be left to the supply officer of First Army in 1914, whose opinion was that the supply regulations, prepared over decades of peace, 'did no special harm'.[72]

As important as the shift from academic to military subjects, and the almost exclusive emphasis on the operational level of war, was the change in the ethos of the academy:

> In accordance with the objects for which the Military Academy is instituted, its course of study must aim at a thorough professional education; it must not lose itself in the wide field of general [academic] studies.
>
> The [academic] teaching may take the form of lectures, which appeal merely to the comprehension and the memory of the hearer, while in the military subjects, everything depends upon the pupil learning to apply and to make the most of the knowledge which he acquires. It is, moreover, essential to bring about an active process of mental give and take between teacher and pupils, so as to stimulate the pupils to become fellow workers. The awakening effects of co-operation like this will never be seen where the one only expounds and the other only listens.[73]

The aim of the War Academy from 1888 at least was to produce officers with a profound practical understanding of their profession, able to fit in with the methods of the General Staff. Learning for its own sake was seen as a diversion.

Balancing this more narrowly technical education was the final examination at the end of the three-year course at the War Academy. Unlike all the previous examinations, 'This time personal factors, such as character, general education, manners, personality, played a role, in addition to pure military merit'.[74] It is difficult to see how such factors could be tested in a purely written examination. The course on General Staff service, however, ended with a three-week-long staff ride.[75] According to the 1888 'Order of Teaching', this staff ride 'offers the opportunity of testing the capacity, knowledge, and endurance of each officer – of finding what he can do'.[76] This is precisely the environment in which non-academic factors could be tested. Such emphasis upon commandability at the operational level, rather than merely technical planning, served to balance the more narrow teaching of the academy.

On the basis of their performance in the final examination, War Academy students received the gradings which largely determined their future careers. The best graduates, graded fit for service with the General Staff, were attached to that corps for a period of one or two years. The remainder joined the *Höhere Adjutantur* (administrative staff), became instructors in the various military schools, or returned to line service.[77]

## *Training in the General Staff*

Following the final staff ride in July of the third year, those officers graded fit for the General Staff rejoined their regiments until March of the following year.[78] This period of line service may have been designed to refresh the staff officers' experience of 'real' soldiering and so prevent them becoming isolated from the rest of the army. A further aim may have been to allow line officers to see that the staff officers did indeed represent the cream of the officer corps.

Each spring, about 45 officers began a probationary period with the Great General Staff in Berlin. For the next one or two years, they underwent an intense period of training, in which their capacity for hard work, prolonged concentration, swift handling of large quantities of data, as well as their potential as senior staff officers and as commanders at up to army level, were stretched and tested. At the end of this time came yet another examination: only four or five would be judged of a sufficiently high standard to become permanent members of the General Staff.[79]

Permanent appointment to the General Staff was by no means the end of an officer's training. For their rank, officers of the General Staff held positions of great responsibility. Hindenburg, for example, was operations officer of 1st Division when only a senior captain and was chief of staff of VIII Corps as a colonel.[80] In the German system of dual command, such staff officers were expected to be the junior partners of their commanders, commanders three or four ranks senior to them. If a General Staff captain was to be taken seriously by his divisional commander, it was essential that he have a level of training not far short of that enjoyed by his commander, at least in certain key areas. In short, for the General Staff system to be effective, its officers had to be made into generals while still of field rank.

The entire General Staff corps underwent a continuous programme of map exercises and staff rides. The aspirant officers attached to the Great General Staff were given a tactical map exercise to solve every week, in addition to their already-heavy work load and entire Great General Staff, including the aspirants, took part in two or three large-scale strategic exercises each spring. Some exercises, the *Kriegsspiele*, ran for months under the personal direction of the CGS, who also led the entire Great General Staff in two staff rides each year.[81]

In the late 1930s, the German Army published several volumes detailing the exercises set by Schlieffen. Each winter, he would set the officers of the Great General Staff up to five separate map exercises. Most involved whole armies and at least one would be from the enemy point of view.[82] In his *Kriegsspiele*, Schlieffen extended Moltke's practice of allowing junior officers to fill very senior positions. For example, in one of Moltke's last exercises, in 1886, Hindenburg, although only promoted to major in the previous year, commanded the entire Russian Army.[83] Schlieffen allowed even the aspirant officers to play in such senior posts.[84]

> In 1903, some officers suggested that the forces were too large and 'it was not the business of junior officers to lead armies and groups of armies.' On this point the Generalfeldmarshal said at the conference [which concluded the exercise]:
>
> 'I do not presume, gentlemen, on what grounds many of you should not be placed at the head of an army. In any case, I hope that you will be called upon to lead a corps or a division, or, at least, will, as General Staff officer, stand by the side of one of the higher commanders. You must, therefore, be in a position to appreciate the movements of an army. Only thus, if your corps or division is given an independent task – and this will often happen in a future war – will you be qualified to arrive at a decision which will be for the benefit of the whole.'[85]

Officers continued their training even when away from Berlin, while serving in the *Truppen-Generalstab*. The education of all the General Staff officers in his formation, both the officers of his own staff and also those serving as divisional operations officers, was a particular duty of the chief of staff of a corps.[86]

Not only did this exhaustive round of training and exercises develop the command potential of General Staff officers, such that the views of even its junior members were to be given considerable weight, but also 'the opportunity for discussion and airing of his views enabled the Prussian CGS to establish a definite school of thought'.[87] The existence of such a school of thought was central to the effective employment of directive command.

## The Position of the General Staff within the Army

The grip of the General Staff on the operations of the German Army, already tight due to its monopoly of the key staff positions, was strengthened further by the accelerated promotion enjoyed by its officers. Members of the General Staff were promoted to the rank of captain an average of one year before their contemporaries and reached the rank of major some four years earlier.[88] In a system of promotion otherwise largely based on seniority, such accelerated promotion meant that General Staff officers were younger than other officers of the same rank and therefore had more time in which to reach senior rank before retirement.

Thanks to Daniel J. Hughes' exhaustive analysis, the extent of the General Staff's hold on senior positions may be examined. Between 1871 and 1914, 2,443 officers held the rank of *Generalmajor* (equivalent to brigadier-general).[89] Of a sample of 2,120 of these officers, 296 (13.96 per cent) had been members of the General Staff.[90] Since only 2.14 per cent of officers were members of the corps,[91] General Staff Officers were approximately seven times more likely to attain the rank of *Generalmajor* than were other officers. Moreover, General Staff officers reached that rank at a younger median age than did others (about 50 years old compared to about 53½).[92]

The speed with which General Staff officers were promoted was not only because they received preferential treatment at the hands of the Military Cabinet, which controlled promotion, but also because of the German practice of compelling poor-quality officers to take early retirement.[93] Since it was unthinkable that a General Staff officer would fall into this category, General Staff officers inevitably became proportionately more numerous among the senior ranks.

Hughes gives final positions held before retirement for 2,015 of the 2,443 officers who reached the rank of *Generalmajor*,[94] of whom 253 (12.56 per cent) had been members of the General Staff. Whereas 52.27 per cent of non-General Staff officers (921 of 1,762) retired as brigade commanders, only 23.32 per cent (59 of 253) of General Staff officers did so. Of the 1,035 officers who held a position above that of brigade commander,

194 (18.74 per cent) were from the General Staff, nine times their proportion in the army as a whole. Of the key posts of corps and army commanders, 37 of 105 (35.24 per cent) and nine of 16 (56.25 per cent) of the officers who retired when holding these positions respectively had been members of the General Staff.

Hughes' figures show that not only were the key staff positions held by members of the General Staff, but a very high proportion of senior command positions were also held by officers who had been members of that corps. Since these senior commanders had already absorbed the doctrine of the General Staff, they were likely to follow the intent of the CGS closely and effectively, and would usually accept the advice of their more junior General Staff operations officers.

This type of 'hot-house' environment for the production of young generals carried with it considerable risks. The main danger was that the General Staff might become isolated from the rest of the officer corps. This could take two forms. First, members of the General Staff could face considerable jealousy and resentment, owing to their enjoyment of accelerated promotion and the powerful positions which they held. Some brigade commanders may not have taken kindly to receiving orders from junior General Staff majors acting as the junior partner of the divisional commander. The fact that line commanders were impotent as regards General Staff officers, due to their protection by the CGS, may have increased this feeling of resentment. Second, by concentrating on staff work and operations, the General Staff ran the risk of its officers becoming out of touch with the realities of war at the tactical level, as indeed they did with regard to logistics.

Precisely in order to combat these dangers, the General Staff operated a system of alternation in assignments. Officers (other than those of the technical branches of the General Staff, who would never command units) were not permitted to remain in one branch or area for too long, but were posted regularly between service with the *Grosser Generalstab*, with the *Truppen-Generalstab* and with line units. This last was held to be of particular importance and no officer could be promoted without having successfully commanded a line unit.[95]

Hindenburg's career was typical of the more successful General Staff officers.[96] Commissioned in 1865, he successfully sat the entrance examination for the *Kriegsakademie* in 1873. At the end of the three-year course, Hindenburg served six months with his regiment before spending one year attached to the Great General Staff in Berlin. In April 1878, he was promoted to captain and posted to the headquarters of II Corps. In 1881, he became operations officer of 1st Division. In 1884, after seven years of continuous staff duty. Hindenburg took over command of a line infantry company. The next year, promoted to major, he returned to the Great

General Staff, followed by a period as operations officer of III Corps. During both of these postings, Hindenburg also lectured on tactics at the *Kriegsakademie*. In 1889, he was transferred to the War Ministry. In 1893, after a second seven-year period of continuous staff duty, he became commander of Infanterie-Regiment 91. Three years later, Hindenburg was appointed chief of staff of VIII Corps. He commanded 28th Division from 1900 to 1905, when he took over command of IV Corps, 29 years after leaving the *Kriegsakademie*. Of this time, nine and a half years had been spent in line postings, 12 years with the *Truppen-Generalstab* and only seven years in the cloistered environment of the Great General Staff and War Ministry in Berlin. Although Hindenburg had spent the majority of his service in staff positions, he had none the less had considerable contact with line troops.

The time that General Staff officers spent commanding line units and serving with the *Truppen-Generalstab* ensured, at least theoretically, that they remained in touch with the tactical level. Service with line units also gave line officers an opportunity to see what these staff officers were like at 'real' soldiering. During such service, General Staff officers' efficiency reports were written by their line commanders alone. Since a poor report could seriously damage an officer's future career, the fact that most General Staff officers' careers did not so suffer suggests that they were of at least average competence in line posts.

The German system of selection and training of General Staff officers was effective in its aim of producing a highly-trained cadre of officers imbued with a common doctrine, the basic requirement of directive command, but it did this at some cost. By concentrating so strongly on operations and tactics, the system resulted in a definite narrowing of outlook, as we have already noted with regard to logistics.

While the General Staff was able to recognise its limitations in certain areas and willingly turn for advice to the appropriate experts, as with artillery tactics in 1917,[97] this was not always the case. Curiously, the General Staff appears to have been more ready to accept advice in directly military matters than elsewhere. Bismarck's struggles with Moltke over grand strategy during the Franco-Prussian War were notorious, while Ludendorff's interference in economic and diplomatic affairs during the First World War played no small part in Germany's eventual defeat.

Even in its own special sphere of operations, the General Staff appears to have been too narrowly technical on occasion, as in 1914, when it had prepared only one plan for war, regardless of the circumstances. Schlieffen's obsession with the need to defeat France in as short a time as possible, with its consequent emphasis upon rapid mobilisation and deployment, ignored the diplomatic possibility that France might not be involved in the war. The casual infringement of Belgian neutrality, with its inevitable involvement of Britain in the war, was a classic example of the narrow military-technical concentration upon mobilisation rather than battles.

## The General Staff and Army Training

The General Staff was responsible neither for the training of troops nor for the writing of field regulations. These duties, along with other administrative matters, were the domain of the War Ministry.[98] Nevertheless, the influence of the General Staff upon these matters, both as a corps and through its individual members, was considerable.

The only direct control over troops enjoyed by the General Staff was during the annual *Kaisermanöver*.[99] The training value of the manoeuvres during the 1890s appears to have been limited, since the Kaiser personally commanded one of the contending armies and insisted that he always won. He also had a 'predilection for picturesque cavalry charges'. The realism of the manoeuvres was greatly increased after Moltke II insisted that the Kaiser no longer play an active part. [100] The *Kaisermanöver* became a continuous exercise, without daily pauses to reorganise and Moltke used them to test different combat formations, attacks against an enemy using French principles of defence and the relative merits of envelopment and breakthrough operations.

The manoeuvres ended with a detailed critique by the General Staff. The subjects raised demonstrate that the General Staff sought to extend the use of its philosophy beyond operations and into the field of tactics. Under Moltke II, the critiques were used: to express concern that the offensive spirit of the infantry should not be permitted to become an *Angriffshetze* (attack frenzy), as was the case in France; to urge greater use of entrenchments; to question the usefulness of cavalry for close reconnaissance; to emphasise the importance of artillery support and the need for artillery to identify friendly and hostile positions; to restate the necessity for combined-arms action in the attack; and to point out the greater effectiveness of flank or rear attacks; and underlined the importance of peacetime training for attacks on fortified positions. While the General Staff could exercise influence on the army as a whole through the *Kaisermanöver*, its power should not be overstated. A number of criticisms appeared year after year in the General Staff critique, showing that little notice had been taken by the troops,[101] and shortly before the First World War the critiques themselves were no longer circulated, on the insistence of senior generals, incensed by the sharpness of their criticism.[102]

The influence of individual members of the General Staff on the rest of the army is difficult to assess. Officers of the *Truppen-Generalstab* at corps and division level were responsible for the preparation and running of manoeuvres and exercises within their formations. Their influence was probably dependent upon whether the formation commander supported their plans and criticisms. Such support was most likely from commanders who had themselves been members of the General Staff. General Staff officers in non-General Staff posts may also have had some influence. Although the General Staff had no formal role in the writing of field regulations, individual General Staff officers were transferred to the War Ministry to help produce new manuals. Hindenburg, for example, was involved in writing new regulations for field engineers and heavy artillery in 1889.[103]

## Directive Command from 1890 to 1914

The German Army stagnated under von Schlieffen, CGS from 1890 to 1906. In the face of an ever-worsening military balance, Schlieffen became obsessed with the panacea of the single decisive battle of annihilation by means of a double envelopment, based on his faulty understanding of Hannibal's victory over the Romans at Cannae in 216 BC. In his quest to deny the enemy any room for effective response, that is, to have tempo, Schlieffen became ever more restrictive of his own commanders. Ignoring Moltke's maxim that it is impossible to plan a major engagement in advance, Schlieffen insisted that his subordinates follow his orders to the letter.[104] He planned the advance of his armies to be like 'battalion drill', controlled from OHL by the CGS, linked to his armies by a row of telephones on his desk.[105]

There were many critics of Schlieffen's policies, such as General von Schlichting, who 'strongly defended the right and duty of Prussian officers to act on their own initiative, accepting personal responsibility for their actions'.[106] Nevertheless,

> If the regulations demanded from the commanders that they should foster the spirit of responsibility amongst their subordinates, they certainly were not assisted in this task from above, for every officer in whose command something unusual happened that smacked of an offence against regulations felt the ground tremble beneath his feet.[107]

The extent of the decline, however, should not be overstated. Regarding directive command, Schlieffen himself said,

> Various incidents may happen which may necessitate a certain deviation from the original plan ... It will not be possible to ask the

> commander for orders in this case, since communications may not work. The corps commander will be faced with the necessity of arriving at a decision of his own. In order that this decision should meet the ideas of the commander-in-chief he must keep the corps commanders sufficiently informed while, on the other hand, the latter must continuously strive to keep in mind the basic ideas of all the operations and to enter into the mind of the commander-in-chief.[108]

While this appears similar to Moltke's teaching, it is noteworthy that Schlieffen considered that independent judgement was necessary only if the situation changed and if communications did not work: Moltke assumed this to be the normal state of affairs, Schlieffen hoped to eliminate such uncertainty.

Schlieffen retained the outward forms of directive command and indeed extended it as regards the General Staff. He seems, however, to have been unwilling to permit the independence and flexibility of subordinate commanders which the doctrine required if it was to be applied in practice. One result of this was that the officers commanding armies in August 1914, groomed for high command by Schlieffen, proved almost uniformly lacking in determination and initiative.

Moltke II sought to return to the command system of his uncle: 'The Supreme Commander needs to be intelligently helped by the initiative of army commanders. The latter, on their side, should always think in terms of the general situation and try unceasingly to conform to it.'[109] The overall plan was once more intended to be adapted to the situation on the ground, rather than being blindly applied. Within four years of his succeeding Schlieffen, most of the army's basic manuals had been revised, manuals which in several cases had not been revised for almost 20 years. While some of the new manuals differed only in detail from those issued under Schlieffen,[110] the spirit of the army was considerably changed. Soon after Moltke took charge, a number of works appeared which restated the philosophy of directive command.

Perhaps the most important of these works was an article by Colonel Spohn, entitled 'The Art of Command'. Although not a member of the General Staff (he was second-in-command of Infanterie-Regiment 52 and close to retirement),[111] Spohn so clearly encapsulated the essence of directive command in this article that it is appropriate to conclude this chapter with a number of quotes:

> An order is only justified if, under the actual circumstances of the case, it was absolutely necessary. . . . Every order places the subordinate to whom it is given in a position of constraint . . . but he complies with an order unwillingly if it is dictated merely by the

pleasure of giving orders, or by the desire to magnify one's own importance. . . . Only the man who himself knows how to obey, who has learnt from personal experience how grievous an inopportune or superfluous order can be, and how inexpressibly hard it is, in such a case, to resist the impulse to revolt, only such a man will avoid blunders when he is himself in a position of command.[112]

Modern fighting requires thoughtful leaders trained to be independent. . . . Such leaders . . . are not produced by orders, superfluous in themselves, and beside the mark; but we undoubtedly do get them if we give no more orders than are absolutely essential, and if we praise every independent action, even if it be not altogether apt or appropriate.[113]

Every superior who finds that he has been misunderstood should first look for the fault in himself. . . . The superior knows well enough what he wishes to order, but what he actually has ordered in the excitement of an engagement is beyond his power to judge.[114]

This much is certain, that we can only bring up and train subordinate leaders to have independence, initiative, and fondness of responsibility, if we do not crib, cabin, and confine them . . . to deprive the subordinate commander of the independence to which he is entitled, means robbing him of the pleasure of service and the pleasure of action, and, at the very least, diminishing his interest in his work, and with it the germ of all active endeavour.[115]

No competent officer will adhere to the letter of an order in action, but will pursue the object in view with a proper willingness to accept responsibility.[116]

This much is certain, that superior officers who give their subordinates – in action and everywhere else where it is possible to do so – the independence which is their due, and even demand such power of initiative from them, will never be left in the lurch. They will find their troops, down to the smallest detachments, always in the right place throughout the battle and after the conclusion.[117]

# 2
# The British General Staff and Umpiring

> The Staff College and the General Staff are more concerned in the study of Staff Duties and Organisation than in the art of winning battles. That is one reason why I have always regarded the magic letters psc as being no criterion of Generalship. In fact, I think that the attainment of those letters very often crystallises an already narrow mind into a mere thread of thought!
>
> Major-General Sir Ernest Swinton

> The chief duty of the higher command is to prepare for battle, not to execute on the battlefield. After having clearly indicated to subordinate leaders their respective missions, we must leave the execution to them.
>
> Captain Douglas Haig

## The British General Staff

### *Origins*

The origins of the British General Staff lie in the Crimean War, when the British Army found itself fighting in an area about which it knew little and of which it possessed very few maps. In order to prevent the recurrence of such a situation, a Topographical Branch was established in the War Office in 1855. True to its name, the branch concentrated almost entirely on the topography of foreign countries, 'the nature and strength of their armies were treated as minor matters [and] relegated to the background'.[1] The Prussian successes in 1866 and 1870 provided the impetus for further development. 'It was becoming clearer that the Secretary of State for War needed a responsible source of professional advice to guide him in the creation of defence policy, rather than the hit-or-miss method of asking whomsoever he pleased, as had tended to be the case hitherto.[2]

Cardwell's reform of the War Office in 1870 made the Commander-in-Chief (C-in-C) responsible for providing much professional advice, but 'there was as yet little upon which he [the C-in-C) could rely to aid him apart from his own intuition'.[3] In 1873, this was in part rectified by expanding the Topographical Branch, renamed the Intelligence Department. The director of the new department, Major-General P. L. MacDougall, was charged with

> the collection of all topographical and statistical information which it would be useful to possess in event of invasion or foreign war . . . [and with] the application of such information, in respect to the measures considered and determined on during peace, which should be adopted in war, so that no delay might arise from uncertainty and hesitation.[4]

The department had no influence upon training or operations: 'Such was the concept of staff duties then current that the department was assigned no more than the task of amassing information and presenting it upon request.'[5] Work was begun on the details of mobilisation, 'for the first time in peace', in the late 1870s, largely on the initiative of one of the department's officers, Colonel Robert Home, but his premature death in 1879 brought the work to a halt.[6]

An indication of the limited importance assigned to the Intelligence Department may be given by its transfer in 1874 from the office of the Adjutant-General to that of the Quartermaster-General. Whereas the Adjutant-General was the unofficial deputy of the C-in-C[7] and was responsible for training and discipline, the Quartermaster-General was in charge of supply and transport.[8] Furthermore, since the Quartermaster-General's 'chief duties were regarded as being performed only in wartime, his peacetime responsibilities were very restricted'. In 1880, his entire War Office staff, apart from the Intelligence Department, consisted of just two officers.[9]

Restored to the Adjutant-General in 1882, little further development occurred until the return of Lord Wolseley in 1886. The Intelligence Department was regarded as 'a harmless but rather useless appendage to the War Office'. Wolseley secured a larger financial grant for the department and appointed as its chief Major-General Sir Henry Brackenbury, whom he described as 'not one of the cleverest, but *the* cleverest man in the British Army'.[10] Charged by Wolseley with investigating the measures required to mobilise two army corps, Brackenbury's report helped to precipitate a crisis of self-confidence within the army.

> To mobilise one army corps would mean the purchase of 8,000 extra horses and filling gaps in commissariat, transport, medical and veterinary staff; to mobilise a second would require a further 11,000 horses, and it would possess no regular artillery, no transport corps and no medical staff whatsoever. Even Belgium, with a population one-sixth the size of England's, could field two army corps.[11]

Testifying before the Parliamentary Select Committee on Army and Navy

Estimates in July 1887, Brackenbury stated that the number of staff in his department was 'utterly insufficient' to deal with mobilisation planning. He claimed that the reason Britain could barely produce two corps, despite an annual budget of £14½ million, whereas Germany fielded 19 corps for £19 million, was that the German organisation was superior due to the Great General Staff, which he said was primarily concerned with mobilisation.[12] Other witnesses pointed out that the Great General Staff,

> 'the cause of the great efficiency of the Germany Army', had nothing to do with administrative or executive details but was simply concerned with 'the duties of thought and preparation of plans of organisation and plans of campaign'. In the British War Office, in contrast, except for the small Intelligence Department every other officer was involved primarily with executive and administrative duties.[13]

Yet just as the importance of the Intelligence Department was being stressed, the Treasury was questioning the value of the budget spent on it, on the grounds that a Naval Intelligence Department had recently been created. A request for an increase of 20 per cent in the former's budget was firmly rejected: the Treasury appears to have believed that the army was simply trying to make 'jobs for the boys'.[14]

W. S. Hamer has analysed the situation in the War Office:

> An intelligence department gathers information, it does not assess its value in terms of over-all defence schemes, nor does it arrive at conclusions about the information collected, nor does it initiate action upon it. Such planning is a staff duty, but no such staff existed in the War Office. Between the department for collecting information and the Secretary of State and his policy advisers there was no agency to assess information and to correlate it to the general principles of defence. So far as planning existed it was the responsibility of the Commander-in-Chief. Just as administrative and command duties required to be separated from policy-making functions, so policy-making, staff planning, and intelligence responsibilities needed to be clarified and distinguished. By providing a staff for operations and planning, the gap between making policy and collecting information would be closed.[15]

One consequence of the debate on army reform and the invasion scare of 1888 was the setting up of the Hartington Commission, of which Brackenbury was a member, 'to enquire into the civil and professional administration of the naval and military departments'.[16] Among its main recommendations were the abolition of the post of C-in-C, the formation of a General Staff and the creation of a War Office Council, to consist of four civilian officials and the Chief of Staff, the Adjutant-General, the Quartermaster-General, the Director of Artillery and the Inspector-General of Fortifications.[17]

Little came of the recommendations. One member of the commission, Sir Henry Campbell-Bannerman, dissented from the idea of a General Staff, declaring that 'he was at a loss as to what functions a staff could perform'. While part of his objection was due to a fear that a Chief of Staff might come to be as powerful as the C-in-C, whose influence the recommendations were designed to reduce,[18] Campbell-Bannerman appears genuinely to have had little comprehension of General Staff work: as Secretary of State for War from 1892 to 1895, he failed to appreciate the vital importance of the Intelligence Department collecting maps.[19] Nothing further was done about forming a General Staff until 1895. Although the War Office Council was set up in May 1890, it proved ineffective. Free discussion was hindered by the Secretary of State having absolute control over its agenda, and by the presence on the council of the C-in-C, in lieu of the intended Chief of Staff.

> Either the Commander-in-Chief was supreme, in which case the subordinate military officials would be reluctant to dissent publicly from his views and the purpose of the Council would be nullified, or the Commander-in-Chief was not supreme, in which event his position was ambiguous to say the least.[20]

This difficulty was largely avoided by very rarely calling the council, allowing the individual departments to get on with their separate tasks.[21]

Further reorganisation came in 1895 with the retirement of the Duke of Cambridge, a 'bow and arrow' general, who had been C-in-C since 1856. The powers of the new C-in-C, Lord Wolseley, were greatly reduced, making him in effect 'primus inter pares'. The War Office Council continued as before, the only change in membership being the substitution of the Inspector-General of Ordnance for the Director of Artillery. Although now intended to meet more often, the council met only six times between 1895 and 1901.[22] The Intelligence and Mobilisation departments were reassigned to the C-in-C, making him in effect the Chief of Staff,[23] but his position was still ambiguous. Although required to exercise 'general supervision' over all the military departments, he had no authority over them.[24] Wolseley, angered by this reduction in the power of his office, attempted to reassert its primacy and insisted that the Adjutant-General report to the Secretary of State only through him.[25]

Lord Roberts, who succeeded Wolseley, restored much of the C-in-C's power. He was given 'control' over the Adjutant-General, the Director of Mobilisation and Military Intelligence (DM&MI) and the Military Secretary in November 1901 and he continued to 'supervise' the other departments.[26] Roberts created the post of DM&MI by merging the Intelligence Department with the Mobilisation Department. This officer, who became a member of the War Office Council,[27] was intended to have the same status as the Adjutant-General.[28] This was not fully achieved, since the DM&MI remained a temporary major-general, whereas the other military members of the council were substantive lieutenant-generals.[29] The DM&MI, Sir William Nicholson, attempted to expand his department, but an enquiry by the financial department of the War Office revealed considerable confusion in the rest of the army as to its function and hostility to its expansion. The Adjutant-General, Kelley-Kenny, was violently opposed to its very existence, while Ian Hamilton and John French considered advance planning for campaigns to be a futile exercise, since there were so many unknown variables.[30] The new system lasted only three years before being swept away by the reforms of the Esher Committee.

### *The Creation of the General Staff*

Just as it appeared that the C-in-C had regained his previous power, the post was abolished as one of the recommendations of the War Office (Reconstitution) Committee of 1903–4. The committee consisted of only three men:[31] Lord Esher, formerly a member of the Royal Commission on the War in South Africa;[32] Admiral Sir John Fisher, who became First Sea Lord in October 1904; and Sir George Clarke, secretary to the Hartington Commission.[33] Its main recommendations were the abolition of the post of C-in-C, the reform of the War Office Council and the creation of a General Staff.

The War Office Council became the Army Council on 6 February 1904.[34] Its Military Members were the Adjutant-General and the Quartermaster-General, and the new offices of Chief of the General Staff (CGS) (redesignated Chief of the Imperial General Staff (CIGS) in 1909) and Master-General of the Ordnance.[35] Although the CGS was granted many of the powers of the old C-in-C, the new post was weak in a number of ways. First, although the Army Council and the post of CGS were created in February 1904, the General Staff only came into official existence on 12 September 1906.[36] For the first two and a half years of the new system, when the various departments were settling down to their new relationships, the department of CGS barely existed. This is likely to have limited his influence over the other departments.

The second main weakness was the status of the CGS. Although designated First Military Member of the Army Council and required to 'supervise' the other departments, as had the C-in-C, the CGS was barely even 'primus inter pares'. It had already been found that assigning an officer responsibility for the efficient running of a department without giving him the power to intervene directly was to put him in an ambiguous position. While this system may have operated with a degree of effectiveness under the C-in-C, it may be doubted that it did so under the CGS. The C-in-C was respected by the other heads of departments as the professional head of the army. Since promotion to the post of C-in-C was open to all senior officers, they had an incentive to maintain its powers. The CGS enjoyed no such moral superiority. Since the post was intended to be on a parallel and separate promotion ladder to the Administrative Staff, the other heads of departments had little incentive to maintain its powers, rather the opposite. The CGS was not so much a down-graded C-in-C as an up-graded Director of Mobilisation and Military Intelligence, the most junior member of the War Office Council.

The British General Staff was divided into two parts: the War Office staff and the staff of the regional commands. The duties of the former were laid down as being

> to advise on the strategical distribution of the Army, to supervise the education of officers, and the training and preparation of the Army for war, to study military schemes, offensive and defensive, to collect and collate military intelligence, to direct the general policy in Army matters, and to secure continuity of action in the execution of that policy.[37]

Although these responsibilities were considerable, an examination of the War Office staff's three directorates[38] indicates that their actual power was limited. The Directorate of Military Operations was concerned only with planning. Whereas the German CGS was the commander designate of the entire field army, his British counterpart was primarily the chief military adviser to the Secretary of State for War and had no direct powers of command: only in 1916 was the CIGS permitted to issue orders in the name of the government, a power cancelled in 1918. Apart from this brief period, all reports and orders were channelled through the Secretary of State,[39] who was usually a civilian politician. The Directorate of Staff Duties was primarily responsible for appointments to and instruction of the General Staff, the appointment of instructors to the Staff College, the instruction and examinations at the Staff College, the education and examination of officers for promotion, military publications and military history. To carry out this wide range of duties, the directorate had precisely nine officers.[40] The 13 officers of the Directorate of Military Training were responsible for Home Defence, training and manoeuvres in the United Kingdom and for schools of training. Responsibility for schools of training gave little real power, since the three combat arms (cavalry, infantry and artillery) had no central schools, it being considered that the training of these arms was solely the concern of commanding officers.

The powers of the 144 officers of the General Staff in the regional commands[41] was equally limited. Officers of the German *Truppen-Generalstab* were above the rest of the staff in status, by virtue of their being the commander's junior partner. Their counterparts in the British Army enjoyed no such precedence. Although the Staff Manual (War) of 1912 stated that it was the duty of a General Staff officer to offer his advice to the commander, 'it was rather easier to suggest this novel practice than to legislate for its acceptance'.[42] The British General Staff officer remained very much his commander's subordinate, a view strongly held by Sir John French, who became CIGS in 1912 despite the fact that he had neither been to the Staff College nor served on the General Staff. Shortly after taking up his new post, French told Staff College students that many difficulties could be overcome,

> if you endeavour to comprehend clearly the definite line of demarcation which exists between the function of the commander and the function of the Staff. It is the duty of the Staff to present all the facts of the situation to a commander with perfect accuracy and impartiality and then to take the necessary measures for carrying his decisions into effect.

He concluded that staff officers should be but tools in the hands of the commander.[43]

Even the General Staff officer's position as chief of staff was threatened. As Henry Wilson confided to his diary in October 1904,

> The proposals of Douglas [the Adjutant-General] and others were that in every command the Administrative staff officers were to be *much* senior to the General Staff which I feared would lead to the gradual extinction of the newly formed General Staff and the glorification of the Administrative Staff into the old and pestilent form of Chief Staff Officer.[44]

This indeed is largely what occurred. From 1909, each senior commander had two chiefs of staff, for the General Staff and the Administrative Staff, both with the right of direct access to the commander.[45] Thus, whereas a German commander received advice and reports from only one source – a General Staff officer who could ensure that operations received top priority – a British commander had two potentially conflicting sources of advice. Since the administrative chief was the more senior of the two staff officers, it is likely that his was the more dominant voice.

### *Selection of General Staff Officers*

The Esher Committee recommended that the General Staff should form a 'blue-ribbon' elite, although not a separate corps. Its members should serve for a maximum of four years before returning to regimental duty and should receive automatic accelerated promotion. While on the staff, they should wear a distinctive uniform and come under the command of the CGS.[46] It was hoped that higher command posts would come to be all but confined to officers who had served satisfactorily in the General Staff at the War Office.[47] Three issues were highly contentious: which officers should be eligible for service on the General Staff; how officers should be chosen; and whether accelerated promotion should be limited to the General Staff alone.

The Esher Committee proposed that General Staff officers be recruited mainly from the Staff College,[48] making it a *corps d'élite*. Although upheld by the Hutchinson Committee,[49] there was considerable pressure for other criteria to be used in addition. French, for example, urged the current CGS, Lyttelton, to retain the right to appoint non-psc (passed Staff College) officers,[50] while two members of the Hutchinson Committee recommended that the majority of General Staff officers should be selected from those who had served on the Administrative Staff (the staffs of the Adjutant-General and the Quartermaster-General). The two officers, who happened to represent this branch, feared that a more elitist system would result in only second-rate officers entering the Administrative Staff and that 'jealousy and friction may perhaps result'.[51] One of them, Brigadier-General Miles, resented the implied denigration of administration: 'Administration is sometimes spoken of as if it were pure indoors work. But it is not so; there is no better practice than drawing up large bodies of troops in ceremonial.'[52] He neglected to explain for what it was that this was better practice. In 1906, he arranged for officers to attend special courses at the London School of Economics, designed to prepare them for higher appointments in the Administrative Staff. The course was intended to be a rival to the General Staff-controlled Staff College in the supply of staff officers, and instructors from the Staff College were excluded from the lectures.[53]

Two points emerge from the question of which officers should be eligible for service on the General Staff. First, there was to be no strict separation between the General Staff and Administrative Staff, due to a belief that General Staff duties were not dissimilar to those of the Administrative Staff, a concept totally at variance with German thought. Second, considerable efforts were made to prevent the General Staff attracting the best officers, largely because of branch rivalries. This indicates that combat at the operational level was by no means the over-riding priority in the British Army that it was in the German Army. On the contrary, there was a distinct concentration on the administration of friendly forces. We have noted the dangers of an over-concentration on operations, as occurred in the German Army, but the British emphasis on administration was probably more damaging to combat effectiveness.

The second question concerned how officers should be selected for the General Staff. Lord Haldane favoured the German system, in which officers were chosen by the CGS, on the recommendation of the War Academy, but this option was rejected,[54] on the grounds that the CGS did not know officers well enough to draw up a list of General Staff officers fairly[55] and that such powers would make the CGS too dominant.[56] It was decided, on the personal advice of the king, that a list of officers eligible for General Staff service, the 'General Staff list', should be drawn up by the Selection Board.[57] The board, which also controlled promotion to colonel and above, consisted of the Inspector-General of the Forces, the seven regional commanders-in-chief and the four military members of the Army Council.[58] The only one of these 12 officers directly concerned with General Staff duties was the CGS himself. While he might have a considerable degree of moral authority, it is clear that the CGS was by no means dominant even in the selection of his own staff. It was possible for the Administrative Staff to pack the list with their own nominees.

The Esher Committee recommended that officers should receive accelerated promotion for service on the General Staff 'in all cases',[59] giving a considerable career boost (thereby improving recruitment to the General Staff) and this would in time have resulted in the majority of senior posts being held by such officers. This proposal met with considerable resistance and compromises were soon suggested. The Hutchinson Committee recommended that General Staff officers be rewarded with a good posting, particularly the command of a battalion.[60] This was opposed by the CGS, Lyttelton, on the grounds that such a posting was in fact a disincentive, as the command of a battalion was considered a heavy duty.[61] In 1906, it was agreed that only 'approved service' on the General Staff should bring accelerated promotion,[62] but in 1907 the Army Council decided that accelerated promotion should be awarded for good service in any staff post, not just in the General Staff.[63]

## The Staff College

In the British Army, neither staff officers nor the training provided by the Staff College were regarded with great esteem. The Duke of Cambridge was not alone in considering graduates of the Staff College to be 'very ugly . . . and very dirty officers'.[64] There was little emphasis on formal training when it came to filling staff posts: 'Though officers possessing a psc were too few to fill all available staff appointments, there was still no guarantee that the successful graduate from Camberley would receive a staff posting.'[65] The combination of the limited supply of pscs and the diversion of some even of these to other duties meant that 'in 1899 nearly half the staff appointments were filled by untrained regimental officers'.[66] Of the 460 generals and staff officers who served in the Boer War, only 120 were psc,[67] while shortly after that war, only seven of the 52 officers at the War Office were psc.[68] When the General Staff was formed, there was fierce opposition to possession of a psc being mandatory for admission to the new body, with Sir John French arguing that an experienced regimental officer could be as good a staff officer as one with a psc.[69]

*Selection for the Staff College*

In the German Army, competition for places at the War Academy was fierce, with over 1,000 candidates for only 160 places by 1914, a ratio of about eight to one. In Britain, the ratio of applicants to places at the Staff College was between four and five to one, with 101 candidates for 24 places in 1904, and 185 for 36 places in 1913.[70]

Four factors, however, undermined the claim that the officers who secured places at Camberley represented the cream of the army. First, 'many regiments, not only the cavalry, shunned the establishment as a pedagogical talking shop'. 'It was the proud boast of the Gordon [Highlanders] that none of their officers had ever entered the Staff College or ever would. To permit oneself even to breathe the name of such a place was held to be excessively bad "form".'[71] Only 38 cavalry officers attended between 1856 and 1881.[72] Sir James Edmonds claimed that at least one battalion commander would only recommend incompetents and refused to put forward good men, in order to keep them in the battalion.[73] This practice was not restricted to the more obviously conservative corps: Edmonds' pay as a captain in the Royal Engineers was stopped while he attended the course, on the grounds that he was not employed on corps business.[74] Many able officers were therefore unable to seek entry to the Staff College.

The second factor was the quota system. Originally, selection for the Staff College was purely by examination, although no regiment could have two successful candidates in a single year. In the 1880s, this system was replaced by a system of quotas, each arm being guaranteed a certain number of places each year. Of the 28 places open to competition in 1886, the quotas were: Cavalry and Infantry – 18; Royal Artillery and Royal Engineers – 6; Indian Army – 3; Royal Marines – 1. This system was not without its flaws:

> A ludicrous situation occurred in 1886 when Royal Artillery officers filled 7 out of the top 8 positions [in the examination results] and an Engineer the eighth. At the other end only 13 infantry and cavalry officers qualified for 18 places, so that 5 who had failed to qualify were admitted . . . The gunner officer who came seventh with 2,407 marks was excluded while a Rifleman who came thirty-second and 'failed' with 1,585 marks was admitted. In the previous year,

> Ordnance Corps officers occupied 10 of the first 12 places and 4 of them were excluded by the same rule. Clearly, without some such restriction there would have been the serious disadvantage of the Ordnance Corps virtually monopolising first the Staff College, and later the senior staff posts throughout the Army, but on the other hand it could hardly be claimed that Camberley was getting the best brains when such anomalies occurred nearly every year.[75]

The third problem was that comparatively few officers actually passed the entrance examination. This does not appear to have been due to the pass mark being set too high. Indeed, the examination was a test almost more of physical endurance than of intellect, with 42 hours of examination over two weeks.[76] At least one part of the problem appears to have been poor quality examiners. Edmonds complained about the marks that he was awarded in two papers in which he was expert and was told that these examiners would not be used again. Nor was his the only case of difficulty with examiners. When Edmonds became an examiner himself, he was told to fail only five per cent of the candidates, no matter what marks the others achieved.[77]

The final factor which undermined the elite status of those entering the Staff College was the system of nominations, introduced in the 1880s, under which a certain number of places each year were in the gift of the C-in-C. The only requirement was that the officer nominated had scored at least half marks (later dropped to three-eighths) in the entrance examination.[78] Nomination allowed some of the problems of the quota system to be alleviated[79] and could permit a certain flexibility, such as in the case of Haig, whose overall score was sufficient to win a place but who failed the paper in mathematics by only 18 marks[80] (four and a half per cent). Nevertheless, nomination introduced a subjective element, based upon connections and patronage, into the selection system. Further, although nominees were officers unable to win places at the Staff College through their own ability, their contacts in high places meant that they usually secured the best staff postings after graduation.[81] It is of note that the number of places available for nomination increased far more than did those open to competition. In 1886, there were 28 places open to competition and four nominations.[82] By 1913, there were 36 places for competition, but 15 nominations.[83]

### *Training at the Staff College*

Edmonds reported that the two-year course was not strenuous. His corps, the Royal Engineers, considered it a long holiday,[84] a view perhaps justified by Edmonds finding time to write a weighty history of the American Civil War, while his fellow sapper, Macdonagh, was able to qualify as a barrister.[85]

Not all students put their time to such practical use: in the late 1880s, Horace Smith-Dorrien 'seems to have spent more of his time between the kennels and the stables, except when at Epsom, Ascot, or Hawthorne Hill. Legend says that after he had been there three months he was found wandering about the corridors asking the way to the library.'[86]

The German War Academy had a lecturing staff of 42, of whom 20 were officers of the Great General Staff and 16 were university professors. The British Staff College had a staff of nine.[87] In 1896, only one of the nine had any combat experience (Henderson as a subaltern in 1882) and 'only Major Simpson, who taught Staff Duties, had been on the staff, but in the Intelligence Division, and about the workings of that institution he was conspicuously silent'.[88] Edmonds was highly critical of the instruction provided:

> As carried out the syllabus seemed designed to complete one's neglected military education rather than to prepare one for staff work . . . What actually happened in the first year was that we sat at a few lectures . . . and heard what amounted to no more than the reading of some paragraphs of the regulation books (mostly out of date) and some pages of military history.

While much work was done in the field, this consisted largely of drawing and simple field engineering.[89] There appears to have been little training in staff duties or in tactics, the core subjects at the War Academy, although this was in part rectified in the second year. The new commandant, Colonel Hildyard, set numerous tactical field exercises, although these all involved forces under brigade size. The only war game was the annual contest between the Senior and Junior divisions of the college.[90] In common with a number of other officers, Edmonds considered the most useful part of the course to be the time spent on attachments to other arms. He himself served with the 6th Dragoon Guards, the 37th Battery Royal Field Artillery and the 4th Battalion King's Royal Rifle Corps.[91] His period on a brigade staff was less successful, as the Brigade Major used his presence as an opportunity to go away on holiday.[92]

Perhaps the greatest contrast between the German War Academy and the British Staff College was in the attitude to examinations. The Germans placed great weight upon examinations, requiring all students to meet a high standard in order to be permitted to continue the course. The British repeatedly reduced the importance of examinations and abolished some altogether. The reason for this difference in approach appears to have been due to fundamentally different perceptions of what was tested in an examination. Essentially, the Germans employed examinations to test an officer's power of judgement, whereas the British used them to test his memory.

The British system was characterised by 'cramming'. The level of detail required, the breadth of the syllabus and the length of the reading lists made it impossible to digest the material taught. Only by cramming could officers pass the examination.[93] The effort required was considerable: Haig spent over nine months with a private tutor before attempting (and failing) the Staff College entrance examination.[94] With examinations so firmly based upon the regurgitation of facts, rather than on judgement, near perfect scores were possible: Edmonds scored 98.8 per cent in his captain to major promotion examination in 1894.[95] Even the reproduction of passages from textbooks was permitted, one officer being letter perfect on sections from Hamley's *Operations of War*.[96]

The unsatisfactory nature of the system was repeatedly remarked upon, but no one appears to have suggested changing the system to test judgement and so render cramming valueless. The problem was that 'the difference between absorbing and cramming was too subtle for some officers . . . to grasp – especially since cramming was what they had been encouraged to do since they were young boys'.[97] The solution adopted was to progressively reduce the importance of examinations. The entrance examination was circumvented by increasing the proportion of places reserved for nominated candidates. The examination at the end of the first year of the course became a formality, such that 'no one regarded it seriously'. Edmonds recalled one incident in which, 'I was trying to help a lame duck (a nominee) when the invigilator came up. I expected trouble; all he said was, "It's no good prompting him, you must dictate it to him", and proceeded himself to do so.'[98] Henry Rawlinson, commandant from 1903 to 1906, and his staff, 'were not unduly influenced by the marks gained by students in the examination at the end of the first year; they took men as they found them, and judged them mainly by the impression they felt they would make on those who met them as staff officers later'.[99]

'Wully' Robertson, commandant from 1910 to 1913, gave even less weight to examinations, although he emphasised practical skill in the field.[100] The final examination had already been abolished by Hildyard in the 1890s.[101] In these circumstances, there was effectively no objective measurement of a student's ability. Even the final assessment was vague. The British appear to have been loth to withhold the magic letters 'psc' from even those officers whose confidential reports strongly recommended that they not be employed on the staff. Only in 1911 was recommendation for or against service on the General Staff made separate from the award of a psc.[102]

Officers of the German General Staff were the acknowledged cream of the officer corps, selected largely by merit through objective examination. Their training was rigorous and exacting. Since some 160 graduates were produced by the War Academy each year, of whom only a handful became members of the General Staff, sufficient trained staff officers were available for the administrative duties of the *Adjutantur* (personnel staff) and the *Intendantur* (logistics staff). While many British psc officers were undoubtedly of high quality, the selection and training system did not give them the same status as their German counterparts. Since the Staff College produced only 30 to 50 graduates each year, there were insufficient trained staff officers available for there to be any question of allowing only the best to serve on the General Staff. In 1914, there were only 447 pscs in the whole army.[103] Since many of these were senior officers holding commands, there were approximately the same number of General Staff positions as there were psc officers to fill them. As a result, not only were there hardly any trained staff officers available for service on the Administrative Staff, despite the importance of its duties, but it was not possible to develop a distinction between those officers who were merely psc and those who were members of the General Staff, a distinction central to the German system.

Up to a third of entrants to the Staff College owed their places to patronage, while others were there more because of their arm of service than their ability. Once at the Staff College, award of a psc was almost certain. Robertson dismissed only two students during his three years as commandant, one for academic reasons, the other, a very capable student, for breaking King's Regulations by refusing to grow a moustache.[104] Although the quality of training provided at the Staff College improved considerably in the decade before 1914, it was still possible for an officer to gain a psc without having to prove himself in any serious examination. Since officers whose patrons secured them nominations were both less tested at the Staff College and more likely to gain the better staff postings, the aura of position by merit enjoyed by the German General Staff was not shared by the British General Staff. Finally, since junior General Staff postings were open to non-psc officers with patrons, the status of the corps was further undermined.

### *The General Staff and Command*

The failings of the system of selection for the General Staff were compounded by the actions of members of the corps. The behaviour of Haig, one of the key figures in the creation of the General Staff, provides an example:

> If staff officers are in awe of the commander, there is a danger of loyalty becoming blind. In order to function properly, the staff must be composed of able and intelligent men possessing the courage to question their commander. As Haig himself often stressed, a premium must be placed upon independence. It is up to the leader

> himself to ensure that these requirements are satisfied. Few succeed. The failure to choose staff officers with independent minds is often an indication of weaknesses in the commander's own character. He may want the staff to be a convenient counter-weight to outside criticism and may, as a result, seek officers with whom he feels comfortable. Likewise, he might feel threatened by intelligent subordinates, high fliers who could be potential successors. Consciously or sub-consciously, he might select intellectual inferiors in order to reduce the threat subordinates pose. Being surrounded by inferiors also boosts the ego of the commander, providing him with confirmation of this ability to lead . . . Whilst [Haig] recognised that modern war demanded efficient and outspoken staff officers . . . when he began for the first time to choose a staff of his own, he displayed many of the weaknesses outlined above.
>
> Obsequiousness was a predominant characteristic among those closest to him. In choosing a personal staff, Haig stressed harmony; he wanted a 'band of brothers'. Honesty and integrity were less important than an amiable temperament. He had little patience for men with the same qualities which had characterised him during his days as a staff officer. It was no concern (and some positive attraction) if subordinates held him in awe. These weaknesses negated his otherwise progressive attitude towards the staff and staff training.[105]

Haig's tendency to ignore his own teaching was shown in 1912, when he returned from India to take over I Corps at Aldershot. He brought with him two members of his Indian staff, Captains Baird and Charteris. The staff at Aldershot referred to this as the 'Hindu Invasion'.

> Haig's action was indeed worthy of scorn. The man who had struggled, while Director of Staff Duties, to turn the staff system into a meritocracy, was here engaging in patronage pure and simple. Neither Baird nor Charteris had been to Camberley; their staff experience was minimal; and the greater part of their careers had been spent in India. Their main qualification for this impressive promotion was their ability to please their master.[106]

Not only was the British General Staff unable to assert the degree of independence and leadership of its German equivalent, it was itself unable to escape from the failings of the British command system, with its cult of rank. It was therefore in no position to provide the kind of professional impetus so central to the development of directive command. It is to the British system of command that we must now turn.

## Umpiring

The British Army employed two, mutually contradictory, command systems, which have been termed 'umpiring'[107] and 'restrictive control'. Restrictive control is a system in which subordinates are given orders which lay down their actions in detail and must be obeyed regardless of circumstances. Local initiative tends to be frowned on by commanders, on the grounds that it disorganises the centralised plan. This system of command was standard at the tactical level within the British Army and influenced the operational level, especially during the First World War. More common at the operational level, however, was the system of umpiring.

Umpiring is a term coined to illustrate that practice in which an officer abdicates his command responsibilities. In both directive command and restrictive control, the commander imposes his will upon his subordinates through the assignment of clear objectives, which he then ensures that his subordinates work to achieve. The umpire, by contrast, having indicated a general mission withdraws rather than spur on his subordinates. Whereas both directive command and restrictive control are 'energy positive', in that they force subordinates into action, umpiring is 'energy neutral'.

Three examples may serve to illustrate the dysfunctional effects of umpiring. In the Boer War, both General Sir Redvers Buller and one of his divisional commanders, Lieutenant-General Sir Charles Warren, were 'loth to interfere with their subordinates'. In Buller's case this resulted in his permitting subordinates to employ out-of-date formations, even after he had explicitly admonished them for the practice.[108] Again, Buller allowed Warren considerable freedom of action before the Battle of Tabangama, despite his having already compromised Buller's plan of action.[109]

In the First World War, two of the most important umpires were Hamilton and Haig. Although umpiring was not uncommon within the British Army generally, both Hamilton and Haig may have had this tendency reinforced through contact with the German system of directive command. This influence is most certain in Haig's case. In 1895, Haig wrote a report on a visit he madc to the annual manoeuvres of the Prussian cavalry, in which he emphasised the independence allowed to junior officers in the German Army and sharply criticised those old-fashioned colonels in the British Army, who 'maintain that the colonel should show his authority by a constant interference in the captain's sphere of activity'.[110] In an exercise soon after, Haig stressed the importance of decentralised command and criticised commanders who left nothing to the initiative of their subordinates.[111] His view was reinforced at the Staff College, where he was taught that 'interference of superiors with details really pertaining to subordinates, paralyses initiative'.[112]

Whether Hamilton too was influenced by the German system is less certain. He was, however, exposed to it while chief of the British Military Mission to the Japanese Army in the Russo-Japanese War of 1904–5, since the Japanese Army was closely modelled on the German, even using German manuals in direct translation.[113] Hamilton's own view was that,

> The true commander . . . knows the truth of that great maxim: if the subordinate never makes a mistake, he never makes anything . . . Against the danger of a subaltern's mistake in the execution of his own job, it is but fair to set the risk of a meddlesome superior failing himself in the performance of another's business. The superior is too busy doing someone else's job to attend to his own – too busy with the parts to give his mind to the whole.[114]

It is of note that whereas von Moltke favoured decentralisation of command in order to speed decision making and believed that the officer on the spot was best able to assess the situation, Hamilton appears to have supported decentralisation on the grounds that it avoided the chance of the superior making a mistake.

One of the dangers of umpiring is excessive decentralisation and may be illustrated by the initial landings at Gallipoli.[115] Major-General A. G. Hunter-Weston's 29th Division was to land at five beaches at the tip of the peninsula. While little opposition was met at S, X and Y Beaches, the landings at V and W were repulsed. Rather than exploit from the successful landings, Hunter-Weston concentrated on renewed attempts at V and W Beaches. From his position on the battleship HMS *Queen Elizabeth*, Hamilton could see clearly what the situation was and what should be done to achieve success. He offered Hunter-Weston his entire reserve, two French brigades, for use at Y Beach. The 'energy-neutral' nature of this action is indicated by the reserves being offered rather than assigned.

> The only answer he got was a request for one of them for W Beach. Hamilton's failure to insist on what he saw was the right course exemplifies his refusal to interfere with the man on the spot. Hunter-Weston was a proved fighting soldier, trusted and loved by the commanders and men with whom he served. Hamilton felt he must be allowed to get on with the task that had been entrusted to him.[116]

To call Hunter-Weston a 'proved fighting soldier' appears excessive. He was a freshly appointed brigadier in 1914[117] and had spent much of the six months before the Gallipoli landings training his newly formed division. Despite his display of incompetence, Hunter-Weston was soon promoted to command VIII Corps. Hamilton, therefore, gave excessive freedom to his subordinates, even though he knew they were committing serious errors and he had the power to restore the situation. Yet his intervention at

Suvla Bay[118] was condemned by a committee of lieutenant-generals at the War Office and was an important factor in his being replaced.[119]

While superficially similar, the decentralising inherent in umpiring is very different from that employed in directive command. The umpire often avoids 'interfering' out of an excessive respect for the feelings and reputation of the subordinate. The relationship between the umpire and his subordinate may be considered more important than the successful attainment of the objective. Decentralisation therefore becomes an end in itself. In directive command, the decentralisation of decision making is purely a means towards the end of fulfilling the higher intent most effectively. Since priority is given to the intent, rather than the means, commanders are required to 'monitor' the actions of their subordinates. This monitoring does not take the form of a constant intimidating presence, nor of a demand for frequent situation reports. Rather, commanders are expected to use their own resources, such as liaison officers, radio monitoring and personal visits, to gain an accurate picture of events. If it becomes clear that a subordinate's actions are mistaken and threaten the success of the overall intent, the commander is required to intervene. The German regulations stated:

> Intervention in the operations of individual companies [by the regimental commander] must be restricted to rare and unusual circumstances and is only appropriate, *if the execution of the overall intent appears seriously endangered through the actions of the subordinates* and if there is not enough time to stay within the chain of command with an order.[120]

In the German Army, decentralisation was to be maintained only as long as it assisted the achievement of the intent. If it ceased so to do, commanders were permitted not only to order their immediate subordinates back on course, but even to by-pass them and issue orders 'two-down'. In extreme circumstances, commanders could take over personal command of sub-units, a practice that became common during the Second World War. Indeed, in recognition that circumstances arise that demand close control from above, the Bundeswehr has coined the term *Befehlstaktik* (order-type tactics).[121] At the initial landings at Gallipoli, whereas Hamilton acquiesced to Hunter-Weston's error, a German commander would have been required to order Hunter-Weston to concentrate on the successful beaches and to send his reserves to these. Any question of Hunter-Weston's reputation being harmed would have been considered secondary to the successful achievement of the overall intent.

The second area where the umpire's excessive desire to allow subordinates room for initiative can be dysfunctional is that of orders. For example, Haig believed that having created opportunities for his subordinates to exploit, the commander should outline his broad intent, assign individual tasks and then withdraw.[122] This was similar to the German system, except that the Germans expected the commander to operate actively to support his subordinates.

An essential feature of the German system of directive command was that a subordinate should 'enter into the mind of the commander'.[123] Only in this way could commander and subordinate come to a 'union of views', whereby the subordinate could fully understand the overall intent and his part in it. Commanders therefore had the responsibility to make themselves clear to their subordinates. These, in turn, were required to raise any points of uncertainty. The failure of von Falkenhayn to let the commander of Fifth Army into his thinking has been cited as a major factor in the failure of the German offensive at Verdun.[124] This insistence upon clarity and understanding was in contrast to the reality of Haig's command.

> What [Haig] was thinking about the war as it stood on any particular day, no one, not even his Chief of Staff, could fully make out. He gave his orders quick enough, but never explained them. Moreover, men say he was tongue-tied. If it came to public speaking that was abundantly true. He was anyway a 'silent' man. But such silence was babbling compared with what he said when he gave an oral . . . order. You had to learn a sort of verbal shorthand, made up of a series of grunts and gestures . . . [I recall one briefing which] consisted of D. H. with a pointer in front of a large-scale map, pointing at various spots and making grunting noises with a few words interspersed. 'Never believed' . . . 'Petrol' . . . 'Bridge gone' . . . 'When Cavalry?' and so on . . . I am sure that D. H. felt he had given me a long and lucid lecture on the whole affair.[125]

Since Haig's orders were often difficult to understand, it was essential that his subordinates have open discussions with him, in order that they could share his view of the situation. No such discussions took place. As General Gough reported,

> There were not enough discussions – between the H.Q. Staff and the Army Commanders concerned – when we could sit round a table with all the maps before one, and really thrash out the problems. Haig's conferences were too big and too formal and Army Commanders only attended to hear Haig's plans, never to discuss them.[126]

This absence of discussion was partly due to Haig's reserved character. He was notoriously 'slow of speech and frigid of manner' and this caused him to avoid free discussions with his quicker thinking and more articulate subordinates, such as Rawlinson.[127] Haig's umpiring may in part have been an attempt to distance himself from such uncomfortable situations.

## The Causes of Umpiring

The institutional causes of umpiring were both practical and theoretical. The chief practical cause was that the army's most important function was the protection of India and the colonies. This required large numbers of small garrisons, often of a single battalion. As a result, battalions became highly independent, while opportunities for higher command were severely limited. This in turn led to inexperience and lack of confidence on the part of senior commanders. The theoretical causes were, first, a belief that once an officer became a general, he had nothing further to learn and, second, a misunderstanding of Moltke's system of command.

### *The Regimental System*

The regimental system was largely the creation of Edward Cardwell, Secretary of State for War from 1868 to 1874. In 1872, Cardwell announced that the United Kingdom was to be divided into 'brigade districts', to each of which would be assigned two battalions of line infantry.[128] The brigades were purely administrative, the intention being that each brigade should have one battalion overseas and one in the United Kingdom, although rarely based in its brigade district. Owing to the high wastage caused by the new system of short service and the unhealthy climate of many overseas garrisons, the main function of the home battalions was to produce drafts for their sister battalions. A balance of forces, with 74 battalions in each category, was achieved only in 1908.[129] Before this, there were always more battalions overseas than at home, which caused considerable stress to the system. A further nine battalions of Guards were permanently based in the United Kingdom. While Cardwell's system was well-suited to the demands of Imperial Defence, it encouraged the tendency towards umpiring at the operational level.

British infantry battalions have traditionally been fiercely independent: even Cardwell's 'linkage' of battalions, in which each retained its own number and identity, was very unpopular.[130] When Hugh Childers welded the battalions into single, merged, territorially titled regiments in 1881, often with little historical or geographical logic, the resulting bitterness was considerable.[131] For many years, battalions of the same regiment sought to maintain their separate identities, often with barely disguised hostility to one another.[132] The army, therefore, effectively remained a collection of independent battalions, each with its own sense of identity and tradition. Much of this sense of separateness may be put down to Britain's army being essentially 'private' before 1871. Up to 1748, regiments were raised, equipped and maintained by their commanders, who then 'hired' them to the Crown. Their diverse origins were reflected by a wide variation in titulature, uniform and size.[133] Although repeated efforts were made to exert central control over the regiments, the all-but-literal ownership by colonels of their regiments was ended only in 1871, by Cardwell's abolition of the purchase system, in which officers bought and sold commissions up to the rank of colonel.

A mark of the unique standing of the battalion commander was the fact that he alone was entitled to the distinction of being called a 'commanding officer'; all other commanders were simply 'officer commanding'. While this difference may appear semantic, it was of considerable importance. 'Officer commanding' implies a certain separation between the commander and the unit or formation commanded, as if the commander was only temporary and with limited power. 'Commanding officer' implies no such separation; on the contrary, it emphasises the CO's proprietary power over his unit. It may not be too fanciful to contrast the British terminology with that of the German Army, in which the only officer to have a title similar to that of 'commanding officer' was the commander of a corps, called the *kommandierende General.* As in Britain, the title implied power and ownership, German corps commanders having total responsibility for their formation. Whereas a battalion was incapable of independent action, however, a corps was a self-contained army.

Although Cardwell acted to reduce the proprietary nature of the regimental system, his other reforms encouraged the survival of regimental independence. While the battalions were now linked in pairs, this was purely administrative. Since one battalion was always overseas and the other at home, regimental links had no battlefield importance. For example, the battalions of the Royal Welch Fusiliers met just once between 1880 and 1914, when the 2nd Battalion, while returning from India, stopped briefly at Malta, which was by coincidence garrisoned by the 1st Battalion.[134] While overseas, most battalions were deployed in separate garrisons, with little contact with other units and part of no higher formation. Such isolation naturally nurtured a fiercely independent, inward-looking approach. Although home battalions were integrated into permanent higher formations, their role as draft-producing units kept much of their attention directed overseas, rather than towards forging links with the other units in their formations. Further, since the average length of a battalion's tour was 12 years, each home division could expect one of its battalions to move overseas each year. The upheaval caused by this constant rotation of units must have been considerable.

The effect of the great independence of individual battalions was to limit the authority of formation commanders at the operational level. It may be suggested that formation commanders tended to be wary of issuing direct orders and of imposing their will upon battalions, whose commanders regarded the unit as their personal possession and who could call upon the protection of senior generals through the system of colonels commandant, and which were only temporary members of the formation. It appears that operational commanders tended to direct by suggestion and request, a system of limited force. This tendency may have been increased by senior commanders' limited experience of operational command.

### *The Operational Level*

In 1914, the British Army included 157 battalions of Regular infantry.[135] In Continental terms, this would have warranted headquarters for 13 divisions, six corps and two armies. The actual British peacetime establishment was six divisional headquarters and one corps headquarters, with the personnel for one army headquarters designated. Other headquarters had to be improvised. For its size, the British Army had less than half the number of senior command positions of the German Army.

Both Britain and Germany were divided into military regions, each with its own commander. Each German region provided an entire corps, which would go into battle as a single entity under the regional commander. Six of the seven British regions (Northern, Southern, Eastern, Western, Scottish and Irish) were purely administrative, with no combat function. Only the Aldershot Command was organised on the German model, largely owing to the efforts of Sir John French. In 1904, he reported that the Army Council 'have fully consented to the principle that the First Army Corps [based at Aldershot] should be organised on quite a different footing to the other Commands, and that the staff I work with in peace shall be the staff which I take to war'. Even so, French had to spend much of the next three years resisting attempts to undermine his command's status as a war formation.[136]

Command opportunities overseas were limited. The only permanent formations were in the Indian Army and, before 1914, the Indian government refused to consider sending forces outside the sub-continent. Although many wars were fought between 1870 and 1914, all but the Boer War involved small forces for limited periods. The 'Wars of Empire', while providing ample opportunity for combat experience at the tactical level, were of little benefit in the development of skill at the operational level. The commanders of the six divisions and one corps in Britain were therefore an exclusive band: they alone held command of permanent Regular formations. While other headquarters might be created on a temporary basis for manoeuvres, the officers commanding these had but a fraction of the potential for experience at the operational level of the commanders of permanent formations. Nor did the 14 Territorial Force divisions, formed in 1906, afford much opportunity for generals to gain experience. These formations of part-time soldiers enjoyed only short periods of activity and although expected to fight as whole divisions they never actually trained as such.[137]

Since command of one of the seven permanent formations was virtually the only opportunity a senior officer might have to gain experience at the operational level, effective use of this time was of considerable importance. The evidence suggests that this goal was not achieved. Although an officer might command a formation for four or five years, his opportunities to command it on exercise, or even to devote himself to its training, were limited. At least two of the seven commanders, those of I Corps and 4th Division, had important responsibilities in addition to those of their formations. The problem of balancing his responsibilities may not have been too difficult for the commander of I Corps, who was also C-in-C of Aldershot Command. All the troops of I Corps were based within the Command, while the only part of the garrison not from I Corps was 1st Cavalry Brigade. The position of the commander of 4th Division was almost schizophrenic, in that he was also commander of Woolwich District, home of the Royal Military Academy and depot of the Royal Artillery. The combination of these posts was apparently made for reasons of financial economy. To carry out his duties, this hapless officer possessed two entirely separate staffs.[138] Even in theory, he was unable to give more than half of his time to training his division. In practice, given the nature of administration, it is probable that he spent most of his time running Woolwich District.

There were considerable obstacles in the way of even those commanders able to devote their efforts towards training themselves and their formations. Not one of the six divisions was both concentrated and under a single command. 1st and 2nd Divisions were concentrated around Aldershot, but their Guards battalions were administered by London District. 3rd Division was split between Southern and Western Commands, 5th Division between Irish and Scottish Commands, and 6th Division between Irish and Northern Commands.[139] 4th Division was widely scattered over Eastern Command.[140] Even at brigade level and below, there were only four bases in the country at which all three arms were represented.[141]

With formations so dispersed, the chance for commanders to practise their craft was largely limited to war games in winter and annual manoeuvres in summer. War games, however, 'were never much in favour; in fact, [they were] neglected . . . because they tended to show up incapacity'.[142] No large-scale manoeuvres were undertaken between 1873 and 1898. In 1898, manoeuvres involving 50,000 men, organised into two corps, took place over a three-month period, stopping each evening lest they interfere with the officers' social lives.[143] Presented with bodies of troops larger than any they had seen before, commanders proved unable to meet the challenge of functioning at the operational level: 'senior generals tried to command every battalion as many battles resolved themselves into frontal attacks'.[144]

Umpiring has been defined as the abdication of responsibility by a commander. Unable to cope effectively with his responsibilities, the umpire withdraws from them. This may take the form of a retreat to the sidelines, as Hamilton did at Gallipoli, from where the umpire may proffer advice in the same way as does a soccer trainer in an important match. Alternatively, the umpire may revert to an earlier mode in which he felt more effective and ignore the chain of command.

> If responsibility is not clearly defined, the natural instinct of the superior will continually lead him to interfere directly in the work of his subordinates instead of judging it by its result; the natural instinct of the subordinate will lead him to disclaim responsibility and to do nothing without direct orders. The superior in such a case will be overwhelmed with the details of work that could be done equally well by subordinates, to the neglect of his own proper duties; the subordinate is alternately idle and overworked, ceases to think how the business of his department might be improved, acquiesces in what he knows mistaken, and is only concerned with carrying on his duties sufficiently well not to get into trouble.[145]

Manoeuvres were revived after the Boer War, but their effectiveness in training formation commanders was limited. Divisions were concentrated for only six weeks of the year, of which perhaps four days were spent in army manoeuvres. These four days represented the divisional commander's only practice commanding his formation in the year.[146] Since an officer spent about four years as a divisional commander, his total experience actually commanding a division on exercise was about 16 days. The remainder of the six weeks was spent on manoeuvres within the division. With brigade pitted against brigade, the divisional commander had no opportunity to practise his craft; rather, he acted as the trainer of his subordinates. He would set the scenarios, oversee their course and make criticisms afterwards. In short, he was an umpire and his considerable practice of this role, rather than his short time as a commander, may well have predisposed him to confusing the two. Furthermore, he was not tested in these manoeuvres, nor was he bonded to his formation through shared experience. The sense of separateness, an important aspect of umpiring, was therefore deeply ingrained during these exercises.

The limited opportunities for practising commanders at the operational level meant that senior commanders tended to be inexperienced when leading large forces, as was repeatedly shown in the manoeuvres before

1914. In one year, the two practising armies never even met.[147] In 1899, Buller marched his troops 14 miles before launching them into a one-to-one frontal assault, bringing the exercise to a premature conclusion.[148] In 1913, French commanded a force of two corps attempting to destroy a target force under General Gough. Rather than stay still, as expected, Gough not only manoeuvred but even counter-attacked, ruining French's plans. Rather than note the lesson that enemy action should be taken into account when making plans, French was furious with Gough for spoiling the exercise.[149]

The difficulty of gaining experience was particularly acute for the prospective commander of the BEF, Sir John French. After commanding a division in the manoeuvres of 1904, French was not a player again until 1913. Even in 1913, although playing as an army commander, French was also director of the exercise, the chief umpire. He was therefore 'more concerned with setting problems for his subordinates rather than putting himself under pressure'.[150] His next experience of command was against General von Kluck in August 1914.

### *The Cult of Rank*

The British Army's command system was based on a system which may be termed the 'cult of rank'. Its central tenet was that an officer of a particular rank was *ipso facto* more able and more knowledgeable than any officer of a more junior rank. This applied especially with regard to the superiority of generals over regimental officers. One of the ways in which this belief was expressed was that any suggestions or criticisms made by subordinates were seen as a challenge to the authority of the commander.

When Haig was at the Staff College, 1896–97, he was taught that the comander must be 'larger than life', that he must never be seen to change his mind or to lack a solution to a problem. Underpinning this was the belief that 'the authority of the commander-in-chief is impaired by permitting subordinates to advance their own ideas'.[151] The 'larger than life' persona of the commander meant that subordinates might be so in awe of him, and even a little afraid, that they would hesitate to bring up objections or awkward facts. For example, before the Battle of Neuve Chapelle, Rawlinson apparently did not tell Haig that the German wire in front of his corps had not been cut properly,[152] although this seriously affected the attack.

The cult of rank also prevented questions, opinions or constructive criticisms. At a conference in 1912, one junior officer spoke up to give a possible solution to the problem being discussed: 'There was a frozen silence . . . and afterwards his regimental commander called him in, tore a strip off him, calling him a "young puppy" for raising his voice in the Divisional GOC's presence, and said he had let down the regiment.'[153]

Even when suggestions were asked for, they could receive a hostile reception:

> When Fourth Army attempted to learn lessons from the first weeks on the Somme by asking divisional commanders to write in with comments, there was a considerable reluctance actually to point out mistakes, and when Brigadier General Kentish did so, he was in turn criticised for being a critic![154]

The doctrine that commanders did not need advice may have been a factor in the First World War tendency towards 'chateau generalship', where commanders stayed far in the rear. This was in part because of the difficulty of replacing experienced staff officers and commanders, so that they were forbidden to visit the front.[155] While most commanders' physical bravery was not in doubt, this distancing from the realities of battle may have emphasised the tendency for commanders to see problems as being a result of poor execution, subordinates' incompetence or a lack of 'fibre', rather than the inherent difficulty of the situation. In May 1916, General Montgomery issued a pamphlet of Tactical Notes, in which only one statement was emphasised: 'It must be remembered that all criticism by subordinates of their superiors, and of orders received from superior authority, will in the end recoil on the head of the critics and undermine their authority with those below them.'[156]

*Prolonged Service*

The 'high fliers' of the army tended to spend prolonged periods on the staff, perhaps partly as a result of the limited number of peacetime formation commands available. Since a substantial proportion of this staff duty was at the War Office or the Indian central staff, these officers had little opportunity to develop experience of command and became isolated from the army as a whole. Furthermore, it may be suggested that their powers of command were undermined by the growth of a 'staff mentality'. The extent to which officers destined for high position stayed on the staff may be illustrated by the careers of four officers: Buller, Haig, Robertson and Wilson.

Sir Redvers Buller acquired a very poor reputation owing to his incompetent handling of British forces early in the Boer War. Much of this incompetence may be attributed to his lack of experience at the operational level. When he arrived in South Africa in 1899, Buller had had no experience of commanding troops for over 12 years, apart from in the manoeuvres of 1898 – in which he had performed very badly,[157] having been Adjutant-General from 1890 to 1897.[158] His last command experience had been during the retreat from Khartoum after the death of General Gordon.[159] His second-in-command in South Africa, General White, was in a similar position, having been sent from his desk as Quartermaster-General to command the British forces in Natal on the eve of the war.[160]

Haig's career involved even less time with the troops. Seconded to the Egyptian Army immediately after leaving the Staff College in 1897, Haig spent most of 1898 leading an Egyptian cavalry squadron in the Sudan campaign.[161] On returning to England, he was appointed Brigade Major to French's 1st Cavalry Brigade and went with him to South Africa as his Chief Staff Officer when French was given command of the cavalry division.[162] After a year commanding a group of columns with a mainly defensive role,[163] Haig returned to Britain in 1902, where he spent a year as commanding officer of the 17th Lancers in cramped conditions in Edinburgh.[164] The next ten years saw Haig in a succession of staff posts: Inspector-General for Cavalry in India, 1903 to 1906; Director of Military Training and then Director of Staff Duties at the War Office, 1906 to 1909; and Chief of the General Staff in India, 1909 to 1911.[165] In 1912, when he took over I Corps at Aldershot, Haig was a senior comander with no recent line service.

The absence of line service was all the more apparent in the careers of 'Wully' Robertson and Sir Henry Wilson, who succeeded each other both as commandants of the Staff College and as CIGS. Robertson, who rose from the ranks, did not occupy a single command position between 1891, when as a lieutenant he became a regimental transport officer, and 1919, when he took over the British Army on the Rhine.[166] Wilson's career was similar, with no line command between 1892 and 1915, when he spent a brief period commanding IV Corps.[167]

'High fliers' tended to move from one staff posting to another. While this may have put their administrative abilities to good use, it may be suggested that it greatly increased their tendency towards umpiring. This was in part due to a simple lack of experience of command at the operational level, leading to an uncertainty of touch. It may also have been caused by a growing 'staff mentality'. Staff officers do not command. They rarely have to bear the responsibility of making an important decision quickly, with defeat the consequence of a mistake. On the contrary, staff officers merely request or suggest. This minimalising of responsibility may be greatest in a war ministry, where all the important decisions are referred to a committee dominated by civilian and political influences. In such an environment, the power of command may become atrophied and officers become incapable of acting swiftly and decisively at the operational level in war.

# 3
# From *Stosstaktik* to *Stosstrupptaktik*

> The infantry is the main arm. In combination with the artillery, it overcomes the enemy through its fire. It alone breaks his last resistance. It bears the main burden of the fight and suffers the greatest sacrifice. For this it achieves also the highest glory.
>
> *Exerzier-Reglement für die Infanterie* (1906)

Before the introduction of the man-portable two-way radio, tactical orders had to be given by voice, limiting the frontage a single officer could control to 100 metres.[1] This was reflected in the formations and tactics employed. Every army has its basic tactical unit, the smallest unit to which an independent mission can be assigned, which operates as an entity under the immediate direction of a single commander. Since every member of the unit had to be able to hear the commander's voice, its deployment was limited to that which would keep it entirely within 50 metres of the commander. At the beginning of the period under study, most armies considered the battalion the basic tactical unit. To deploy a unit of this size within reach of the commander's voice required formations to be dense, with soldiers packed virtually shoulder to shoulder. Such formations were viable on a battlefield where most infantrymen were armed with muskets, but the development of firearms during the nineteenth and early twentieth centuries made them no longer so. The standard Napoleonic musket could fire two or three rounds per minute and had an effective range of about 100 metres. The magazine rifles used in the First World War fired 15 rounds per minute to an effective range of 1,000 metres. The result was a near 60-fold increase (six times rate of fire multiplied by ten times range) in the volume of infantry fire and this was augmented still further by the introduction of the machine gun. Commanders faced a dilemma: either they adopted looser formations and accepted reduced control over the troops, or they retained dense formations and risked prohibitively high casualties.

The situation was complicated by the question of fighting power. This concept was developed during the First World War by the German Army, which coined terms to describe the two types of fighting power used at the minor tactical level: *Feuerkraft* (firepower) was that type of fighting power employed in the fire fight and *Stosskraft* (assault power) was that used in close combat. Cavalry and artillery each employed one type of fighting power only;[2] the infantry alone used both types. As firearms improved, cavalry became increasingly vulnerable on the battlefield and artillery was compelled to pull back from the front line and rely on indirect fire, which tended to be considerably less accurate. The key to success became the infantry. Commanders were therefore presented with a second dilemma: victory required the concentration of overwhelming fighting power at the decisive point, but because the individual rifleman possessed limited fighting power, such concentration required the physical massing of troops in dense formations. Dense formations invited prohibitive casualties, but the fighting power of looser formations might not be sufficient at the decisive point. Dense formations offered ease of control and concentration of fighting power, but they presented vulnerable targets to enemy fire. The development of tactics over this period represents the ever-changing dialectic between these factors.

Both the German and British armies experienced sharp internal debates between those who insisted that the traditional *Stosstaktik* (assault tactics, also called 'normal tactics'), based upon bayonet charges by massed infantry, should be retained and those who believed that developments in firearms required major changes in tactics, involving a shift towards looser control and more dispersed formations. (The term 'normal tactics' appears to have originated in the nineteenth century; its use was intended to imply that the new decentralised tactics being suggested by certain theorists were 'abnormal'.)

The 'normal tacticians' supported their argument with two main claims. The first was that fire fights tended to be indecisive. Before the mid-nineteenth century, the firepower available to armies was comparatively limited. Owing to short ranges and low rates of fire, a prolonged fire fight might weaken the enemy, but the troops involved tended to become so tired and disordered as to be no longer capable of launching a bayonet charge to take advantage of the enemy's vulnerability at the end of the fire fight.[3] The normal tacticians argued that the key to victory lay with assault power: an assault by determined infantry or cavalry could achieve in minutes what a fire fight lasting hours might not. They contended that the sight of a charging force, unmoved by the single volley that could be fired against it, would usually be sufficient to cause the defenders to flee almost before the two sides came into contact.

Their second claim was that the result of an assault was decided more by moral than by physical factors. Hand-to-hand combat was a chaotic and bloody affair, which most soldiers would seek to avoid. The essence of the assault was therefore a question of which side would hesitate first. The normal tacticians argued that the most effective means by which the moral power of the attackers could be increased was deployment in dense masses. Colonel G. F. R. Henderson claimed, 'If there is one principle more than another which is important in war, it is that in unity there is strength'.[4] Dense formations steadied the troops' morale, whereas open order was held to be demoralising.[5] The greater the weight of enemy fire, therefore, the greater was the need for dense formations in order to maintain morale.

Even before the general introduction of rifles, great courage was required on the part of troops launching an assault. They were unable to reply to the defenders' fire and were actively inviting the terrors of hand-to-hand combat. It appeared much easier and safer to hold back and rely on fire. This reluctance to assault was more pronounced among less well-trained troops than in troops inculcated with a belief in their own superiority.[6] The normal tacticians therefore emphasised training for the assault and the rigid control it required. They also contrasted the 'glorious' bravery of the bayonet charge with the 'cowardly' nature of a fire fight. Indeed, it is perhaps no coincidence that the British Army's highest award, the Victoria Cross, commemorates a cavalry charge in the face of overwhelming enemy fire. There can be little doubt that the contemporary cult of the *arme blanche* in the cavalry affected the debate on infantry tactics, in that both focused on the perceived superiority of moral factors over technology.

In summary, the 'normal' tactician saw combat as structured and orderly. The fighting power of the infantry was based upon assault power rather than on firepower. Assault power, in turn, was believed to be dependent largely on moral power. Since this moral power was externally imposed, by means of dense formations which pulled the individual forward, the 'normal' tactician argued that mass was central to the fighting power of the infantry. Individual initiative would merely reduce the desired hypnotic effect of the mass and was therefore a positive danger.

The reformers countered these arguments by claiming that, whatever the moral advantages of dense formations, improvements in firearms made them obsolete. Dense masses presented a highly vulnerable target and would suffer casualties sufficient to break the morale of even the most determined mass. In place of clinging to assault tactics, armies should recognise the inherent chaos of the battlefield and seek to exploit it by the use of dispersed formations and low-level initiative.

Developments in tactics from the 1850s may be seen as a gradual rearguard action by the 'normal' tacticians, although the two schools of thought were not to be formed clearly until the 1880s. As the decisive effect of new weapons became impossible to dismiss, conservatives sought to modify the assault tactics to suit the new circumstances yet still retain their fundamental philosophy.

## The Introduction of Breech-Loading Rifles

Technical developments after 1825 greatly increased the firepower available to the infantry: the Dreyse needle gun had a rate of fire of five rounds per minute and was effective up to 700 paces; the Thouvenin thorn rifle fired two rounds per minute to 1,000 paces; and the Minié rifled musket fired one and a half rounds per minute accurately to 1,000 paces, with the advantages that it was simple to operate and that conventional muskets could easily be converted.[7] By the 1850s, the challenge facing commanders was both simple and, apparently, insoluble: 'An increasing number of Europe's infantrymen were carrying rifles which could kill at five times the range of the smoothbore musket. Yet no one had devised a way to make men five times braver, five times as willing to die, or even five times quicker on their feet.'[8] Part of the problem was that the massed formations of the assault tactics were difficult to manoeuvre. In 1904, the Japanese attacked at four times the speed of European troops by employing looser formations.[9]

The Crimean War gave no clear indication of the effect of the new weapons on tactics. Although the French and British used the Minié system, the Russians' heavy casualties could be ascribed as much to the poor quality and small numbers of their skirmishers as to the greater effectiveness of the rifled musket. Nevertheless, when von Moltke analysed the battles of Alma and Inkerman, he concluded that the Russians had over-emphasised shock tactics and that a certain dispersal of troops was necessary in the face of modern fire.[10] The more prevalent opinion, however, was that the Russians had failed to charge home because of their own shortcomings, rather than as a result of the fire directed against them,[11] and that the traditional assault tactics were still valid.

The first real test of the effect of the new technology on tactics came in the Franco-Austrian War of 1859. The French discovered that their rifles were markedly inferior to those of the Austrian infantry. Their response was to emphasise the rapid movement of dispersed formations to within a short distance of the Austrian line, in order to neutralise the longer range of the Austrian rifle. The French then maintained momentum by launching massed bayonet charges after firing only a single volley.[12] The effect was devastating and appeared to demonstrate that assault tactics could still succeed in the face of modern weapons.

This conclusion, however, overlooked several factors which had reduced the firepower of the Austrian infantry: first, the Austrian Lorenz rifled muzzle loader produced a curved trajectory, so that the bullets did not sweep the field in front of the firer;[13] second, the Austrian's poor standard of training in marksmanship and range-taking led to troops wasting ammunition in inaccurate fire at extreme ranges;[14] and, third, a strong tendency towards caution and a reliance on restrictive control meant that the Austrians employed tight formations and were reluctant to manoeuvre, rendering them vulnerable to the French bayonet attacks.[15] The Austrians, having already had their confidence shaken by the limited effect of their firepower, were therefore predisposed to flee from the French assaults. Had the Austrian fire been more effective, the French would have suffered more casualties in coming to close quarters and would not have been able to adopt the dense formations with which they charged the defenders. Even against the Austrians' limited firepower, the French were forced to adopt dispersed formations while moving up to close range, deploying whole battalions in skirmish lines.[16] These lessons were underlined by experience in the American Civil War, leading Moltke to conclude that the firepower of the defence was now much greater than the assault power of the offence.[17]

In 1861, the Prussian Army issued new regulations which sought to adapt the traditional assault tactics to the changed realities of the battlefield. Improved firearms put a premium on the ability of units to manoeuvre rapidly, to take full advantage of cover and to deliver a heavy weight of fire. The Prussians concluded that this could be achieved best by units of company size. For movements outside the zone of enemy fire, however, battalion columns were still considered most effective, while the dispersal of whole companies into swarms of skirmishers was discouraged. The attack of closed formations was retained as the decisive factor.[18] The regulations therefore made a compromise between the rigid control of assault tactics and the decentralisation of command demanded by many reformers. Despite the official adoption of the company as the basic tactical unit, however, the practice of the troops did not alter greatly. During the manoeuvres of 1861, many senior commanders launched battalion columns in frontal attacks against positions without prior fire preparation. While this was perhaps excusable, given that the new regulations were issued only on the eve of manoeuvres,[19] the repeating of these tactics in the manoeuvres of 1863[20] suggested that many officers had doubts about the new system. Minor though the changes introduced in 1861 might appear, they represented a major challenge to traditional systems of command and training.

In a system where the battalion was the basic tactical unit, initiative went no lower than the level of the battalion commander. This officer had served for 20 or more years and could be relied upon to command his unit effectively. The switch to a company-based system meant relying on officers with half that length of service, who had previously been considered capable only of executing direct orders within the framework of the battalion. Nor was this the limit of the decentralisation demanded, for the regulations placed a renewed emphasis on skirmish tactics.

After the defeat at Jena in 1806, the Prussian Army had introduced skirmishers who would advance in dispersed formation ahead of the main body, screening it from enemy fire and attempting to disorder the enemy line by their own fire. This freedom of action was initially granted to one battalion and to the third rank of the other two battalions in each regiment, but it became progressively restrained after 1815, as the army reverted to the close-order drill,[21] until it came to be restricted to the *Jäger* alone. Formed by Frederick the Great, the *Jäger* had developed into a corps of specialists who claimed a monopoly on the use of the rifle. Recruited mainly from experienced woodsmen, 'the *Jäger* regarded themselves not only as soldiers, but also as members of a guild, initiates of an exotic mystery which could be completely mastered only by those trained from childhood'.[22]

The belief that only specialists could be trusted as rifle-armed skirmishers was deeply ingrained. Two problems had to be solved before line troops could be so employed: fire discipline and fire direction. Once troops open fire it is often very difficult to make them stop. Given the high rate of fire of the needle gun, soldiers could expend their entire supply of ammunition within minutes.[23] Troops also tend to open fire at extreme ranges, wasting ammunition and reducing the moral impact of their fire at closer ranges. The solution to both problems was to abandon the practice of forming skirmishers from the third rank of each battalion and instead to deploy complete squads as fire teams. Not only was section fire more effective than individual fire, but whereas the old system had produced a line of skirmishers beyond the control of their officers, the new system kept them in small groups under the command of a non-commissioned officer (NCO), who could control their fire and link them to the company.[24] The requirement for junior NCOs to be leaders rather than merely disciplinarians was a major step, demanding a considerable rise in the standards by which they were selected and trained.

The degree of training required to operate the new system and the amount of control delegated by senior commanders encountered considerable opposition. This opposition was all the greater after the success of the French bayonet charges in 1859. It was reinforced when the Austrians used similar tactics in Denmark in 1864,[25] but that campaign actually indicated that further improvements in technology had in fact rendered assault tactics obsolescent.

Alone among Europe's armies, the Prussian Army had adopted a breech-loading rifle: the Dreyse needle gun. First used in battle against the Danes in 1864, the rifle proved devastating: columns of Danish infantry attempting to charge Prussian positions melted away under the hail of bullets. At Lundby, on 3 July 1864, a Prussian company of 124 men was surprised while bivouacking by a Danish force of 180 men. The Danes immediately launched a bayonet charge. The Prussians waited until they were within 250 metres and then fired three volleys. Driven back by this weight of fire, the Danes attempted to engage in a fire fight. Unable to use cover while reloading their muzzle-loader rifles, the Danes suffered heavily and withdrew. The engagement lasted a total of 20 minutes. The Danes lost 22 men killed and 66 wounded; Prussian casualties were three men wounded.[26] The 'normal' tacticians, however, dismissed the implications of this and other actions. Since the needle gun could fire up to five rounds per minute, three times the rate of the Danish muzzle loaders,[27] the Prussians at Lundby may have fired up to 6,000 rounds at short range, yet caused only 88 casualties. Had the Danes been more determined, it could be argued, they could have charged into contact and made use of their superior numbers. This argument was apparently supported by the fact that most of the casualties were suffered during the fire fight and not at the time of the original charge.

The obsolescence of the concept that a spirited bayonet charge could counteract enemy fire was shown more clearly in the Austro-Prussian War of 1866. The early engagements showed a monotonous regularity of form and outcome: a Prussian advance would be countered by an Austrian bayonet charge, which would be shattered by rifle fire and the stunned survivors driven back. The result was a litany of disaster for Austria. On 26 and 27 June alone, the Austrians suffered 270 casualties to 50 Prussians at Hühnerwasser, 1,048 to 130 at Podol, 5,719 to 1,122 at Nachod, and 4,787 to 1,338 at Trautenau.[28] At Nachod,

> a wounded [Austrian] officer told his captors that the first time his company stood upright to reload, half of them were shot down, and the survivors preferred to continue the fight with empty rifles. The large number of unwounded prisoners included many who surrendered rather than risk further movement in range of the needle gun.[29]

The greatest of the Austrian disasters was at Königgrätz on 3 July 1866. The engagement in and around the Swiepwald, a dense wood 2,000 by 1,200 metres, provided the strongest evidence that the bayonet charges of the assault tactics were no longer effective.[30] In the first stage of the engagement, six battalions of the Prussian 7th Division defeated more than 10 Austrian battalions. In only 30 minutes, the Austrian Brigade Brandenstein was destroyed in a confused fight in the wood. The Austrian muzzle loaders proved utterly unequal to the needle gun, both in rate of fire and in allowing the use of cover. Next Brigades Fleischhacker and Poeckh attacked. The Prussians in the wood had by now dissolved into a mass of small groups. As the dense Austrian masses moved in, the Prussians parted like water, only to close again behind the attackers. Of the 4,000 men of Brigade Poeckh committed, only 1,800 escaped. The final stage was the assault by Brigades Württemberg and Soffaran. Despite heavy casualties, the Austrians almost cleared the wood. At the moment of victory, however, they were ordered to retire to face the decisive outflanking move of the Prussian Second Army. The Austrians had committed almost their entire right wing into the battle for Swiepwald. In less than four hours, the 19 battalions of the Prussian 7th Division had defeated 49 Austrian battalions, of which 28 were destroyed and only 13 remained intact. 7th Division lost about 2,200 men, Austrian casualties were probably about 15,000. Swiepwald showed that the increased firepower of troops armed with breech-loading rifles greatly strengthened their morale, making them ready to fight on despite heavy casualties and loss of formation. Against such a determined defence, a bayonet charge was likely to achieve a Pyrrhic victory at best.

## The Lessons of the Franco-Prussian War

The events of 1866 demonstrated that troops armed with breech-loading rifles possessed overwhelming firepower, even when dispersed and disordered. Nevertheless, the wholesale adoption of dispersed formations was widely resisted. In Prussia, King Wilhelm I clung to the battalion column, which was reintroduced in manoeuvres.[31] Similarly, the French retained the battalion column until 1869.[32] This conservatism was not merely a refusal to accept changed realities: on the contrary, it reflected a serious attempt to deal with the new circumstances of battle.

The events of 1866 confirmed von Moltke's view that modern firearms gave the defence a great advantage over the offence. A relatively small number of infantrymen, deployed in a dispersed formation, could produce a deadly hail of fire. While the tactical defensive therefore became a preferred option, no army could neglect the tactical offensive. Whatever the overall situation, troops would still have to seize ground, requiring them to attack enemy positions. While dispersal appeared ideal for defence, mass was still required for the attack. For a charge to be prepared sufficiently, the attacker must win the fire fight. This phase must not be permitted to become too drawn out, lest the defender move up reserves or the attackers become exhausted. Quick victory in the fire fight required a considerable numerical superiority in the firing line. Once the attack was prepared, mass was needed to ensure superior assault power. The use of battalion columns promised to deliver this mass.

A second factor favouring mass was command. In 1866, the Prussians found that whole units dissolved into swarms of skirmishers. While adequate for defence, such disorganisation made co-ordinated offensive action all but impossible. Had the Austrians at Swiepwald adopted a defensive posture, an attack by the Prussian 7th Division would have been either chaotic or substantially delayed while the units reorganised.

A final factor was the adoption by the French Army of the Chassepot breech-loading rifle, which had an effective range of 1,500 metres, 1,000 metres more than the Dreyse needle gun. By 1870, the French Army had received delivery of one million of the new rifles.[33] The Prussian infantry found itself in the same situation as the French in 1859, of fighting with a firearm greatly inferior to that of the enemy. The Prussians' solution was also similar to that of 1859; the enemy superiority in range must be negated by the rapid movement of dense masses of troops to within the range of the needle gun.[34] Whereas the French in 1859 charged into contact after firing only one or two volleys from close range, however, the Prussians in 1870 intended to conduct a standard fire fight once they had advanced to within the effective range of their rifles.

In the event, the Prussian tactics proved inadequate to solve the problem of superior French rifle fire. In most battles, the Prussians were victorious mainly because of their cannon. Whereas all other European armies relied on bronze muzzle-loading smooth-bore cannon, the Prussian Army deployed Krupp's steel breech-loading rifled cannon. Although the new guns had a far greater range and accuracy than the bronze weapons, no other army had been convinced that Krupp had overcome the problem of burst barrels that had dogged the development of steel guns. The superior design of Krupp's guns was coupled with new tactics which brought the guns forward, but still out of rifle range, rather than keep them back as a Napoleonic grand battery. This combination allowed the Prussian guns to play a decisive role, as at Sedan, for the first time in half a century.

In general, the Prussians found that the use of massed formations against the French in 1870 was ineffective.

> The company columns in which they advanced into action disintegrated under fire into a ragged skirmishing line which quickly went to ground, and which officers and NCOs urged forward in vain. In the woods and close country which lay before the French positions the temptation to 'get lost' was sometimes overwhelming. Only close order could give the infantry confidence, and close order in face of breech-loading rifles was suicidal.[35]

A further problem was that few battles took place on open ground. With the growth of armies and the increased range of firearms, battles took place over a far larger area than in Napoleonic times. Consequently, more terrain features were to be found on the battlefield, while the improved effect of firearms led to a greater use of cover. The effect was illustrated by a German officer who fought at Wörth on 6 August 1870:

> Before the war . . . my regiment and brigade had been very thoroughly trained, but always over open ground and in stereotyped formation. Wörth was our first experience of battle, and you may imagine our embarrassment . . . when we were ordered to advance . . . through [a] dense and pathless wood. . . . The formation to which we were accustomed was evidently unsuitable. . . . It ended in our sending forward a strong chain of skirmishers, with their supports, and breaking up the remainder of the brigade into several columns. . . . We made no progress until [the enemy] flank was turned by other troops . . . [The] normal formation . . . we never attempted throughout the war. On almost every occasion where my regiment was seriously engaged, we fought either in a wood, a village, or in enclosed country, and for neither of these was it in the least adapted.[36]

The combined effect of murderous French fire and splitting up of battalions owing to terrain was to produce a confused seeking for cover:

> When we study the battles of 1870 with maps and books, we are often at a loss to account for the devious wanderings of various companies. If we study the battles on the ground itself, the cause is soon revealed. Tiny depressions, commodious ditches, convenient banks, although often at right angles to the true direction, clearly mark the reason and the course of these meanderings.[37]

Despite the clear evidence that only open-order tactics were effective in the face of modern firearms, the revised German regulations of 1873 persisted in retaining the company column as the basic tactical unit.[38] Once again, the reasoning appeared sound. German attacks had regularly ground to a halt, with whole formations dissolving into skirmish lines, unable to advance in the face of enemy fire and forced to rely on flank attacks by other units. The battles of Spicheren, Wissembourg and Fröschwiller all followed this basic pattern.[39] Perhaps the most drastic instance was at Fröschwiller, where almost the entire Bavarian 4th Division came to be extended into a single skirmish line that was easily checked by the French.

Whereas skirmish lines often proved incapable of effective offensive action, it appeared to some that close-order units might still be able to succeed. The attack of the Prussian Guard Corps at St Privat on 18 August

1870 is often cited as proof that close-order attacks were no longer possible. Nevertheless, although the corps suffered 8,000 casualties in 20 minutes,[40] it was subsequently argued that the assault could have succeeded. Colonel F. N. Maude pointed out that the French positions had not been prepared adequately by artillery bombardment and that an attacking force double the size of the Guard Corps would have been more appropriate to the situation. Yet the Prussians advanced to within 600 paces of the French position. Had the Prussians possessed better rifles, Maude suggested, they would have had a 'fair chance' of winning the fire fight and launching a successful assault.[41] This argument appeared to be supported by evidence that the effectiveness of the French fire actually reduced as the range decreased. The greatest number of casualties were suffered at ranges between 1,200 and 1,500 metres, whereas fewest losses were suffered at between 500 and 600 metres, despite the fact that the Prussians remained at this range for over an hour while awaiting the flank attack by the Saxon Corps.[42] This, however, was in fact more because of poor French musketry than any inherent principle of rifle fire and so Maude's conclusions were based on weak evidence.

There was a fierce debate within the German Army after 1870 as to the correct lessons of the Franco-Prussian War. Rather than attempt to draft regulations based upon first impressions, the army waited for conclusions to be reached, notably from the General Staff history of the war. Having allowed time for the fog of war to clear, the Germans published new regulations for the infantry in 1888 and for the artillery in 1889. These regulations marked a dramatic advance in tactical doctrine.

The 1888 regulations made a decisive break with the past. Up to this time, the assault power of the infantry had been considered primary. The main purpose of the infantry's fire was to prepare the charge, which was seen as the decisive factor. The new regulations held such assault tactics to be impossible against modern weapons and replaced them with a system of *Feuertaktik* (fire tactics). Under the new system, the firepower of the infantry was dominant and the charge was relegated to the taking of positions already cleared by the fire. With the shift in emphasis from assault to fire, the basic combat formation also shifted from the column to the swarm of skirmishers. The days of 'normal tactics' were declared over.[43]

> *The infantry fight will as a rule be decided by fire action* and this is brought into fullest use in dispersed order. Fire in close order is the exception.[44]

> Fire in dispersed order is the main combat means of the infantry. This fire may of itself not only repulse the enemy and prepare one's own attack, but even, under certain circumstances, achieve the decision. In most cases, an overwhelming fire, concentrated on the

> decisive points and brought up to close range, will have such an effect that the final charge is made against positions already abandoned or only weakly held by the enemy.[45]

> Our infantry, with its excellent musketry training, is able to repel any *frontal* attack by its fire. The enemy will suffer immense losses in the attack, and once repulsed, his confidence will be so severely shaken that he will hardly attempt to renew the attack.[46]

The *Schützenswarm* (swarm of riflemen) became the basic combat formation.[47] While close order was retained for reserves, owing to its ease of command, it was to be used in the front line only at the moment of a decisive charge and even then only in combination with dispersed order.[48] 'Large units in close order within effective enemy infantry fire can expect extremely serious losses in a very short time.'[49]

A sharp distinction was drawn between the encounter battle and the attack on a prepared position.[50] In an encounter battle, speed of deployment was essential in order to win the advantage over the enemy.[51] Against a prepared position, such impetuous forward pressure would be suicidal. A carefully planned attack was required, whose central feature was the attainment of fire superiority.[52] The first stage was the deployment of forces at the edge of the zone of effective fire. This would be followed by an artillery battle, in which the attackers' artillery sought to neutralise the defenders' guns and then prepare the enemy infantry for attack. In the next stage, swarms of skirmishers worked their way forward to a point as close as possible to the enemy position. From there, they engaged the defenders in a fire fight, seeking to wear them down. The regulations noted that the more concentrated was the fire, in terms of both time and space, the greater was its moral effect on the enemy.[53] The final stage was the assault of the enemy position. Support troops were to be held close behind the skirmishers in order to be able to launch an assault at a moment's notice. This stage was by far the most dangerous and the regulations warned against launching the charge prematurely:

> So long as fire superiority has not been won or at least the enemy appear considerably shaken, the attack can be carried out only with heavy losses. It is therefore necessary to await the fire effect before leading the final assault. The required results may best be judged from the skirmish line; this line recognises first when and where the enemy resistance slackens, it can make swiftest use of all advantages, and it is primarily from here that the impulse to carry out the assault will come. It is therefore the duty of the close-order bodies to follow the skirmish line at once, to support it and to protect it against counterattacks.[54]

A vital aspect of the attack was envelopment. The flanks were the only vulnerable points of an infantry unit.[55] For this reason, the attacker should always seek to deploy forces to fire on the flanks of the enemy. This was difficult for troops to achieve if already in contact and so was to be attempted by reserves or by forces deployed especially for this purpose.[56] The suggestion that the impulse for the assault might come from the skirmish line rather than from a senior commander in the rear was a sign of the changed attitude to command displayed by the new regulations. For the first time, the concept of directive command was made official doctrine at the level of minor tactics.

The 1888 regulations encapsulated von Molkte's philosophy of issuing only essential orders and rarely interfering in tactical arrangements.[57] While the doctrine was nowhere made explicit, the regulations repeatedly emphasised that higher commanders were forbidden to intervene in the actions of subordinates unless those actions seriously endangered the overall plan.[58] The regulations made it clear that the primary role of the higher commander was to support his subordinates through the allocation of reserves[59] and the supply of ammunition.[60] 'These views are valid down to the command of the lowest levels.'[61]

The extent of the decentralisation of command and the freedom given to even junior commanders and soldiers was considerable. The regulation's creed was 'Omission and neglect carry a heavier charge than an error in the choice of means'.[62] The individual soldier was no longer required to adopt a particular posture, but could adjust to his individual situation: 'This encourages the rifleman's strength of judgement, bodily dexterity, daring and self-confidence, great intelligence in the use of terrain, as well as continuous attention to his leader.'[63] The development of these characteristics in his men was considered one of the main duties of an officer.[64] A natural tension existed between the need to guide subordinates and the need to allow free rein to their initiative. If either aspect were allowed to become dominant, the delicate balance would be upset.

> These requirements are fulfilled if no more is ordered by the higher ranks, as must and can be ordered by them, and if the executing ranks work together for the assigned task and do not misuse the independence given them in an arbitrary way. . . . The independence asserted within such boundaries is the foundation of great results in war.[65]

## The Conservative Reaction

Although the 1888 regulations represented a major advance in tactical thought, they were out of date almost from the moment they were issued.

In 1884, Germany had become the first major power to issue its entire force of infantry with a magazine rifle, the 11 mm Mauser.[66] This was replaced in 1888 by the 7.9 mm Mannlicher rifle, the *Gewehr '88*, which used smokeless powder. 'It was the most up-to-date rifle of any in use at that time.'[67] Soldiers now carried more ammunition and produced a higher rate of fire than ever before. Furthermore, by eliminating the clouds of smoke given off by black powder, troops could now both see to greater ranges and no longer gave away their positions when they fired. Although the new regulations were issued at the same time as the *Gewehr '88*, they were not an expression of the tactics demanded by that weapon; rather, they encapsulated the lessons of the Wars of Unification of 20 years before.[68]

The year 1888 marked the end of the period in which the lessons of the Wars of Unification could be applied directly, because advances in technology made those lessons increasingly less applicable. Since there was no major Continental war between 1871 and 1914, the writers of manuals found themselves in the difficult position of having to assess the effect of new weapons on tactics with only peacetime experience to guide them. The period 1888 of 1914 was particularly rich in technical advances. The German Army introduced the small-calibre magazine rifle in 1888, quick-firing guns in 1896, the barrel recoil device for guns in 1906 and the machine gun in 1908. At the same time airships, and aeroplanes, telephones and indirect-fire devices were also developed.[69]

Despite these advances in technology, there was resistance within the army against changing tactics. Indeed, in certain important respects, the army actually regressed. While this resistance was in part because of an understandable reluctance to abandon the manual of 1888, based upon war experience, for the uncertainties of peacetime experience, there was also a powerful tendency towards conservatism.[70] A number of senior officers favoured a return to close order on theoretical grounds, while many junior commanders preferred the assault tactics as a result of erroneous lessons from peacetime training. The basic cause of this conservatism appears to have been a faulty evaluation of the balance between technology and morale.[71]

The theorists were led by Jakob Meckel and Wilhelm von Scherff,[72] who favoured the old 'normal tactics', based upon assaults by troops in close order, and rejected absolutely the idea that modern firearms produced an annihilating effect. Meckel strongly opposed the current emphasis on flank attacks. He argued that this undermined the troops' resolve, for even in an envelopment the enemy would form a front, the very thing soldiers were told was impregnable. Meckel attacked the 'aversion to casualties' which the concentration on flanking action apparently demonstrated and recommended massed frontal infantry assaults on points prepared by a heavy artillery bombardment. Casualties would be severe, but soldiers simply had to accept this. Scherff originally supported the belief that frontal attacks were ineffective: even if the enemy line was penetrated, the attacker would be himself enveloped. Scherff altered his position in 1897, complaining that the 1888 regulations, by emphasising the need for careful preparation and the use of envelopment rather than frontal attack, encouraged an aversion to decisive combat. He argued that open order was only a limited expedient and that the close order of the old assault tactics was more effective in the assault, because it permitted easier co-ordination of the whole attack force.

The proponents of the assault tactics held fundamentally different views on command to those expressed in the 1888 regulations. Whereas the latter emphasised initiative at all levels, the 'normal' tacticians believed that uniform rules were needed to ensure the combination of individual actions into an effective whole.[73] They argued that the troops should be relieved of the question of how they should carry out their tasks and be allowed to concentrate on the actual performance of those tasks. Essentially, the 'normal' tacticians doubted the ability of troops to reach a sufficiently high standard of training as to be able to cope with the demands of directive command.

At unit level, there was again a strong emphasis on the traditional tactics.[74] Over the long years of peace, the devastating effect of modern firearms came to be underestimated. With this central pillar of reality weakened, the need for open-order tactics became less obvious. Most units returned to close order, which was easier to inculcate and allowed the company commander to retain close control over his men.[75]

Just when the decline in the army's tactics was at its greatest, war broke out in South Africa. The Boer War (1899–1902) was generally seen as the first test of the new technology, whose lessons would be directly applicable to a European conflict. Every major power, including Japan, sent observers, and the German General Staff even published its own study of the war. This noted that although the British regulations bore a close resemblance to those of 'the great continental armies', the British infantry showed a consistent disregard for the vital need to establish superiority of fire before an assault. Although the British repeatedly altered their deployments during the war in an attempt to improve their capabilities, their failure to grasp the principle of fire superiority was considered by the German General Staff to be the real cause of the persistent defeat of British attacks.[76] In Germany, after a brief return to the fire tactics laid down by the 1888 regulations,[77] the troops reverted to close order, as the difficulties of commanding troops in dispersed order appeared insoluble and the lesson from South Africa that modern firearms made close order suicidal was not sufficiently clear on the manoeuvre grounds of Europe.

The Russo-Japanese War (1904–6) proved to be of considerable importance for German tactical devlopment. All the new weapons developed over the previous two decades were used and the Japanese employed the German 1888 regulations in an unaltered translation. Indeed, the Japanese had preferred not to adapt the manual to take account of their own experience, but had decided to wait for the next German edition, which they intended again to adopt unaltered.[78] After analysing the course of the war, most German military thinkers concluded that the 1888 regulations were basically sound, but that they were no longer fully appropriate to modern circumstances.[79] The army responded by issuing a series of new manuals between 1906 and 1911.[80]

The *Exerzier-Reglement für die Infanterie* of 1906 gives a clear idea of the resulting tactical doctrine.[81] Although based upon the principle of fire superiority,[82] they were less emphatic in this regard than the regulations of 1888. While the 1888 edition had warned against launching an assault prematurely, the 1906 manual emphasized the importance of developing the infantry's offensive spirit: 'Its actions must be guided by the single idea, "Forwards against the enemy, whatever the cost!"'[83] This error was compounded by the belief that the achievement of fire superiority was a once-and-for-all event and that movements by platoons and even companies in close order would then be possible.[84]

The assault was to be delivered only after fire superiority had been achieved. The new regulations differed from those of 1888 by insisting that the artillery battle should no longer be seen as a separate phase, but should flow into the infantry battle.[85] The artillery was to support the infantry principally by suppressing the defenders' artillery. It was also expected to assist the attack by engaging at close range any targets threatening the infantry. This was to be done by attaching individual batteries to the infantry, to give fire support until the last moment before the assault.[86] The achievement of fire superiority was to be judged by a slackness of enemy fire (owing to casualties and men going to ground) and its growing inaccuracy (owing to men not aiming properly as a result of fear).[87] The attacker was to seize this opportunity: 'The defeat of the enemy is consummated by thc assault with fixed bayonets'.[88]

The 1906 regulations were in many ways a retrograde step from those of 1888. The key factor was a limited acceptance of the argument that modern fire was not as annihilating as had been claimed. If fire was less overwhelming, there was less need for open-order tactics and consequently less need for decentralised command. The 1906 regulations therefore led to a more stereotyped model of tactics than had the previous edition.[89] Despite these failings, the manual was still in advance of the main body of Continental doctrine. It emphasised the importance of soldiers being imbued with independence of thought and deed, so that they acted even when their superiors were absent.[90] Where possible, the regulations avoided laying down binding rules; instead they preferred to show the advantages and disadvantages of actions, leaving it to the commander on the spot to choose what was best suited for this particular task.[91] The new regulations, however, suffered the same fate as had those of 1888, in that much of the infantry chose to ignore the rules laid down and retained the close-order approach of the assault tactics, with their restrictions on individual initiative.[92]

## Training

An important factor in the retention of the assault tactics was a deep-seated distrust on the part of many senior commanders of the ability and willingness of ordinary soldiers and junior officers to make effective use of the freedom given them by open order tactics. Von Scherff insisted that the size of the smallest tactical unit was determined primarily by the need for it to be commanded by an officer: a platoon.[93] Only an officer could be relied upon to operate effectively. Doubts were even expressed regarding the ability of junior officers, which was of central importance for determining which system of tactics should be employed:

> Normal formations for attack and defence are requisite . . . in armies in which the tactical training of commanders and subordinate leaders is deficient and where it is feared that the latter will abuse the latitude allowed them. Where such normal formations are prescribed, it is assumed that hard and fast rules are requisite for training; that the average officer cannot be expected to estimate a situation correctly and arrive at proper decisions; and that the majority of them must be given definite rules for combat if they are to render any service at all.[94]

Were such doubts justified?

For most German men, military service began on 1 October of the year in which they reached the age of 20. Although every male was liable for service, each year group numbered 600,000, double the number needed, even after a subtantial increase in the size of the army in 1913 meant that 305,000 men were required annually.[95] The army was therefore able to adopt fairly strict selection criteria. There appears to have been no prejudice against recruits from an urban background. Indeed, it was considered that men who could quickly learn the skills needed for industry were likely to be equally adept at acquiring military skills,[96] particularly as the advance of technology made skills increasingly common to both areas. Once conscripted, men served for two years in the *Activ* (standing) army.[97] Their training was regulated by two principles: the *Felddienstordnung*

(Field Service Regulations) of 1908 laid down that 'The training of troops in peacetime is regulated by what will be required of them in war'[98] and that the *Exerzier-Reglement dür die Infanterie* (ERfdI) of 1906 stated, 'The training [of troops] is correctly directed if it does that which war requires and if nothing must be unlearned on the battlefield which was learned in peacetime.'[99]

Since men served for only two years in the standing army, there was considerable pressure to bring them to a sufficiently high standard of training in the limited time available. This pressure was intensified by the need to make conscripts combat-ready after only one year, the period served by half the men in a unit each summer, in case war should break out. The result of this pressure was that the conscript 'was kept busy from dawn in a combination of intense physical activity and a fairly demanding intellectual programme requiring memorisation of ranks, order, responsibilities, and weapons nomenclature – all likely to be completely unfamiliar'.[100] Of each day, the German soldier would spend between five and six hours on drill and tactical training, two hours on fatigues and two hours in lectures, a total of some ten hours. This may be compared to an average of six hours' duty per day in the British Army at that time. In general, as one senior British officer noted, 'the whole training outlook [in Germany is] more business-like and thorough [than in Britain]'.[101] At the end of two years, men were discharged into the *Reserve*, in which they served for a further five years.[102] Although no longer serving full time, members of the reserve were liable for front-line service upon mobilisation. Their skills and fitness were maintained by their being recalled to the colours for two weeks each September.[103]

The standard of training that could be achieved was raised by four factors. First, since all conscripts were enlisted at the same time and at roughly the same age, a uniform system of training could be applied. The second factor was the permanence of the organisation of formations in the German Army. There was therefore no disruption of training as a result of the rotation of units and personnel between home and overseas postings as there was in the British Army. This permanence also allowed units to concentrate on the single goal of preparing for a major Continental war. The third factor was the responsibility granted to commanders for the training of their men:

> Every commander, from the company commander upwards, is responsible for training his subordinates according to the regulations. His choice of means may be limited as little as possible. Superiors are required to intervene as soon as they notice misunderstandings and backwardness.[104]

The effect of this decentralisation was that company commanders were usually given a free hand in the training of their men.[105] This had two results. First, senior commanders were able to train the formations directly under their command, rather than spend their time devising training schedules for sub-units. They also had the time to monitor the training which took place, enabling them to identify errors at an early stage.[106] Second, the troops were trained in the units in which they would go to war and by the officer who would lead them.[107] For this reason, the German Army largely rejected the idea of centralised schools.

The final factor affecting the overall quality of a unit was the proportion of reservists needed to bring it up to war strength. In peacetime, active units were held at about two-thirds of their official war strength.[108] On mobilisation, all that was necessary was to recall the annual contingent discharged the previous autumn, men familiar to the officers and with their skills still fresh. By contrast, 61.8 per cent of the mobilised strength of the BEF in 1914 were reservists.[109] The British recognised this problem before the war: 'A German squadron, battery or company officer will recognise his command after mobilisation whereas our officers will not.'[110]

The German Army recruited NCOs for the active army from the ranks and from special NCO training schools.[111] Three-quarters were men identified during their active conscript service and persuaded to re-engage (*kapitulieren*). After a period of two years' further training, the *Kapitulanten* were promoted to NCO rank. The remaining NCOs were graduates of a special schooling programme designed for boys hoping for a military career. From the age of about 14, these boys attended one of the nine *Unteroffizier-Vorschulen* (NCO preparatory schools), which provided a general education and paid particular attention to physical development. When they reached the age of 17, the pupils moved to one of the eight *Unteroffizier-Schulen* (NCO training schools), where they received a purely military education for a further two years. Upon satisfactory completion of the course, they were posted to regiments with the rank of *Unteroffizier* (corporal). The training received by these aspirant NCOs was of a high standard. In the opinion of one British officer, 'When they leave [the NCO training] school . . . they are as efficient as the average British subaltern of, say, five years' service'.[112]

The quality of German NCOs had declined towards the end of the nineteenth century.[113] With the rapid spread of industrialisation in Germany at this time, the army had found itself unable to attract young men of intelligence and ability. A major effort was made to improve the prospects of military service and so improve the quality of the NCO corps. This programme appears to have produced three main inducements. The first was that the education provided by the *Unteroffizier-Schulen* was free,[114] attracting men of ability but with limited financial resources. The second inducement was the raised status of the NCO, with privates being required to salute them and stand to attention when addressing them, just as they would an officer.[115] The most important inducement, however, was the introduction of the *Zivilversorgunschein* (civil service certificate), whereby the government guaranteed to provide public employment for those men who satisfactorily completed 12 years service as an NCO. This incentive proved sufficient to attract the necessary quality of applicant[116] and ensured a constant influx of younger men and the retirement of the old.[117] The system also created a pool of experienced retired NCOs who could be recalled to the reserve in time of war.

The *Zivilversorgunschein* system was not without its faults. 'Evidence suggests that [the] ongoing, successful attempt to modernise [the NCO corps] generated the unwelcome side-effect of virtually institutionalising physical and emotional abuse of the rank and file.'[118] The promise of a civil service post on retirement from the army was dependent upon an NCO possessing a satisfactory record: 'A non-commissioned officer in the Imperial Army was judged by results.'[119] He was put into a difficult position by having his future career dependent upon his achieving the required standard with the soldiers assigned to him, yet having no official power to impose punishment. Punishments had to be imposed by an officer and an excessive number could affect an NCO's grading in his final report. The resulting stress was expressed in the frequent unofficial abuse of recruits and in the suicide rate among NCOs being higher than that of privates.[120]

Most officers in the active army had been educated at one of the 11 *Kadettenhäuser* (cadet schools), which provided a free education to boys intending to join the officer corps. The quality of the education given by these establishments was unexceptional and sometimes poor. Nevertheless, it appears to have been superior to that provided by the private schools attended by most British officers. The opinion of one British officer educated in a *Kadettenhaus* was that 'Of the general education provided by the college . . . I have nothing but praise'.[121] The schools did not over-emphasise military subjects: the *Fänrichsprüfung* (ensign's examination) taken upon leaving the school included French or English, Latin and mathematics. An interest in literature, drama, fine arts and music was also encouraged.[122] The candidates achieving the highest grades in the examination were immediately commissioned with the ranks of *Leutnant* (second lieutenant). The remainder attended one of 11 *Kriegsschulen* (war schools) for a period of nine months, during which time they held the ranks of *Fähnrich* (ensign). At the end of the course, they were posted to regiments with the rank of *Leutnant vorläufig ohne Patent* (second lieutenant temporarily without a commission). If approved by their brother officers they were finally commissioned.[123] Since promotion was mainly by seniority, the year gained by those scoring highest in the ensign's examination was an important incentive for hard work at the cadet school.

A less common route to a commission was through service as a *Fahnenjunker* (probationer), open to men who had achieved *Abitur* (the qualification allowing university entrance) or passed the ensign's examination. The probationer usually served some nine months in the ranks, being promoted to corporal after three months. If considered suitable, the probationer then took the same war school course as did those from the cadet schools.[124] Those commissioned by this route were therefore about one year junior in seniority to their contemporaries who had attended the cadet schools. Competition for a commission was often fierce, it being common for there to be 20 applicants for one place. The commanding officers of regiments, who were responsible for recruitment to their units, were therefore able to demand high standards in their choice of candidates.[125]

Officers were under great pressure to achieve high standards: 'The officer's career depends entirely on the results he is able to achieve in the training of his men.'[126] In 1891, Colonel Henderson noted,

> The officers of the Imperial [German] Army are under constant supervision. Their tactical capabilities undergo incessant tests. So ruthless is the system of rejection, that a few mistakes in field manoeuvres lead to speedy retirement. The application of the system is short and sharp. . . . The hint of a brigadier that an application for sick-leave will be favourably considered is enough, or an explanation of the mistakes committed in presence of the whole of the officers of the battalion. So precarious is the tenure of command, that one often hears the remark that So-and-so goes to bed with his Pickelhaube on one side and a silk hat on the other, for he does not know whether, when he wakes up, he will find himself soldier or civilian.[127]

Not only was an officer fully responsible for the training of his own unit, with superiors carefully monitoring his performance but intervening only in the case of error,[128] but he was also required to serve a posting with another arm of service,[129] in order to prevent him from developing an insular, single-arm attitude. Further, his training included a requirement to master the skills of commanding units larger than that normally assigned to him: during the annual manoeuvres, every officer was given a command higher than his own and was forced to retire if he performed poorly.[130] The same system operated in regard to promotion: 'An officer was fit for promotion or he was not; in the latter case he was given the option of requesting permission to retire. . . . When an appointment was vacant, the best man available was put into it, regardless of his rank.'[131]

The German Army placed considerable reliance upon the reserve. One of the greatest surprises of 1914 was the German use of reserve formations of corps size in the front line. While the senior posts were filled by active officers, most of the junior officers and the NCOs were from the reserve. A small proportion were retired members of the active army, either officers with less than 18 years' service or NCOs who had completed 12 years. Most were products of the system of *Einjahrig-Freiwillige* (one year volunteers), under which

> young men of good education who undertook to clothe, feed and equip themselves during their period of service, and who attained a satisfactory standard of proficiency in their duties, were permitted to transfer to the Reserve as 'aspirant officers' [*Offizier-Aspiranten*] at the end of one year's service only.[132]

During their year of active service, the *Einjährige* were given experience of command by being promoted to *Gefreiter* (lance-corporal) after six months and to *Unteroffizier* (corporal) three months later. Those who reached the necessary standard were required to serve for a further eight weeks in each of the two years following their transfer to the reserve. There was then a second examination. Those who passed were commissioned into the reserve, while the remainder became reserve NCOs.[133] Once commissioned, they were liable for a further three annual training periods of four to eight weeks each.[134]

Only the best of the *Einjahrig-Freiwillige* became officers. Of the 64,000 men who volunteered for this service in 1912,[135] only one-quarter were accepted. Since there were only 29,000 reserve officers,[136] only half even of those accepted as *Einjährige* were finally commissioned. Those considered unsuitable for commissioning but retained as NCOs formed a reservoir of talent from which shortages of officers could be filled in wartime. The rigor of the selection process accounts in part for the high status enjoyed by the holders of such commissions, particularly those few who were promoted to major. 'A widely circulated story had it that an old and famous professor, granted an audience with the kaiser and asked to make a request, raised his glaucomous eyes and, with a shaking voice, begged to be made a second lieutenant of the reserve.'[137]

## From *Feuertaktik* to *Stosstrupptaktik*

### *The Tactical Problem*

In August 1914, the German Army expected a war based upon infantry fighting power. While artillery was seen as important, its main function was considered to be the suppression of the enemy's guns, primarily by means of direct fire. Freed from hostile artillery fire, the attacker's infantry would work up to the enemy, covering its movements by its own fire. Once established at close range, the attacker would use his firepower to defeat the enemy in a fire fight, which would be won when the enemy began to waver. The attacker would take immediate advantage of this weakness to launch a bayonet charge, which the enemy would be unlikely to face. Having taken the position, the process would be repeated against the next enemy force.

The greater part of the infantry's firepower was expected to be produced by rifle fire. Machine guns were introduced into the German Army in 1908[138] as a result of experience in Manchuria. Initially, one company of six guns was assigned to each regiment.[139] Its fire was considered equivalent to that of up to six platoons (about 250 rifles)[140] under field conditions. Since the regiment included over 2,500 riflemen,[141] the machine-gun company was believed to account for only ten per cent of its total firepower. Further, since the machine gun weighed between 34 and 40 kilograms,[142] its suitability for use in the attack was limited. German doctrine held that machine guns were best suited to provide enfilade fire support at that critical moment of the attack when the movement of friendly infantry to the assault impeded supporting artillery fire.[143] While recognising the machine gun's limitations, the Germans were sufficiently convinced of its value that in 1912 it was decided to assign a machine-gun company to each battalion.[144] This process appears to have been nearing completion for the active army in 1914, with 233 companies being formed in that year alone.[145] Most active regiments went to war with two six-gun companies, but one-third of reserve regiments still had no machine guns at all.[146] Nevertheless, tactics were still based upon rifle fire.

The realities of combat in 1914 soon revealed two flaws in the pre-war image of battle. The first lay in the belief that direct fire was still an effective option for field artillery. This illusion was quick to be shattered, as at Le Cateau, on 26 August 1914, when General Sir Horace Smith-Dorrien's British II Corps turned to face its German pursuers.

> Brigadier Headlam, in command of the 5th Division's artillery, was as familiar with the modern methods [of indirect fire] as any other officer of his rank. But, like many officers of similar vintage, he rather regretted the disappearance of the old traditions that went hand in hand with the old tactics. It was not that the modern method was inefficient . . . but it lacked gallantry. Some senior officers, mostly retired, went so far as to growl that it was downright ungentlemanly. . . . General Headlam did not approve of the carefully chosen positions where the guns now waited for action. He wanted them out in the open. He wanted them placed as close as possible to the infantry in order to give the infantry the closest possible support.[147]

Seven batteries, totalling 42 guns, were redeployed by Headlam's order. Their new positions were completely exposed to fire from the advancing Germans and 'salvoes of shells crashed down on gun after gun in succession',[148] while in the 11th Battery 'every officer had fallen, and so many men that only enough were left to work a single gun'.[149] Finally, the order was given to withdraw the guns.

> The teams of the 122nd Battery galloped up. . . . As they came within view of the enemy, they were struck by a hurricane of shrapnel and of bullets . . . but still they went on. The officer in charge of the teams was killed and one team shot down in a heap before the position was reached; but two guns of the 122nd Battery were carried off without mishap. A third was limbered up, but the horses went down instantly. It was an extraordinary sight: a short wild scene of galloping and falling horses and then four guns standing derelict, a few limbers lying about . . . and dead men and dead horses everywhere. It was then decided to abandon the remaining guns and also those of the 124th and 123rd Batteries, which were in an even more exposed position. . . . Altogether, twenty-four field guns and a howitzer were lost in this part of the field; considering that the batteries were practically in the firing line, it is astonishing that any were rescued.[150]

The British lost a total of 38 guns at Le Cateau.[151] Of these, 25 were lost by the seven batteries deployed to use direct fire and only 13 by the remaining 19 batteries that employed indirect fire. The losses among the direct-fire guns were therefore five-times higher in proportion to those among the indirect-fire guns. The days of direct fire were clearly ended.

The second flaw in the pre-war image of battle was in the concept that 'Opportunities for using machine guns are fleeting and frequently local'.[152] In both the British and German armies, machine guns were seen primarily as a mobile reserve of firepower, to be used at decisive moments. The only real difference in doctrine was that while the Germans sought to use the six guns of a regiment en masse,[153] the British preferred to use them in pairs.[154] Much of the basis for the doctrine of 'fleeting opportunities' was the belief that machine guns were unsuited to prolonged fire, because of a growing inaccuracy as they overheated[155] and their enormous consumption of ammunition. In both armies, however, there were officers who disputed this official perception and who recognised the potential power of the machine gun, both in firepower and relative invulnerability to the attacker's fire.[156] One of these was von Schlieffen, whose writings in retirement indicate a greater awareness of modern firepower than he had shown while in office.[157]

Although the plan that bore his name was characterised by a commitment to the offensive, Schlieffen was greatly concerned with the problems of defence. This was a direct consequence of his decision to mass the bulk of his forces on the right wing for the decisive envelopment through Belgium, leaving only three corps to cover the front south of Verdun,[158] precisely the sector on which the French Army was likely to launch its strongest attack. The way to resist this attack occurred to Schlieffen only in retirement. In 1909, he argued, 'The best reserves are motor-loads of cartridges following up behind',[159] indicating that he saw the key to successful operations to be a reliance upon the firepower of machine guns, which alone would require such quantities of ammunition. Machine power was to replace manpower.

This idea was taken further in Schlieffen's final memorandum of 28 December 1912, in which he noted that a corps was now too large for its components to be employed to best effect. His solution was to merge active and reserve formations and reduce the size of each corps from 24 to 20 battalions and from 144 to 90 field guns. The greater flexibility of the new organisation would allow better use to be made of the available resources and no reduction was therefore necessary in the front assigned to each corps. At the operational level, the dangerous distinction between active and reserve formations would be eliminated and the forces removed from each corps would be sufficient to create 16 new corps.[160] At the tactical level, the reorganisation would recognise the increase in the firepower of formations following the introduction of machine guns and quick-firing guns, which would now provide the bulk of a formation's fire capability. Schlieffen argued that the infantry's tactics, as laid down by the 1906 regulations, were no longer appropriate in the face of this fire.[161] Although his ideas were ignored at the time, the experience of war brought their rapid adoption. By the end of 1915, the majority of German divisions had been reorganised to consist of nine battalions of infantry and 36 field guns.[162] These reductions were matched by an increase in the numbers of machine guns and heavy artillery pieces.

The views of those officers before 1914 who had disputed the official doctrine that machine guns were merely 'weapons of opportunity' were substantiated at Neuve Chapelle, on 10 March 1915. Owing to the inaccuracy of two freshly arrived siege batteries, a 400-metre sector of the German front trench remained largely unscathed by the British bombardment. When 2/Scottish Rifles and 2/Middlesex advanced, they were met by a hail of fire from two German machine guns.[163] 'It was thought at first that the attack had succeeded in reaching the German trenches, as no one behind could see and not a man returned. The dead bodies of the attackers were found lying in rows in the 11.15 a.m. advance.'[164] One officer and 64 men of Jäger-Bataillon 11 had killed 1,000 British infantrymen, largely by means of their two machine guns.[165]

It was therefore clear by early 1915 that the pre-war image of battle had been severely flawed when it held that direct fire would be the main function of field artillery and that machine guns were merely weapons of opportunity. The realisation of these flaws led to a tactical problem: how was the attacker to achieve superiority of fire sufficient for a successful assault in these new circumstances?

The key factor remained the firepower of the defending infantry. The fire of massed riflemen, however, had been replaced by that of machine guns. Once installed in concrete emplacements, these were all but invulnerable to the attackers' rifle fire. Only a direct hit from a high-explosive shell could destroy them and the accuracy required was such that only observed fire could be effective. This presented a further problem: if the guns employed direct fire, they would have the necessary accuracy but would suffer unacceptable losses; if they employed indirect fire, the guns would be protected but the telephone links to forward observers were too vulnerable and too inflexible for reliable communications in a fluid battle. With the artillery of both attacker and defender forced to employ indirect fire, counter-battery fire became far more difficult and so most artillery fire came to be directed against the infantry. The defender's artillery could produce devastating effects, often sufficient to halt an attack.[166] Such an effect was far more difficult for the attacking artillery to achieve.

The armies of the First World War were faced with only two possible solutions to the tactical impasse: either separate firepower and assault power, by relying on masses of indirect-fire guns to make up for their inaccuracy by sheer weight of fire, leaving the infantry merely to 'mop up'; or combine the two elements of function, by restoring firepower to the infantry, allowing it to overcome resistance by means of its own integral firepower. In short, was firepower to be a bludgeon in the hands of the artillery, or a scalpel in the hands of the infantry?

## *The Development of* Stosstrupptaktik

The problem of the attack in position warfare may be divided into three phases: the break-in, the breakthrough and the break-out.

The break-in consisted of those operations designed to seize the forward sector of the enemy defensive system and to dislocate that system as a whole. In general, this phase was marked by the degree of forward planning and preparation possible, since the attack was made from a secure line against a fixed enemy position. There were therefore comparatively few unknown variables. For this reason, attempted break-ins were usually successful throughout the war.

Having broken into the enemy position, the attacker moved to the breakthrough phase, in which he attempted to puncture the enemy defensive system. Whereas the break-in could be made under relatively ordered conditions, the breakthrough required troops to act in the midst of uncertainty and chaos, it being impossible to predict accurately the effects of bombardment, casualties and enemy manoeuvres. The attacker's difficulties were increased by the fact that his own infantry was exhausted, depleted in numbers and nearing the limits of artillery support, whereas the defenders were now fighting on their own ground, close to their guns and with fresh reserves. For these reasons, the breakthrough was considerably more difficult than the break-in and the first successful breakthrough on the Western Front was in March 1918.

The break-out was the most challenging of the three phases. Once the attacker had broken through the enemy defensive system, he had to maintain the momentum of his advance in order to prevent the defender sealing off the penetration. Whereas the defender could bring up fresh reserves by rail, the attacker had to push his forces through the narrow gap in the enemy line, a gap across a roadless wasteland under constant artillery fire. Because of these problems, this operation proved beyond the capabilities of all armies in the First World War on the Western Front and was first achieved in the very different conditions of 1940.

Within each phase, combat at the lowest tactical level may be divided into three sub-phases. First, enemy strongpoints and machine-gun emplacments had to be destroyed, which required the firepower of artillery pieces. Second, enemy fire had to be suppressed and the fire fight won. This again required firepower, primarily in the form of machine guns and mortars. Third, it was necessary to seize enemy positions, by means of assault power. The successful repetition of these three sub-phases through each of the main phases was essential if a break-out was to be achieved, although success in the break-out phase was probably at least as dependent upon efficient logistics as it was upon effective tactics.

Once the lines on the Western Front stabilised into position warfare in November 1914, it rapidly became clear to the German commanders that the fire tactics, even when correctly employed, were no longer effective in the prevailing conditions. The solution developed was termed the *Stosstrupptaktik* (assault squad tactics).[167] Initial developments took the form of ad hoc experiments by units in the field.[168] Field guns were brought close behind the front line, as had been recommended in the pre-war regulations.[169] The fire of these guns was devastating at the short ranges of position warfare, but standard field guns proved unsuitable. The enemy could quickly disable the gun crew[170] and bringing the guns up overnight into camouflaged emplacements was possible only in the break-in. In subsequent phases, when their fire was particularly valuable because the infantry had advanced beyond the range of the indirect-fire guns, the field guns could be concealed only with great difficulty and were therefore highly vulnerable. Further, since the standard German field gun, the *Feldkannone '96*, weighed 945 kilograms,[171] manhandling it across the devastated battlefield was almost impossible.

Another experiment was the use of armoured plates, originally designed to protect machine-gun crews, by groups of three men, of whom one carried a shield made of two such plates with which he attempted to cover himself and his companions from fire. While this gave a very limited degree of protection from hostile fire, it did nothing to solve the problem of winning the fire fight. The defender's fire was therefore still sufficient to kill the attackers, despite their shield. A further idea was the use of hand grenades. The German Army had developed several types of grenade after the Russo-Japanese War, but in 1914 most were stored in fortresses. Their utility in the siege-type conditions of trench warfare soon became obvious, since they gave the individual soldier far more assault power[172] than did a bayonet. As early as the autumn of 1914, officers such as Leutnant Walter Beumelburg of 2 Pionier Bn. 30 saw the value of grenades for clearing trenches. The system of working along a trench (*Aufrollen*, rolling up) proved more effective than a frontal assault, even when the attackers had no grenades.[173]

One of the most important functions of the German General Staff was the identification, development and promotion of new ideas. Oberstleutnant Max Bauer, a key figure at OHL, [174] was given responsibility to gather and test new ideas and equipment, and to disseminate the best of these throughout the whole army. To this end, Bauer formed three *Front-Versuchstruppen der OHL* (front experimental units of OHL) to test *Minenwerfer* (trench mortars), *Flammenwerfer* (flamethrowers) and *Sturmkannonen* (assault cannon) respectively.[175] The personnel of all three units were *Pioniere* (combat engineers), traditionally the arm involved in developing experimental equipment.[176] The units concerned with the development of trench mortars (Major Lathes) and flamethrowers (Hauptmann Reddemann) proved highly successful. Both continued to develop and disseminate their equipment and tactics throughout the war, while also providing detachments for key attacks.[177] Essential though their role was, the most important of the three units was that concerned with assault cannon. It was within this unit that the various weapons and tactics were combined and the assault squad tactics developed.

On 2 March 1915, OHL ordered the formation of a *Sturmabteilung* (assault detachment) to test a new lightweight 3.7 cm assault cannon. The new unit consisted of two companies of engineers and a detachment of 20 assault cannon, totalling 649 officers and men. Its commander was Major Kalsow, after whom the unit was named.[178] Sturmabteilung Kalsow spent two months testing its equipment and developing new tactics, using full-scale copies of entrenchments. These tactics involved using the assault cannon to make gaps in the enemy defensive works by direct fire from the front trench during the preparatory bombardment. When the barrage lifted, small parties of engineers would advance, protected by armoured shields, and clear paths for the assault cannon, which would then be manhandled forward under covering fire from the infantry in the German front line. Having thus achieved a break-in, the cannon would engage machine guns and artillery posts with high-explosive shells and use grape shot against enemy infantry. Under the cover of this fire, mixed *Sturmtruppen* (assault squads) of engineers and infantry would attempt to break through the enemy defences.[179]

Sturmabteilung Kalsow was committed into combat during June and July 1915. Despite its specialist training and equipment, the unit was immediately split into its component parts: the engineers being used to build positions and the guns permanently emplaced in the front line, in direct contradiction of their intended role. Casualties were heavy, 184 men and six guns being lost in the first fortnight alone, and the results disappointing. The one discovery of value was that the 3.7 cm guns were too light, being no more effective than machine guns or mortars, while their pronounced muzzle flash made them easy for the enemy to locate and direct artillery fire against.[180] When the unit came out of the line, it was found that the replacements for its heavy losses were of such poor quality that six weeks would be needed to bring it back up to the required standard of training. Before this process was complete, Kalsow had been replaced. As Bauer later wrote, 'The first commander of the battalion . . . was an engineer and regarded his unit as such. Later, I found an outstanding commander in the form of Hauptmann Rohr, equally distinguished as a person and as a soldier, and from then on the battalion made rapid progress.'[181]

Rohr took over the assault detachment on 8 September 1915, ten days after it had been transferred to Armee-Abteilung Gaede. Despite his junior rank, Rohr was an obvious choice to command the experimental unit. Before his transfer, he had commanded No 3 Company in the Garde-Schützen-Bataillon.[182] The unit was one of only 18 active battalions of light infantry in the German Army, which represented the elite of its infantry. These units were ideally suited for the development of new infantry tactics. Each had received a machine-gun company before the outbreak of war,[183] giving them a great awareness of firepower, while they had a reputation for rapid manoeuvre in battle. The Garde-Schützen-Bn had gained considerable experience of the key features of the front, notably the Hartmannsweilerkopf,[184] where the assault detachment would test its tactics. Furthermore, it had formed its own elite assault company on 2 March 1915[185] and it appears likely that this had been commanded by Rohr. He was therefore an ideal figure to make the realities of infantry combat clear to an experimental force of engineers.

As soon as he took over command of the assault detachment, now reinforced by six machine guns, four light mortars and six flamethrowers, Rohr began a period of rapid evaluation of ideas and equipment. In this he co-operated closely with Reddemann, commander of the experimental flamethrower unit, Garde-Reserve-Pionier-Bn 3. In only a few weeks, these two officers developed the *Stosstruppgedanke* (assault-squad concept),[186] which was to remain the basis of German infantry tactics for 30 years. Rohr quickly identified the flaws in the tactics developed by Sturmabteilung Kalsow. The armoured shields had been a failure, as they were ineffective against shell fire and reduced the mobility of the men carrying them to such an extent as to counteract the limited protection afforded against bullets. Moreover, even had the shields been more effective, little would have been gained. The German infantry regulations stated that an assault should be made only against an enemy on the verge of collapse. The armoured shields, while protecting the attacker, did not address the problem of laying down effective fire on the defender, preparatory for the assault, the essence of fire tactics. The idea of the assault cannon leading the assault was flawed also, since there was no armoured vehicle, that is, a tank, to carry them. Without such a vehicle, the guns were too slow and too vulnerable for the tactics to be effective.

Recognising the inadequacy of indirect-fire artillery, Rohr emphasised the importance of organic heavy weapons, *Truppwaffen*[187] (squad weapons), within infantry units. While indirect fire was still essential for general suppression, the squad weapons enabled particular targets to be engaged with speed and precision. Their presence restored firepower to the infantry and so filled the gap in capabilities caused by the eclipse of the rifle. The infantry was once again in a position to prepare its attacks by its own organic fire and to judge the moment for assault by a slackening of the enemy's fire.

The squad weapons may be divided into two pairs of mutually complementary weapons, each pairing meeting a different requirement for firepower. The first pair, that of *Infanterie-Geschütz* (infantry gun) and trench mortar, provided fire sufficient to destroy obstacles and machine-gun emplacements. The second pair, of machine gun and *Granatenwerfer* (grenade firer), supplied a flexible reserve of firepower with which to engage enemy infantry and win the firefight.

The first infantry guns were unsatisfactory. The 3.7 cm assault cannon fired too light a shell and was too easily located.[188] Rohr tested a battery of 10.5 cm mountain howitzers in the assault role. He may have been influenced by their use by the Japanese to support infantry attacks in 1904–5,[189] but he found the guns too cumbersome for trench conditions. Experiments were made with remounting captured Russian 7.62 cm guns and the standard German field gun, the 7.7 cm *Feldkannone '96*. Fifty *Nahkampfbatterien* (close-combat batteries) were formed with this equipment. In 1918, a purpose-built gun was issued, the Krupp *Infanterie-Geschütz '18*, which weighed only 300 kilograms and fired a 7.7 cm shell to 2,000 metres. Owing to limited production, only 53 batteries of this excellent gun were formed. In the mobile conditions of 1918, the Germans reverted to their pre-war doctrine and attached conventional field gun batteries to infantry regiments as *Begleitbatterien* (accompanying batteries), the guns to be used singly or in pairs.[190]

The infantry gun was a powerful weapon. Its range allowed it to engage any target within the enemy defensive zone, including the field guns and heavy machine guns deployed towards the rear of that zone, whose fire was of decisive importance to the defence. Its rate of fire, accuracy and shell weight also made the infantry gun ideal for use against unexpected enemy machine-gun nests or concrete pill boxes. Despite its considerable capabilities, however, the infantry gun was only a partial solution to the problem of achieving direct firepower. A field gun, even on a smaller mounting, was still vulnerable to enemy fire and its mobility was such that it could not keep up with a deep advance. Its main use was during the initial break-in or in restoring the momentum of an attack held up by an enemy strongpoint.

The second support weapon employed in the new tactics was the 7.6 cm trench mortar,[191] which was relatively light and mobile. Its high trajectory enabled it to fire at targets at close range, which was difficult for indirect-fire artillery.[192] It also meant that the shells fell almost vertically from the sky and so even deep trenches gave little protection.[193] With its greater mobility and effective (if relatively less accurate) fire, the trench mortar proved complementary to the infantry gun.

The complementary pairing of infantry gun and mortar was repeated at a lighter level by the machine gun and grenade firer. The grenade firer had a maximum range of 300 metres and was easily dismantled into two man-portable parts.[194] Its relatively light weight and ease of assembly and disassembly, enabled it to keep up a steady rate of fire, yet still stay in close touch with the infantry. It was versatile, using both direct and indirect fire, and its accuracy and high rate of fire made it ideal for engaging targets with great flexibility.

The final squad weapon was the machine gun. The basic German machine gun was the *Maschinengewehr '08*, a variation of the belt-fed, water-cooled Maxim gun. Although highly effective in defence, it was too heavy[195] to be used in the attack. A lighter model, the *Maschinengewehr '08/'15*, was produced, but this was almost as heavy as the older model when modified for the assault role.[196] None the less, by the end of the war each infantry company possessed six of these guns.[197] The British Lewis gun was generally a better weapon and extensive use was made of those captured.[198]

Since the individual infantryman was no longer required to participate in the battle for fire superiority, infantry formations and equipment were remodelled. Whereas the pre-war emphasis had been on firepower, the new emphasis was on assault power. Perhaps the most obvious result of this shift in emphasis was the abandonment of linear formations of riflemen in favour of small groups of grenadiers.[199] The linear formation had been designed to place the maximum number of rifles in a position to engage the enemy. With the abandonment of fire tactics, this formation merely obstructed the field of fire of squad weapons. In addition, widely spaced lines were unsuited to effective use of cover, did not concentrate force at the decisive point and were difficult to command and manoeuvre. All of these factors made linear formations inappropriate for a force emphasising assault power. Conversely, the small group was ideally suited to this function.

As a consequence of this shift in function, the equipment of the infantryman required adaptation. 'The principle of *identical equipment of all infantrymen* was broken *for the first time*.'[200] The rifle was often abandoned, since its fire was unnecessary while its weight reduced mobility and its length made it unsuitable for close combat. In its place was put a family of hand grenades, the infantryman's 'pocket artillery'.[201] Because of its explosive effect, ease of use and the number that could be carried, the hand grenade proved ideal for close combat and so greatly increased the assault power of the infantry.

The Germans coined a generic term for weapons employing assault power: *Nahkampfmittel* (weapons of close combat). These were not simply edged weapons, such as the bayonet. Rather, included under this term were all weapons used in a battle to capture or defend a position during the assault, including grenades and flamethrowers.

The primary weapon was the grenade: 'The hand grenade is regarded by the Germans as an indispensable weapon in trench warfare, both for offensive and defensive use.'[202] The Germans used three main types of grenade: stick, egg and rifle. The stick grenade, *Stielhandgranate*, was the most common type of German grenade. Its relative lightness (300 grams) and the extra leverage given by the handle, meant that it could be thrown up to 50 metres, even when lying prone,[203] and a soldier could carry up to eight.[204] Two main types were used: one with a five-and-a-half second fuse,[205] the other fused to explode on impact.[206] An unusual feature of the stick grenade was that it produced blast rather than splinters.[207] The reason was that in an assault fragmentation grenades would be more dangerous to the attacker, who was in the open, than to the defender, who was under cover. The egg grenade, *Eierhandgranate*, was a small fragmentation design. Its long range and splinter effect made it ideal for use in defence.[208] The final type of grenade was the rifle grenade. The initial version proved unsatisfactory, but a more effective design with a range of 200 metres was issued in 1917.[209]

The Germans first introduced a man-portable flamethrower, with a range of 20 metres, in 1912 and improved the design in 1917.[210] The oil used was deliberately of a type that gave off thick clouds of black smoke. This was partly to cover the attacking troops, but was mainly intended to increase the moral effect of the weapon.[211]

The Germans had found the traditional combination of rifle and bayonet to be unsuitable for the conditions of trench warfare. They considered the problem functionally: the rifle with bayonet combined firepower with assault power, therefore any replacement must address both of these capabilities. Although the firepower of the infantry was no longer of importance in the battle for fire superiority, it was still necessary for the infantry to have some fire capability. Targets would appear beyond grenade range and a total reliance on edged weapons in close combat was considered undesirable. In place of the cumbersome rifle, the infantry adopted a carbine, the *Gewehr '84/'98*, and pistols.[212] In 1918 certain units were issued with a *Maschinenpistole* (submachine gun), considered ideally suited to requirements.[213] An edged weapon was also needed and the bayonet was therefore replaced with a dagger.

The German Army identified the fact that the traditional equipment of the infantryman, the rifle with bayonet fixed, was unsuited to the conditions of trench warfare. The speed with which this problem was understood and steps taken to correct it, through the development of alternative weapons and tactics, indicates strongly that communication from the front-line troops to the higher command was close. This adaptability to the realities of war suggests a high degree of professionalism.

The Germans had rejected the use of linear formations in favour of more compact groups. It was therefore necessary to decide at what level these groups should be formed. Since the main reason for the eclipse of infantry firepower was the vulnerability of large masses of troops to enemy fire, the logical assault grouping was of section size. Rohr called these section-sized units *Stosstrupps* or *Sturmtrupps* (assault squads). Each squad consisted of eight men and an NCO.[214] This proved to be the most effective size both for command purposes and for best use of the terrain. The system evolved naturally, for similar squads were formed by a number of units in combat as early as the autumn of 1914.[215]

The essence of assault squad tactics developed by Hauptmann Rohr was that the attacking infantry should be able to react rapidly and effectively to enemy resistance (see Chapter 8 for details of the tactics). The key to this was the decentralisation of command so that individual sections could operate on their own initiative according to the situation, within the context of the whole. This required a very high standard of training, particularly among NCOs, because of the need to manoeuvre in close combination with fire support from the squad weapons. It was only because direct command, and therefore rigorous training, were ingrained in the German Army that assault squad tactics could be adopted successfully.

# 4
# Restrictive Control and Timetable Tactics

> [It is] a tradition deeply ingrained in the whole Army . . . that the chief task of each rank is not the doing of the work of that rank, but the controlling of the work of the ranks below.
>
> L. S. Amery, *The Problem of the Army*

A key figure in the development of British tactics before 1914 was Colonel G. F. R. Henderson. Henderson first came to prominence in 1891, with the publication of his article, 'Military Criticism and Modern Tactics',[1] while he was Instructor in Tactics at the Royal Military College, Sandhurst. In this article, he ardently supported the central argument of the 'normal' tacticians: that troops had to be kept under close control if they were to be effective. Such control was impossible over dispersed troops and the 'normal' tacticians believed that the advantages of closely controlled close-order formations outweighed the greater flexibility of dispersal. It is of note that Henderson's criticism was directed at the Prussian company column.[2] The Prussians, however, had found this formation to be too dense and inflexible and had frequently dispersed even companies into swarms of skirmishers.[3] Henderson was therefore arguing against a formation he considered too dispersed, but one that the Prussians had already abandoned as too concentrated.

> 'Extended order is the rule, close order the exception': 'great clouds of skirmishers and small tactical units, that is the form for infantry.'
>
> These were the cries that were heard on all sides after 1870, in England as well as on the Continent. But in England there were men who saw the dangers and the exaggeration of the new theories, who held that close order was now, as heretofore, the backbone of the attack, extended order no more than an essential accessory. Nor did they – and here the army was always with them – accept the necessity of breaking up the battalion and of sacrificing unity to the initiative of the subordinate leaders. To their views opinion has veered round . . . close order whenever it is possible, extended order only when it is unavoidable.[4]

Henderson strongly opposed initiative below battalion level:

> Whilst the startling doctrines . . . as to the absolute independence of the subordinate leaders had much to do with the dispersion of units and the difficulties of command in the battles of August and September 1870, the well-known pamphlet of Prince Frederick Charles, 'On the Art of Fighting the French' was directly accountable for even greater evils – for the reckless impetuosity of the German officers of every rank. Such was the general impatience to anticipate the enemy, to seize the initiative, and to force on him the defensive, that it almost seems as if the *furia Francese* was a veritable nightmare.[5]

> The company had become free from all control and interference. It was in the hands of its own leader to do with as he pleased. Not the slightest tie bound it to its own battalion. . . . The line of battle became formed of a number of small bodies, each fighting for itself, and wandering to and fro across the battlefield as the judgement or ambition of its immediate leader might dictate. Nor were single *Züge* [platoons] always to be restrained. Unreasonable initiative often carried them far away from their companies.[6]

Henderson was equally critical of the Prussian tendency in 1870 of attempting to avoid enemy fire by the use of cover:

> Another cause of confusion was the habit the troops acquired of swerving to one flank or the other in order to seek cover, and thus abandoning the line of direction. This was not confined to individuals; but whole companies, or the greater part of whole companies, acted in this respect with wonderful unanimity. . . . Tiny depressions, commodious ditches, convenient banks, although often at right angles to the true direction, clearly mark . . . the course of these meanderings. Cover exercised a magnetic influence, to which the unity of the battalion . . . opposed no counter-attraction.[7]

The basic reason for Henderson's objection to the Prussian company column was a perceived need for order on the battlefield:

> The Germans have preferred to recognise confusion as an inevitable evil, and endeavour to minimise it by training their men in peace to such control and obedience as is possible under such untoward circumstances. . . . But it is well to ask whether [that] is all that is necessary. Is it not wise, whilst doing all in our power to evolve order out of disorder, to begin at the very beginning, and to endeavour to prevent that disorder assuming abnormal dimensions?[8]

Essentially, Henderson emphasised the need for senior commanders to know precisely the location and activity of every unit:

> Against a civilised enemy . . . the individual battalion would play but an insignificant part. It would form but one amongst many units, for a decisive attack would be seldom committed to any force less than a division, and it is even probable that a whole army corps . . . would be called upon to undertake the operation. In any movement made in such strength as this, order and precision are the most important considerations. . . . Now, if every battalion engaged in the firing line were to adopt a different formation, and, if the commanders were left to their own initiative, such might well be the case, it would be difficult in the extreme to preserve the necessary intervals between the component parts of the attacking force. For an operation of this kind a normal formation is absolutely necessary.[9]

Henderson believed decentralisation of command could lead only to chaos and inappropriate formations. That commanders might be sufficiently well trained so as to be able to adopt the correct formation on their own initiative was foreign to him. British regulations therefore ensured that 'the unity of the battalion was scrupulously respected; and [that] the leaders of the units in the fighting line . . . were neither encouraged to manoeuvre nor permitted to deviate from the line of direction the commander had assigned'.[10]

Since the British rejected decentralisation and the manoeuvring this would produce, they were compelled to rely on frontal attacks at the tactical level:

> [In the British drill book,] little stress is laid on flanking fire or flanking movements. . . . This omission makes clear . . . that flank attacks and the development of flanking fire . . . are held to be the province of the superior authorities: they are not within the province of those officers whose commands merely form units of the whole force. On the contrary, instead of encouraging excessive exercise of initiative, the paramount importance of order, of the cohesion of the attacking body, and of maintaining the true direction is inculcated on every page. . .
>
> Secondly, the instructions of the drill book are principally concerned with the execution of a frontal attack. There is no disposition manifested to shirk the difficulties of such an operation, but neither is there timid insistence on those difficulties. . . . Moreover . . . the success of the frontal attack is considered well within bounds of possibility.[11]

The rigidity resulting from restrictive control at the tactical level produced a vicious circle. The more adherence to strict regulations was insisted upon, the more individual initiative was repressed. The more individual initiative was repressed, the greater the need for strict regulations. Even in 1891, Henderson had some inkling of this problem, yet brushed aside the inherent paradox.

> The groundwork of an officer's education should be the tactical regulations: the drill-book, and the drill-book alone. When every word and every principle contained therein has been tatooed into his brain, theoretically and practically, so that it is impossible for him to act otherwise than in accordance with them, then, and not till then, let him be introduced to grand tactics and the operations of war.[12]
>
> [But] there are men so bound by regulation and method as to have lost all power of initiative, who are incapable of assuming responsibility, whose only guide in battle is the drill-book, and who have lost the ability of adapting principles to circumstances.[13]

Henderson could offer no solution to this problem other than faith in the quality of the British soldier:

> English soldiers are brought up with the idea that obedience is of more importance than initiative. . . . We have no reason to fear, looking at past history, that initiative will not be forthcoming when it is required; but trained as our officers usually are to look for regulations at every point, it seems unwise to trust them entirely to their own resources in the most important work they have to undertake.[14]

This article led to Henderson being appointed Professor of Military Art and History at the Staff College, Camberley. For the next seven years, he was to exercise a major influence on the attitudes to command of the future leaders of the army, including Haig, Allenby, Byng, Rawlinson, Robertson and Kiggell.[15] Ironically, Henderson reversed his position in 1899, with the publication of 'The Training of Infantry for the Attack'.[16]

Henderson rejected his own 'normal-tactics' argument and called for a new approach, similar to that employed by the German Army. Replying to those who argued that the 'normal' formation was the most suitable, he retorted, 'All systems . . . which depend on explicit regulations make but small demands on the intelligence of the individual officer, and for that reason, if for no other, they are quite inadequate to the exigencies of modern warfare'.[17] Henderson argued that training should concentrate upon the goal of producing commanders able to adapt general principles to each unique situation, citing a German officer who had fought at Wörth in 1870:

> We certainly did well for young and inexperienced soldiers; and the reason was that . . . our officers, including the captains and subalterns,

> were used to responsibility; they had been to a certain extent trained to exercise their own judgement, and to devise methods of overcoming unexpected difficulties, without continually asking for orders. This pulled us through.[18]

## After the Boer War

Henderson's revised views were confirmed by his experience as Director of Intelligence to Lord Roberts in the Boer War[19] and he worked hard to convince the army that he was correct. He published two more articles[20] and was appointed by Roberts, now C-in-C, to rewrite the *Infantry Drill Book*.[21] Henderson now explicitly rejected the dogma of restrictive control:

> It was mechanical discipline, absorbing all individuality, forbidding either officer or man to move or to fire without a direct command, and throwing no further responsibility on the subordinate leaders than that of merely passing on orders and seeing that they were obeyed ... that was still the ideal of the British army in 1899. The system had certainly been modified. ... But the principle was resolutely adhered to of keeping everything in hand by means of precise orders, of formations in which every man acted in accordance with a carefully defined routine, and of a continual looking to, and dependence on, supreme authority. ... In fact there was a constant endeavour to make battle conform to the parade-ground, to apply drill of the most mechanical character to the bullet-swept field, to depend for success on courage and subordination, and to relegate intelligence and individuality to the background.[22]

His belief in the need for thinking soldiers was firmly restated in his draft *Infantry Drill Book*, and in the *Combined Training Manual* of 1905, which was based upon it.[23]

> Success in war cannot be expected unless all ranks have been trained in peace to use their wits. Generals and commanding officers are, therefore, not only to encourage their subordinates in so doing by affording them constant opportunities of acting on their own responsibility, but they will also check all practices which interfere with the free exercise of the judgement, and will break down, by every means in their power, the paralysing habit of an unreasoning and mechanical adherence to the letter of orders and to routine, when acting under service conditions.[24]

The extent to which British tactics were changed should not be underestimated.[25] Attacks were to be made by skirmishers moving forward in dispersed order, with intervals of up to 15 paces. Once at short range, a decisive fire superiority was to be achieved by thickening the firing line to one man for every three paces. The dispersion deemed necessary made independence of action by individual soldiers essential. Victory in the fire fight was considered decisive, but the signal for the assault was to be given by the brigade commander. The use of machine guns and single field guns was recommended in the case of a deliberate assault.

The process of reform was largely halted by Henderson's premature death in 1903[26] and Roberts' enforced retirement in 1905. Henceforth, the development of tactics was the responsibility of the newly formed General Staff. The result was a gradual reversion to the normal tactics of a decade earlier. Ironically, the agents of this reversal were mostly officers whom Henderson had taught at the Staff College, before his conversion to decentralised tactics. The debates within the General Staff are revealed in the reports of its annual conferences.

The question of artillery support for the infantry was discussed at the 1908 conference.[27] Officers showed that they were aware of the need for fire to be kept on the defender until the last possible moment before an assault. The value of howitzers was stressed, since their steep trajectory allowed them to fire over friendly troops more easily than could cannon. There was general agreement that the supporting artillery should continue firing even when the attacking infantry were close to the enemy position. One officer recounted an incident in South Africa where a shell had landed only 40 yards in front of the attackers, yet had harmed none of them. Lieutenant-Colonel Edmonds reported that senior German officers considered 300 metres the narrowest safety margin, despite the protests of junior officers, while the Japanese laid down a margin of 100 metres. Although the British appear to have been in advance of other European armies on this question, they subscribed to the general underestimation of the effect of defensive fire on artillery and therefore considered its capability for indirect fire to be unimportant.

The problem of the infantry fire fight was introduced by Colonel Du Cane at the 1909 conference.[28]

> While the whole of our regulations lay down that the fight is won by the side which obtains superiority of fire, yet that struggle for superiority of fire is, to a great extent, neglected at manoeuvres. . . . The point that I particularly wish to draw attention to is the conduct of the fire fight itself by the infantry when they reach what is sometimes called the 'final fire position' from which it is intended to deliver the assault. It is often careless and perfunctory. This may, perhaps, be due to the fact that our manoeuvre regulations and training manuals deal to a very considerable extent with the art of

> manoeuvre, and, perhaps, not as fully as they might with the fire tactics of infantry. . . . In fact, we teach our troops how to get into the final fire position, but we do not teach them as much as we ought to do as to what they should do when they get there.

The discussion revealed considerable ignorance of the effectiveness of modern firearms. Brigadier-General May noted that infantry on manoeuvres rarely made use of rifle fire to cover their movements, preferring to rely on artillery support. The infantry, however, followed the same procedure even when there was no artillery present. Colonel Haldane, conversely, rejected the widespread opinion that the density of one man per yard in the firing line laid down in the regulations was absurd, 'an idea for which the South African war is to blame'. Haldane preferred to rely on mass, despite recent combat experience showing that this was no longer effective.

The crux of the matter was revealed by Colonel Stanton, who remarked that the infantry tended to concentrate on the volume of fire produced, rather than its effect. The reason for this was that, as Du Cane stated later in the conference, 'It is extremely difficult to judge whether you have gained sufficient moral superiority over your enemy to allow of a successful assault being delivered'.[29] It is of note that the German Army held the contrary view.[30] The cause of this difference of opinion may have been the contrasting command systems of the two armies. The Germans decentralised the conduct of the fire fight to junior officers and NCOs, who could readily judge the volume and effectiveness of enemy fire. The British, conversely, sought to keep control in the hands of the brigade commander,[31] but this officer was generally too far to the rear to be able to assess accurately whether the fire fight had been won.[32]

The question of the tactical handling of partially trained troops was also discussed.[33] This was of considerable importance for the British, as it was recognised that there would have to be a major expansion in the size of the army in the event of a Continental war. The conclusion reached was that such troops would have to be employed in much more dense formations than would Regular soldiers and that the heavy casualties resulting from such 'timetable tactics' were unavoidable. This view was based upon the experience of the American Civil War and the Franco-Prussian War and did not take account of the great increases in firepower since 1870.

At this time, the British Army had no organisation for the development and implementation of infantry tactics. The School of Musketry at Hythe conducted extensive experiments, but its conclusions could not be enforced on units.[34] Following the discussions at the General Staff conference in 1909, the school 'urged that each battalion should have six [machine] guns instead of two',[35] but this was rejected. Major N. R. McMahon, Chief

Instructor at Hythe from 1905 to 1909, was therefore summoned to the General Staff conference of January 1910.

McMahon's statement at that conference[36] suggests that he recognised that the advent of machine guns and automatic rifles made fire tactics obsolete. He argued that this was all the more true.given that in a major war Britain would have to rely on partially trained troops, who would not have the level of skill necessary for such tactics. His solution was to abandon the concept of the fire fight as a distinct phase of battle. Henceforth, troops should be trained to consider fire as a means to facilitate movement. There should result a dynamic dialectic between fire and movement, 'because heavy fire would be taken as a signal for movement, and movement would be a call for fire'. McMahon argued that superiority of fire was an essential prerequisite for success. Since the majority of riflemen would not be sufficiently well trained to produce the necessary volume of effective fire, this function should be performed by automatic weapons. In defence, a few of these weapons should be able to halt an attack, freeing forces for envelopment and counterattack. For the attack, the solution was the adoption of a light machine gun. This should be issued on the scale of 'at least three times the number of machine guns now available', six per battalion, in addition to the two heavy machine guns already provided.

McMahon's ideas bore a strong resemblance to the *Stosstrupptaktik* (assault squad tactics), which were to be developed by Rohr six years later. It is of note that his suggestions met with a cool reception from infantry officers but were generally supported by officers from the artillery.[37] But although these officers thought his concepts sound, they noted that the provision of the artillery fire support required by these concepts was problematic. Lieutenant-Colonel Furse urged the need for a Forward Observation Officer (FOO), who could direct the fire of the guns from a position near the front line, from which he could view the course of the engagement. The difficulty of achieving this was emphasised. The alternative was suggested of attaching a small number of guns to the attacking infantry, as was done in Germany. The utility of mountain guns in this role was noted, as these could keep up with the infantry and yet still make use of cover.[38]

The idea of decentralising the control of the artillery, either by assigning guns to the infantry or by delegating fire control to an FOO, was not generally accepted. At the 1909 conference, it had been emphasized that an FOO was to send back advice and information only and was not to direct fire.[39] In 1910, the opinion of General Grierson was that, 'he depreciated, most strongly, the command of any of the guns, except in exceptional cases, being taken away from the divisional commander. He said that he never allowed it in the 1st Division.'[40] Senior officers were therefore unwilling to allow the decentralisation of artillery, even though it appeared that the intimate co-operation of guns and infantry required in the attack was almost impossible to achieve by other means.

Furthermore, a direct attack was made on the validity of McMahon's ideas, and indeed on the concept of fire superiority, by Brigadier-General Kiggell. Kiggell was one of Haig's protégés and his views may be taken as representative of the dominant party within the General Staff. It is of interest that Kiggell felt qualified to speak on the matter of minor tactics, despite having had no experience of line service since 1893.

> After the Boer War the general opinion was that the result of the battle would for the future depend on fire-arms alone, and that the sword and bayonet were played out. But this idea is erroneous and was proved so in the late war in Manchuria. Everyone admits that. Victory is won actually by the bayonet, or by the fear of it, which amounts to the same thing so far as the conduct of the attack is concerned. This fact was proved beyond doubt in the late war. I think the whole question rather hangs on that; and if we accept the view that victory is actually won by the bayonet, it settles the point.[41]

Kiggell was essentially arguing for a return to the assault tactics of 40 years earlier. This view was based on a downgrading of the perceived effectiveness of fire, because fire tactics were a response to highly effective fire. The CIGS told the conference that just such a downgrading was to be made in the new edition of *Infantry Training* (1911). The previous edition had stated the principle, 'The decision is obtained by superiority of fire'. This was now to be changed to, 'A superiority of fire makes the decision possible'. McMahon's emphasis on the need for a heavy volume of fire was also distorted to stress the importance of individual accuracy.[42]

There were, therefore, two schools of thought represented at the 1910 conference. McMahon argued that, since the rifle-armed infantryman could no longer produce the volume of fire necessary to achieve superiority of fire, firepower and assault power should be provided by separate bodies within the infantry: the former by automatic weapons, the latter by riflemen. It was but a short step from here to assault squad tactics. Kiggell argued that fire superiority was overrated and that the infantry should rely on the bayonet, a return to assault tactics. This was the dominant school of thought within the General Staff. The School of Musketry's plea for an allocation of light machine guns was therefore rejected as unnecessary on tactical grounds, rather than as a result of financial restrictions.[43]

Kiggell repeated his views at the 1911 conference,[44] arguing that future battles would strongly resemble those of 1870, with rapid movements of infantry supported by direct-fire artillery. Although his arguments were rejected by artillery colonels Du Cane and Furse,[45] they remained General Staff orthodoxy. The final result of this may be seen from the report of the

1914 conference.[46] As Tim Travers points out, 'because there was often no obvious observable linkage between firepower and moral superiority, staff officers basically gave up the game and ultimately emphasized the human assault "at all costs"'.[47]

The British Army went to war in 1914 with tactics reliant upon the assault power of its infantry. The firepower available to support an attack was minimal. The artillery generally favoured direct-fire support for the infantry, despite evidence that modern weapons rendered these tactics obsolete, and the infantry's tactics were based upon the bayonet assault. Nevertheless, great attention had been given in the last years of peace to standards of musketry. Having had his request for light machine guns turned down, McMahon had maintained, 'There is only one alternative left to us. We must train every soldier in our Army to become a "human machine gun".'[48] Every soldier was expected to be able to fire 15 aimed shots per minuute, double the previous rate, and many men achieved 20 or more.[49] The 'mad minute' fire tactics greatly increased the volume of fire produced by the infantry, but this excellence was already obsolescent, as its reliance on dense, linear formations made the British infantry grievously vulnerable to enemy machine-gun fire. The British General Staff ignored this problem, arguing that machine guns were 'weapons of opportunity' and were unsuitable for prolonged fire or for use at long range.[50]

## The Experimental Phase

In 1914, the British Army discovered that its tactics did not match the reality of combat in the First World War. The experience of Headlam's guns at Le Cateau indicated that the use of massed artillery in the direct-fire role was no longer appropriate, while the machine gun was shown to be much more effective than the line of riflemen. The British initially reacted to the obsolescence of their tactics by attempting to restore firepower to the infantry, using ideas similar to those put forward by McMahon in 1910. A careful reading of the *Official History* and the relevant war diaries, reveals that these experiments gave promising results, and that during the spring of 1915 the British techniques were in many ways considerably in advance of those being developed by Sturmabteilung Kalsow. The experiments, however, were abandoned. To understand this process, it is necessary to examine the battles of 1915 (Neuve Chapelle, Aubers Ridge, Festubert and Loos) in some detail.

At Neuve Chapelle, the preparatory bombardment for the initial break-in was to be provided by 340 guns and howitzers,[51] using indirect fire. After registration, the barrage was to last only 35 minutes, in order to achieve surprise. It would not be possible to make corrections during the bombardment, because of the density of the shell fire. This was to be supplemented by nine mountain guns using direct fire. Two guns from 7th Mountain Battery, Royal Garrison Artillery, were attached to the Indian Corps, and seven guns (two from 7th Mountain Battery and five from 5th Mountain Battery) were deployed in support of 7th and 8th Divisions of IV Corps.[52]

8th Division was to attack at 0805 hours with two brigades: 23rd on the left and 25th on the right. It was to seize Neuve Chapelle and break through the German line. 23rd Brigade was assigned two mountain guns and 15th Field Company Royal Engineers. 25th Brigade received three mountain guns and 2nd Field Company RE. The brigade was also supported by eight machine guns and the divisional mortar section.[53] The preliminary artillery bombardment proved to be effective along all but 400 yards of the front to be attacked, the German wire being thoroughly cut and the enemy trenches 'practically obliterated'.[54] Within 20 minutes of the initial infantry assault, the British had broken into the German position on a front of almost one mile.[55] 25th Brigade was completely successful, seizing Neuve Chapelle with little difficulty. The mortar section followed close behind the infantry and reached the village safely. The guns of 5th Mountain Battery were manhandled towards Neuve Chapelle at 1000 hours, but were pinned by enemy fire, one gun being destroyed at 1030 hours.[56]

Opposite 23rd Brigade, however, 400 yards of the German trench remained unscathed, owing to the inaccuracy of a battery of siege guns that had arrived only on the previous day.[57] Since the wire was well cut, the attack could still have succeeded had the mountain guns been able to fulfil their main task of destroying the German machine guns.[58] This they failed to do and the left-hand battalion of the brigade was virtually annihilated by two German machine guns.[59] This failure by the mountain guns was largely because their ammunition was not high explosive (of which First Army had not a single 2.75-inch round) but was shrapnel,[60] which was incapable of destroying the German machine-gun emplacements.

Although a break-in along most of the front had been achieved with comparative ease, the British were unable to turn this success into a breakthrough. Owing to faults in Haig's plan, compounded by delays caused by the system of restrictive control,[61] the British began the breakthrough phase at 1800 hours, almost ten hours after the initial assault, by which time the Germans had brought up substantial reserves. Not only was the defence now stronger than before, but the British artillery was unable to locate the new German line accurately and was therefore ineffective. For these reasons, further attacks achieved little.[62]

7th Division was to move only if the attack against Neuve Chapelle was successful, in order to exploit any breakthrough. It was reinforced by a mobile force, consisting of two guns of 7th Mountain Battery, one squadron of the Northumberland Hussars, a cyclist company and a battery of mobile machine guns.[63] Since no effective breakthrough was achieved, the mobile force was not used and its value remained untested.

At the time, there appeared to be four main lessons from Neuve Chapelle on the question of fire support. First, indirect fire was adequate to cut wire and destroy the enemy trenches during a short bombardment in preparation for a break-in. That GHQ drew this conclusion is shown by a memorandum, issued on 4 April, stating that the outstanding lesson of the battle was that, 'by means of careful preparation as regards details and thorough registration of the enemy's trenches by our artillery, it appears that a sector of the enemy's front line defence can be captured with comparatively little loss'.[64] The failure of the bombardment opposite 23rd Brigade could be dismissed as being because of the late arrival of the guns assigned to that sector, rather than any inherent problem with indirect fire.

Second, mountain guns were of little use in the front line, those supporting 23rd Brigade having been unable to compensate for the failure of the indirect-fire bombardment. If direct-fire weapons were to be employed in support of a break-in, they must be supplied with high-explosive ammunition, which was not available for the mountain guns. Third, indirect fire was effective during a breakthrough only if the enemy could be located accurately. The inflexibility and long response times of indirect-fire guns were serious disadvantages. Fourth, since the infantry could not rely on effective indirect-fire support during the breakthrough, some form of direct-fire capability must be provided.

First Army's plan for Aubers Ridge, 9 May 1915, indicates that note was taken of these lessons. Although the experiments used at Neuve Chapelle had had only limited success, they were to be repeated, in a modified form, and new ideas were introduced. Once again, the new tactical techniques were largely confined to IV Corps, suggesting that its commander, Rawlinson, was more receptive to ideas than were his colleagues.

The indirect-fire bombardment was to last 40 minutes[65] and, despite the fact that the Germans had strengthened their defences considerably since March, it was to be of a similar weight to that used at Neuve Chapelle. Although First Army believed that more guns were needed,[66] no attempt was made to observe whether the results of the bombardment were satisfactory. It appears that Haig was convinced of the validity of the lesson from Neuve Chapelle, that indirect fire was effective. Even while the bombardment was still going on, however, the Germans manned their trenches and fired at the British troops deploying in no-man's-land. As soon as the barrage lifted, this fire redoubled in intensity and crushed the attack. 'It was evident that for the most part the bombardment had completely failed in its primary task, the neutralisation of the enemy's firepower. Adequate lanes had not been cut in the wire . . . and very few gaps had been made in the German 6-feet-high breastworks.' An illustration of the difficulties faced by senior commanders in directing their forces was that the assault went ahead, even though the commanders of 1st Division (Haking) and I Corps' artillery (Fanshawe) were in a fortified house only 300 yards behind the front line.[67]

IV Corps had noted the ineffectiveness of the mountain guns at Neuve Chapelle and at Aubers Ridge provided direct-fire support to the assault by different means:

> Two guns of the 104th Battery, XXII Brigade RFA, [were] brought up during the night [before the assault] into specially prepared emplacements in the front breastwork, within 350 yards of the enemy's line. One of these guns, that on the right, breached several gaps of five to six yards in the German wire and breastwork, using HE shell; but the other, owing to weaknesses of the floor of the emplacement, was not able to shoot with accuracy.[68]

Both attacking battalions of 24th Brigade faced very heavy German fire when they advanced from their trenches. Despite this, one officer and 30 men of 2/Northamptonshire were able to enter the German line through a gap made by the effective gun on the right. 2/East Lancashire, on the left, were shot down without making any gain. The effectiveness of even standard 18-pounder field guns,[69] when secretly emplaced in the front breastwork, was indicated.

The third lesson of Neuve Chapelle was that the infantry required integral direct-fire heavy weapons if a successful break-in was to be converted into a breakthrough. According to the *Official History*,

> In view of the experience of Neuve Chapelle – where the infantry had been held up by various strongpoints on which the artillery could not concentrate either with sufficient rapidity or accuracy – 'infantry artillery' was to be attached to infantry brigades for close support of the assault. It was to consist of batteries of trench mortars . . . and 3-pdr Hotchkiss or mountain guns, carried on lorries or armoured cars.
>
> Besides a section of a field company RE, a small force of mounted troops and cyclists to assist the advance beyond the German front line [that is, during the latter part of the break-in phase] was allotted to each brigade, and in addition a section of a mountain artillery battery and four trench mortars with which to engage the enemy machine guns in any strongpoints that might be encountered.[70]

The forces allocated to 24th and 25th Brigades[71] were almost identical to those used by the division at Neuve Chapelle. The difference was one of purpose, rather than of organisation: at Neuve Chapelle the forces were assigned to the initial assault only, whereas at Aubers Ridge they were to support the infantry during the latter part of the break-in. Due to the failure of the initial assault, however, the attack never reached the phase for which they were intended. Unlike the two field guns of 104th Battery, the mountain guns were not in the front line at the start of the attack, but were 1,500 yards to the rear, with orders to move up after the initial assault. They played no part in the preliminary bombardment, and by the time they reached the front line, it was clogged with casualties from the already-failed attack.[72]

The two 3-pounder Hotchkiss guns mounted in armoured cars were ordered to drive up and down a certain stretch of road behind the British lines and fire at the Germans, and to withdraw if engaged by enemy artillery.[73] They appear to have done little damage to the enemy.

Another innovation was tried within 7th Division, which was intended to exploit any break-in achieved by 8th Division. The division was supported by a squadron of cavalry, a mobile machine-gun battery, a battery of 1.5-inch trench mortars, two field companies RE, two 13-pounder guns from T battery RHA and one 3-pounder Hotchkiss gun on an armoured lorry, while two guns of XIV Brigade RFA had teams ready to move up behind 22nd Brigade.[74] This force appears to have been formed in response to the lesson from Neuve Chapelle that indirect-fire support was ineffective during the breakthrough and that the infantry required its own integral direct-fire capability. The experiment was not tested, since the failure of 8th Division's attack meant that the division did not go into action.

Although most of the innovations prepared for Aubers Ridge were not used in that battle, owing to the failure of the initial assault, by mid-May 1915 the British had developed a number of promising solutions to the problem of the attack in position warfare. These ideas were still only in the initial stages of development and weaknesses remained. Nevertheless, the use of a hurricane bombardment, supplemented by field guns in the front line, and the attachment of light cannon, mobile machine guns and engineers to the infantry in order to provide integral direct-fire support during the breakthrough, were important advances and were ahead of the concepts being developed at the same time by Kalsow, whose unit consisted of cannon and engineers alone.

Curiously, Aubers Ridge marks the turning point in British tactical development, away from ideas of integrated bodies of infantry and heavy weapons that would ensure the provision of effective direct-fire support during the breakthrough, in favour of a separation of firepower and assault powers: Pétain's concept of '*L'artillerie conquiert, l'infanterie occupe*'. The *Official History* reports that Haig concluded that

> the German defences were so strongly built, and the machine guns so well placed that a rapid infantry assault with distant objectives, preceded by merely a short, sudden and intensive burst of artillery fire, was no longer a practicable operation. He now proposed to follow the French method of a long methodical bombardment of the German defences by heavy artillery . . . in order to ensure the destruction of the enemy's wire and the demolition of the machine-gun emplacements and strongpoints before the infantry was sent forward.[75]

Haig appears to have drawn the lesson from Aubers Ridge that indirect fire was not in fact as effective as had been thought after Neuve Chapelle and that careful observation of the fire was necessary to ensure that the preparation was adequate. Far from being solved, the problem of the break-in remained dominant in British thought. For this reason, attention was again focused on this aspect of battle, at the expense of developments for the breakthrough. This was shown at the Battle of Festubert, on 16 May 1915.

For the preliminary bombardment, the British gathered 433 guns and howitzers. The bombardment was intended to last 36 hours and was to follow a definite programme. The artillery was carefully registered, every round fired was observed, and the damage inflicted on the German positions was determined by patrols. Towards the end of the prescribed period of the bombardment, Haig asked the commanders of the attacking divisions whether they were satisfied with the effectiveness of the bombardment, another innovation. 2nd and 7th Divisions replied that they were, but the Meerut Division requested that the assault be postponed by 24 hours. Haig agreed to this request.[76]

IV Corps was not involved at Festubert, but 7th Division took part, under the command of I Corps. Its sector was wide and the indirect-fire bombardment was supplemented by direct-fire weapons: 'Six guns, with old motor tyres on the wheels to deaden the sound of movement, [were] brought forward overnight into emplacements prepared in the British front breastwork. These guns fired high-explosive shell at the German parapet with considerable success.'[77] Despite the care with which the bombardment had been observed and the additional use of field guns in the front line, the initial assault was met with heavy German machine-gun fire. 20th Brigade was halted once the front defences were captured and the two lead battalions of 22nd Brigade had lost almost two-thirds of their strength by the time they reached their objectives. Further advance was prevented by enfilade fire. The supporting units attached to 7th Division, No.1 Trench Mortar Battery, 54th and 55th Field Companies RE and two guns of 7th Mountain Battery,[78] appear to have been of little effect.

At Festubert, the British had succeeded, although with difficulty, in breaking into the German defensive system. It had proved impossible to convert this break-in into a breakthrough. It appears that the primary lesson that Haig drew from the battle was that a prolonged bombardment was the key to the break-in, this being the main difference from the tactics used at Aubers Ridge. This is apparent from his plan for Loos, on 25 September 1915.

Haig's original plan was to attack with only two divisions, since he was of the opinion that First Army possessed insufficient heavy artillery for a larger attack. The attack was subsequently expanded to six divisions, chlorine gas being used to compensate for the lack of artillery.[79] A total of 941 guns, of which only 47 were heavy pieces, was deployed for the bombardment, which was to last four days. The fire was directed by a detailed programme based upon careful examination of aerial photographs and was closely observed.[80] Although reports on the eve of the battle revealed that the German wire was by no means adequately cut and that the enemy defensive works had not been effectively destroyed (the bombardment was so light that the Germans believed it was a feint),[81] they were ignored, the British relying upon the poison gas to kill the German defenders and reduce the effect of the defensive obstacles. This it did, in those areas where it reached the German positions.

Only two of the innovations developed during the spring were employed at Loos. 7th Mountain Battery was deployed in support of the attack, four guns being assigned to I Corps and two to IV Corps.[82] The latter were attached to 47th Division and were emplaced in the front line on the night before the attack, their task being to destroy German machine guns in the enemy front line. The 2.75-inch mountain gun's unsuitability to this role was demonstrated once more, where two machine guns escaped the bombardment and caused considerable loss before being overrun.[83] It appears that no field guns were used in the direct-fire role, despite the success of the guns so used at Aubers Ridge and Festubert. The second innovation was the use of mobile machine guns. By September 1915, the BEF possessed 18 batteries, of which five were engaged at Loos. Their role appears to have altered since the spring, when they were intended to provide fire support during the breakthrough, since the only battery mentioned by the *Official History* was used to help consolidate ground already taken, rather than to assist in a further advance.[84]

The stagnation and abandonment of the tactical innovations developed during the spring of 1915 appears to have been largely because the General Staff remained convinced of the validity of the infantry doctrine of 1914,[85] which emphasised the importance of linear formations of bayonet-armed riflemen. The official view was expressed clearly in the pamphlets issued by the General Staff. SS 119, 'Preliminary Notes on the Tactical Lessons of Recent Operations', issued in July 1916, stated, 'It is the spirit of the bayonet that captures the position';[86] and SS 135, 'Instructions for the Training of Divisions for Offensive Action', issued in December 1916, noted that 'The rifle and the bayonet is the main infantry weapon'.[87]

This retention of the pre-war linear, bayonet-based tactics was a key factor that blocked the development of the innovations of spring 1915. As we have seen, linear formations became a liability once the development of maximum firepower, their *raison d'être*, was no longer necessary. With troops deployed in long lines, it was difficult for direct-fire support weapons to find a clear field of fire. This may in part explain the failure to develop infantry artillery. The provision of firepower was therefore left to indirect-fire weapons:

> The assault no longer depends upon rifle fire supported by artillery fire, but upon the artillery solely with very slight support from selected snipers and company sharpshooters. The decisive factor in every attack is the bayonet.[88]
>
> The consequence was that the artillery now became the chief weapon of offence, while the infantry arm, dethroned from its place as queen of the battlefield, became its kitchen maids or 'moppers-up', and any method or procedure was accordingly regarded as a matter of minor importance. For this reason alterations urgently needed, such as a drastic overhaul of the chain system of command and the working out of a new doctrine for the infantry attack to meet the challenge of the German defence organisation, received little or no attention.[89]

This was reflected in a vital difference between the efforts made by the British and German armies to solve the problems of the attack in position warfare. As we have seen, the Germans assigned responsibility for the development of new techniques to a senior officer at OHL, Oberst Bauer. He in turn set up three experimental units that were intended to examine and test new tactics and weapons. Permitted to concentrate fully on this task, and enjoying high-level support, these units could make important advances in doctrine, as Rohr was to show in December 1915.

The situation in the British Army was very different. In June 1915, GHQ established an 'Inventions Committee, composed of officers of the General Staff, Royal Artillery and Royal Engineers. Its duties . . . were to examine inventions connected with trench warfare . . . and to undertake experimental work.' The committee was quickly replaced by an unofficial Experimental Section RE, under the Engineer-in-Chief. The section grew to a maximum size of only two officers and 18 men and, although it did valuable work testing 'gadgets',[90] it was inadequate to develop and test a new tactical doctrine, yet no other body appears to have existed at GHQ that might undertake this vital task.

Furthermore, whereas Sturmabteilung Kalsow was a permanent unit concerned solely with the development of new tactics in the field, the British relied upon *ad hoc* groupings of forces. Thus, the guns of 5th Mountain Battery were assigned to the brigades of 8th Division only three days before the attack at Neuve Chapelle, while those units attached to the division for Aubers Ridge joined brigades only two days before that attack.[91] While such short periods of attachment might have been appropriate if a new doctrine had been already developed and disseminated, they were inadequate for the careful experimentation necessary for the actual development of such a doctrine.

In summary, the British Army had neither a section at GHQ directly concerned with the creation of a new tactical doctrine nor did it possess, or seek to create, a force dedicated to testing and developing such a doctrine. There was therefore comparatively little effort directed towards the solution of the problem of low-level tactics in position warfare. The important developments in technique of spring 1915 were consequently largely neglected.

The detailed consequences of the British retention of assault tactics may be understood through a functional analysis of the three aspects of combat required within each phase of battle: firepower to destroy enemy emplacements and machine guns, firepower to achieve fire superiority and assault power to seize positions.

By May 1915, the British had come some way towards providing the firepower needed to destroy enemy emplacements and machine guns, by the use of direct-fire field guns, mortars and mountain guns. Although field guns emplaced in the front line shortly before an assault had proved their effectiveness in the break-in phase at Aubers Ridge and Festubert, the idea had been abandoned by the time of Loos, because of the switch to prolonged bombardments by indirect-fire artillery. Since the effectiveness of these bombardments could be determined by the use of observers, and deficiencies could in theory be rectified, there appeared to be no need for guns to be risked in the direct-fire role. Reliance upon indirect fire alone had the added advantage that all the guns could be kept under close central control, a preference for which was apparent among British commanders even before the war. Yet as early as May 1915, German machine-gun emplacements, the key to the defence, were proof against all but a direct hit.[92] The difficulty of achieving such accuracy using indirect fire was one factor in persuading the British to rely on long preparatory bombardments, the sheer number of shells fired making a direct hit more probable. The reliance upon indirect fire was retained despite the fact that this form of bombardment was found to be inadequate on every occasion, as at Loos.

The question of command appears to have been considered of greater weight than that of tactical effectiveness. The problem was not to be resolved until the introduction of predicted shooting late in 1917.

A second potential source of firepower to destroy enemy positions during the break-in was the mortar. These were assigned to the artillery in the British Army, to the engineers in the German Army. The reluctance of artillerymen to leave their cannon and horses for an unimpressive 'old bit of drain pipe' partly explains the limited development of mortars in the British Army. Although artillery mortars were deployed, they were used primarily for wire cutting, until the availability of a new fuse made indirect-fire howitzers more effective at this task and the mortars became redundant.[93]

Firepower to destroy enemy positions was also needed during the breakthrough and break-out phases. The experiments of May 1915 included attempts to use light mortars and mountain guns to fulfil this requirement. At the start of the war, the British did not have a single type of mortar, nor were any under design.[94] Although several types were extemporised in France and were used at Neuve Chapelle and Aubers Ridge, the first effective design was the Stokes mortar. The initial order for 1,000 was placed in August 1915, after the Ministry of Munitions had spent months fruitlessly trying to convince the War Office that the weapon was suitable.[95] Despite its simple design, the Stokes mortar had a range of 400 yards and was potentially as accurate as the German light *Minenwerfer*. The main flaw in the design was that the mounting was too heavy for the weapon to be used in a mobile role, as was required in the breakthrough. If the mounting was discarded, as was frequently the case, the tube then being steadied by hand, the weapon lost much of its accuracy.[96] It was unpopular with the infantry because it attracted hostile fire and eight men had to be assigned to each weapon to carry its ammunition supply. Nevertheless, it became the basic mortar employed by British troops and provided a vital element of heavy-weapon support to the infantry after the break-in.

The second potential source of firepower with which to destroy enemy machine-gun emplacements during the breakthrough was the mountain gun. The use of such guns in this role had been suggested by Brigadier-General May at the General Staff conference of 1910.[97] In 1914, the Royal Garrison Artillery included 12 batteries of mountain guns: by 1918, there were 44 batteries.[98] Given that a considerable number of mountain guns were available, it might be expected that May's suggestion would have been acted upon and a number of these batteries used on the Western Front, but this was not the case.

Only three mountain batteries served in France.[99] The 2nd, 5th and 7th Mountain Batteries were shipped to Britain from their garrisons in Egypt and India in the autumn of 1914 to form III Pack Artillery Brigade. The brigade sailed for France on 9 December 1914, where it was at once split up, with 2nd Battery assigned to 4th Division in II Corps, 5th Battery to 3rd Division in III Corps and 7th Battery to 8th Division in IV Corps. The batteries fought with some success, but GHQ decided that they were unsuited to trench conditions and would be better employed in the terrain for which they were designed. The three mountain batteries therefore left France for Salonika in December 1915. GHQ may have been influenced in its dismissal of the 2.75-inch mountain gun by its poor design, which made it difficult to handle.[100] Furthermore, little high-explosive ammunition was available, making the gun ineffective against machine-gun emplacements.

In February 1917, a new mountain gun, the 3.7-inch pack howitzer, was introduced into service. It had none of the design defects of the old 2.75-inch gun and was to remain in use until 1960.[101] Although the new weapon was directly comparable with the infantry guns then being employed by the German *Sturmbataillone*, the British appear not to have considered using the 3.7-inch pack howitzer in that role and not one of these weapons was sent to the Western Front. That the howitzer was capable of performing the close-support function was demonstrated in the 1930s, when the Royal Artillery proposed attaching 18 of the guns to each infantry division for precisely this purpose.[102]

The second need was for firepower with which to achieve fire superiority. The vital need for the enemy's fire to be overcome before an assault was launched had been clear even before the war. We have noted, however, that both the Germans and the British believed that the achievement of fire superiority was a once-and-for-all process, after which open movement was possible. This error was compounded in the British Army by the assumption that fire superiority would be achieved after a given time, a consequence of control being retained by commanders too far to the rear to be able to judge the level of enemy fire by personal observation. In battle, the British believed that the preliminary bombardment would have won the fire fight and that little further fire support was necessary. The net result was that attacks were often launched without fire superiority having been achieved and without any covering fire to suppress the enemy. The *Official History* considered this to be a key factor in the failure of the attack at Aubers Ridge.[103]

Although the British Army never introduced a weapon comparable to the German *Granatenwerfer* (grenade firer), it did issue an excellent light machine gun: the Lewis gun, first deployed in July 1915. By the end of that year, each battalion had been assigned eight of these weapons, the number of light machine guns urged as a minimum by McMahon in 1910. This total was doubled, to 16, towards the end of 1916 and was doubled again, to 32, a year later. The final allocation, reached in July 1918, was 36 guns per battalion.[104] This gave two guns to each platoon, the scale adopted by the German Army early in 1917.[105] Although some senior officers had urged the creation of mixed platoons, consisting of two rifle sections, one grenade section and one Lewis gun section, as early as the autumn of 1916, this was not officially accepted until the end of 1917,[106] thereby delaying the development of integrated platoon tactics. The Lewis gun proved of great value in the offensive role of suppressing enemy fire in order to allow infantry to assault.

The final aspect of combat within each phase of battle was the need for assault power with which to seize positions. The Germans had found that the most effective close-combat weapon was the grenade. The British had only one type of hand grenade in service in 1914: introduced in 1908, its design was primitive and dangerous. A wide variety of new designs were produced, both official and locally made, but the first effective type was the No. 5 Mills bomb, accepted for service in May 1915.[107] By July, 16,000 had been delivered and 11,484 were available at Loos. Although production of the Mills bomb was to reach 800,000 per week by July 1916,[108]

> it was well into 1917 before it could be said to be in almost universal use on the Western Front . . . The 'No. 5' grenade weighed 1 lb. 5 ounces [600 grams], and men were trained to throw it 30 yards. It was a thoroughly hazardous weapon in the assault, since 30 yards was within its lethal range if it exploded in the open, especially on hard ground. The five-second time fuse of the 'No. 5' was initiated when the grenade left the hand . . . In the confined space of a trench bay or dugout the effect could be murderous, though erratic: the detonator was not centrally placed and the fragmenting of the casing was unpredictable.[109]

The Mills bomb was ill suited to both attack and defence. In the attack, its fragmentation effect made it at least as dangerous to the thrower (in the open) as to the enemy (in a trench). In defence, its short range meant that the enemy could not be engaged until the last moments of an assault. The flaws of the Mills bomb were readily apparent, as were the advantages of the German concept of a family of grenades, yet little effort appears to have been made to improve the British equipment.

A number of British officers had recognised the value of the grenade soon after the war had begun. During the winter of 1914–15, IV and Indian Corps had each formed special grenade detachments[110] and their performance was considered to be generally satisfactory. When IV Corps asked its six brigades for lessons learned from Neuve Chapelle, three responded by emphasising the value of grenades, with 20th Brigade noting that they had a 'very great moral effect and caused many surrenders'.[111] This approach continued in some parts of the army and was reflected in pamphlets such as 'Notes on some Bombing Operations in the Reserve

Army',[112] issued in October 1916, that emphasised the value of grenades and also the necessity for close co-operation between bombers, Lewis guns, rifle grenades, Stokes mortars and snipers. While developments closely parallel to German ideas were being made, they were neither widespread nor accepted by the General Staff, which made repeated statements disparaging the value of grenades.[113]

The emphasis upon close control and indirect fire also resulted in the infantry losing its main pre-war source of integral firepower, the two heavy machine guns assigned to each battalion. While the creation of the Machine-Gun Corps may have improved technical efficiency, it may be suggested that the price was high, in that it separated the weapon from the infantry. The problems were illustrated by Major R. M. Wright, who had served in the Machine-Gun Corps during the war and had noted how relations between that corps and the infantry steadily deteriorated.[114]

In 1914, each infantry battalion had contained its own 'small and highly-trained machine-gun section', which came under the direct command of the battalion commander. The result was close co-operation between the infantry and machine guns within the battalion. The brigading of these sections into brigade companies and then into divisional battalions, while improving co-operation between machine-gun sections, did so at the cost of reducing co-operation with the infantry. From being a valued and integral part of the battalion, the machine-gunners became just another drain of men from the battalion. The natural response was that infantry commanders tended to use the corps as a dumping ground for their worst men.[115] 'Mutual confidence began to dwindle, and this lack of the complete understanding and sympathy . . . had a gradual but marked effect on the relations between the machine-gunners and the infantry, increasing the difficulties of securing perfect cooperation between them.'[116]

This separation of infantry and machine guns was widened by the development of indirect fire by the machine-gunners. While this was partly a response to the difficulty of employing direct fire in support of infantry using linear formations, it may also have resulted from the new Machine-Gun Corps seeking to justify its independent existence by creating a separate function for itself.[117] Such behaviour is not uncommon among military organisations, a similar example being the emphasis placed upon strategic bombing, and the simultaneous down-grading of close air support, by both the Royal Air Force and the United States Air Force after they became independent services.

The use of indirect fire by machine guns had been rejected before the war on the grounds that it was wasteful of ammunition and that the guns were needed in the front line. Its introduction meant that the guns tended to be deployed to the rear, leading to a feeling of abandonment on the part of the infantry. This was reflected in the infantry believing that the machine-gunners enjoyed a pampered existence and fired off belts of ammunition simply to boil water for tea.[118] Indirect fire also led to the creation of an artillery-type mentality on the part of the machine-gunners.[119] Machine-gunners 'unashamedly admitted' that during the German counterattack at Cambrai in November 1917 they had continued to fire on their pre-set indirect-fire targets, even when within sight of highly vulnerable formations of German troops. As Major-General Sixsmith wrote, 'After all that the British had suffered from machine guns in their attacks against the Germans, this seems too much to bear'.[120]

The absence at GHQ of a structure, such as the German *Sturm-bataillone*, through which needs from the front could be fed back and assessed, meant that British thought remained mired in the problems of the initial break-in. There was therefore little pressure for the development of concepts for the breakthrough and the break-out, and consequently little effort put into determining the requirements for success in those phases. This concentration upon the initial break-in phase only, and the demand that heavy weapons be centrally controlled, undermined the promising innovations of spring 1915. The British infantry retained its pre-war reliance upon linear, bayonet-based tactics until late 1917, while developments in fire support focused primarily upon indirect fire. Although this system was adequate to achieve success in the break-in, its inflexibility made the conversion of a break-in into a breakthrough almost impossible (see Chapter 5). One consequence of this was that British attacks became a series of set-piece break-ins, rather than a dynamic progression from break-in to break-out (see Chapter 6). The cycle was broken largely by the restoration of movement on the Western Front in 1918, caused primarily by improvements in artillery tactics, the use of tanks and the exhaustion of the German Army after its spring offensives.

## Training

After the First World War, it was clear that, by comparison with both the French and the Germans, British troops had had a low level of military skill. It became orthodoxy to make a sharp distinction between the pre-war Old Army, portrayed as having reached a pinnacle of excellence, and the wartime New Army, whose deficiencies were blamed on the government's short-sightedness in its defence policy before the war. This was the line taken by Brigadier-General Edmonds in the *Official History*. In the preface to the volume covering the second half of 1915, Edmonds wrote,

> General Joffre complained that the young French troops, owing to lack of trained officers, could only go straight on and could not

> manoeuvre in battle. The new British divisions could not even keep straight on. . . . Other things being equal, success after the original deployment has been accomplished is largely a matter of sound doctrine and good leading, particularly leading by battalion and company leaders, and in the final stages by noncommissioned officers and brave individuals in the ranks. In 1915, a year after the outbreak of war, among the hastily collected staffs and improvised officers and NCOs, the standard of military knowledge, though in the circumstances extraordinarily high, was not high enough to command success. It was absurd to think that it could be. War is not a thing that can be quickly grasped by any person of intelligence or waged by any one of spirit dressed in military uniform and armed. . . . The awful slaughter and pitiably small results of the battles of 1915 were the inevitable consequences of using inexperienced and partly trained officers and men to do the work of soldiers, and do it with wholly insufficient material and technical equipment. The British nation had failed to keep up an adequate force, and had neglected to make reasonable preparations for war, in particular to provide for rapid expansion.[121]

In the years before and immediately after the Boer War, the British Army was unfit to engage in a major Continental war. This was in large measure a consequence of the army's continued reliance on assault tactics. This system, otherwise known as 'timetable tactics', in which the battalion was the smallest tactical entity and victory was sought through the clash of bayonet-armed masses, made few demands of either soldiers or junior officers beyond a strict obedience to orders. Since little was required of troops, the quality of recruits was of minor importance. Indeed, men of low intelligence and initiative would respond best to the inculcation of obedience. Britain was therefore able to retain a system of voluntary enlistment in which the inducements to service were so low as to make only those with no other prospects of employment willing to put themselves forward – 'conscription by poverty'.

The length of service, reduced to seven years in 1908, was not long enough to provide a secure career, but was too long for it not have a detrimental effect on a man's future civilian life. Since soldiers received little training in skills applicable to civilian life, military service substantially reduced a man's future employment prospects. The army was therefore seen with considerable hostility by many families.[122] The result was that of those offering themselves for military service almost half came from unskilled trades,[123] while more than 90 per cent were unemployed at the time of volunteering. The low standard of these applicants is indicated by the fact that most failed to meet even the low physical standards required by the army: height, five feet three inches; chest, 33 inches; weight, 112 lbs.[124] The quality of recruits to the British Army was therefore substantially lower than that enjoyed by the German Army, which could call upon the country's best men through conscription.

The limited intelligence of recruits was of little importance for assault tactics, and this was reflected in the army's priorities in training.

> The main moral quality required of the soldier . . . was discipline – an unquestioning readiness to go anywhere at the word of command. By continuous practice the soldier learnt to carry out automatically, and without a thought of consequences, the orders which were shouted at him. The complete hypnotization of the soldiers by their officers was looked on as the ideal of training. Discipline supplied the place of courage, and intentionally superseded both reason and will.[125]

To achieve the discipline required for assault tactics, the army imposed a strict system of regulations upon the troops: 'supervision was omnipresent and individuality was systematically stamped out of the recruit'. The result was troops that were 'bred to deference and lacking in initiative'.[126] Such troops could not be relied upon to carry out tasks on their own and depended on precise orders. This meant that the British Army required larger numbers of officers and NCOs than did other armies in order to ensure the constant presence of authority. This constant presence, in turn, increased the troops' dependence on external control.

With the main aim of training being the inculcation of discipline, which could be largely achieved during recruit training at the regimental depot, there was not the same degree of urgency in field training as was to be found in the German Army. This was revealed both in the amount of time spent in training each day and in the way in which this time was spent. In 1905, Brigadier-General Henry Wilson estimated that the average British soldier trained for five hours each day, in contrast to eight hours by a German soldier.[127] The German syllabus included lectures on organisation and weaponry and emphasised practical and field training. British training concentrated on drill and physical exercise. 'If only the same amount of energy were put into the development of the stunted and neglected brains of our recruits as is put into the development of their chests and forearms, the result would be an incalculable increase in the fighting value of our forces.'[128] The limitations of British training at this time may be illustrated by a marksmanship competition held by Aldershot Command in 1902: of 1,210 rounds fired by the 12 best shots, only ten bullets hit the target. The results were not published.[129]

Once the necessary level of discipline had been attained, there was comparatively little further training required to make troops fit for assault tactics. To fill the time left after drill and other training, the men were employed in fatigues.

> Under the existing system, everything that is connected with the maintenance and upkeep of the barracks and of the regimental life generally is supposed to be done by the soldiers themselves. The result is that in an ordinary garrison town an enormous proportion of soldiers are always employed on a number of miscellaneous clerical and 'fatigue' duties. All this work could be much better and more efficiently done either by reservists or by civilians from outside.[130]

There were numerous examples of troops spending much, if not all, of their time on fatigue duties, such as carrying coals or delivering post, while receiving minimal combat training.[131] Seen from the perspective of assault tactics, however, such practices made sense, in that they kept the troops busy and reduced costs, while ensuring that the maximum number of men were available for service in the event of war.

The last years before the First World War saw improvements, notably as regards marksmanship,[132] but the basic approach appears to have remained unchanged. The deadening belief in assault tactics meant that manoeuvres were often unrealistic, with the limited importance accorded them being shown by soldiers being issued only three or four rounds of blank ammunition for each day, yet half of the annual allocation being returned unused.[133] Even the improvement in marksmanship may have been of limited value, 'for a good target shot need not necessarily be a battle marksman. For the latter a cool head is of more value than all the marksmanship skill of the target range.'[134]

Once war broke out, the Regular Army relied upon reservists to bring it up to war strength. These were supplied by the Regular (145,347), National (215,451) and Special (63,933) reserves. The army's formations were augmented by the divisions of the Territorial Force.[135] The Regular Reserve consisted of men who had recently left the colours. The terms of their enlistment made them liable for service in the reserve for five years after discharge. The National Reserve was made up of retired regular soldiers who were no longer legally liable for reserve service, but could be expected to volunteer. While the personnel of both these reserves had completed a substantial period of regular service, a considerable number of them had been away from the colours for many years, in which time there had been substantial changes in organisation, weaponry and tactics. They did not receive refresher training, other than an annual musketry course. The Special Reserve consisted of civilians who underwent a period of six months' full-time training, after which they were liable for an annual refresher course lasting one month.[136]

Since most of the 209,000 Regular and Special Reservists were needed to bring the units of the BEF up to war strength, and to provide replacements for casualties, the only additions to the army's force pool were the 14 divisions and 14 yeomanry brigades of the Territorial Force. Formed from the obsolete Militia and Volunteers in 1908, the force had not been altogether successful. Although the planned strength of 302,199 men was less than half that originally intended, the actual strength of the force had peaked in 1909, at 270,041 men. By 1913, numbers had declined to 245,779 men, with one in six of these being too young for active service. The fighting value of the force was further diminished by the fact that fewer than one in five of its men had served for four years or more, it was equipped with obsolescent equipment,[137] and it was still organised on the out-dated eight-company system. Finally, the amount of time allocated for training was so minimal as to make its members little better than civilians. In 1911, Lord Roberts calculated that the number of hours of training undertaken by a Territorial soldier in two years was equal to that done by a German soldier in only 16½ days, meaning that a Territorial would have to serve for 100 years to do as much training as a German conscript did in two years.[138] To external observers, the value of the Territorial Force in a major war was questionable.[139]

During the First World War, Britain formed 51 new infantry divisions, of which all but nine served overseas. Most were formed in the first few months of the war, when it was intended that they should be ready for active service after six months, the same length of time originally laid down for bringing the Territorial Force to combat readiness. In the event, shortages of trained officers and NCOs, and of equipment of every kind, made this target unattainable. The pre-war Territorial divisions required an average of 8.7 months training before sailing overseas, while those of the New Armies needed 9.4 months. The Second-Line Territorial divisions, which received lowest priority for equipment and personnel, and were frequently used to provide drafts to units already at the front, took 27 months to reach combat readiness.[140] Even then, they appear to have been of exceptionally low quality.

The timetable issued by the Army Council for training the new divisions allocated the first three months to recruit training. The fourth month was to be given over to company-level training, the fifth and sixth months to training battalions and brigades. The final week was earmarked for divisional training. Of the initial recruit training, almost half the time was to be devoted to drill and a quarter to musketry.[141] The emphasis on close-order drill, of little value for either fire tactics or assault squad tactics, indicates a continued belief in the importance of discipline,[142] and thus a retention of assault tactics. Drill generally received even more time than was scheduled because of the slow delivery of weapons, reinforcing the tendency to train troops for timetable tactics based on blind obedience.

THINGS TO DO...

Phyllis
home 1(802)863-1718
cell #

WiLLY (860) 677-1678
Barry (860) 584-5651
LyNS (work) (860) 628-9000
cell # (860) 517-8041

Sup: Alee
3-11
(860) 918-0834

In 1918, Haig considered that British recruits needed nine months' training in Britain and a further six months' in France before they were ready for battle. At that time, the French trained recruits for a total of six months yet still produced better soldiers.[143] For most of the war, as before, training in the BEF was the responsibility of individual formation commanders. The result was a wide range of schools at GHQ, army and corps level.[144] Only with the appointment of Lieutenant-General Sir Ivor Maxse as Inspector-General of Training in July 1918 was an attempt made to lay down a coherent policy from GHQ. Even then, Maxse's powers were largely advisory. He himself noted that he had been appointed only as the result of intense pressure on GHQ from London and that Haig, having conceded this point, had no intention of making use of him.[145]

The main responsibility for training rested with the division, the largest permanent formation in the army. Since the GHQ policy of frequent rotation of divisions through battles kept them constantly on the move, however, it may be doubted whether many of these formations were ever settled long enough to achieve a very high standard in their own training schools and courses.

Corps were in a better position to organise training, since they were more settled and had the resources to set up instructional schools. The school run by Maxse's XVIII Corps during 1917 may be taken as representative of the best of these establishments. Five types of courses were run, and were attended by a total of 3,142 men over four months.[146] One course was designed to improve the skills of platoon commanders and sergeants, another trained men for promotion to NCO, while two others trained Lewis gunners and signallers. The most important courses were the Special Battle Courses, which lasted three days and were designed for divisions joining the corps for a battle. Two officers from each company in the division were required to attend. Generals, staff officers and battalion commanders were also invited to attend and usually accepted. The main purpose of the course was to explain the ground and the battle situation, identify appropriate tactics and give suggestions for training. Unusually, the evenings were spent in free discussion.

Two factors undermined the potential benefits of higher formation schools. The first was the traditional freedom given to the divisional commander to train his own formation as he saw fit, without interference from above. This freedom generally precluded even the pointing out of errors. The prevalence of this attitude was shown in a letter written by Maxse to Fifth Army, after a divisional commander had complained about an order to send men to the XVIII Corps school.[147] The tone of the letter was somewhat apologetic, suggesting that Fifth Army generally supported the divisional commander's authority and his right to make such a complaint: 'It is always unpleasant for a Corps Commander to have to interfere with the training of a division and he should only do so in the case of those divisions which appear to him to require it.' Maxse pointed out that ten other divisions had been happy to send their company commanders on special courses at the corps school. The brigade and battalion commanders of 39th Division had been so impressed by the course that they had themselves voluntarily attended. Only one divisional commander had objected. The impression none the less is that Maxse had received a reprimand for interfering in the internal affairs of a division.

The second factor undermining training was the rate at which the British rotated divisions between corps. This may be contrasted with the German practice of leaving divisions in one place for as long as possible. Maxse noted that it was not unusual for a British corps to command 20 different divisions over the course of one year and that his own corps had seen 30 divisions, half the entire BEF, pass through during 1917.[148] This constant movement brought two problems. First, coherent training was all but impossible in the absence of an overall policy laid down by GHQ. The result was summed up in 1918 by Guy Dawnay, deputy Chief of Staff at GHQ:

> There is no doubt that our training system is neither perfectly co-ordinated nor evenly distributed through the armies. I am constantly being told by divisions moving from corps to corps and from army to army that they are being taught different doctrines as they move from one command to another.[149]

Second, training often received a low priority. With a division forming part of his corps for a matter of weeks only, the corps commander had neither the time in which to determine the division's standard of training,[150] nor the incentive to remedy any defects, since the division would soon be someone else's responsibility.

Without pressure for efficiency from higher commanders, many divisional commanders appear to have allowed training to be all but abandoned. After a visit to the Second Army area in August 1918, Maxse noted of the GSOs 2 of the corps and divisions that he had seen, 'The question of visiting battalions, etc., and seeing if they are organised or training on sound lines apparently never strikes them'.[151] Of the 30 divisions that passed through XVIII Corps in 1917, Maxse considered that only two had reached a high standard of training, while a further 12 were trying. In his opinion, fully 16 of the divisions were simply not bothering with training.[152] Under this system, many battalions fell into near chaos. Maxse noted that even the number of platoons within a battalion might vary widely both from the regulation number of 16 and from the number within other battalions of the same brigade, with men being assigned to platoons and sections on an *ad hoc* basis.[153] He believed that

> This ignorance arises from the fact that our officers are not taught elementary tactics and that those whose business it should be to instruct them are sometimes themselves uninstructed. Moreover, the time and opportunities afforded for even company training are so meagre in the course of a year that only a few determined men train their formations to fight battles.[154]

Although the failings of the army's training system were apparent, GHQ made little attempt to impose a coherent approach until the appointment of Maxse as Inspector-General of Training in July 1918. It was a common complaint that GHQ showed little interest in the corps and army schools. In 1916, Haig even ordered the corps schools to be abolished in favour of divisional schools, but the decision proved unworkable and was soon reversed. In August of the same year, Henry Wilson complained that First Army school had not received a single paper from GHQ since it was set up and that none of the senior officers at GHQ had bothered to visit the establishment. Reviewing the evidence, Tim Travers was driven to refer to 'a GHQ system that simply did not exist'.[155] Even after Maxse had been appointed, he was given little power.

This apparent disinterest in training on the part of GHQ may be contrasted with a general insistence upon discipline, in the form of formal compliments and polished equipment. These two factors serve to suggest that the army's senior commanders retained their pre-war approach, based upon the rigidly disciplined assault tactics, throughout the war, with dire consequences for the fighting power of British troops.

# 5
# The Battle of Thiepval, 1 July 1916

> Most of the [British] attacks broke down under our barrage fire, and if they did not a comparatively small number of rifles, and certainly machine guns when a few remained undamaged, sufficed to repel them. Only in those instances where the garrison of our trenches was originally weak, and had been put out of action by the enemy's artillery fire, did the British succeed in penetrating into our trenches.
>
> SS 494: 'Extracts from the Reports of German Formations Employed on the Somme, 6th Bavarian Reserve Division' (19 September 1916)

The Battle of the Somme was Britain's biggest offensive to date, twice the size of Loos in both length of front attacked and number of troops employed. It began on the middle day of the middle year of the war and may be taken as an example of the extent to which British tactical thought had developed in the first half of the war. Further, the British Army had not been engaged in a major battle since the end of Loos, nine months earlier. The British had therefore had ample time in which to analyse the lessons of 1915 and adapt their procedures accordingly.

The initial assault on the Somme was made by 14 divisions, and the narrative for this day alone filled over 150 pages in the British *Official History*. The sheer scale of the battle makes a detailed tactical analysis of the whole impossible here. The approach taken therefore is to focus on one section of the battle, the attack of X Corps against Thiepval. The points brought out regarding this action are generally applicable to the battle as a whole. The X Corps attack is of particular interest, since one division, 36th (Ulster), captured most of its objectives, while the other division, 32nd, was bloodily repulsed. The reaction of the British commanders to this unexpected situation, that ended with 36th Division's gains being lost, highlights certain important elements of the British command philosophy.

## The British Plan

At the Staff College, much of Haig's training had been based upon the concepts of Napoleonic warfare. Central among these concepts was that of the 'advanced guard': 'This was the entity that reconnoitred, protected the main body of the army, then attacked and pinned the main enemy army, drew in his reserves, deceived him and found weak points so that the decisive blow could be struck.'[1] By 1910, Haig had developed a more aggressive form of the concept. The functions of reconnaissance and protection of the main body were now less important, while the other functions had been transformed into a vigorous preparation that 'was supposed to take place along the entire battle front to wear out the enemy, draw in his reserves and find or create a weak point for the decisive attack'. This aggressive posture was emphasised still further in the succeeding years.[2]

Haig's original plan for 1916 appears to have been based upon his development of the Napoleonic advanced-guard concept and consisted of three phases. First, the German forces on the Western Front as a whole were to be 'worn down', in order to reduce the enemy's reserves. This was to be followed by a preparatory action lasting some two weeks, which would draw in the remaining German reserves. Finally, there was to be a decisive attack: the weakened German forces would be unable to prevent an Allied breakthrough and subsequent break-out.[3] The potential results of such a break-out had been illustrated by the Germans against the Russians at Gorlice-Tarnow in 1915. The first two phases had been shown to be an essential preliminary to any decisive attack. One of the lessons of 1915 was that even if a breakthrough of the German First and Second Positions were achieved, the arrival of fresh enemy reserves by rail could block any attempted break-out.[4]

Haig's original conception of the first 'wearing-down' phase was for a large number of relatively minor attacks along the whole length of the Western Front, in effect an intensification of the existing British practice of trench raids. As early as February 1916, however, Haig began to doubt whether this could produce significant results without also involving heavy British losses.[5] His solution, agreed with the French commander, Joffre, was to merge the first two phases.[6] This 'wearing-out' attack was to be executed on the Somme, where the line held by the British and French armies met and where combined operations were accordingly easier to organise. The battle was therefore designed as a feint only. The main British effort, Haig's *Schwerpunkt* (focus of energy), was to be in Flanders, centred on Ypres.[7] The offensive planned was similar to that actually carried out the following year at Passchendaele. Preparations for this Flanders offensive continued in parallel with those for the Somme throughout the first half of 1916.[8]

The preliminary battle on the Somme was intended to be primarily a French affair. Joffre originally promised to provide up to 45 divisions, three times as many as the British could supply. Sixty divisions was almost twice the number Haig had calculated as the minimum necessary for a major battle.[9] Such a force could probably have inflicted substantial losses on the Germans in the two weeks allocated to the preliminary phase, fulfilling the 'wearing-out' requirement, and would have pinned much of the enemy reserve. The number of divisions promised by the French fell steadily as their losses at Verdun mounted. At the end of April, Foch told Haig that he hoped to have 38 divisions available.[10] A month later, by which time the French had suffered almost 185,000 casualties at Verdun,[11] the force allocated was to be between 22 and 26 divisions.[12] Two weeks after that, on 6 June, only three weeks before the Somme offensive was to begin, Joffre cut the French contribution again, to only a dozen divisions.[13]

Verdun caused considerable alteration to the function of the Somme battle. Whereas Haig and Joffre had in February agreed to merge the 'wearing-out' and 'reserve-pinning' battles, Verdun made the French unable to conduct a major wearing-out fight and also made such a fight apparently less necessary. By the end of June, German casualties at Verdun had reached almost 200,000 men, considerably more than even the initially planned Allied attack with 60 divisions could have inflicted in the two weeks allocated to it. In effect, the 'wearing-out' battle was being fought at Verdun. Indeed, at one time Haig considered the possibility that Verdun might make even the 'reserve-pinning' battle on the Somme unnecessary.[14]

Haig's intentions for offensive action in 1916 appear to have been somewhat unfocused.[15] This was a consequence of his not having designated a definite *Schwerpunkt*. On the one hand, he planned to fight the decisive battle in Flanders, with the Somme designed as a feint to draw in and pin German reserves. On the other hand, even with the French providing only 13 divisions, the combined Allied total for that battle was 27 divisions. This was far more troops than Haig had had in any of his 1915 battles, yet these had on several occasions come near to achieving a breakthrough. Haig therefore had hopes that the Allies might succeed in making a decisive breakthrough on the Somme.

The importance of having a *Schwerpunkt* should not be underestimated, the core of the concept being the focusing of maximum effort at the decisive point. If the Somme was to be only a feint, the minimum of resources should be expended on it, sufficient only to fulfil its strictly limited objective of pinning the German reserves. This would leave the maximum resources available for the decisive effort in Flanders. If the Somme was to be the decisive effort, all available resources should be devoted to it, with preparations for the Flanders battle either abandoned or that operation converted into a feint. The consequence of Haig having no *Schwerpunkt* was that his aims for the first stage of the Somme were somewhat contradictory, a compromise incompatible with the concentration of effort inherent in that concept. Preparations for both offensives were to go ahead, hopefully deceiving the Germans as to the location of the main attack. The offensive would be started on the Somme. According to its progress, the battle could either be abandoned in favour of the Flanders battle, or it could be converted into the decisive battle.

The Intelligence Branch at GHQ predicted, correctly, that the Germans would need at least five days to move an extra five divisions into the Somme area,[16] giving Haig a narrow 'window of opportunity'. If the initial break-in was successful, the British could commit further forces and have hopes of achieving a breakthrough before the Germans could react. If the initial attacks brought only limited success, they would still serve to draw in German reserves and so prepare the ground for a decisive attack in Flanders. This compromise meant that the Somme was allocated more resources than were needed for a feint, but fewer than were needed for a decisive attack. If insufficient success was achieved initially and the battle was abandoned, the extra resources allocated to the Somme would probably have been misplaced. Conversely, if the Somme was made into the decisive effort, it would be the resources expended in preparing the Flanders battle that would have been misplaced. For a force whose resources were as limited as were those of the British Army at this time, any inefficiency in the use of resources was certain to make victory over the Germans more difficult.

Another result of Haig's decision to keep his options open as to the location of the decisive battle was that he needed to achieve major results on the Somme within a very short period. If the Somme was to become the decisive effort, the initial results had to be on a considerable scale, to make up for there having been no previous battle to pin the German reserves. Conversely, if the German reserves were to be drawn in soon after the battle started, it was necessary to threaten a breakthrough. Haig's *Schwerpunkt* for the first phase of the Somme was therefore a deep advance.

Haig's *Schwerpunkt* led him to overrule the opinion of Rawlinson, the army commander on the spot, who considered that a methodical attack gave greatest prospect of success, and insist that Fourth Army set its formations objectives deep within the German defensive system. Haig was therefore attempting to achieve a decisive success with forces sufficient only for a large-scale feint.

### *The Artillery Bombardment*

Central to the success or failure of the initial British attack on the Somme was the preliminary artillery preparation. In his original proposal, submitted to Haig early in April 1916, Rawlinson noted that the operation could employ either an intense bombardment lasting five or six hours, or a longer and more methodical, though less intense, bombardment of between 48 and 72 hours duration.[17]

Rawlinson's memorandum discussed the merits of the two types of bombardment. With regard to their moral effect, he noted that that of an intense bombardment was greater, but that that of a prolonged bombardment was still 'very great indeed'. The factor he considered decisive was the need for an intense bombardment to take place during daylight, so that the fire could be adjusted by observation in order to ensure its accuracy, since the inaccuracy of the bombardment at Aubers Ridge had been the main cause of the repulse of the initial infantry assault. Since the movement of troops in daylight was not possible, the attack forces would have to move into position during the previous night and remain in the trenches during the bombardment. Here they would be exposed to the inevitable enemy counter-bombardment, which would cause casualties and reduce morale. Rawlinson argued that a prolonged bombardment would permit the infantry to attack in the early morning, with deployments covered by darkness. He therefore proposed a bombardment lasting between 50 and 60 hours.[18] Haig's response was to emphasise the greater surprise and moral effect of an intense bombardment and he urged Rawlinson to reconsider.[19]

Rawlinson's revised proposal again argued in favour of a prolonged bombardment. Rawlinson pointed out that surprise was unlikely even if an intense bombardment were employed, in part because the French had already decided to use a prolonged bombardment. Furthermore, the extent of wire to be cut and the number of strongpoints to be destroyed were too great for a short bombardment to be effective. Also, since the Germans possessed many strong shelters, only a long bombardment which isolated and destroyed these shelters, would have any major effect on morale.[20] Haig now gave way and agreed to a methodical bombardment,[21] which should 'be continued until the officers commanding the attacking units are satisfied that the obstacles to their advance have been adequately destroyed'.[22]

Rawlinson's original timetable[23] devoted the first day to wire-cutting only, with the destructive bombardment planned to last four days, increased to six due to bad weather.[24] It was carried out by 1,070 field guns and 467 heavy guns,[25] manned by 50,000 gunners,[26] firing 1,508,652 shells,[27] at a cost of £6 million.[28] These figures, far in excess of anything the British had enjoyed up to that time, led to a strong sense of optimism among senior commanders. With one million shells allocated to cut the German wire and a further half million heavier shells for trenches, dug-outs and strongpoints, such optimism appeared soundly based. Surely this weight of fire would destroy the German defences, leaving them ripe for capture.

Both Haig and Rawlinson repeatedly emphasised that 'nothing could exist at the conclusion of the bombardment in the area covered by it' and that the infantry need only walk over and occupy it.[29] Not only did the events of 1 July show this to have been but wishful thinking, an analysis of past experience would have demonstrated the limits of the artillery firepower available. Such an analysis does not appear to have been made, nor did any organisation exist to make one. Up to the beginning of June 1916, there was no effective artillery organisation above division level in the BEF.[30] Even after this deficiency had in part been rectified, there ensued a long-running struggle in which the General Staff sought to block the creation of a separate artillery staff, despite the ignorance of most General Staff officers regarding artillery.[31]

The first question regarding the effectiveness of the bombardment was the number of guns available. Although there were far more guns, especially heavy guns, the length of front attacked on the Somme was such that only a limited increase in density was achieved. On the Somme, the British had about one field gun for every 21 yards of front and one heavy gun for every 57 yards.[32] Although the number of heavy guns was more than four times greater than at Loos (467 to 110[33]), their density along the front was only about one and a quarter times as great.[34] At Loos, Haig had argued that he had enough guns for an attack by two divisions only and had extended his plan to involve six divisions in view of the intended use of poison gas.[35] The density of guns on the Somme was therefore little more than half that which Haig had considered necessary nine months earlier, when the German positions were considerably less strong. The British density of 32.2 heavy guns per mile may be compared with the 87.5 heavy guns per mile employed by the French on their sector on the Somme.[36] Even with this density, it was not possible to obliterate the defenders, as the Germans had discovered at Verdun in February 1916.[37] The German troops were told they would find only corpses, but were met by heavy small-arms fire as soon as they moved into the open.[38]

The second question concerned the objective of the bombardment, which was primarily the destruction of the German defensive works.[39] This would in effect convert the battlefield from a fortress into open terrain. Was this perhaps what Rawlinson meant when he said nothing would exist after the bombardment? If achieved, this would enable the attackers to move freely into contact, thereby reducing the effectiveness of the defenders' fire and consequently, their morale. A secondary objective was noted by Rawlinson in his revised proposal: unless relieved every 48 hours, the German troops' morale would 'break under the strain' of a prolonged bombardment. Reliefs were therefore to be a particular target for fire.[40]

It appears that the British artillery preparation was based upon the idea of producing a collapse in the morale of the enemy by means of an assault preceded by fire. The effectiveness of the artillery was therefore to be measured not so much in the killing of German soldiers, but rather in the destruction of field works and the psychological strain imposed on the enemy. While the killing of the German garrison would assist the attack,[41] this approach held that the garrison depended primarily for its effectiveness upon the psychological state of the troops, which was in turn affected by the state of the physical defences.

The difficulty facing the British high command was how to assess that psychological state. As we have noted, the British system of restrictive control tended to concentrate decision-making in the hands of senior commanders. At this stage of the First World War, this meant that important decisions were rarely taken below corps level. Before the war, the assessment of the enemy's psychological state had been left to brigadiers, who had found the task extremely difficult from their position 1,000 yards behind the front line. By 1916, the assessment was to be made by corps commanders. Since corps headquarters were between five and ten miles behind the front line,[42] it was virtually impossible for these officers to assess the enemy's psychological state with any accuracy. This was reflected on the Somme by Haig's initial insistence that the assault be made only once commanders were satisfied with the efficacy of the artillery preparation[43] being dropped and the assault directed to follow a bombardment of fixed length,[44] as at Loos. This suggests that, as had been the case before the war, there was a tendency to assume that a given number of shells would destroy the defences and that the enemy position would therefore be ripe for assault after a set time had elapsed, rather than this being tested by direct observation.

With the British plan based upon the assumption that the German defenders would be on the verge of psychological collapse when the infantry assaulted, it is necessary to examine the other side of the hill, to assess whether such a collapse was likely.

## The German Defensive Position

### *The Physical Defences*

After the initial war of movement in 1914, the Somme became a quiet sector. Both French and German high commands were content with this state of affairs,[45] needing to concentrate resources for 'decisive' battles elsewhere along the front. By the summer of 1916, the Germans had enjoyed over 18 months of comparative peace in which to build defences, and they had taken full advantage of this time.

In constructing their positions, the Germans had incorporated a number of lessons learned from the battles of 1915. The result was a defensive position of exceptional strength:

> The original wire entanglement, five to 10 yards in breadth, had now grown into two great belts of entanglements, each about 30 yards broad and 15 yards apart. Masses of barbed wire of double and treble thickness were interlaced to iron stakes and trestles, three to five feet high, and made an impassable barrier except for small gaps left here and there for German patrols to pass through. The front line, from being a single trench or breastwork, had become three lines of trench 150 to 200 yards apart, one for the sentry groups, the second (*Wohngraben*) for the front-trench garrison to live in and the third for the local supports. . . . Concrete recesses had been dug deep into the parapet from which the sentries could observe either directly or with a periscope. The dug-outs . . . had now been tunnelled to a depth of 20 to 30 feet and at intervals of 50 yards, each capable of holding some 25 men; and at each end wooden steps led up a steep shaft to daylight in the front trench system. The intermediate line of strong-points (*Stützpunkte*), about 1,000 yards behind the front line had been perfected. . . . Communication trenches led back to the Reserve, now called the Second Line, which was as strong and as heavily wired as the first, and, being out of effective range of the mass of the enemy's field batteries, would it was believed force the enemy's artillery to make a new deployment before preparing it for assault. . . . A Third Line, about 3,000 yards behind again, had been begun in February and was almost completed before the Somme battles opened.[46]

The first obstacle facing an attacker was the wire in front of the German First Position. If this was not cut effectively, the prospects for the assaulting infantry were poor. With the belt of wire entanglements being 75 yards wide, the British faced 1.9 million square yards of wire on their 25,000-yard front. To cut through this obstacle, the British allocated approximately one million shells, two-thirds of the total used in the artillery preparation, but it remained a daunting task: 'Before the invention of the [106] instantaneous fuse [in 1917], HE churned up the wire but left a formidable obstacle.'[47] For this reason, shrapnel was preferred by both the General Staff and artillery experts.[48] The effectiveness of shrapnel against the thick wire used by the Germans, was, however, questionable.[49] Furthermore, up to one-third of all British shells were 'duds', because of poor manufacture.[50]

During the night of 30 June–1 July, a matter of hours before the assault was due to begin, the British sent patrols into no-man's-land to check the state of the German wire. Concern as to the effectiveness of the bombardment is indicated by the patrols carrying wire-cutters, to clear further gaps. The results were varied, but generally the wire was best cut in the south, near the junction with the French, and worst cut in the north. On the X Corps front (Map 1), towards the northern end of the attack sector, the wire in front of Thiepval and Gommecourt appeared largely untouched, as was that north of the Leipzig Salient. The same was true of the wire facing 8th and 29th Divisions, to the right and left of X Corps respectively.[51]

In general, the British artillery had not been able to cut the German wire effectively. Difficult though this task was, it was not without solution: at Aubers Ridge, two 18-pounders had been emplaced in the front line. The floor of one of the emplacements had been weak, making the gun there inaccurate, although it had still been able to do considerable damage to the German defences. The second gun had used HE to blast several gaps in both the German wire and the breastwork. In only a few minutes' firing, a single gun had made breaches sufficient for one company.[52] Extrapolating from this, it is possible to suggest that 150 such guns, firing a total of perhaps 3,000 rounds over 40 minutes, might have been as effective in clearing the German wire on the Somme as were the 1,010 guns firing 1,000,000 rounds over seven days actually used. The idea had been recommended by the General Staff in February 1916,[53] but not a single gun was so employed on the Somme.

When Haig agreed to Rawlinson's proposal for a prolonged bombardment, he had specified that it should 'be continued until the officers commanding the attacking units are satisfied that the obstacles to their advance have been adequately destroyed'.[54] This could be difficult to judge: at Aubers Ridge, the failure of the 40-minute preparatory bombardment was obvious to the front-line troops even before it ended, but the assault could not be cancelled, even though the commander of 1st Division and the I Corps CRA were in a fortified house only 300 yards behind the front line.[55] On the Somme, an instant decision was not demanded, news that the wire was not properly cut being brought back by patrols several hours before zero. No action was taken as a result of these reports. This may have been partly a result of the dropping of Haig's requirement that the effectiveness of the bombardment be directly assessed in favour of a simple assumption that the scale of the bombardment was such that it 'must' have been adequate. For example, the commander of VIII Corps, Hunter-Weston, told his subordinates that the enemy wire had been 'blown away' and that the troops could walk in, even though those very subordinates 'could see [the wire] standing strong and well'.[56]

The main reason for no action being taken with regard to the patrols' reports appears to be that senior officers did not look to patrols to provide reliable information, rather patrols were seen as a way to boost the troops' morale, although in fact the reverse was true.[57] Units which reported that the bombardment was not effective were actually rebuked by formation

MAP 1
Thiepval, 1 July 1916: German Defences

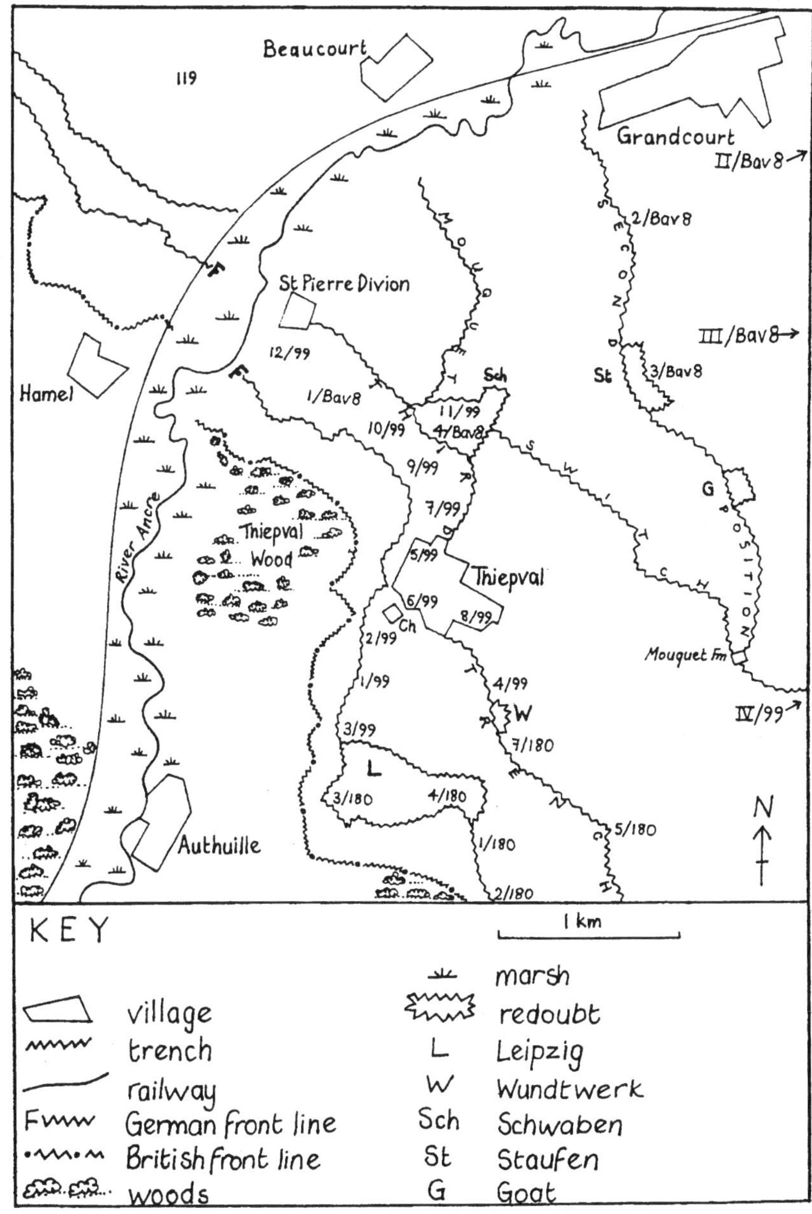

staffs for being scared,[58] the reports presumably being dismissed as fabrications designed to have the assault abandoned. The principle underlying 'normal tactics', that troops could not be trusted but must be closely controlled from above, led senior British commanders to discount reports that did not fit their preconceptions and to consider their own troops more of a problem than the Germans.[59]

Beyond the German wire, lay the First Position:

> The front-trench system was on a forward slope where it had been sited in the autumn of 1914, at a time when a long and wide field of fire was considered essential and when artillery observers were posted in the front line. It was therefore in full view of the enemy's ground observers, to whom the excavated chalk subsoil gave all the evidence they required.[60]

While the placing of the German position meant that it enjoyed good observation of no-man's-land and the British trenches, the convex shape of the chalk slopes meant that much of the area behind the British lines was dead ground.

Opposite X Corps,[61] the Germans had strengthened the front trench by building two strongpoints, in Thiepval village and the Leipzig salient. Both stood on the high ground of the Thiepval spur, which gave them a commanding position over no-man's-land. On the western side of Thiepval village, the Germans made use of the large, virtually shell-proof, cellars of the houses to create a series of interconnected machine-gun posts. The chateau was similarly fortified. The machine guns in these positions were mutually supporting and enfiladed much of the X Corps front. The second trench was intended primarily as living accommodation for the German garrison and was provided with numerous deep dug-outs, each with two exits. The third trench was again strengthened by strongpoints: the Wonder Work (Wundtwerk), the eastern side of Thiepval village, the Schwaben Redoubt and the hamlet of St Pierre Divion. Each was a self-contained mini-fortress, designed to block any penetration through the front trench. In addition, 1,500 yards behind the First Position, a single trench linked Grandcourt and Mouquet Farm to the rear of the Schwaben Redoubt. This Intermediate Line contained regularly-spaced machine-gun posts and served to delay any force which broke through the First Position, giving time for the Second Position to be fully manned. The Second Position, linking Grandcourt and Mouquet Farm, was of the same design as the First Position, with extra strength provided by Stuff (Staufen) and Goat (Zollern) redoubts. The Third Position, three miles behind the Second, was again of the same design. Summing up, the *Official History* noted,

> Altogether, from its natural position and the skill with which the defences had been developed in 18 months' work, the sector was of extraordinary strength, requiring all the art of the gunner and of the engineer to dislocate and destroy its strongpoints and obstacles before there could be any hope of a successful infantry assault.

The British artillery fired 500,000 shells at the German positions during the week-long preliminary bombardment seeking to perform just such a preparation.

> During . . . 25 June, the fire of the British heavy batteries increased. . . . Their shells crashed into the German trenches, the ground shook and the dug-outs tottered. Here and there the sides of a trench fell in, completely blocking it. . . . By evening some sectors of the German front line were already unrecognisable and had become craterfields. . . . During the afternoon [of 26 June] aerial torpedoes . . . fired from heavy mortars in the British front line, made their first appearance. Coming down almost perpendicularly from a great height, these monsters bored deep into the ground and then burst. Tons of earth and great blocks of chalk and rock were hurled into the air, leaving craters, some 12 feet deep and 15 feet in diameter. Only deep dug-outs of great strength could stand the shock and the weaker ones were crushed to atoms with all they contained. . . . Shells from a British rival to the German 'Big Bertha' shrieked through the air against the redoubts and principal strongpoints. . . . [27 and 28 June] brought a similar picture of continuous devastation. . . . [30 June] was a repetition of the previous six days. The German front defences no longer existed as such. . . . the trench itself had gone. A succession of shell craters replaced it. . . . The look-out shelters and bomb-proof observation posts were now a heap of ruins, a mass of twisted steel rails and broken blocks of concrete. All the communication trenches had also been blocked and many of them completely destroyed.[62]

From the British side of no-man's-land, it appeared that the artillery had largely achieved its objective of destroying the German defensive positions, thus compelling the enemy to fight in the open. The bombardment had largely obliterated the German trench system, but this was of limited benefit, as in so doing it had created several hundred thousand shell craters:

> The various German diaries, as also statements made by German prisoners taken at the time, show that the shell craters were considered as good or better for defensive purposes than the original trenches; in the trenches their position was known, but when they lay

> among the craters it was impossible to locate them. The defence was also made more mobile, as the men could rapidly take up fresh positions in other shell holes either in front, in rear, or facing the flank.[63]

Martin Middlebrook estimated there were about 1,000 specially built machine-gun posts facing the British attack.[64] Assuming this figure to refer to the whole defensive system, including the Third Line, this would correspond to one post for every 300 yards of trench, with extra posts in the numerous strongpoints. It should be noted that the number of machine-gun posts was substantially greater than the number of actual machine guns available.

The British artillery faced two problems in trying to destroy these posts. The first was the initial identification of the posts. The *Official History* notes that one machine-gun post opposite the left front of 108th Brigade (see Map 2, page 145) 'was used from the top of a shaft, entered by a tunnel from the bank alongside the railway in the Ancre valley. Like many others, this emplacement was not unmasked until the attack had been launched'.[65] The second problem was in actually hitting those machine-gun posts which had been located. The British put Thiepval under a heavy bombardment, knowing it to be a German strongpoint: not a single machine-gun post was destroyed. The obliteration of the village, which so encouraged the British commanders, served only to add protective layers of rubble over the posts.[66] Even had every machine-gun post been destroyed, the effect on the German defence would not have been very great: the machine guns themselves were kept in the relative safety of the dug-outs during the bombardment and could have been used with almost equal effectiveness from shell holes.

The prime aim of the British artillery bombardment, the destruction of the German defensive works, was not achieved. The German wire, the most serious obstacle, was properly cut in few areas and was barely damaged in a number of sectors. The enemy trenches had been largely obliterated, but the resulting crater field was if anything a stronger defensive position. Most of the machine-gun posts remained undamaged. If the physical defences had survived the bombardment, what of the soldiers who were to man them?

### *The Defenders*

The main sector of front to be attacked by the British was defended by XIV Reserve Corps (Generalleutnant von Stein), part of Second Army (General Fritz von Below).[67] On mobilisation in August 1914, it had consisted of two reserve divisions, 26th and 28th, which followed the standard organisation, of two brigades of two regiments. In both divisions, one regiment was from the active army. In peacetime, a number of active divisions had an extra brigade or regiment, which was attached to a reserve formation on mobilisation. 26th Reserve Division received Infanterie-Regiment 180 from 54th Brigade, 27th Division. 28th Reserve Division's active regiment was subsequently replaced by Infanterie-Regiment 163, from 81st Brigade, 17th Division, via 17th Reserve Division.[68] Since reserve units were originally formed on a cadre of 25 per cent active troops and the reservists had received annual refresher training, the quality of reserve formations was probably little lower than that of active formations. In March 1915, the corps was reinforced by 52nd Division, one of 19 divisions created from units taken from existing divisions, which were reduced from four to three regiments.[69] 52nd Division received Infanterie-Regiment 66 from 13th Brigade, 7th Division, and 84th Brigade (Infanterie-Regimente 169 and 170) from 29th Division. The formation was considered equivalent to an active division.

German organisation became increasingly variable during the first half of the war, as regiments were detached and machine-gun units of various sizes attached, without any overall scheme. It was only from the second half of 1916 that the number of regiments and machine guns in each division became standardised. This variation was revealed in a British intelligence report on XIV Reserve Corps in March 1916.[70] Of the corps' three divisions, 26th Reserve Division consisted of 13 battalions and 40 machine guns, 28th Reserve Division of nine battalions and 60 machine guns, and 52nd Division of nine battalions but only 41 machine guns. The ratio of machine guns to battalions in the three divisions was therefore 3:1, 6½:1 and 4½:1, an overall average slightly more than twice the pre-war allocation. The number of guns increased between the date of the report and the start of the Somme offensive, so that each division probably had sufficient guns to allocate one to each company, with extra guns in the various strongpoints.

XIV Reserve Corps had held the same stretch of front since October 1914, during which period it had suffered few casualties. In June 1916, therefore, the majority of the soldiers were still the product of the pre-war army. With their peacetime experience sharpened by 18 months of active service, their standard of training is likely to have been high.

The attack of the British X Corps was directed against the sector of the line held by Generalmajor von Soden's 26th Reserve Division. All four of the division's regiments were in the line, in north to south order 121, 119, 99 and 180. The main thrust of X Corps was against Reserve-Infanterie-Regiment 99 [RIR 99], a four-battalion regiment. RIR 99 was deployed with three battalions in the First Position, each with three companies in the front trench and the fourth company in one of the strongpoints in the third trench, and the fourth battalion in the Second Position[71] (Map 1). It was supported by elements of Bayerisches-Reserve-Infanterie-Regiment 8 (Bav8), part of 10th Bavarian Division, which was in the process of being deployed when the British infantry attacked. This regiment had two companies of its first battalion, I/Bav8, in each of the First and Second Positions, with its other two battalions in reserve. The sector of RIR 99 was therefore defended by 28 companies: ten in the front trench, four in the reserve trench, six in the Second Position and eight in the Third Position. If the troops facing the X Corps attack on the flanks of RIR 99 are included, the Germans had 32 companies compared to 144 British companies.

There are no reliable figures for the number of casualties suffered by the Germans during the preliminary bombardment. It is, however, possible to make a very rough estimate, based on figures given by Captain G. C. Wynne for Messines in May 1917.[72] He calculated that the 6,000 shells fired at each German regiment per day caused only about 40 casualties, an average of 150 shells per casualty. This figure cannot be applied directly to the Somme, owing to a number of differences between that battle and Messines. At Messines, the Germans were considerably more widely spaced and enjoyed the protection of numerous reinforced-concrete shelters. Conversely, the British artillery was rather more skilled and accurate by 1917. It may be suggested that 75 shells per casualty would represent an upper estimate for the effectiveness of the Somme bombardment. This consisted of 1,500,000 shells, of which two-thirds were used to cut the German wire and would have caused few casualties. With approximately one-third of all British shells being duds, the total number of functioning shells directed at the German positions was about 335,000. With 75 shells required to cause each casualty, it may be estimated that the British bombardment cauused about 4,700 casualties. This is, of course, only the roughest of estimates.

The vast majority of the British shells fell on the area defended by the 34 battalions of XIV Reserve Corps, whose battalions averaged 800 men, giving a total infantry force of about 27,000 men. The figure of 4,700 casualties would represent slightly more than 17 per cent of this force. Even with casualties being more concentrated in the battalions holding the First Position, it is probable that over three-quarters of the defenders remained unscathed. The bombardment, however, was uneven in its effects. Some German units suffered very few casualties, whereas others, such as 9/99, were decimated.[73]

The British high command was well aware that the bombardment could not hope to kill all the German defenders, but believed that a prolonged bombardment would undermine the enemy's morale. In his revised plan of 19 April 1916, Rawlinson stated:

> A long bombardment gives the enemy no chance of sleep, food and ammunition are difficult to bring up, and the enemy is kept in a constant state of doubt as to when the infantry assault will take place. His troops in the front line must be relieved every 48 hours, or they will break down under the strain.[74]

German accounts, indicate that Rawlinson had greatly overestimated the moral effect of the bombardment on the defenders:

> For seven days and nights they had sat on the long wooden benches or on the wire beds in the evil-smelling dug-outs, some 20 feet and more below ground. The incessant noise and the need for constant watchfulness had allowed them little sleep and ever-present, too, had been the fear that their dug-outs might at any time become a living tomb from which escape would be impossible. Warm food had seldom reached them during the bombardment, so that they had had to live on the supplies, three dumps each of 2,000 rations in each company sector . . . previously stored in the front line.[75]

The German defenders, while very tired, had not been deprived of food, nor had they required relief, even though the bombardment lasted seven days. In general, they do not appear to have found the strain too great. Much of the reason for this was identified by John Keegan. He calculated that the 500,000 shells fired at the German defences weighed 12,000 tons. He then noted,

> Out of the 12,000 tons, weight of shells delivered onto the German-occupied area, only about 900 tons represented high explosive. And the greater part of that small explosive load was dissipated in the air, flinging upwards, to be sure, a visually impressive mass of surface material and an aurally terrifying shower of steel splinters but transmitting a proportionately quite trifling concussion downwards towards the hiding places of the German trench garrisons. Each 10 square yards had received only a pound of high explosive, or each square mile about 30 tons.[76]

By comparison, the Allies in 1944 delivered an aerial bombardment of 800 tons per square mile during Operation Goodwood, and that in minutes rather than days, and still found the defenders capable of vigorous action.[77]

### *Doctrine*

At this stage in the war, German defensive doctrine emphasised the rigid defence of positions. When General Fritz von Below communicated the defensive doctrine of OHL to Second Army in August 1915, he began by stating, 'The fundamental principle is that the *first line* must be held at all costs'.[78] Visiting von Below's headquarters on 2 July 1916, von Falkenhayn echoed this statement: 'The first principle in position warfare must be to yield not one foot of ground; and if it be lost to retake it by immediate counterattack, even to the use of the last man.'[79]

On 19 May 1916, Stein issued a pamphlet to XIV Reserve Corps laying down the doctrine by which it was to defend its positions.[80] In it, he echoed a statement in Below's pamphlet that the most effective method of holding a trench line was the use of effective flanking fire from machine guns.[81] Stein noted that this allowed the garrison of the First Position to be reduced. Few machine guns should be deployed in the front trench, rather they should be positioned in the second and third trenches, so that they could fire over the front trench. This deployment, in effect, served to widen no-man's-land by up to 200 yards, the distance between the first and second trenches, thus giving the defenders a greater field of fire. The second element of the doctrine was the immediate counterthrust. For a short period after capturing a position, an attacking force is usually at its most confused and disordered. Stein considered that a counterthrust launched at this time would find it comparatively easy to recapture a position. The concept of envelopment was considered central to the counterthrust. The greatest danger from an enemy penetration was that the gap created in the defence might be widened. A deep penetration could be more easily plugged than a wide penetration. For this reason, the units on either side of a penetration were required to counterthrust the enemy flanks.[82] This both prevented a broadening of the penetration and attacked the enemy at their weakest point.

## The British Infantry

In the absence of any detailed manuals issued by GHQ for operations below division level, Major-General A. A. Montgomery, Fourth Army chief of staff, expanded some of Rawlinson's ideas into a pamphlet of tactical notes, which he presented as a final draft on 11 April 1916. The pamphlet was published on 17 May,[83] by which time Haig's chief of staff, Kiggell, had incorporated much of it into his own pamphlet,[84] SS 109: 'Training of Divisions for Offensive Action', published on 8 May.[85] Kiggell's pamphlet copied Montgomery's reliance on linear tactics.

Both pamphlets emphasised the central importance of mass and of strict discipline and therefore suggest that British faith in 'normal tactics' had been in no way diminished. The attack was to be made in a number of waves. Following long tradition, every unit, down to the battalion, was to be divided into three parts, fighting, support and reserve, usually in the proportions 2:1:1, each divided into a number of waves, usually four. As both pamphlets stated, 'Experience has shown that to capture a trench a single line has usually failed, two lines have sometimes failed but sometimes succeeded, three lines have generally succeeded but sometimes failed and four or more lines have usually succeeded'.[86] As General Sixsmith points out, 'The author probably had in mind the countryman's adage, "One log can't burn, two won't burn, three may burn, and four logs make a fire"'.[87] Although Montgomery complained, 'The temptation is often to try and carry a position by weight of numbers', this was precisely what the system of waves was designed to do. This tendency was further strengthened by his assertion, 'Each line of assaulting troops must leave its trenches simultaneously and make the assault as one man. This is of the highest importance.'

Montgomery claimed that much of the reason why rigid timetable tactics had to be employed was that the troops could not cope with anything more advanced:

> We must remember that owing to the large expansion of our Army and the heavy casualties in experienced officers, officers and troops generally do not now possess that military knowledge arising from a long and high state of training which enables them to act instinctively and promptly on sound lines in unexpected situations. They have become accustomed to deliberate action based on precise and detailed orders.

The statement that troops had become used to deliberate actions based on precise and detailed orders is revealing. Montgomery himself pointed out that, 'Officers and men in action will usually do what they have been practised to do or have been told to do in certain situations.'[87] In effect, he was arguing that the troops could not manage without detailed orders because that was all that they had ever been given, yet he went on to emphasise the importance of rigid discipline:

> It has been rightly said that this war will be won by superior discipline and moral [sic]. We undoubtedly started with the disadvantage of pitting an undisciplined nation against a disciplined one. . . . No opportunity, therefore, must be lost of inculcating discipline into the troops. . . . Things which may appear trivial matters to those who have only lately joined the Army are really of great importance, such as saluting, cleanliness, tidiness in dress, manner when speaking to their superiors, strict observance of orders and instruction, absence of stragglers, etc. All these inculcate a habit of obedience and self-respect. Men must learn to obey by instinct, without thinking, so that in times of stress they will act as they are accustomed to do.

The extent to which this demand for rigid obedience could go may be illustrated by two examples. Edmonds reported that, on a tour of the trenches, General Allenby, then commander of Third Army, once abused a man for not being correctly dressed. The discovery that the man was in fact dead was dismissed by Allenby as being irrelevant. He also complained of the poor state of repair of the trenches, despite their having been shelled recently.[88] Even senior officers were not immune to such treatment: shortly after visiting the War Office with Lieutenant-General Du Cane in the summer of 1918, General Maxse received a letter from the adjutant-general of the BEF informing him that a complaint had been received from the War Office that the two lieutenant-generals had been improperly dressed, 'in that they were wearing Sam Browne belts without any brace', contrary to Army Council Instructions.[89] As Tim Travers has pointed out, it was considered 'more important to stress control and discipline of one's own troops than worry about the enemy'.[90] This was nowhere more explicit than in the one sentence that was underlined in Montgomery's pamphlet: 'Finally, it must be remembered that all criticism by subordinates of their superiors, and of orders received from superior authority, will in the end recoil on the heads of the critics and undermine their authority with those below them.'[91]

In his *Tactical Notes*, Montgomery laid down that the assault was to be delivered at a 'steady pace'. While he noted that 'occasions may arise where rapid advance of some lightly equipped men ... may turn the scale',[92] this tactic does not appear to have been employed. Instead, the infantry were ordered to advance at a pace of 100 yards in every two minutes, less than two miles per hour.[93] With no-man's-land averaging 600 yards in width, it would take 12 minutes to reach the German line. In 1910, Major McMahon had told the General Staff conference that automatic weapons could inflict up to 60 per cent casualties on a wave of infantry in as little as one minute.[94]

In an attempt to make the troops more self-sufficient, each soldier was loaded down with 66 lbs of equipment.[95] Many men in the rear waves were required in addition to carry such things as rolls of barbed wire or long poles with which to signal to the artillery. The average load of these men appears to have been in the region of 80 lbs.[96] The *Official History* considered that such a weight 'made it difficult to get out of a trench, impossible to move much quicker than a slow walk, or to rise and lie down quickly'.[97] While accepting that a lighter weight of equipment would have been better, John Terraine has taken great exception to this statement and has given a number of examples of troops carrying loads considerably heavier than 66 lbs for long periods.[98] Every one of these examples, however, is of troops *marching* and one even notes that packs were thrown off to fight.[99] As Oberst Wilhelm Balck wrote in 1911, 'It is advisable for infantry to remove packs for an attack; such tremendous physical exertions await the troops that everything ought to be done to reduce the load carried by the individual man'.[100] As it was, the *Official History* noted that the men of 32nd Division were already 'dog-tired' even before the attack began, from the labour of digging assembly trenches and bringing up supplies.[101] Their exhausted state was probably typical of the majority of the assaulting troops.

## The Battle

### *The Initial Assault*

Zero hour was set for 7.30 a.m. on 1 July 1916. The British had wanted it to be earlier, just before dawn, but the French had insisted on the attack taking place in full daylight, in order to allow the artillery to observe their fire. It was only with difficulty that the British had managed to convince the French to abandon their preferred attack time of 10.00 a.m.[102] This possibility of using more accurate observed fire was not taken up by the British, who retained rigid artillery fire plans. The decision to attack at 7.30 a.m. meant that the main argument advanced by Rawlinson in favour of a prolonged bombardment, that it allowed the attack to be launched at dawn, was no longer valid.

Each day during the bombardment, the British had fired a concentrated barrage on the German positions, as if in preparation for an imminent infantry assault. These barrages had lasted 80 minutes and had been fired at a different time each day. On the day of the assault, the barrage was to last only 65 minutes,[103] from 6.25 a.m. to 7.30 a.m. The hope was that the Germans would expect it to last a further 15 minutes and so be surprised when the attack took place. At zero, the guns bombarding the German First Position were to shift their fire from the front trench to the third trench.[104] This was to be the signal for the infantry to move.

X Corps attacked with 32nd and 36th (Ulster) Divisions and held 49th (West Riding) Division in reserve. The attacking divisions each held one brigade in reserve and three of the four attacking brigades had one battalion in reserve and one in support, while the fourth brigade attacked with all four battalions. Each battalion had two of its four companies in the first wave. The initial attack by X Corps was therefore made by 20 companies. These were faced by ten German companies in the front and support trenches and a further four companies in the reserve trench of the First Position. All 14 companies could engage the British advance. As a result, although the British enjoyed overall numerical odds of more than four to one, the effective odds were little better than three to two.

X Corps was to seize the German First Position between the Leipzig

Salient and St Pierre Divion (inclusive), with the divisional boundary running just north of Thiepval (Map 2). The lead brigades were to secure the redoubts in the reserve trench and then seize the Intermediate Line: the break-in. The reserve brigades were to move through this line and assault the Second Position, the attack being timed for 10.10 a.m.: the breakthrough. 49th Division, allocated to Gough's Reserve Army, was to carry out the pursuit:[105] the break-out.

32nd Division attacked with 97th Brigade on the right and 96th Brigade on the left. The commander of 97th Brigade, Brigadier-General J. B. Jardine, had been an observer at the Russo-Japanese War ten years before and had noted the importance of the infantry following close behind the artillery barrage. At the final rehearsal for the attack, Jardine had suggested to Rawlinson that the infantry should be closer to the barrage than the 100 yards being practised, recommending they be only 30 to 40 yards behind. Rawlinson was sceptical and unimpressed when told this was Japanese practice.[106] Not to be put off, Jardine ordered his two lead battalions to send their first waves into no-man's-land at 7.23 a.m., so they were only 40 yards from the German wire when the barrage lifted.[107]

The results of the 97th Brigade attack were directly dependent on the previous artillery preparation.[108] On the right, 17/Highland Light Infantry (HLI) found the wire well cut and were able to enter the Leipzig Redoubt before the Germans could come out of their dug-outs. On the left, 16/HLI faced heavy machine-gun fire even before the barrage lifted. The German wire had few gaps cut in it and all were covered by fire. A party of sappers with Bangalore torpedoes was shot down. Half the battalion was lost before the wire was reached and most of the survivors went to ground. Once the limited surprise of the initial assault had worn off, the brigade was unable to make further progress. An advance by 17/HLI towards the third trench was halted by fire from the Wonder Work. Attempts to renew the assault by the brigade's two other battalions succeeded only in giving limited reinforcement to 17/HLI. One member of 16/HLI later described seeing German soldiers standing on their parapet, taunting their opponents.[109] Once the artillery barrage lifted, the attack was conducted with almost no covering fire, allowing the Germans to shoot at the British troops virtually undisturbed. The Germans immediately brought elements of several companies forward and attacked the British troops in the Leipzig Salient from both flanks, while at the same time blocking any attempt to widen the gap in their line. This counterthrust drove the British back into the Leipzig Redoubt, but could do no more, because of heavy casualties and the exhaustion of the supply of hand grenades.[110]

96th Brigade met with almost total disaster.[111] The left battalion, 15/Lancashire Fusiliers, had also crept into no-man's-land during the bombardment, taking up positions 100 yards from the German wire. As

MAP 2
Thiepval, 1 July 1916: Initial Attack

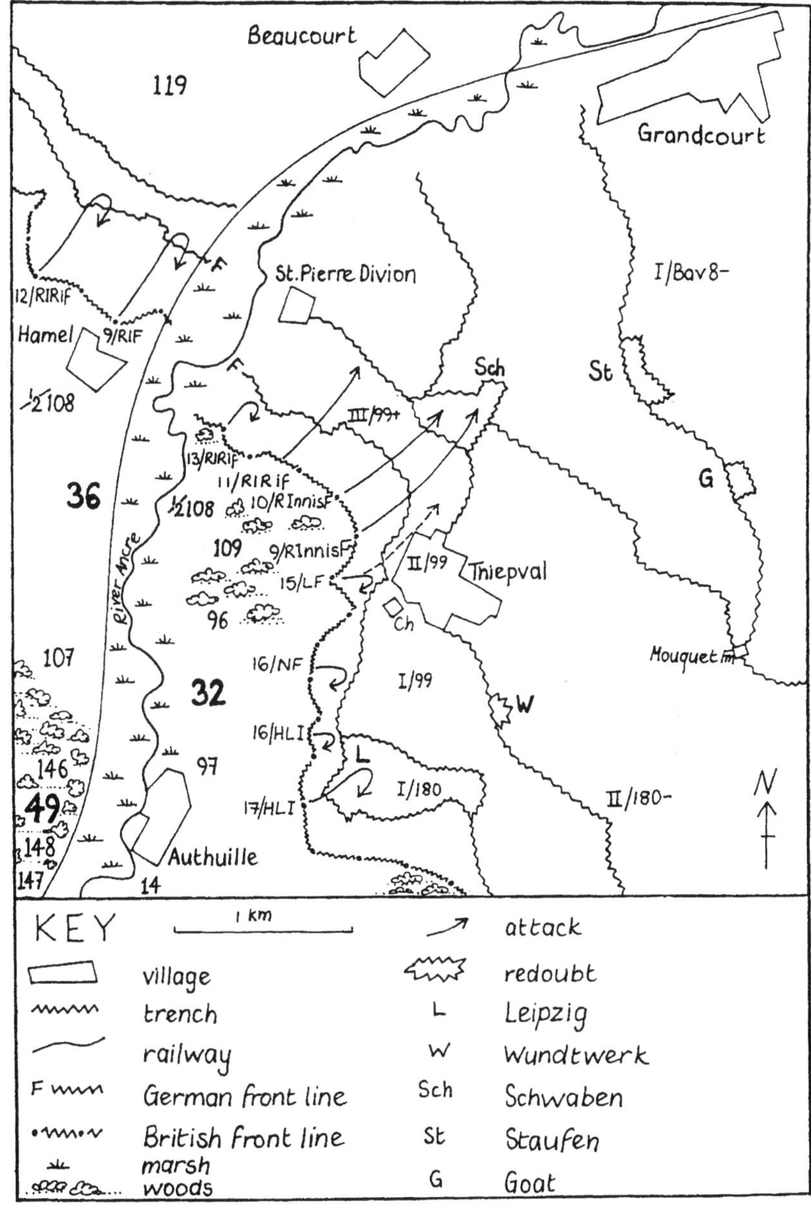

soon as the barrage lifted, the brigade was heavily engaged. 'The impossible had happened. Human beings *had* lived through that awful fire; and, from their machine guns, cunningly concealed in concrete emplacements, they poured a murderous leaden stream of bullets into our men.'[112] This fire, combined with heavy shelling, halted the British attack. None of the right battalion, 16/Northumberland Fusiliers, reached the German positions. About 100 men of 15/Lancashire Fusiliers entered the enemy line at Thiepval, but were immediately engaged in a vicious mêlée,[113] the survivors veering to the left, where they joined the victorious Ulstermen. Attempts by the remainder of the brigade to renew the attack and relieve the men of 15/Lancashire Fusiliers, who it was thought held part of Thiepval, were repulsed with ease. The situation was summed up by the history of 16/Northumberland Fusiliers:

> On the riven, tortured ground between the opposing trenches was written, in human bodies, the epic of Tyneside's heroism and Britain's might. The men of the attacking companies had moved forward in perfect unison until the deadly fire had stayed their progress. Not a man had wavered. After nightfall they were found in straight lines, as if the platoons had been 'dressed' for parade. Gloriously they had attacked; gloriously they had made the great sacrifice. The silent lines of majestic dead epitomised the soul of Britain.[114]

36th (Ulster) Division attacked with two brigades, 109th on the right and 108th on the left.[115] As with 32nd Division, the success or failure of the attack was largely determined by the effectiveness of the preliminary bombardment. Opposite 109th Brigade, the gunners had done their job well:

> The positions had suffered exceptionally heavily under the days-long hail of iron. The trenches had all but disappeared, obstacles swept away and dug-outs demolished. 9/99, west of the Schwaben Redoubt had shed its blood particularly heavily. . . . One machine gun in the redoubt did not even manage to fire; shortly before the enemy attack a direct hit knocked out the machine gun and most of the crew.[116]

The lead battalions of the brigade, 9/ and 10/Royal Inniskilling Fusiliers, moved out into no-man's-land at 7.15 a.m. and took up positions 100 yards from the German wire. This was well cut and the Ulstermen were able to capture the first two trenches before the Germans could properly man their line. The machine guns of 9/ and 10/99 were overrun moments after they opened fire.[117] The garrison of the Schwaben Redoubt was able to offer little more resistance. The Intermediate Line was largely empty and was captured by 8.30 a.m. The brigade had taken all its objectives, had captured 400 prisoners and had effectively annihilated III/99.

South of the River Ancre, 108th Brigade attacked with 11/ and 13/ Royal Irish Rifles, with 15/Royal Irish Rifles of 107th Brigade in support. Here too, the lead battalions moved into no-man's-land just before the bombardment ended. 11/Royal Irish Rifles on the right shared in the success of the neighbouring 109th Brigade. On the left, the men of 13/ Royal Irish Rifles were mown down by the fire of 12/99, 1/Bav8 and the machine guns in St Pierre Divion. To one Ulsterman, the rows of bodies looked like 'sheaves of corn on the ground'.[118] North of the Ancre, the brigade attacked with 9/Royal Irish Fusiliers and 12/Royal Irish Rifles. Both began to advance at 7.28 a.m. and at once started to suffer casualties:

> In combination with their machine guns and rapidly established artillery barrage, the parts of Reserve-Infanterie-Regiment 119 [in this area] defeated the attack, in places right in front of the English trench. Where the enemy had pushed in along the Ancre, he was annihilated. In places, the defeated assault troops lay in shell-holes very close to the German position. From these they began a fire fight with remarkable bravery. Nevertheless, their efforts were in vain. The German defensive fire swept them aside, the attack was here a pitiable failure.[119]

A few men of 9/Royal Irish Fusiliers penetrated the German line, but finding themselves alone and under fire from all sides withdrew. The Germans were back in possession of their front trench by 8.00 a.m.

The situation on the X Corps front at about 8.30 a.m. was generally one of failure (Map 2). 32nd Division's attacks had been repulsed, except on the extreme right, where one battalion had a tenuous grip on the Leipzig Redoubt. It was, however, erroneously thought that part of Thiepval had also been captured. Most of 36th Division's assault had also come to nothing. The only real success was on the front of 109th Brigade, which had reached the German Intermediate Line. This was the only sector of the corps front where an effective break-in had been achieved.

### *The Second Phase*

The original plans of both the British and the Germans had gone awry. The Germans had not been able to hold the First Position and now faced the threat of the Ulstermen creating a major breach in their defences. Conversely, most of the British attacks had failed, leaving several units holding isolated sections of German line. Senior commanders on both sides now needed to make critical decisions and could no longer rely purely on plans laid down in advance. These decisions primarily involved how and where to use reserves, essentially the only means by which they could influence the battle. In this regard, the commander of X Corps, Lieutenant-General Sir Thomas Morland, was in a better position than Generalmajor von Soden of 26th Reserve Division. Morland's reserves consisted of almost five full brigades, a total of 18 battalions, more than had been committed to the original assault. Soden had only 14 companies, most of which were miles behind the front, and a recruit battalion. It was at this stage that the difference in the command philosophies operated by the British and German armies became decisive.

### THE BRITISH

One of the key features of the First World War was the difficulty in maintaining communication with units once they had begun an attack.[120] Troops who had gone 'over the top' were almost as remote from their commanders as if they had been in the wastes of Antarctica. The defenders were hardly in a better situation. The preliminary bombardment had cut virtually all the telephone wires in the zone of battle, even though these had been buried six feet deep.[121] There was therefore a zone some 2,500 yards wide, between the British front line and the German Second Position, in which communications depended primarily on runners. Visual means of communication were tried, but the smoke covering the battlefield made them largely ineffective. Even if runners managed to deliver their messages safely, in itself a hazardous task, there tended to be such a lapse of time between their dispatch and their arrival as to make the news largely out of date. The experience of Colonel Dickens of Queen Victoria's Rifles (1/9/London) was typical: 'For two hours after zero, no news whatsoever was received from the front, all communications, visual and telephonic having failed. Beyond answering appeals from the Brigade for information, we had leisure to observe what was going on.'[122]

If it was not possible to communicate with the troops once they had attacked, some way had to be found by which the battle could be fought without communications. The solution adopted by the British was wholly in accordance with their philosophy of restrictive control: since troops could not be trusted to act effectively without direct orders, such orders must be provided in advance. The effect of this attempt to 'preordain the future'[123] may be illustrated by the orders governing the artillery barrage and by the restrictions placed on the movements of officers within battalions and brigades.

The orders given to the artillery were rigid in the extreme. In his *Tactical Notes*, Major-General Montgomery stated,

> Experience has shown that the only safe method of artillery support during an advance is a fixed timetable of lifts to which both the infantry and artillery must rigidly conform. . . . No changes must be

> made in the timetables by subordinate formations without reference to Corps Headquarters or confusion is sure to ensue. If divisions or brigades depart from the programme and call the artillery fire back because part of the line is held up it means that either the neighbouring bodies of troops who have not been held up will probably come under the fire of their own artillery or at least will be held up by it. Generally speaking the best method to break down the resistance is for the lifts to go on as arranged and for the bodies of each flank to push on, thus taking off the pressure from the front of the troops held up.... Should, however, it be considered advisable by the Corps Commander to bring the lift back *ample previous warning must be sent to all concerned* and the programme readjusted to meet the altered situation... This re-bombardment is difficult to arrange and should not be resorted to if it can be avoided.[124]

The effect of this rigidity was to make the artillery very slow to adjust to a situation outside the original plan. For example, in X Corps, part of 14th Brigade was pinned by German fire while moving up to support 86th Brigade at 8.45 a.m. With alterations to the artillery timetable having to be made by corps headquarters, it was not until 12.05 p.m. that the British artillery could be brought back to support 14th Brigade.[125]

Only in two places on the X Corps front was the order to adhere rigidly to the artillery timetable disregarded. On the extreme right of the corps attack, an artillery commander observed that 17/HLI were pinned in front of the Wonder Work. He communicated this information to Brigadier-General Jardine and was given permission to shift the fire of two batteries to cover the Highlanders' retreat to the Leipzig Redoubt.[126] On the extreme left of the corps, the failure of the 108th Brigade attack north of the Ancre was observed and permission requested to bring the barrage back on to the German front line. This permission was refused, but the barrage was nevertheless brought back.[127]

The ban on departures from the pre-planned timetable would have been less serious if a number of guns had been allocated to divisions for close support. Some guns were indeed so assigned, but the number appears to have been small and unevenly spread across the Fourth Army front. XIII Corps orders stated that 'certain batteries' would be assigned in this way.[128] X Corps appears to have used only two guns in this role, with orders to engage machine-gun posts near Thiepval, using indirect fire; however, one suffered a premature burst that put both guns out of action.[129]

Having been ordered to adhere precisely to the artillery timetable, many gunners appear to have become rather detached from the battle:

> On the whole we had a very delightful day, with nothing to do except send numerous reports through to Head Quarters and observe the

> stupendous spectacle before us. There was nothing to do as regards controlling my battery's fire, as the barrage orders had all been prepared beforehand.[130]

A similar rigidity was to be found in the orders which restricted the ability of officers to accompany their units in the attack. In his *Tactical Notes*, Montgomery had laid down,

> The guiding principle is that the Commander of an Infantry Brigade should be where he can best control such reserves as he has at his disposal. . . . Personal influence on the battlefield can, generally speaking, be seldom brought to bear under modern conditions, and it is by timely use of his reserves and artillery that a Commander can influence an action. . . . The fact that he is near or far from the firing line is of comparatively small importance. . . . It is essential that communication from front to rear should not be lost.[131]

The result of this insistence on commanders staying in communication with their superiors was a network of officers sitting in telephone boxes rather than leading their troops.[132] They were linked to their commanders, but were separated from their troops and so knew little of what was actually happening. At its extreme, entire brigades were sent into no-man's-land with every officer above company level ordered to remain behind, rendering co-ordination between different units and arms all but impossible.[133] This removal of command was made worse still by the practice of leaving all battalion and company seconds-in-command behind, along with ten per cent of the unit, in order to leave a cadre on which to rebuild the unit.[134]

Ironically, having ensured that his troops attacked without their commanders, in order that he might retain communication with those officers, and having concentrated all decision-making into his own hands, General Morland proceeded to place himself in an advanced observation post from which he was virtually out of communication with his headquarters.[135] Nevertheless, by about 8.30 a.m., he had a fair idea of the results of his corps' initial attack, and was essentially faced with a simple choice: should he commit his reserve to reinforce the successful attack of 109th Brigade or to renew the failed attack of 96th Brigade?

At 8.32 a.m., Major-General Nugent of 36th Division asked corps headquarters whether he should commit 107th Brigade according to the plan, to move through 109th Brigade in the Schwaben Redoubt to attack the Second Position, since the troops on both flanks had been repulsed. After a delay of almost 40 minutes, General Morland decided that it should not be committed, but 107th Brigade had by then already crossed no-man's-land, reaching the German Second Position at 10.00 a.m., where it was delayed by the British artillery barrage for ten minutes.[136]

At about the time Morland made his decision, Major-General Perceval, commander of 49th Division, learned of 36th Division's success and 32nd Division's failure. He immediately concluded that his entire division should be thrown in to exploit the Ulstermen's gains. Wishing to impress the value of this course of action on Morland personally, he hurried the two miles to the latter's observation post. On arrival, he was told merely to move one brigade into Thiepval Wood to replace 107th Brigade. His suggestion for turning the German position from the 109th Brigade penetration was 'declined'.[137] This marks the turning point of the X Corps battle. General Morland's fateful decision to withhold his reserve until the situation around Thiepval had been resolved, despite the recommendations of all three of his divisional commanders that forces be sent to reinforce the troops in the Schwaben Redoubt in order to turn Thiepval from the north,[138] was a direct result of the British Army's command system. Indeed, given that system, his decision may have been the best in the circumstances. Officers and men had neither the experience nor the training required for the difficult operation of mounting a flank attack from a penetration in the enemy position.

The British soldiers' inability to carry out anything but the simplest of manoeuvres may have owed more to their commanders having little faith in their capabilities than to any actual deficiency in potential skill. At Loos, one battalion had moved through a gap in the defences and taken prisoner an entire German battalion that had previously repulsed three frontal attacks by two brigades.[139] On the Somme, the Ulstermen sent patrols down the Intermediate Line to within 500 yards of Mouquet Farm and found it clear (Map 2). Had troops been available to occupy this line, the entire German First Position opposite 32nd Division would have been enveloped and would probably have been captured. This was indeed precisely what the Germans feared.[140]

The responsibility for the failure to exploit this potentially decisive opportunity must rest with the British high command and its belief in restrictive control. British commanders were well aware of the effectiveness of 'soft-spot tactics'. At the weekly army commanders' conference on 15 June 1916, Haig had stated,

> Reserves must not be wasted in impossible frontal assaults against strong places. They should rather be thrown in *between* these strong places to confirm success where our advance is progressing favourably and to overcome the enemy's centres of resistance, which are holding up neighbouring troops, by attacking them in flank and rear.[141]

While this was sound practice, the army made little attempt to make its implementation possible. Immediately before noting the value of flank attacks, Haig had emphasised the central importance of a uniformly linear advance:

> Isolated advances by detachments, pressing forward beyond the reach of support, should be avoided. The ground gained is difficult to hold because the enemy can concentrate against these small bodies. The most gallant men are thus lost in vain. In the advance of the infantry therefore we should aim at such uniformity as will ensure mutual support.

There was certainly no hint that formations should actively seek to envelop the enemy in preference to relying on frontal attacks.

Commanders made little effort to train their men to make flank attacks, or even to alert them to the potential benefits of such actions.[142] Official pamphlets concentrated on the frontal attack. The statement in SS 135, 'Instructions for the Training of Divisions for Defensive Action', that 'All troops must move direct on their objective. Complicated manoeuvres, such as wheels and forming to a flank, must be avoided when possible',[143] was typical of the doctrine being laid down by the General Staff. Reliance on simple maoeuvres was all the more necessary when all but company officers were ordered to stay behind in the British trenches. If senior commanders were to retain control over their formations once these had entered no-man's-land, by means of detailed orders given in advance, only the simplest of manoeuvres was possible. The consequence was to make the frontal attack the basic tactic.[144]

Morland's decision to concentrate on the attempt to capture Thiepval by frontal assault was in accordance with his focus of energy, which was the maintenance of an ordered, linear advance. An envelopment from the Schwaben Redoubt would have involved a level of confusion and decentralisation of command unacceptable in the British command system. Even though the unauthorised attack of 107th Brigade had extended the penetration almost to the Second Position, making a breakthrough possible, Morland devoted the rest of the day to repeated attempts to capture Thiepval by frontal assault, despite the failure of every attack. No assistance was sent to the Ulstermen until 9.00 p.m.[145]

### THE GERMANS

The British attack on Thiepval was reported to Generalmajor von Soden at 7.20 a.m., almost as soon as the British left their trenches and before the barrage had lifted.[146]An hour later, he received news of the capture of the Schwaben Redoubt and immediately ordered the divisional reserve to man the Second Position. This force consisted of II/Bav8, 1st Machine-Gun Company (MGK)/Bav8 and 1/Musketen-Bataillon 1 (an automatic-rifle unit[147]), and had been on alert in the Third Position, four miles behind the front line, since 4.30 a.m. The order was delayed by half an hour, as there was no telephone link to the force. Until this reserve could arrive, the German divisional artillery put down a barrage on the Schwaben Redoubt and the Intermediate Line. In the First Position, the men of 1/Bav8 and 7/99 built barricades across their trenches and blocked attempts by the Ulstermen to widen their penetration.

The news that the British had captured the Schwaben Redoubt reached Generalleutnant von Stein, the corps commander, at about 9.30 a.m. The delay in this information reaching XIV Reserve Corps from 26th Reserve Division was caused by Stein having to move his headquarters because of British shelling at about 7.30 a.m. He was to be shelled out again the next day.[148] Stein appreciated the situation and concluded that the Schwaben Redoubt was the key to the entire defensive position of 26th Reserve Division, some four miles of front. Accordingly, he ordered that the redoubt be recaptured immediately.

Soden responded by placing the operation in the hands of Generalmajor von Auwäter, commander of 52nd Reserve Infantry Brigade (Reserve-Infanterie-Regimente 99 and 119). By this means, Soden left the recapture of the Schwaben Redoubt to a commander who was familiar with the ground and the troops involved. This decentralisation of command both shortened the decision-making loop for the operation and also allowed Soden to concentrate on fighting his division as a whole, rather than become absorbed by one sector. Soden ordered Auwäter to attack at once and not to wait until II/Bav8 arrived. Auwäter had already decided to recapture the Schwaben Redoubt by envelopment (Map 3). Each of the three attacking forces was to be based on one of the battalions of Bayerisches-Reserve-Infanterie-Regiment 8. Auwäter issued the orders for this operation at about 10.15 a.m., just as 107th Brigade's attack on the Second Position was being repulsed. An hour later he placed the execution of the operation in the hands of the Bavarians' commander, Oberstleutnant Bram, who had just arrived at Auwäter's headquarters.

The commanders of I/ and III/Bav8 issued their orders for the counter-thrust at 10.45 a.m. Such was the weakened state of the Second Position and the weight of British artillery fire, supplemented by air attack, however, that preparations for the attack were delayed. This delay was increased by the presence of isolated groups of 107th Brigade who had forced their way into the Second Position.

Soden was becoming increasingly impatient. The Schwaben Redoubt was the key to the entire divisional position, and the Germans believed that the British had recognised its importance and had therefore deliberately concentrated their forces against it.[149] In fact, British troops were spread evenly along the whole Fourth Army front. The German troops holding the Second Position and the flanks of the penetration were perilously

MAP 3
Thiepval, 1 July 1916: Second Phase

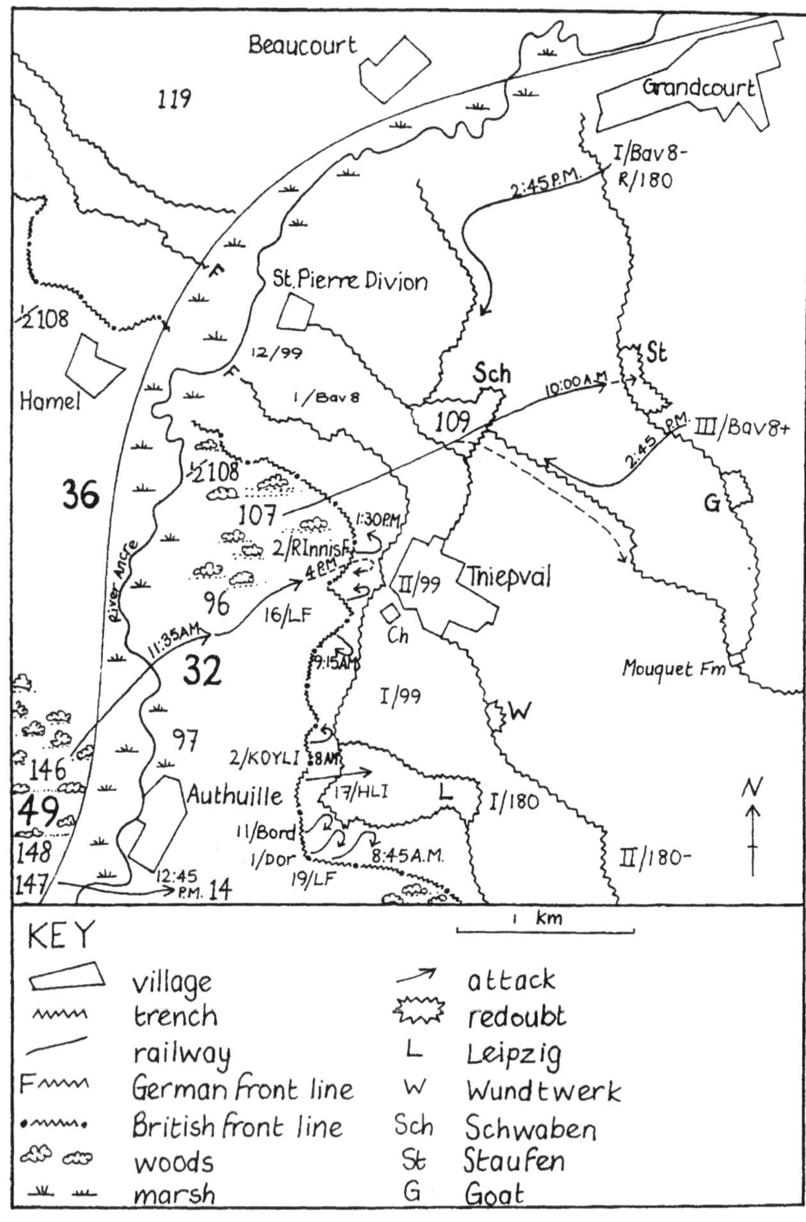

weak. A strong, co-ordinated push outwards by 36th Division might well have overwhelmed the defenders. Apart from the handful of companies in the Second Position, the Germans had no reserves available: two battalions from Infanterie-Regiment 185 were assigned by XIV Reserve Corps, but would not arrive before evening.

Bram reached Stuff Redoubt at 1.00 p.m. The area had seen little activity in the three hours since the attack of 107th Brigade was repulsed. British troops, however, still held small sections of the position and more men lay near the front trench and might capture it if reinforced. Bram saw that speed was of the essence. He had been given full authority to conduct the recapture of the Schwaben Redoubt by Auwäter. By this further decentralisation of command, Auwäter allowed himself to concentrate on his brigade as a whole and put the operations around the Schwaben Redoubt in the hands of an officer on the spot, who knew the troops involved and could act immediately according to the circumstances.

Bram found that II/Bav8 had suffered heavily during its approach march and had lost its way, while I/Bav8 in Grandcourt was out of communication. Bram decided to attack at once with III/Bav8 alone, reasoning that 'a prompt counterthrust with fewer, but immediately available, forces gave a better prospect of success than a later attack with all the assigned troops'.[150] The British artillery fire slowed the German preparations so that Bram's attack had to be timed for 3.00 p.m. At 2.45 p.m., however, I/Bav8 attacked independently from Grandcourt. III/Bav8 immediately responded by launching its own attack. The British were driven back and the Intermediate Line recaptured. With only six companies, the Germans had sealed off the British penetration and recovered half the area lost.

## Conclusion

Although the Schwaben Redoubt was not finally recovered until 10.30 p.m., the attack by I/ and III/Bav8 around 3.00 p.m. marked the turning point of the day's battle in this area, the inevitable consequence of General Morland's decision at 9.10 a.m. not to reinforce 36th Division's success. For almost five hours, a gap 2,000 yards wide had existed in the German position, in an area vital to the defence of a long stretch of front. The Germans had recognised the decisive importance of this sector and had allocated all their available reserves to closing the gap. The British, clinging to the idea that a broad, linear advance was necessary, had concentrated on renewing the failed frontal attacks on Thiepval. The first reinforcements sent to the Schwaben Redoubt, numbering only eight companies, arrived at 9.00 p.m.,[151] over 12 hours after the position was first captured.

The loss of the opportunity presented by the Ulstermen's seizure of the Schwaben Redoubt was also the result of the different command systems employed by the British and German armies. The British, seeking to pre-ordain the future, laid down rigidly detailed orders in advance, orders that did not take into account any serious deviation from the plan. They required the minimum of initiative and perforce relied on the simplest of tactics. In order that senior commanders might retain control over their formations, commanders at every level, down to and including battalion commanders, were ordered to remain behind when their troops attacked. The result was that the British troops went into action virtually leaderless, making detailed orders all the more necessary. Meanwhile, commanders found themselves in communication with their superiors but out of communication with their troops. In effect, X Corps left its brain behind when it attacked.

Although commanders were in communication with their superiors, their role was largely passive. Having passed back information about their units' situation, they were expected to wait for orders: the cult of rank operated to block low-level initiative. It also made senior commanders unwilling to listen to suggestions from subordinates, even when these were better informed, as when General Morland rejected Major-General Perceval's plan to use 49th Division to support 36th Division. Had Morland accepted this idea, X Corps might have won an important victory.

Whereas the British forces tended to be leaderless and lacking in an ability to assess the situation, the German forces enjoyed leaders at every level who were well forward and who were ready to act on their own initiative, according to the circumstances. The attack by I/Bav8 from Grandcourt, which set off the decisive recapture of the Intermediate Line, was launched by a battalion commander who was out of communication with his superiors but who knew the importance of recapturing the Schwaben Redoubt.

The results of 1 July 1916 represented a major defeat for the British: only one corps reached all its objectives; total casualties were 57,470, of whom more than one-third were killed.[152] German casualties are impossible to determine with accuracy: based on figures given by a number of regiments, Martin Middlebrook suggested a total of 8,000, of whom 2,200 were prisoners.[153] X Corps suffered 9,643 casualties, of whom over half were in 36th Division,[154] which thus paid the price of its success. The corps inflicted perhaps 2,000 casualties, of whom probably 500 were prisoners, mainly in the battle for the Schwaben Redoubt.

X Corps had virtually nothing to show for this expenditure of blood. The few footholds gained in the German front line were soon given up and the old battle lines restored. It need not have been so. Despite Haig having set over-ambitious objectives for his forces and having trusted too much in the effectiveness of the preliminary bombardment, a major breakthrough was almost achieved. The failure to follow up the initial success of 36th Division was largely the result of the British Army's system of restrictive control. This led to inflexible manoeuvres and an emphasis upon the techniques of the break-in, where this approach to tactics was at its most effective, owing to the possibility of detailed advance planning. This concentration on the break-in alone meant that troops were not trained for the more complex manoeuvres, such as envelopment, required in a breakthrough.

# 6
# The Evolution of Elastic Defence

> The secret of effective defence lies in depth. By depth and by the fullest exploitation of the ground and by camouflage, the defence becomes invisible. In this way . . . an attack . . . can be met with continual surprises . . . And the aim of this defence is to be ready at all times to meet any enemy thrust, any shift of his thrust point [*Schwerpunkt*], not by opposing it frontally by a line but by swallowing up . . . the attack.
>
> Major F. O. Miksche, *Blitzkreig*

From November 1914 until November 1917, the French and British armies made repeated efforts to break through the German defences on the Western Front. Although no breakthrough was achieved, the pressure put on the German defensive system was enormous. This may be illustrated by the number of shells used. In the first eight days of the Somme, June–July 1916, the British artillery fired 1,732,873 rounds: the total for the whole battle was 27,768,076 rounds. In the first eight days of Messines, June 1917, the British expended 3,258,000 shells.[1] The rate of increase was to be maintained: in one 24-hour period in September 1918, the British were to fire 943,847 rounds.[2] On several occasions, Allied attacks came near to penetrating the entire defensive zone and the casualties inflicted on the German defenders, even when attacks were repulsed, were grievous.

The Germany Army's response was a dynamic evolution of its defensive doctrine, in an ongoing attempt to counter both advances in Allied offensive doctrine and Allied numerical and material superiority. The success of this process is indicated both by the fact that the Allies never did achieve an effective breakthrough, even in the last months of the war, and by the retention by the German Army of the resulting doctrine, with only slight amendation, for more than 20 years after 1918.[3] This evolutionary process provides an excellent example of the mutual interaction of command, training and tactics. Throughout, advances in one area were possible only because progress in the other two areas had created a sound basis for further development: rapid evolution in one area alone would have been untenable.

Command was the most important of the three areas. The German system of decentralised command allowed a greater flexibility in tactics and also meant that officers were permitted to hold views that did not follow existing doctrine. This freedom of thought repeatedly resulted in fierce debates within the army, which senior commanders actively sought to encourage. Both characteristics served to create a fertile environment for the development of new ideas and procedures.[4] A very high standard of training at every level was demanded by decentralisation of command. One consequence was that troops were better able to cope with the greater demands of the new tactics and that commanders were more ready to listen to their subordinates, since their professional competence was beyond question. Tactics, finally, provided the driving force behind the evolution of new procedures, because of the urgent need to respond to Allied attacks: the reality of the battlefield provided a merciless test of command and training, highlighting ineffective approaches and demanding ever higher standards.

The evolution of defensive tactics by the German Army during the First World War may be seen as the development of three central concepts. As was the case with the system of decentralised command, the German terms for these concepts appear to have been coined only after the concepts themselves had been developed. The first concept was the depth of the defence. The defender could either seek to hold a line rigidly, *Linienverteidigung* (linear defence), or could fight a flexible battle within a deep defensive zone, *Flächenverteidigung* (area defence).[5] The key features here were the depth of the defensive system and the freedom of action given to the defending troops. The second concept was the extent to which the defence was to be made invisible, *die Leere des Gefechtfeldes* (the emptiness of the battlefield).[6] By this means, the planning of an enemy attack was made more difficult, the accuracy of a hostile bombardment reduced and the achievement of surprise by the defender made easier. The third and final concept was the aggressive posture of the defence, *Schlagfertigkeit*.[7] In its general usage, this word means a 'quickness at repartee' and implies an ability to respond at once to another's remark with a better remark of one's own. In the military context, the term may be translated as 'immediate responsiveness'. A defence can aim to hold ground passively, or it can respond to attacks by launching its own counterattacks. The scale and timing of any counterattacks included in a defensive doctrine are indicative of the level of *Schlagfertigkeit* intended.

## Pre-War Doctrine

Between 1870 and 1914, the German Army placed great emphasis on the offensive, as indeed did most other European armies. The time assigned to defensive training was generally limited and this was reflected in the army's manuals. The *Exerzier-Reglement für die Infanterie* of 1888 devoted only a single paragraph to the defence,[8] a total of two pages.

The manual laid down that the essence of the defence was the development of maximum firepower. The rifle line was therefore to be as strong as circumstances required. Supports and reserves were to be brought closer than in the attack, but the reserves were to be kept out of enemy fire as much as was possible. Each defensive sector was to be under a single commander and have its own reserve. If more than a passive defence was intended, as was generally expected to be the case, as large a force as possible was to be held back as a *Hauptreserve* (general reserve). The deployment of troops for positional defence was therefore to be sparing.

Although the front line was to be strong, the emphasis on reserves being held back gave the defence a certain depth. The requirement for these reserves to be out of enemy fire implied that they should be out of sight, or invisible. The strength of the reserve showed an intention to fight the defensive battle in an aggressive manner, seeking to seize 'tempo'. Finally, the insistence that each defensive sector be a single *Kommando-Einheit* (command unity), with its own reserve, gave each sector its own commander, able to fight his own battle.

The 1906 edition of the *Exerzier-Reglement für die Infanterie* paid rather more attention to defence than had the 1888 edition, 20 paragraphs[9] compared to one. The new paragraphs, however, were shorter than before and filled little more than five pages. Overall, the new regulations laid down a similar form of defence to that of 1888. There was, however, a slightly greater emphasis on depth. The instructions underlined the effectiveness of infantry fire and the relatively small forces required.[10] A broad field of fire was considered essential.[11] The fire of the infantry was to be integrated with that of the artillery, which was to take up positions enabling it to maintain fire up to the last moment of an enemy infantry attack. The guns were to deploy 600 metres behind the infantry,[12] in order to avoid fire directed against one hitting the other.[13]

In general, only one defensive position was to be held, although forward positions could be used to force the enemy to deploy early.[14] The main position would not normally be a continuous line, but would consist of a series of battalion or company sectors.[15] *Lücken* (gaps) could be left between these sectors, as long as they were well covered by fire.[16] Invisibility was considered of great importance. Supports and reserves were to be hidden either by dead ground or by field works.[17] Regarding artificial cover, the regulations emphasised, 'Fieldworks lose a large part of their value if they make it easier for the enemy to identify the position'.[18] Dummy trenches could be dug to deceive the enemy and to attract his fire.[19]

Although a passive form of defence was recognised, the emphasis was on the offensive form.[20] Commanders were to deploy their forces in such a way as to leave the maximum available for the general reserve, with which to achieve a decisive result.[21] This reserve was to be placed sufficiently far to the rear to have room to deploy.[22] A counterattack against forces that had broken into the defensive position was considered very effective, because of the enemy's disorganisation, but the opportunity was considered fleeting. It was generally held to be better to repulse an attack in front of the position.[23] With regard to command, the 1906 regulations retained the previous requirement that each sector have its own commander, with his own reserve,[24] although this was not emphasised as strongly as in 1888.

When war came, the Germans found that much of this doctrine was obsolete, because the effectiveness of modern firearms had been seriously underestimated. The pre-war belief that massed infantry with a broad field of fire were needed for the defence proved false. Such formations laid themselves open to devastating long-range artillery fire from the attacker, whose guns, using indirect fire, were almost immune to the defender's counter-battery fire. Artillery support against the attacking infantry was also more difficult to organise than had been anticipated, owing to problems in maintaining communication between infantry and guns. Finally, decisive counterattacks proved impossible, since the defender did not have sufficient forces to produce a reserve large enough to have a major effect.[25]

## The First Experiments

The pre-war German doctrine had been based on the expectation that defensive positions would be held for only short periods before resuming the offensive. The infantry regulations made no mention of such details as communication trenches or latrines, although these were covered in the manual of the *Pioniere*.[26] The first defences in 1914, therefore, consisted of only a single trench line. Wire obstacles, ignored in the infantry regulations, were swiftly adopted when it became obvious that there was to be no immediate return to the offensive. Similar considerations led to the various battalion sectors being linked to form one continuous trench.

With the trench system running the entire length of the Western Front, from Switzerland to the North Sea, and with the need to deploy large forces in the East, the German Army experienced an acute shortage of manpower. Since it was necessary to bring troops out of the line for rest and to maintain reserves available to counter Allied attacks, the Germans found that it was no longer possible to place large numbers of troops in the front line. A revision of the doctrine was necessary, which initially took place on an *ad hoc* basis.

The evolution in doctrine up to the spring of 1915 may be illustrated by the defences which faced the British attack at Neuve Chapelle on 10 March.[27] The depth of the position had increased from the 600 metres laid down before the war to 2,500 metres. The front line consisted of a single trench line, held by about half the defending companies. About 1,000 metres behind the front line was a line of *Stützpunkte* (strongpoints), sited roughly 800 metres apart. These concrete machine-gun posts were placed in such a way that they could cover the intervening ground and act as *Anklammerungspunkte* (centres of resistance) should the front line be penetrated. A proposal by local commanders to link the strongpoints with a second continuous trench had been rejected by the corps commander, in the belief that the front line would be held less stubbornly if there were such a fall-back position. The artillery was deployed 1,500 metres behind the strongpoints, the crews being too vulnerable to small-arms fire closer to the front line. Individual batteries were emplaced in the line of strongpoints. A second artillery position, 2,500 metres further to the rear, was under construction.

The defending forces were to some extent deployed in depth. Approximately half the available troops were in the front line, with a density of about one man to every three metres of trench. The supports, about one-quarter of the total force, were deployed 2,500 metres behind the front trench, outside effective field artillery range. The reserves were 3,500 metres further back still, in billets. Forces from the general reserve could be on the scene in about 24 hours.[28] With the opposing trench lines little more than 100 metres apart, it was not possible to disguise the front trench, which was therefore vulnerable to observed enemy artillery fire. The use of aerial photography by the British meant that the strongpoint could not be completely hidden, but their small size and careful location in dead ground made them difficult to spot from the ground and so made observed artillery fire less effective. The only real invisibility achieved was with regard to the supporting companies, which were kept out of sight. The Germans recognised that an enemy attack was likely to be able to capture stretches of the front trench, since it was vulnerable to artillery fire and thinly garrisoned. The supports and reserves were therefore expected to fight an aggressive battle to hurl back the attackers and to recover the old front line. This counterattack was to be made before the attackers had time to consolidate their gains.

The British attack followed a brief but intense artillery bombardment. The German wire and breastwork were largely swept away and the garrison killed or stunned:[29] four companies were annihilated. Where the bombardment had been less accurate, however, two machine guns in the front trench of one company were able to kill about 1,000 British attackers. The defenders here were overcome only after a second, more accurate, bombardment.[30] The effectiveness of machine-guns was shown again by the strongpoints, which were each occupied by two guns from the support companies during the initial British bombardment. From these emplacements, the German defenders could bring enfilade fire from at least four machine-guns against any British advance deeper into the defences.[31] Owing to faults in its command system, the British attack force was not able to mount an effective assault on the line of strongpoints until the second day of the battle, 11 March. The attack was prepared by a short artillery bombardment, which failed to hit the German positions because these had not been accurately located. The British infantry then moved forward, only to be mown down by the machine guns of three strongpoints. 'Six German machine-gunners, almost unaided, stopped the whole offensive.'[32]

In accordance with the doctrine that the front line should be recaptured if lost, regardless of its tactical value, the Germans prepared a counterattack as soon as the news was received that the British had penetrated the line on the morning of 10 March. Since the local reserves were insufficient to do more than contain the British attack, a brigade was sent from the army reserve. An attack was planned for dawn on 11 March, to be delivered with the bayonet and without prior artillery preparation. The brigade was unable to reach its start positions in time and the attack was postponed. The British were therefore given time to consolidate their positions.[33] German doctrine differentiated between two types of counterattack. The *Gegenstoss* (immediate counterthrust) was designed for use against an attacker still disorganised by his assault. The *Gegenangriff* (deliberate counterattack) was a larger, more methodical operation, for use against an attacker who had had time to consolidate his new positions.[34] Unable to prevent the British consolidating, because of the delay in bringing up reserves, the Germans launched a counterattack at dawn on 12 March. The preparations had been hasty and it was repulsed with heavy losses. Again, machine guns were crucial to the defence, in this case that of the British. The position now stabilised on the existing lines.[35]

Neuve Chapelle serves to illustrate certain key factors in defence in position war. The pre-war German doctrine had been based on infantry-fire. Since the rate of fire of each rifle was low, the necesary firepower could be achieved only by massing infantrymen in a single dense line, with a broad field of fire. This deployment was difficult to conceal and left comparatively few troops available as a reserve for counterattacks. The result was a linear, inflexible defence. The experience of war showed that massed infantry were extremely vulnerable to enemy artillery fire and that it was not possible to prevent an attacker entrenching himself only a few hundred metres away from the defended line. It was also found that machine-guns possessed substantial firepower even over prolonged periods and were effective with a narrow field of fire. It became possible to hold a line primarily with machine-guns, protected by infantry, and keep the greater part of the defending forces back for the counterattack. The small size of the machine-gun posts made them relatively easy to conceal, and reserves could be held outside the range of the attacker's field artillery. The result was a shallow, but more flexible defence. Interestingly, such a system was outlined by von Schlieffen in 1905,[36] and the line of strong-points built behind the German front line in the winter of 1914–15 appears to have been a partial implementation of his ideas.[37]

The events at Neuve Chapelle gave three main lessons: first, a single line of machine-guns was insufficient, a second line being required behind the front line; second, forces that could be located could be destroyed by artillery before an attack, showing the need for invisibility; third, reserves had to be sufficiently close behind the lines to launch a counterthrust before the attacker could consolidate. These lessons were underlined by the British attacks at Aubers Ridge and Festubert. The German position had been given a little more depth by the construction of a second trench 200 metres behind the front line and of communication trenches, with fire steps on both sides in order to channel any penetration, to the rear. The main change was the construction in the front trench of strong machine-gun emplacements, able to resist all but a direct hit from a large shell.[38] No other changes were made to the defence.

The British attack at Aubers Ridge on 9 May was a failure, more a result of British errors, such as the artillery bombardment being insufficient,[39] than of the strength of the German position. The new machine-gun emplacements, however, from which most of the execution was done,[40] proved almost impossible to locate. 'One battery commander, who spent the whole day in the front trenches, reported that he failed to discover the position of a single machine-gun.'[41] The attack at Festubert took place on 16 May after a prolonged artillery bombardment. Although more effective than at Aubers Ridge, the bombardment was again unable to locate a number of the German machine-gun posts. The importance of the second line of machine-gun posts was again demonstrated. The machine-guns which had not been located, and the use of shell-holes and convenient ditches by the German reserves, produced a defence that was difficult for the attackers to see and so to counter, showing the value of invisibility. Finally, the German reserves were again too few and too far to the rear to launch an effective counterattack.[42]

The defensive system employed by the Germans at Festubert, however, was already out of date. On 13 May, von Falkenhayn had issued two reports prepared by the headquarters of Third Army on the lessons of the French attack in Champagne in February 1915.[43] Faced by heavy French pressure, Third Army had developed a defensive system of great strength and flexibility. A single trench line was soon found to be inadequate. By the close of the battle, a network of trenches 2,500 metres deep had been dug, which,

> superficially, had an irregular and unsystematic appearance, but which, in reality, represented the results of a carefully thought out, complete and minutely organised scheme. . . . We have learnt by experiment and experience that what was required was not one or even several lines of fixed defences, but rather a fortified zone which permitted a certain liberty of action, so that the best use could be made of all the advantages offered by the configuration of the ground, and all the disadvantages could as far as possible be overcome.[44]

The spreading of the defence over an area also made its camouflage easier. The Germans had found that enemy observation of positions resulted in their destruction.[45] This was to be avoided by three means: first, the main defensive zone was to be placed on a reverse slope. It was, however, considered essential to maintain possession of the crest line in front of this zone.[46] Second, positions should be made as inconspicuous as possible.[47] Third, there should be a large number of positions, including dummies, in order to divide the enemy's fire.[48] Regarding counterattacks, the Germans noted that a counterthrust by neighbouring troops before the enemy could consolidate any gains was most effective. If it was too late for this, a counterattack, 'carefully prepared by artillery, mortars and rifle grenades', should be employed, attacking from all sides at once.[49]

The defensive system consisted of three main elements. First was a zone of positions covering the ground from the forward slope back to the 'main line of defence' on the reverse slope. This consisted of a number of lengths of trench with a good field of fire, behind which were listening posts, observation posts and positions for a few mortars and machine-guns.[50] The second element was the 'main line of defence'. This was perhaps 200 metres below the crest on the reverse slope and its field of fire was considered of small importance.[51] The final element of the system was a second zone, behind the main line of defence, which was filled with lengths of trench, designed to channel and block a penetration. Command posts, observation posts and heavy weapon positions were also built here.[52] Positions through the defensive system were to be provided with flanking works, particularly for machine-guns, obstacles and dug-outs, each with two entrances.[53] Battery positions were to be similarly fortified[54] and were to be used as rallying points if the line was pierced.[55] Direct fire by heavy weapons was considered to be essential in the confusion after the line had been penetrated, and was to be provided by mortars and 'infantry guns', placed within or close behind the infantry position and under infantry command.[56]

The basis of the defence was to be fire. This was provided primarily by artillery, which could often halt an attack by itself,[57] and by machine-guns, which were most effective when employing flanking fire.[58] Much of this fire was to be direct, but artillery observers were placed well forward in strong shelters, linked to the guns by direct telephone lines.[59] The defensive fire and the layout of the positions served to separate the attacking infantry from its supporting artillery. The attackers were then to be fragmented, channelled into killing zones, and hit immediately by a counterthrust, while their disorder was at its greatest. There was little emphasis on large-scale counterthrusts by the general reserve. The battle was to be fought primarily around the main line of defence: although a complete Second Position was constructed, 2,000 metres behind the rear of the First Position,[60] it was intended as a precaution against an enemy breakthrough, rather than as an integral part of the initial defensive battle.

The construction of deep defensive works was a major drain on resources, which were therefore concentrated where the need was most pressing. Until mid-1915, this was the sector of the Western Front where the Germans faced the French. Falkenhayn considered the British incapable of delivering an effective offensive and left the minimum of forces to face them.[61] This sector of front being seen as 'quiet' may account for its defences not being modernised in accordance with lessons learned in Champagne until the summer of 1915. After Festubert, the Germans realised the need to provide stronger defences against the British and a Second Position was constructed, as had been done in Champagne. This proved its worth at Loos, on 25 September 1915. By using chlorine gas, the British were able to neutralise the German First Position and the row of strongpoints on part of the attack front. Pressing forward, British troops stumbled onto the Second Position, which had not been damaged by the initial bombardment and which the Germans had by this time been able to man. Both the initial attacks and a subsequent attack by 21st and 24th Divisions were destroyed by machine-gun fire from this position.[62]

During the spring of 1915, the first stirrings began of what was to become a major debate within the German Army concerning the principles of defence. The debate appears to have begun in the Operations Section of the OHL branch concerned with the Western Front, the main body of OHL being on the Eastern Front at this time. Whereas the British counterpart to this section dealt only with actual operations, the German organisation was also responsible for examining tactical developments.[63] It was in this capacity that Oberst Max Bauer set up experimental units to test flamethrowers, mortars and assault cannon early in 1915.[64] The debate began over the question of the means by which the First Position should be held[65] and it is of note that all sides accepted that the pre-war doctrine was too inflexible and had to be altered. The debate was therefore not about whether the existing doctrine was still valid but rather about how it could be changed to suit the new circumstances.

One view, taken by the head of the section, Oberst Fritz von Lossberg, was that the position should be held rigidly. He accepted, however, that the enemy might penetrate this position and that positions in depth were required in order to halt any further advance. Reliance should be placed on flanking machine guns to hold the position, with infantry distributed to launch immediate counterthrusts against the flanks of any penetration. Essentially, although penetrations of the First Position were to be expected, they should be avoided if at all possible and should be driven back immediately if they occurred. Lossberg's view was dominant at OHL and was expressed in the pamphlet, 'Essential Principles for the Defence of Positions', issued in August 1915 by Second Army in response to an OHL instruction.[66] Even this limited level of flexibility, in which small units launched counter-thrusts on their own initiative, was resisted by many formations, steeped in the rigidity of pre-war doctrine, and OHL was compelled to send General von Claer to the front to enforce the new doctrine.[67]

The other main point of view was held by a small group of junior General Staff officers at OHL, led by Oberst Max Bauer. Realising that any attempt to hold the First Position rigidly would require troops to be massed in the forward trenches, where they were vulnerable to enemy artillery, this group argued for a thinner forward garrison and consequently for a more flexible system of defence. Wynne states that their ideas were crystallised after they saw a plan for a defence in depth given in a captured French document.[68] Since, however, the system already adopted by Third Army in Champagne was considerably more developed than that given in the French document, it appears more likely that the idea for a defence in depth came from within the German Army. The French document therefore provided evidence to support an existing point of view, rather than to inspire a new approach.

Rather than accept that enemy participations of the First Position were inevitable but regrettable, they suggested that such penetrations should in fact be actively *encouraged*. With the garrison of the First Position reduced and concentrated in strongpoints, larger forces would be available to launch counterthrusts against the enemy penetrations. Cut off from support by the line of strongpoints in the First Position and out of supporting artillery observation on a reverse slope, the attackers would fall easy prey to the large-scale counterthrusts which the larger reserves could deliver. It would then be relatively easy to restore the defenders' control of the whole of the First Position.[69] The ideas had a number of points in their favour. First, they would reduce the effectiveness of the enemy artillery by making the defenders more dispersed and deployed further behind the front line, that is, by giving the defence greater depth. Second, the defence would be less position-based, giving it invisibility. Third, the defence would be converted into an active, aggressive battle, based on immediate responsiveness, in which the superior training of the German troops would be most effective.

The key factor that led to the initial rejection of Bauer's ideas was that of command, since many officers still distrusted the capabilities and fighting spirit of the troops.[70] This was indicated, for example, by the initial unwillingness to link the strongpoints with a continuous trench, on the grounds that this would weaken the troops' resolve to hold the front trench at all costs.[71] This mistrust had been at the heart of 'normal tactics' and had repeatedly blocked moves to decentralise tactics. As before, this philosophy was compelled to change, as the realities of the battlefield showed that control and mass were no longer effective. It is a sign, however, of the relative freedom of thought permitted within the German Army, and the General Staff in particular, that Bauer's group was permitted to hold dissenting opinions and develop ideas.

The arguments at OHL remained unresolved when the British and French armies attacked in Artois and Champagne on 25 September 1915. In Champagne, the French achieved considerable success, causing the German Third Army to consider a short withdrawal. When Falkenhayn briefed the Kaiser on the situation, he was accompanied by Lossberg, who expressed strong disapproval of the proposed retreat. Doubtless to his surprise, Lossberg was promptly appointed Third Army chief of staff, despite his junior rank.[72] So began his extraordinary career as the German Army's expert on defence.

Although a member of the General Staff, Lossberg was a fighting soldier by temperament. Before leaving OHL for his new posting, he wrote to his wife, 'I am leaving this place of dusty documents and am going to Champagne, where there is fresh air. There I shall be in my element among soldiers and shall be able to breathe again.'[73] Arriving at Third Party headquarters, he had a brief interview with his new superior, General von Einem, and then went on a personal inspection of the threatened sector of line. Rather than simply view the area on a map or from an observation post in the rear, Lossberg's instincts led him almost to the front line itself. Here he could see the situation as it really was and judge the atmosphere of the defence. This exposure to raw reality was to produce an important change in his views on defence.

Lossberg subsequently appears to have presented the new defensive scheme that he instituted in Champagne as entirely his own idea.[74] It consisted of a number of positions and zones with a total depth of 8,000 metres. The front of the system consisted of a lightly held outpost zone, placed on a crest line. Behind this, on the reverse slope, was the First Position, consisting of several trench lines. Relatively few troops were deployed here, but these had strict orders to hold their positions rigidly. Behind the First Position was a zone 2,500 metres deep, occupied by supports, artillery observers, direct-fire heavy weapons and some field guns. The rear of this zone was marked by the 1st *Rückwärtige* (Rearward) Position, built on the forward slope of the next ridge line, giving clear observation across to the rear of the outpost zone. It was manned by the local reserves and protected more artillery observers and guns. A further 2,500 metres to the rear was the 2nd Rearward Position, again on a reverse slope and providing cover for elements of the general reserve. This system was in fact very similar to that already adopted by Third Army in February 1915.[75] The main change was that the First Position was now more thinly garrisoned and the majority of the defenders were employed as successive waves of counterthrust forces. The firepower of the garrison of the First Position was maintained at a high level, despite the reduced manpower, by a shift from rifle fire to machine-gun fire. The result was that the initial defence remained strong, but the counterthrusts were far more powerful.

While at OHL, Lossberg had argued against Bauer's group, supporting the doctrine that the First Position should be heavily manned, in order to prevent enemy penetrations and to ensure sufficient forces were available within the position to launch immediate counterthrusts against those penetrations that did occur. Having seen the situation on the ground, Lossberg's belief that the First Position should be held rigidly was reinforced. The fact that large numbers of troops in the position had surrendered as soon as they found the enemy behind them strengthened his conviction that the garrison must be inculcated with the need to hold its position to the last man, even if surrounded.[76] Lossberg realised, however, that enemy penetrations of the First Position could not be prevented and that a strong garrison here merely resulted in severe losses. He now saw the value of the suggestion urged by Bauer's group that the First Position should be held more thinly and the majority of the defenders be employed for counterthrusts. By this means, casualties would be reduced and it would be easier to defeat the inevitable enemy penetrations. This provision of strong counterthrust forces, deployed in depth, was Lossberg's main contribution to the Third Army defensive position.

With counterattacks playing an ever more important role in the German defensive doctrine, the various types of counterattack started to become more clearly defined. Two forms of counterthrust came to be identified. The first was carried out by small, squad-sized groups within the First Position, as an immediate response to an enemy attack. What this involved is indicated by an order issued by Reserve-Infanterie-Regiment 235 on 12 December 1915, which required every platoon to have at least six grenade specialists, who were to launch immediate counterthrusts, without waiting for orders, should the enemy attack.[77] This manoeuvre came to be termed a *Gegenstoss in der Stellung* (counterthrust within the position). The second form of counterthrust was undertaken by company- and battalion-sized reserves, supported by artillery and heavy weapons, which would move forward from behind the First Position to attack enemy penetrations before they could be consolidated. This manoeuvre came to be termed a *Gegenstoss aus der Tiefe* (counterthrust from behind the position).[78] If the reserves were unable to launch a counterthrust before the enemy was able to consolidate, a counterattack should be employed. This would be a carefully planned, large-scale attack, often prepared over several days.[79]

In addition to these forms of counterattack, the Germans on several occasions planned to make major attacks, designed to dislocate enemy preparations for an offensive. Such an operation was proposed (although never carried out) in April 1916, by which the Sixth Army was to disrupt the British preparations for an offensive at Ypres.[80] This form of counter-offensive, as well as counterattacks against a large-scale enemy break-through, was subsequently termed a *Gegenschlag* (counterstroke).[81]

The key to these developments was the German system of command. Lossberg made great efforts to ensure that the higher commanders and their staffs maintained close touch with the troops and listened to their views:

> Any free time he could spare he went visiting the front-line commanders and in personal reconnaissance of difficult sectors of the position; he also divided the army front among the officers of his staff and each had to visit the battle area of his sector twice a week and ask the junior local commanders their requirements. These were forwarded to the divisional staffs concerned and, if reasonable, had to be attended to at once. Colonel v. Lossberg mentions that the reward he received for these untiring efforts to ease the privations of the front-line units was the grateful recognition he was invariably given on his visits to them. He found this relationship between Army headquarters and the front line invaluable.[82]

## The Somme

The experiences of Third Army in Champagne during September 1915 did not alter the basic defensive concept of the German Army, that the front line should be held rigidly, expressed in the old Prussian saying, '*Halten was zu halten ist*' (Hold what is to be held). Lossberg's belief that the troops could not be relied upon to fight on when surrounded had been reinforced by the number of soldiers who had surrendered in such circumstances. His thinning of the front garrison and emphasis on counter-thrusts by reserves were the result more of an appreciation that a dense garrison was too vulnerable to the attackers' artillery, than of a desire for greater flexibility in the defence *per se*. The response of OHL to the Allied material superiority was to order a major strengthening of the defensive fieldworks, in the belief that stronger positions would reduce the effectiveness of the enemy artillery and so allow a more dense front garrison. Lossberg's system in Champagne was considered little more than a temporary response to inadequate defences, rather than a permanent counter to Allied artillery fire. That this return to earlier practice was officially endorsed is shown by Falkenhayn's comment, 'The first principle in position warfare must be to yield not one foot of ground; and if it be lost to retake it by immediate counterattack, even to the use of the last man'.[83]

With the need to thin the front garrison apparently reduced by stronger field defences, Falkenhayn ordered a reversion to the doctrine developed in Champagne in February 1915. Although the defensive system now consisted of three full positions, with a further line between the First and Second Positions, the battle was to be fought in the First Position only and half the available troops were deployed here. Most were placed in the second trench, which was well equipped with dug-outs. The first trench was held largely by the flanking fire of machine guns. Maximum use was to be made of the depth of the First Position, with machine guns being placed towards the rear of the position but able to cover the ground in front. The infantry garrison was ordered to counterthrust any enemy penetration at once, considered the best way to recover ground.[84] The front line remained on a forward slope along much of the Western Front, so that it might have a wide field of fire.[85] This suggests that the German high command's belief in the strength of its field works led it to discount previous experience that artillery could destroy any position, given time.[86] With the front garrison now more dense, it was believed that fewer penetrations would occur and that there was therefore less need for a strong counterthrust reserve behind the position. The absence of a strong reserve brought the Germans close to disaster at Thiepval on 1 July 1916.

Shortly before midnight on 1 July 1916, von Lossberg was appointed chief of staff of Second Army, which faced the Allied attack on the Somme.[87] Lossberg almost certainly already knew his new commander, General Fritz von Below. The two men would have had contact while Lossberg was deputy head of the Operations Section of OHL and it is likely that they had co-operated in the production of Below's report on the Allied offensives of September 1915.[88] Together, they were to fight the British on the Somme for the next five months.

Falkenhayn's belief that the construction of strong field works was an effective counter to Allied material superiority, making defence in depth unnecessary, was shown to be wholly unrealistic. A pamphlet issued by the British General Staff in October 1916 noted:

> One of the most important lessons drawn [by the German Army] from the Battle of the Somme is that, under heavy methodical artillery fire, the front line should be only thinly held, but by reliable men and a few machine guns, even when there is always a possibility of a hostile attack. When this was not done, the casualties were so great before the enemy's [i.e. British] attack was launched, that the possibility of the front line repulsing the attack by its own unaided efforts was very doubtful.[89]

Lossberg at once returned to the principles he had developed in Champagne, holding the First Position lightly and keeping most of the troops back for counterthrusts. The system of three positions, with an Intermediate Line between the First and Second Positions, was retained and strengthened. The position served both to block enemy penetrations and to protect reserves before they were committed. Despite the increased depth of the defensive system, however, Lossberg retained his insistence on the rigid defence of the front line. In the report he wrote for Ludendorff after the battle had ended,[90] he bluntly asserted:

> It is absolutely essential to remember that, in spite of 'defended areas', the fighting must take place in the foremost line and, if this is overrun, for its recapture . . . As a matter of principle, every unit must fight in that portion of the foremost position which is given to it to defend. The voluntary evacuation of a position, or of portions of a position, can lead to most disastrous results for the troops on the flanks. The voluntary evacuation of positions must, therefore, only take place with the express permission of the Higher Commanders, who are in a position to realise its effects on the troops on the flanks and on other arms (artillery).[91]

Lossberg understood that even a dispersed front-line garrison was vulnerable to enemy artillery fire and that troops were naturally disposed to attempt to avoid this fire by moving away. He noted that movement to the side was rarely effective, because of the Allied bombardments, and that it ran the danger of the enemy suddenly occupying the vacated position. Movement to the rear was equally ineffective, because the bombardment of the ground behind the position was hardly less than that on the position itself. The only acceptable movement was therefore forward. Even then, Lossberg considered this suitable only 'in the case of good troops who are well trained in initiative and in rapid counterattack',[92] and he emphasised the need to defend the First Position rigidly:

> During the battle of the Somme, the methodical evacuation of portions of the position depended on obtaining permission from Army Headquarters and every evacuation of positions, even to the

> smallest extent, carried out on the responsibility of the individual commander was forbidden. Every man was obliged to fight at that point at which he was stationed; the enemy's line of advance could only lead over his dead body. Army Headquarters believes that it was owing to this firm determination to fight, with which every leader was inspired, that the enemy, in spite of his superior numbers, were destroyed in face of the steadfast, closely knit ranks of our front line troops.[93]

Parallel to the increase in the depth of the defensive position, the concept of invisibility was also evolving. The idea of placing positions on reverse slopes, developed in Champagne, was applied by Lossberg to the Somme. This made British artillery observation more difficult and so reduced the effectiveness of bombardments. Although this advantage was made less important by the use of observation aircraft by the British, whose control of the air was initially uncontested,[94] artillery observation from the air was greatly inferior to observation from the ground. The imperative need for positions to be on reverse slopes was clear and was fully accepted by the majority of the German Army. Equally, the importance of retaining control over the crest line was emphasised.[95]

Under the constant Allied bombardment, the German positions were rapidly reduced to a mass of shell-holes, which the garrisons hurriedly linked together to form *ad hoc* trenches. Obstacles, communication trenches and dug-outs ceased to exist in this zone of desolation.[96] A number of units found that even this form of position was quickly seen by the enemy and chose instead to live in separate shell-holes, covered by waterproof sheets.[97] Since these sheets blended into the landscape, the British were unable to locate the German defenders accurately, with the result that engagements repeatedly took the form of an ineffective bombardment followed by a failed infantry attack. Lossberg objected strongly to this practice, even if the shell holes were connected.[98] While his objection was partly based on the greater physical demands that shell-hole positions placed on the defenders, his main concern was that command was far more difficult in these circumstances. With troops dispersed and invisible, artillery barrage lines could not be laid down with accuracy, organised resistance and counterthrusts were all but impossible, and commanders found it difficult to inspire their men. Lossberg therefore advocated the retention of continuous trench lines, despite their being more easily located by the enemy. These trenches, however, came to be used primarily as living accommodation and rallying points, with the troops moving forward into shell-holes to face an attack.[99]

The main area of development was that of counterthrusts. The holding back of troops to act as a counterthrust reserve had been one of the most important innovations introduced by Lossberg in Champagne. As a consequence of Falkenhayn's reversion to the earlier doctrine, the principle had been largely discarded in the defence schemes initially used on the Somme, but the impossibility of holding the First Position with only the thin garrison made necessary by the weight of enemy artillery fire required a renewed emphasis on the counterthrust by reserves from behind the position, although the counterthrust from within the position was still considered fundamental to the defence.

> Immediate counter[thrusts] carried out on the bold initiative of subordinate commanders in the front line, nearly always succeeded. Whenever possible, these counter[thrusts] were delivered from a flank by bombing parties. Frequently, just a few stout-hearted men were able to drive out the enemy.[100]

The strength of British attacks, and the small forces assigned to the First Position, however, frequently made large-scale counterthrusts necessary. As in Champagne, these were carried out by reserves deployed behind the First Position in a series of waves, each wave of increasing size. Once an enemy attack was identified, these reserves were to move forward, each wave occupying the positions vacated by the previous wave.[101] In this way, a continuous forward pressure was maintained against enemy penetrations. The enemy became progressively exhausted, having continually to face fresh troops. This exhaustion could be increased if a heavy artillery barrage was put down behind the enemy, cutting them off from support or reinforcement.[102] The results could be dramatic: one German division noted, 'British troops, even when they had broken through in large numbers, were incapable of exploiting their success and allowed themselves to be made prisoner without offering resistance.'[103]

Counterthrusts were effective only if the enemy had not had time to consolidate their gains. When this was the case, recourse had to be made to a counterattack. The first requirement for a counterattack was for commanders to gain a clear idea of the situation, on the basis of which they had to decide whether the ground lost was worth the likely expenditure of force involved.

> It frequently happens that parts of positions which have been tenaciously defended against many assaults are finally lost owing to their being situated on the forward slope or forming a salient, being thus unduly exposed to the force of the enemy's fire before the assault takes place. If such points are retaken by a methodical counter-attack, the troops are deliberately placed once more in what has already been recognised as an unfavourable position, and there is once more a risk of suffering heavy casualties and a danger, which

> should not be underestimated, of again losing the position which has just been recaptured. When this is judged to be the case, the higher commander must, after coolly weighing the consequences, forbid a methodical counterattack in spite of the importance of acquiescing in and supporting every effort on the part of the troops to regain lost ground.[104]

The counterattack could be made with heavy artillery support, or could attempt to surprise the enemy by dispensing with artillery preparation. Fresh troops were almost always required[105] and might be led by elite assault parties,[106] at this time supplied by divisional *Sturmkompagnien* employing the assault squad tactics developed by Hauptmann Rohr. The importance of fire support from machine guns for both counterthrusts and counterattacks could not be overemphasised.[107] Although Lossberg planned a number of large-scale counterattacks during the early stages of the Somme, they had to be cancelled as insufficient forces were available.[108] By late August, losses were running so high that Below was compelled to forbid all but the most local counterattacks except those he specifically approved.[109]

The vital ingredient that allowed the new doctrine to operate dynamically was the increasing decentralisation of command. The main factor compelling the Germans to grant ever more extensive room for initiative to ever more junior subordinates was the need for counterthrusts to be made before the enemy could consolidate. The time during which an attacker is vulnerable to a counterthrust tends to be very short. This may be illustrated by an incident recounted by a British Guards lieutenant, whose platoon had just seized an enemy position after a fierce fight.

> The reorganisation for some 20 minutes was not good at all. We were completely shattered. Our hearing was very badly impaired by the noise. We were being physically ill because of the adrenalin build-up inside us and we had very little ammunition or, to be quite frank, very little spirit left for much more of a fight. We simply sat around. We were very cold and I think that a lot of people for this period of 10 to 20 minutes simply didn't want to do anything else and it took a great deal of effort from the Junior Noncommissioned Officers to get people moving again, to get the circulation going and start sorting out their weapons and standing by for anything else that might happen. We did expect to be counterattacked and I think for that period we probably could not have done a great deal about it. However, after 20 minutes, when the company sorted itself out, the casualties were moved off . . . and we were resupplied with ammunition, things got a lot better and the Guardsmen were able to take up defensive positions. Had we been attacked then, it would have been a different story![110]

Although this incident occurred in the Falklands War of 1982, the temporary state of psychological exhaustion, resulting in disorientation and lethargy, may be taken as typical of infantry combat throughout modern times, including the First World War. The critical factor here is the short duration of this incapacity. A counterthrust would have to be delivered within minutes if it was to take advantage of it. While a series of small-scale counterthrusts might serve to prolong the period of incapacity, giving time for a larger counterthrust to be organised, the basic requirement for an immediate response (*Schlagfertigkeit*), remained unchanged.

The Germans found that, under battle conditions, a message took an average of between eight and ten hours to pass from divisional headquarters to the front line.[111] Such delays were incompatible with immediate responsiveness. Two main measures were employed to speed up reaction times. The first was to ensure that every commander had adequate reserves, over which he had full control.

> Even the Company Commander must, in no circumstances, neglect to provide himself with a reserve consisting of a few groups and, if possible, of machine guns as well. The Sub-Sector Commanders must also have at all times sufficient troops at their disposal to be able at once to drive the enemy out, by means of a counter[thrust], should he succeed in penetrating into the position.[112]

While local reserves were sufficient for small-scale counterthrusts, more radical measures were necessary if larger counterthrusts were to be launched quickly enough. The solution adopted was a rationalisation of the command system. Each division deployed all three regiments forward, each with one battalion in the front line, one in support and the third in reserve, thus making each sub-sector of the defensive zone the responsibility of a single regiment. Within each sub-sector, executive command over the entire regiment was given to the commander of the front battalion, designated the *Kampftruppenkommandeur* (KTK) (combat troops commander). This officer, regardless of his rank or seniority, enjoyed full command over the three battalions of his own regiment and also over all reinforcements sent from outside. He therefore had the ability to respond immediately to any enemy penetration. The KTK was enabled to concentrate entirely on fighting the battle. All administrative duties, such as ammunition supply, evacuation of wounded and readiness of reserves, were performed by the regimental commander.[113] A similar rationalisation was carried out higher up the chain of command:

> The real weight of the fighting rests on the shoulders of the Divisional Commanders, on whom devolves full responsibility for the maintenance of their sectors. Divisional Commanders must, therefore, be

> given control of all the organs of action available in their sectors, with the exception of guns employed on special tasks and, in exceptional cases, Corps Artillery Groups detailed for special long-range objectives. They must at the right time allot to their subordinate commanders both their own reserves and the reserves placed at their disposal by superior authority; these subordinate commanders must, in their turn, make local arrangements for the employment of these reserves on the battlefield. The Divisional Commander must exert a continuous and keen influence on the whole control of the action; this will be ensured by accurate reconnaissances on the ground and by maintaining daily personal touch with his troops and their commanders.[114]

As with the regiment, the corps commander supported the divisional commander primarily by taking over administrative duties, leaving the latter free to focus entirely on the battle.[115] The chain of command was therefore simplified from five stages (corps to division to brigade to regiment to front battalion) to only two (division to front battalion), each with full control over its sector of front.

An important factor in this decentralisation of command was that higher commanders made considerable efforts to ensure that they were well informed yet also ensured that this did not involve distracting subordinates with continual demands for reports. At every level, formations set up their own observation posts, linked directly to the headquarters, which reported on the situation.[116] This was supplemented by frequent visits to lower headquarters. Almost every day, von Below, often accompanied by Ludendorff himself, visited three or four divisional commanders at their battle stations. These interviews, usually attended by the corps commander also, were found to be of great value in producing a united approach.[117] In addition to accompanying Below on these visits, Lossberg spent much time in the front line itself, in order to determine the exact situation of the troops, their morale and endurance.[118]

The doctrine of holding the First Position rigidly, but with a thin garrison, and of employing reserves to throw back enemy penetrations by means of counterthrusts imposed great demands on the troops. This was reflected in the importance given in official pamphlets to the need for a very high standard of training. The strains facing the front garrison were extreme. Spread in small groups throughout a zone of unconnected shell-holes, under constant artillery fire and rarely seeing company or even platoon commanders, the need for a soldier to possess 'the highest possible degree of self-reliance, so that he may know how to act during the critical periods of his own or the enemy's atttacks' was central.[119] Junior officers and NCOs had to display a 'whole-hearted disinterestedness and self-sacrificing care for subordinates'. Battlefield proficiency had to be of a high order. Every soldier was to know how to use all types of German hand grenades, most were to be familiar with enemy grenades and officers had to be able to work a German machine gun. Machine-gunners were trained to bring their weapons out of a dug-out and into action within 30 seconds. The launching of counterthrusts, whether by a single man or a whole regiment, was to be ingrained. The troops were to follow the practices developed by the storm battalions. In order to give time in which training could be completed and the latest lessons incorporated, troops were, if possible, to be given about 14 days behind the lines before going into battle. This also allowed commanders to become familiar with the ground and the situation of operations.[120]

Although Lossberg's new defensive doctrine allowed the Germans to prevent an Allied breakthrough, the cost was heavy. Allied casualties on the Somme were in the region of 600,000, of which over 400,000 were British. In the British *Official History*, Edmonds initially proposed that German casualties were also about 600,000,[121] but later revised this estimate to 680,000.[122] In 1938, Liddell Hart and Wynne calculated that the figure was about 500,000,[123] though Wynne later proposed 465,000 as the true total.[124]

The German Army could not afford to suffer almost half a million casualties in another battle, even if the Allies lost even more heavily. Although Lossberg's doctrine had succeeded on the Somme, a similar battle in 1917 might bring defeat by exhaustion. A new doctrine had to be found.

## Elastic Defence in Depth

The opportunity for change came at the end of August 1916. Falkenhayn's position had become increasingly weak as the summer progressed. In June, the Eastern Front had come close to collapse in the face of the Brusilov Offensive. In July, the last attempt to capture Verdun failed and the Germans began to lose the ground so painfully gained.[125] The final straw came on 27 August, when Rumania declared war, an event Falkenhayn had predicted impossible before mid-September. The following day, the Kaiser summoned Hindenburg, then commander-in-chief of the Eastern Front, for consultation. Falkenhayn responded by resigning.[126] He was replaced as Chief of the General Staff by Hindenburg, with Ludendorff as his First Quartermaster-General, with joint responsibility.

Although the declaration of war by Rumania was the ostensible reason for Falkenhayn's removal, it is likely that his conduct of the Somme battle was perhaps the most important factor. Bauer recorded that when

Ludendorff took over from Falkenhayn, he and his colleagues at OHL felt as if an enormous weight had been lifted from them,[127] since they had been totally opposed to Falkenhayn's rigid system of defence on the Somme. Since Bauer had already been instrumental in the removal of Moltke in 1914,[128] it is possible that he played as important a part in the replacement of Falkenhayn. This appears all the more likely since Bauer was an enthusiastic disciple of Ludendorff,[129] probably as a result of working with him when he was Moltke's designate-chief of operations between 1911 and 1913.[130] Ludendorff, in turn, had been one of Schlieffen's pupils and some of the defensive ideas developed subsequently appear to have originated with his old teacher.[131]

Both Hindenburg and Ludendorff had spent the war on the Eastern Front, apart from a brief period in August 1914. Although operations here were generally less expensive in terms of casualties than in the West, Ludendorff claimed 'It was always my endeavour to achieve success at the least possible cost. Troops may take pride in bearing heavy losses and succeeding in spite of them. The commander must have a different point of view.'[132] Applying this philosophy to the Western Front, Ludendorff concluded,

> Without doubt [the German infantry] fought too doggedly, clinging too resolutely to the mere holding of ground, with the result that the losses were heavy. The deep dug-outs and cellars often became fatal man-traps . . . The Field Marshal and I could for the moment only ask that the front lines should be held more lightly, the deep underground works be destroyed and all trenches and posts be given up if the retention of them were unnecessary to the maintenance of the position as a whole and likely to be the cause of heavy losses.[133]

Ludendorff believed that the defence had to be made in greater depth and more invisible, while the garrison was to be allowed more flexibility.[134] This inevitably involved a greater emphasis on the counterthrust.

Upon arrival at OHL, Ludendorff came across the same group of progressive officers, led by Oberst Bauer, who had argued for greater flexibility with Lossberg a year earlier. Finding himself in complete agreement with their views, Ludendorff resolved to issue a new doctrine on defence, the first time the subject was dealt with in an official manual since the *Exerzier-Reglement für die Infanterie* of 1906. He summoned Generalleutnant von Hoehn to OHL, to write a preliminary paper, *Die Abwehrschlacht* (The Defensive Battle). This formed the basis for the new manual, *Die Führung in der Abwehrschlacht* (The Conduct of the Defensive Battle),[135] written by Bauer and Hauptmann Geyer.[136] Published on 1 December 1916, it was issued down to division level.[137] A companion manual, *Allgemeines über Stellenbau* (General Principles of Field Position Construction) was also produced.[138]

Ludendorff's own description of the new defensive system reveals how the concepts of depth (*Flächenverteidigung*), invisibility (*die Leere des Gefechtefeldes*) and immediate responsiveness (*Schlagfertigkeit*) were expressed, and how they linked with a fundamental need for highly decentralised command and excellent training:

> In sharp contrast to the form of defence hitherto employed, which had been restricted to rigid and easily recognised lines of little depth, a new system was devised, which, by distribution in depth and the adoption of a loose formation, enabled a more active defence to be maintained. It was of course intended that the position should remain in our hands at the end of the battle, but the infantryman need no longer say to himself: 'Here I must stand or fall', but had, on the contrary, the right, within certain limits, to retire in any direction before strong enemy fire. Any part of the line that was lost was to be recovered by counter [thrust]. The group [of eight men], on the importance of which many intelligent officers had insisted before the war, now became officially the tactical unit of the infantry. The position of the NCO as group leader thus became much more important. Tactics became more and more individualised.[139]

Bauer's manual recognised that the pre-war defensive doctrine, which generally regarded defence as merely a preliminary of a renewed offensive, was no longer appropriate to the circumstances of position war:

> The aim of the defence of in a battle is to make the attacking force fight itself to a standstill and use up its resources in men, while the defenders conserve their strength. . . . The defence should not be based on the employment of the largest possible number of men, but must rely principally on its armament (artillery, trench mortars, machine guns, etc.). . . . The Higher Command should not make it a rigid and unconditional rule that ground cannot be abandoned. It should so conduct the defence that its own troops are on favourable ground, while the attacking force is only left ground unfavourable for its operations. . . . Distribution in depth forms the basis of all preparations. . . . The commander of the defence must not abandon the initiative in his conduct of the fighting.[140]

The manual placed great emphasis on the need for depth in defence:

> The distribution of the infantry must be based on economy of force, bearing in mind that, under a heavy bombardment of long duration,

> well constructed defences and a strong garrison offer no sure guarantee for the repulse of attackers by a purely passive defensive.[141]

The defensive system was normally to consist of three zones. The first was the *Vorfeldzone* (forward zone), which was designed for ordinary trench warfare, to be lightly held while giving protection against surprise and enemy artillery observation of the defensive system.[142] It was usually to be 400 to 1,000 metres deep, although it could in practice be up to 3,000 metres deep, and was garrisoned by perhaps half a company on a regimental front.[143]

Behind this zone lay the *Grosskampfzone* (battle zone). The positioning of this zone was entirely independent of that of the forward zone and was made without regard to the abandonment of ground. The sole criterion was its suitability for defence against a major attack. Although the two zones might sometimes coincide, the different defensive requirements for battles and ordinary trench warfare meant that the battle zone normally lay behind the forward zone. There could be a gap between them, but it was preferred that they should merge into each other.[144] The zone was to be between 1,500 and 2,500 metres deep[145] and was held by two battalions of each regiment,[146] which also provided the garrison for the forward zone. Behind the battle zone was to be at least one *rückwärtige Kampfzone* (rearward combat zone). In order to prevent a simultaneous artillery attack on both zones, the front of the rearward combat zone was to be at least 3,000 metres behind the front of the battle zone.[147] In the event of a major enemy attack, it was to be occupied by the reserve battalion of each regiment.[148]

Not only was the garrison spread in depth, the frontage assigned to formations were also wide. Each division was to defend a front between 2,500 and 3,250 metres.[149] Since divisions usually deployed their three regiments side by side, each regiment held about 1,000 metres of front. With the combined depth of the front two zones averaging 3,000 metres, each regiment held 300 hectares with two battalions, equivalent to only one soldier per 50-metre square.

Every zone was designed for defence in depth. Each included several trenches, irregularly placed 150 to 400 metres apart, connected by numerous communication trenches. Between the lines and scattered throughout the zone were numerous strongpoints and *Anklammerungspunkte* (rallying points). These were to be gradually linked by further trenches, while numerous diagonal switch lines were also to be dug. The result of this complicated mass of positions was that

> The enemy who has broken through should eventually find himself surrounded in front and flank by fire trenches and obstacles and it should then be possible to annihilate him by means of well hidden

> machine guns and trench mortars, and also by the guns told off to deal with ground inside our front line.[150]

The new doctrine rejected Lossberg's belief that the front position must be held rigidly:

> The garrisons of the foremost trenches must be weak, but they should not be tied rigidly to one point when they can no longer find cover and may, within certain limits, change their position in order to escape from very intense bombardment. Experience shows that no matter how carefully the enemy directs his fire, there are points within every area allotted to a unit in which this fire is less effective. It is, therefore, a question of observing the fall of the enemy's fire and of avoiding the areas in which it is most intense, by advancing, moving to the flanks or falling back on the nearest supports. The best method is to advance, as this is the quickest way of escaping from the enemy's fire.[151]

Great emphasis was also placed on the need for positions to be invisible:

> The resistance of a defensive zone cannot . . . be based solely on the strength of its organisation; even one which is strong in itself must always yield in the course of time to very heavy concentrated fire of the enemy. It is therefore most important to cause the enemy to spread his fire both in time and space. The more works, therefore, of all kinds that there are in and between the defensive zones, the more they are scattered and the less they are recognisable by the enemy's ground and air reconnaissances, the more difficult it will be for him to spot the important points, and to concentrate his fire on them, and the more ammunition and time must he employ for the destruction of the defensive works. By this method of organisation, the enemy will be deceived as to the relative importance of the various works, his fire will be misled and the garrison saved from the effect of his preparatory bombardment. . . . The inconspicuousness of all works from both ground and air becomes of decisive importance. . . . The use of labour for purposes that do not contribute to fighting ends, but merely make works look pretty or unnecessarily tidy, is forbidden.[152]

Positions were to be built on reverse slopes, except when friendly artillery observation over them would not be possible.[153]

The new manual gave the strongest importance to the need for a high level of immediate responsiveness. Although the small forward garrison was to make every effort to repulse an enemy attack, penetrations were inevitable. These were to be cut off from further support by artillery fire and any further advance halted by fire from small arms and heavy weapons.

> The difficult situation in which the enemy now finds himself must be utilised *without waiting for further orders*. The detachments of the trench garrison . . . and the supports lying ready behind the foremost trenches, whose task must have been so drilled into them as to become second nature, must counter [thrust] immediately and recapture the front line. . . . The enemy must be annihilated to the last man by the use of the hand grenade and the bayonet in hand-to-hand fighting.[154]

Only the small *Sicherheitsbesatzungen* (emergency garrisons), who manned a few key posts and were distinguished by white arm bands,[155] did not take part in these counterthrusts within the position. The result was 'These tactics cause the fighting to take place not *in*, but *for* the front line'.[156]

It was recognised that the front divisions might not be able to eject the enemy or to hold his attack through their own unaided efforts. In this case, the front garrison was urged to fight on as long as possible, even if surrounded, in order to prevent the enemy consolidating and so allow time for a counterthrust by formations from the general reserve, which were termed *Eingreif* divisions.

> Though usually translated as 'counterattacking', '*Eingreif*' means 'interlocking' or 'gearing into' and thus conveys the idea that the divisions sent up . . . to counterattack enter into the framework of the battle, under one of the divisional commanders already engaged, regardless of seniority.[157]

This counterthrust was to receive maximum fire support, be led by assault squads and be combined with renewed efforts by the front garrison. The manual emphasised, 'The success of the attack depends not on the strength of the forces engaged in it, but on the resolution with which it is carried out, the co-operation of all arms and rapidity of execution'.[158] If an immediate counterthrust could not be made, a counterattack should be carried out. This was to be carefully prepared over several days, in order to allow thorough planning and training to take place. It was emphasised that a counterattack should not be made automatically, but only if the ground to be recaptured was worth the anticipated losses and expenditure of ammunition.[159]

The conduct of the battle was placed in the hands of the divisional commanders, with corps headquarters providing support. Continuity was considered vital to an effective defence and corps headquarters were therefore to remain in place for as long as possible. Divisions had to be rotated more frequently, but their sectors were to be of sufficient depth that they could withstand prolonged periods of battle. It was seen as important for a senior commander 'to gain, by means of personal reconnaissance, a thorough knowledge of the ground and the trenches in his sector. Only thus will he be in a position to conduct the fight properly and maintain the necessary personal touch with the troops.'[160]

The flexibility given to the defenders of the forward defences placed greater demands on the troops than ever before. Ludendorff noted, 'Having regard to the ever more scanty training of our officers, NCOs and men, and the consequent falling-off in discipline, it was a risky business'. A major effort was made to ensure that the troops were sufficiently skilled to carry out the new tactics. Each army set up a wide variety of training courses and particular attention was paid to the development of company officers and NCOs. Courses in tactics and musketry were ubiquitous. Machine-gunners were comprehensively trained, with a special practice ground assigned to the *Scharfschützen* (sharpshooter) detachments. Similar establishments were set up for mortars, signallers and engineers, where officers from other arms were also trained. The artillery too honed its skills.

> Training was carried on without interruption, both in and behind the line. The life was much the same as in peacetime. Everywhere efforts were made to fit the army for its heavy task and to keep its losses within bounds. . . . Of course, all our leaders . . . made every effort to prevent the troops from becoming tired or stale under training. Physical rest was an absolute necessity for the maintenance even of discipline and it was only by adequate periods of relaxation in rest billets that men could gradually recover from the heavy moral strain.[161]

The new doctrine made equally great demands on divisional commanders and their staffs. In order to inculcate these officers with sound and clear ideas on the defensive battle, two schools were set up, at Sedan and Solesmes (later Valenciennes),[162] whose commandant, General Otto von Moser, later published his wartime diaries. Moser was a brigade commander when he was seriously wounded on 2 September 1914. He commanded 107th Division for a year before being transferred to command 27th Division, which spent August 1916 on the Somme.[163] He therefore had considerable experience of divisional command in position war.

Moser was appointed on 1 January 1917 to command a Testing and Instructional Division, a complete war-strength formation, with which he was to test the new defensive doctrine and teach it to senior officers. A great deal of work was involved. Not only did the exercise ground assigned to the school have to be extended, involving the evacuation of three villages, but the positions for both friend and foe had to be laid out and constructed. These had to suit the ground and also provide a clear and convincing presentation of the new doctrine. In laying out the positions, Moser had to take account not only of the new manual on defence but also of the changes that it made necessary in all the other manuals. Moser received a copy of the new doctrine only in mid-January, but fortunately found himself in full agreement with it.[164]

Moser quickly concluded that the main focus of the course must be that of a *Divisionskommandeur-Schule* (divisional commanders' school). The 'duties and rights' of the divisional commander in the defensive battle would be examined in theory and then tested on the practice ground. In parallel with this process, the school would have to test and develop new tactics, pieces of equipment and positions. The rich store of experience held by the officers attending the courses would be of great value in this task, but he was well aware of their faults. Although their experience was rich, few had an overall view of tactics or had the time, or inclination, for further learning. Moreover, many of the students had received the command of a division only a few months before and had been given no extra instruction in their new duties. They therefore retained a certain narrowness and the outlook of their original arm of service. Since the new doctrine placed greater responsibilities on the divisional commander than ever before, practical and effective instruction was essential.[165]

The first course ran from 8 to 16 February 1917 and was attended by about 100 officers from the Western Front. Major von Bockelberg and Hauptmann Geyer came from OHL to observe and assist. Moser noted that the event was a great success and that the formula of morning lectures and afternoon exercises was shown to be correct. The presence of so many experienced officers, as well as the two representatives from OHL, led to lively discussion and improvements in both the course and the doctrine. Certain artillery and corps officers expressed concern at the decentralisation of command to divisional level but were won over by Moser. The war game with which the course ended was of particular value in proving the correctness of the new doctrine and showing how the battle should best be fought.[166] A second course was held from 20 to 28 February and was attended by officers from both Western and Eastern fronts. Three senior Austro-Hungarian staff officers came as observers. Visitors included Ludendorff, Crown Prince Rupprecht and General Fritz von Below. Again, the course was a great success. Moser conducted a third course from 4 to 12 March, which was attended by a number of allied representatives and led to further refinements of the doctrine. On 18 March he left to take over command of XIV Reserve Corps and was succeeded as commander of the school by General von Wenniger.[167]

While the new defensive doctrine was accepted with few reservations by most officers, strong objections were raised in some quarters about the flexibility given to the front garrison. Not even the personnel of OHL were unanimous in its support. Ludendorff admitted, 'The controversy raged furiously in my staff; I myself had to intervene to advocate the new tactics'.[168] The leader of the objectors was von Lossberg. His opposition to flexibility being given to the front garrison was forcefully put on 8 September 1916, at the first conference held by Ludendorff after Falkenhayn's replacement.[169] Lossberg continued to argue his case even after the publication of Ludendorff's new defensive manual. As we have seen, the pamphlet 'Experience of the German First Army in the Somme Battles',[170] issued on 30 January 1917 and largely written by Lossberg, continued to emphasise the importance of rigidity in the front garrison.

> It is a tribute to General Ludendorff's flexibility of vision that he not only allowed Colonel von Lossberg's memorandum . . . to be circulated, unexpurgated, to all German divisions but even had it incorporated in full in a new [*Ausbildungsvorschrift für die Fusstruppen im Kriege* (AVF) (Training Manual for the Foot Troops in War)]. It may be that the opposition had led him to question the wisdom of some of the instructions given in [Bauer's] textbook and possibly accounts for the statement in his *War Memories* that [Bauer's] defensive-battle textbook was 'completed' by the [AVF] issued eight weeks later, although it contained such a contradictory doctrine for the conduct of the defence within the battle zone.[171]

The fact that Ludendorff not only permitted Lossberg to maintain his contrary views but even circulated them throughout the German Army suggests that Ludendorff was by no means dogmatic in his support of Bauer's doctrine. Ludendorff's main aim was to develop the most effective doctrine possible, regardless of its origins, and he believed that a free debate was the best means by which this could be achieved.

The other main objection to the doctrine of elastic defence in depth was based on the belief that the *Eingreif* divisions would not be able to launch their counterthrusts before the enemy had consolidated his position. The leading proponent of this view, General von Hoen, argued for a rigid forward defence designed to prevent enemy penetrations where possible, with the *Eingreif* divisions employing carefully planned counterattacks to eject those penetrations that did occur. Although Lossberg accepted the concept of the *Eingreif* divisions making counterthrusts, he too doubted whether these divisions could launch their attacks quickly enough.[172] On this point Ludendorff stood firm.

## The Perfection of Defence in Depth

Despite the number of pamphlets and training courses that the German high command employed in trying to disseminate the doctrine of elastic defence, many formations were slow to adopt the new concepts. This was probably due to a combination of a reluctance to decentralise command

and the narrow concentration on one's own sector of front noted by Moser. The urgent need to implement the new doctrine, and the dire consequences of a failure to do so, were graphically demonstrated at Verdun in December 1916 and at Arras in April 1917.

The French attack at Verdun on 15 December was the final act of that ten-month battle. After a methodical six-day bombardment twice as heavy as that at the start of the Somme, the French assaulted with eight divisions. The German defence collapsed: the entire battle zone and its garrison of 14,000 men was lost. Ludendorff responded by sacking the army and corps commanders. The reasons for the disaster were simple: first, the garrison had remained in its deep dug-outs too long, allowing itself to be overrun; second, the reserve battalions and the *Eingreif* divisions had been held too far to the rear and had therefore arrived only after the French had consolidated their gains.[173] Both errors resulted from a failure to emphasise the importance of immediate responsiveness.

Although OHL issued a pamphlet on 25 December detailing the lessons of the Verdun battle, similar errors were made at Arras four months later. For a variety of reasons, the German defensive system along this sector of front had not been reconstructed as required by the new doctrine. In particular, the forward garrison was still employing deep dug-outs rather than the shallow *Mannschafts-Eisen-Beton-Unterstände* (MEBUs) (personnel reinforced-concrete shelters). The length of time required for troops to emerge from these deep dug-outs seriously reduced their immediate responsiveness. The commander of Sixth Army, General von Falkenhausen, intended to fight the battle in accordance with the more rigid principles advocated by von Hoen. Despite the fact that the strongpoints in the battle zone were obsolete both in design and distribution, it was emphasised that they 'were to be the main centres of resistance of the new defence system and that they were to be held at all costs, even though surrounded by the enemy, to make easier the counterattack by the troops from the back of the battle zone'.[174]

The British preparatory bombardment was again more than twice as heavy as on the Somme. Although relatively few casualties were caused, the German positions were obliterated and the garrison exhausted. After a final five-minute hurricane bombardment, the assault was launched at 5.30 a.m. on 9 April. The German front battalions were largely overrun before they could react. Parts of the support battalions suffered the same fate, but most of these troops hurriedly fell back to the rear of the battle zone where they halted and formed a rough line. Counterthrusts were out of the question, there being too few troops available. Surrounded and apparently abandoned, the garrisons of most of the forward strongpoints withdrew to this new line. Only a handful of the strongpoints were defended.[175] The battle had thus far shown the vital need for the forward garrison to occupy MEBUs rather than deep dug-outs, so that they could respond immediately to an attack. It had also demonstrated the ineffectiveness of static strongpoints.

Ludendorff's doctrine had been based on the expectation that the enemy would penetrate deep into the battle zone; indeed it had practically invited such an event. The enemy, far from artillery support and disorganised after the assault, would then be ripe for large-scale counterthrusts, conducted by the *Eingreif* divisions. Although five divisions were available at Arras, no such counterthrusts took place. Falkenhausen appears to have been convinced by the doubts expressed by Hoen and Lossberg regarding the feasibility of launching large-scale counterthrusts by the *Eingreif* divisions before the enemy could consolidate. He therefore held them well behind the battlefield, in order to relieve the front divisions after two days.[176] They were presumably to recapture the ground previously lost by means of a counterattack. Under this plan, any strongpoint surrounded in the battle zone would have to wait at least two days for relief, and this may account for the tendency for their garrisons to withdraw rather than try to hold out.

It soon became apparent that the defeat was caused by Sixth Army ignoring the new doctrine and not by any flaws in the doctrine itself.[177] As a sign that the concept of the *Eingreif* divisions had been fully accepted there were calls for each *Stellungsdivision* (position division) to be assigned its own *Eingreif* division, which Ludendorff was forced to reject on the grounds that the extra formations were not available.[178] Fortunately for the Germans, the British were unable to launch a co-ordinated attack to exploit their initial success until 14 April. By that time the defence had been transformed.

On the morning of 11 April, von Lossberg was appointed chief of staff of Sixth Army. Since First Army, his previous posting, held the sector on the left of Sixth Army, Lossberg was well aware of the situation around Arras. He demanded, and was granted, *Vollmacht*[179] over the defence on the Sixth Army front, in order, Wynne believed, to allow himself to ignore Ludendorff's new doctrine and employ his own more rigid system.[180] Lossberg followed his usual practice of conducting a personal reconnaissance of the front before making his plan for the defence. The first formation he visited was XIV Reserve Corps, commanded by Moser.[181] This may have been of some importance for Lossberg's subsequent decisions, for Moser had put Ludendorff's doctrine into full effect and had repulsed with ease a British attack around Bullecourt. The success of the new doctrine in its first test must have made an impression on Lossberg, who had previously rejected it as demanding too much from the troops. Leaving Moser, Lossberg visited the two other corps headquarters, several divisional headquarters, a number of artillery observation points and finally walked to the foremost line. The importance of this personal observation of the battlefield, at considerable physical risk, can scarcely be overestimated. As a consequence of this tour of inspection, Lossberg modified his opposition to granting flexibility to the forward garrison and accepted that a rigid defence was not possible in the circumstances along part of the battlefield.[182]

The defensive system as reorganised by Lossberg[183] is of particular interest because in it he made use of both competing doctrines of defence. South of the River Scarpe, he used his extraordinary eye for ground to identify an almost continuous reverse-slope battlefield some 12 miles long. Along most of this sector, the battle was to be fought in accordance with the doctrine which he had developed in Champagne and on the Somme. This doctrine relied on separating the attacker's artillery barrage from his infantry in a battle zone out of sight of the enemy's observers.

The conditions necessary for this were not available in certain parts of the southern sector and were altogether absent north of the river, where British control of the Vimy Ridge gave observation over the entire German position. In these circumstances, the British would be able to ensure that their infantry enjoyed the protection of an observed barrage right up to the limits of field artillery range. Almost any form of defence, rigid or mobile, would simply be pulverised in this sector. Lossberg therefore adopted a variant of Ludendorff's doctrine in these vulnerable sectors. A lightly held battle zone would compel the British to launch a full-scale attack, in the face of which the Germans would withdraw. At the rear of the zone, by which point the British infantry would have outrun their artillery support and be exhausted and disorganised, the bulk of the defenders were to launch a powerful counterthrust. Fresh, and with heavy artillery support, the German infantry would drive the British back to their original positions, relying on intermingling with the enemy to avoid the British artillery fire. Lossberg admitted that the tactic was risky, but argued that it was the only possible method in the circumstances.

In the exposed sectors, the disrupting effect previously produced by the system of rigidly held strongpoints was now largely achieved by fire alone. The first element in this was *Vernichtungsfeuer* (annihilating fire) by the artillery on the enemy's trenches and on no-man's-land as soon as an attack began. The second element was fire from heavy machine guns, which were no longer static in defended localities, but were to provide mobile fire support within the battle zone. The 15-gun sharpshooter units, one of which was allocated to each division, were deployed at the rear of the battle zone to act as a rallying line and to provide fire support for the *Eingreif* divisions. The garrison was deployed in depth, in order to make the enemy more vulnerable to fire as he exposed his flanks and so that troops could be held back for counterthrusts. The defenders were carefully camouflaged, making accurate fire direction more difficult for the British artillery and allowing the German soldiers to achieve surprise against the British infantry attacks.

The main means of holding ground was large-scale counterthrusts by the *Eingreif* divisions. The relative deployment of forces between the forward zone, the battle zone and behind the battle zone was now 2:2:5. The troops gathered behind the battle zone in readiness to launch the counterthrust from behind the position, therefore, now numbered more than half of the total defenders. Although Lossberg was somewhat unwilling to decentralise command over the *Eingreif* divisions, the necessity for their intervention in the battle being made at precisely the right moment led him to devise a system by which a single code-word from the front divisions would start the *Eingreif* divisions forward, once they had been released by the army headquarters.

Almost as soon as he had finished making these dispositions, in which he accepted the basic validity of Ludendorff's doctrine, Lossberg modified his orders. As it became clear that the British would not be able to support their attacks with the overwhelming artillery fire that had been feared, Lossberg saw less reason to modify his former insistence on a rigid defence. The defence was therefore altered, with elastic defence allowed only in those few areas best suited to counterthrusts.[184] Both systems proved effective, as was shown by the fate of two attacks made on 14 April. On that day, the British VII and VI Corps each made an attack with two battalions designed to seize hills from which much of the German defensive system could be observed, in preparation for a general advance.

The VII Corps attack[185] was undertaken by Queen Victoria's Rifles (QVR) and Queens' Westminster Rifles (QWR) of 56th Division, the objective being Hill 92 on the Wancourt Tower Ridge. Opposing the assault were three companies of Infanterie-Regiment 61, deployed in a scattered mass of small posts. The defensive zone lay on a reverse slope devoid of natural cover and was, for this reason, to be held rigidly, rather than by means of Bauer's mobile defence in depth. Since the crest of the ridge was in their hands, the Germans rightly assumed that the British would not have been able to locate their defensive dispositions. This was well known to the British troops also, with the consequence that, as the QVR history records, 'to most of us the enterprise appeared to be over-rash'. With little information as to where the enemy actually were, the preliminary bombardment 'only had the effect of warning the Germans that an attack was on foot'. The assault, at 5.30 a.m., was swiftly repulsed. The QWR history reports, 'As soon as the leading waves of infantry had gone over the Tower Ridge and started down the further slope they were met by murderous machine-gun fire. . . . There were hardly any survivors from the leading waves.' The QVR history notes that the attacking infantry quickly lost touch with the supporting barrage, 'with the result that our men . . . were at the mercy of the German infantry and machine guns, who were able to come up from cover and open a devastating fire'. By 8.00 a.m., the Germans had regained complete control of the defensive system. Casualties were 629 British (two-thirds of the attacking force) to 49 Germans.

The VI Corps attack[186] was delivered by the Newfoundland and 1/Essex battalions of the 29th Division, with orders to capture Infantry Hill, an advance of about 1,200 yards. Holding the defences here were troops of 3rd Bavarian Division, principally from Bayerisches-Infanterie-Regiment 23. The forward zone consisted of two shallow trenches and was under British observation. The battle zone behind it, however, was shielded from view by Infantry Hill and was filled by small copses and depressions, which provided ample cover for counterthrust forces. The attack was preceded by an hour-long artillery bombardment, which caused many of the defenders of the forward zone to withdraw or move to the flank. The British infantry attacked at 5.30 a.m. and found little opposition. After pausing to consolidate on the German front line, the British resumed their advance, the Germans falling back before it, and reached their objectives at about 7.00 a.m. Believing the operation over, the troops began to dig in.

At this point, a German artillery barrage on no-man's-land cut the attackers off from support and severed telephone communications with their guns. Soon afterwards a small body of German infantry moved from the flank to recapture the old front line, thereby sealing the breach. Trapped within the defensive system and out of sight of artillery observers, the men of the Newfoundland and 1/Essex battalions on the reverse slope of Infantry Hill found themselves engaged by fire and counterthrusts from three sides. One hundred and fifty British troops surrendered and the remainder fled back over the crest of the hill, only to be shot down. An essential factor of this stage in the action was the way in which each German company operated on its own initiative within the context of the whole. Since the troops were never left idle, waiting for orders, the defenders were able to maintain the momentum of their operations and so retain tempo and prevent the British recovering their balance. The Bavarian regimental histories note that the men now saw the value of the four months spent in training for the new defensive tactics and were convinced of their superiority to the British, despite the latter's advantages of material and ammunition.

By 10.15 a.m. the Germans had regained their positions, captured 300 prisoners and 20 machine guns, and inflicted 1,148 casualties (out of 1,514 attackers). German losses are impossible to determine but were almost certainly fewer than 500 men. Since the greater part of the battle took place on a reverse slope, as far as the British were concerned, two entire battalions had simply been swallowed whole by the German defensive system. Similar events occurred throughout the remainder of the British offensive, as the British high command failed to grasp the importance of reverse-slope positions and attacked only the strongest parts of the German line. Such was von Lossberg's disbelief at this British policy that he maintained his strongest reserves in the north, where the British enjoyed excellent observation over the German defences, which were therefore very vulnerable, rather than the south, where the British actually attacked and were consistently repulsed.[187]

Early in June, OHL issued a pamphlet of lessons learnt from the British and French offensives in April (Arras) and May (the Nivelle offensive),[188] which again emphasised the importance of depth, invisibility and immediate counterthrusts. The most interesting feature of this pamphlet is that it appears to reveal a change in attitude towards the decentralisation of command among many officers. Perhaps the most important of these officers was Lossberg himself. In his pamphlet 'Experience of the German First Army in the Somme Battle', he had emphasised the importance of retaining cohesion in the defence in such a way that battalion commanders could still direct their units as a whole.[189] This had been written as a direct rebuttal to Bauer's pamphlet, 'Principles of Command in the Defensive Battle in Position War', which proposed to replace the battalion with the section as the basic tactical unit.[190] Now, only six months after opposing moves to extend decentralisation of command below battalion level, Lossberg was a key figure in the writing of a new pamphlet that actively advocated such decentralisation. Such had been the effect of his experience at Arras that Lossberg was again prepared to abandon views he had previously championed, now that he had been proved incorrect.

The OHL pamphlet stated that commanders must exercise their initiative and conduct an active defence. Lower level commanders must be given 'a certain amount' of freedom in choosing tactics. While troops should hold on if surrounded, the pamphlet stated that few positions should be held rigidly and that a timely withdrawal would not harm morale. Lossberg's former contention that morale would be strengthened by a grimly determined defence was replaced by a call for an active and aggressive stance. The counterthrust was central to this and must become second nature. It was not the numbers committed but rather the way in which they were handled that was decisive.[191] Although Lossberg and his supporters clearly still had reservations about the flexibility inherent in Ludendorff's doctrine, shown by lower commanders being given only 'a certain amount' of freedom, the experience of Arras and the Nivelle offensive, both of which had shown that those troops that fell back remained effective whereas those that held their ground were overrun, had convinced them that such freedom was both effective and necessary. They may have been reassured by the extensive training programme introduced by Ludendorff to improve the quality of the German troops and so make the soldiers better able to implement the new doctrine.

On 8 June 1917, Lossberg was again appointed chief of staff of a defeated army. This time he went to Fourth Army, which had been forced out of its positions on the Messines Ridge on the previous day. This defeat was partly because the local commander had failed to provide adequate forces for the counterthrust from behind the position and partly because of overwhelming British material superiority, including mines that obliterated the German forward zone at the start of the battle.[192] The British preparations for the Passchendaele offensive, which again ignored the importance of artillery observation, were clearly visible to the Germans even before Messines. Lossberg therefore had almost two months in which to formulate his defensive scheme before the British attacked again on 31 July. He spent two weeks in careful observation of the prospective battlefield and analysis of tactics before issuing an order on 27 June in which he detailed the method by which the battle was to be fought.[193] This order shows that he intended to employ a modified version of the doctrine he had developed on the Somme.

The basis of the defence was to be the counterthrust from behind the position by the *Eingreif* divisions. The organisation employed for these formations was adapted from that of the Roman legions of the third century BC.[194] As in the Roman system, the defence was organised into three sections. The first, the *hastati*, denoted the forward garrison and was to face the initial attack. The second section, the *principes*, consisted of one regiment from each *Eingreif* division, which was held ready to launch an immediate counterthrust from behind the position. Since Frederick the Great had used a similar system, this section was also referred to as *Fredericus Rex*. The final section, the *triarii*, was made up of the remainder of the *Eingreif* divisions, which were held well back and under cover in order to keep the troops fresh. In battle, if the *principes* were called upon to launch a counterthrust, their place would immediately be taken by a regiment of the *triarii*. By this means, the troops of the *Eingreif* divisions were kept fresh, yet a constant flow of forces was maintained available for immediate use in a counterthrust. These counterthrusts were to be carefully prepared in advance: all leaders down to company level were to make a personal reconnaissance of the ground and maps giving the detailed deployment of the front divisions were to be held by the *Eingreif* divisions.

Enemy troops who penetrated the defensive position were temporarily disordered, in unknown ground and without artillery support. They were therefore vulnerable to counterthrust. The vital importance of seizing this opportunity quickly was emphasised by Lossberg calling for '*den sofortigen Gegenstoss*' (the instant immediate-counterthrust). The enemy was to be given no time to consolidate. After the British had been driven out of the position, the *Eingreif* forces were to be withdrawn and the previous deployments restored as soon as possible in order to avoid an over-dense forward garrison.

In contrast to Ludendorff's doctrine, the attacker was not to be drawn into the depths of the position but was to be repulsed by the front garrison if possible. It was only because he accepted that the front garrison could not normally achieve this, given the dispersion forced by the weight of the enemy artillery fire, that Lossberg placed so much emphasis on the counterthrust from behind the position. Even though the enemy would probably enter the defensive system, 'nevertheless the garrison, even of the foremost line of shell-holes, must fight in their positions till the last man, and even though surrounded'.[195] Lossberg also ordered, however, that these troops must not remain in their trenches but must employ assault squad tactics to conduct an aggressive and mobile battle within the battle area assigned to them. While a few troops were designated as permanent garrisons and were not to take part in the counterthrust from within the position, even these were not to be static.

Lossberg's order of 27 June reveals that the differences between his doctrine and Ludendorff's had narrowed considerably as a result of the experience gained at Arras. Lossberg now trusted junior commanders sufficiently to allow them limited freedom of movement. His main disagreement with Ludendorff was that he did not believe the troops capable of withdrawing under fire in order to draw the enemy into the position and considered that this would simply result in the collapse of the forward defence.

The events of 31 July showed that Lossberg's compromise was effective. The major British attack that opened the Passchendaele offensive was delayed and disordered by the forward defenders and thrown out of the main battle zone by the *Eingreif* divisions.[196] Lossberg had reached a compromise between his own previous idea of fighting in and for the foremost line and Bauer's idea of fighting behind that line. Lossberg's solution was to do both: the front divisions fought in the front line, the *Eingreif* divisions fought behind it. Although 31 July was in many respects a German victory, the British had seized the forward battle zone and had captured 6,000 prisoners. Total German casualties were probably similar to those suffered by the British, who lost 30,000 men. While the British had not been able to capture their objectives, preventing them from so doing had cost the Germans dearly.

The next major British attack was on 16 August. The German defence was little changed, but the British commanders had abandoned hope of a deep penetration because of the waterlogged condition of the ground and aimed for an advance of only about 3,000 yards. As before, the British were able to seize the forward battle zone but instead of pressing on they then dug in. The *Eingreif* divisions arrived only after the British had consolidated and were repulsed.[197] The British had discovered a counter to the German defensive doctrine. Strong attacks with limited objectives could seize the German forward battle zone and eliminate its garrison, and then defeat the *Eingreif* divisions. This would shift the balance of casualties in favour of the British and so enable them to wear down the German reserves preparatory to a decisive attack. Further, the knowledge that the forward garrison would almost inevitably be eliminated would have serious effects on the morale of the German troops. The third major British attack, on 20 September, followed this pattern precisely.[198]

The German high command believed that the tactics they had employed on 31 July provided the most effective means of repulsing an enemy attack aiming for a breakthrough. Even after the defeat on 16 August, Ludendorff issued a pamphlet underlining the value of this doctrine.[199] He was, however, concerned at these British successes and discussed tactics with the local commanders after each British attack.[200] The Germans realised that the tactics required to defeat a breakthrough attack were not an appropriate counter to a limited attack. The solution appeared to be a partial reversion to the earlier doctrine of a rigid defence of the front line by large numbers of troops. The *Eingrief* divisions would now be employed to make prepared counterattacks against enemy consolidations.[201] Ludendorff disagreed with this change, but felt compelled to accept the opinions of the officers fighting the battle.[202] The revised tactics proved a total failure. The British attack on 4 October enjoyed such overwhelming artillery support that the massed defenders were shattered and easily overrun. Casualties were enormous and the defenders proved unable to prevent the British gaining all their objectives. The new methods were immediately abandoned.[203]

The system employed on 4 October had failed because it had not taken into account the overwhelming material superiority enjoyed by the British. It was precisely this material superiority that had compelled the Germans to develop the principles of area defence, invisibility and immediate responsiveness. The solution to the problems posed by the new British tactics was not a reversion to old practices but rather an extension of these principles. Ludendorff identified the central problem: 'The power of the attack lay in the artillery, and in the fact that ours did not do enough damage to the hostile infantry as they were assembling, and, above all, at the actual time of the assault.'[204] The key to the change was an alteration in the function of the forward zone.[205] Previously just the area between the front line and the main defensive system, it was now to play a vital role. The zone had a depth of between 500 and 1,000 metres and was held by at most two or three platoons on a regimental front. In normal circumstances, these troops would block enemy attempts to send patrols forward to locate the main defensive position. The new order laid down that, in the event of a major attack, the garrison was to fall back 500 metres to the *Widerstandslinie der Vorfeldzone* (line of resistance of the forward zone). This action had the effect of making no-man's-land substantially wider.

The tactic of widening no-man's-land just before a major attack had two main advantages. First, the Germans noted that the British barrage was at its most intense for the first 500 metres behind the front line but was considerably less intense beyond this zone. By voluntarily withdrawing from this area, the Germans ensured that the most powerful portion of the British barrage fell harmlessly into empty space, a classic employment of area defence. The only effect of this expenditure of ammunition was to make the ground almost impassable for the British infantry. Second, it provided a wide zone in which the German artillery could engage the British infantry without fear of hitting friendly forces. This fire, combined with that of the front battalions, could disrupt the British attack even before it reached the main defensive zone.

Having in this way avoided much of the British fire and begun to disrupt the attack, the Germans could then conduct the rest of the defence on the same principles as on 31 July. It was found, however, that stronger forces were required for the counterthrust from behind the position and Ludendorff was eventually compelled to assign a complete *Eingreif* division to each front division.[206] At this time the power of the front division commander was increased by his being given full command over the *Eingrief* division assigned to him, regardless of the relative seniority of the two commanding officers.[207] The new system proved itself over the last month of Passchendaele: although the British captured Passchendaele village, they never again inflicted a serious reverse on the Germans and seized only a waterlogged wasteland of limited military value. Ludendorff therefore ordered the system to be adopted along the entire Western Front.[208]

The doctrine finally perfected after three years of development was a masterpiece of flexibility, perfectly suited to the system of attack used against it. The process of development provides an excellent example of the dynamic interplay between theory and practice and between command and training in the evolution of new tactics. Although the final system was very similar to that advocated by Bauer and Geyer early in 1915, their theory had been tested and modified by experience on the battlefield. The importance of personal observation of conditions on the ground by senior officers cannot be overemphasised. It was this constant first-hand experience of the realities of battle in the forward positions that convinced officers such as von Lossberg that Bauer's ideas were fundamentally correct and were the only effective solution to the problems of the defence in position warfare.

The initial theory developed by Bauer and Geyer was beyond the capabilities of the German Army to put into practice. It demanded commanders at every level to direct their forces with minimal guidance for above and required troops to perform complex manoeuvres on their own initiative and while under heavy fire. The scepticism of many officers was not unfounded. It was only through a major programme of training, in which everyone from private to general was taught how to fulfil their own part in the doctrine, that the Germans were able to bring that doctrine into effective reality.

# 7
# 'Blob' Defence

> The general organisation of the defence was adapted from the Germans, as laid down in the manual *Allgemeines über Stellenbau* [General Principles of the Construction of Field Positions] issued . . . on 15th Aug[ust] 1917. This book, copies of which were captured soon after issue, summed up the enemy's experiences after nearly three years' defensive warfare on the Western Front.
>
> Brigadier-General J. E. Edmonds,
> *The Official History of the Great War: Military Operations: France and Belgium, 1918*

By December 1917, it was clear that the British Army was unlikely to be able to conduct major offensive action during 1918. Haig had calculated that the BEF would require 615,000 replacements during that year if the current tempo of operations was to be kept up. He was offered 100,000.[1] The situation of Britain's allies was similarly unfavourable. The French Army had suffered serious mutinies after the failure of the Nivelle offensive in April and could now be relied upon for no more than minor offensive operations. The Italian Army, worn out by its own failed offensives, had collapsed at Caporetto with the loss of over 300,000 casualties. Eleven British and French divisions had to be sent to restore the front. Most seriously, the entire Eastern Front had disintegrated, with both Russia and Romania suing for peace. The only glimmer of hope was that the Americans were coming. Eight months after its declaration of war in April 1917, however, the United States had only 130,000 troops in France.[2] It was estimated that by August 1918 the effective force available would have increased only to 18 divisions.[3]

As a consequence of the defeat of Russia, Germany enjoyed a temporary numerical superiority over its enemies. Between November 1917 and 21 March 1918, the Germans redeployed 40 divisions from the Eastern Front to bring the total in the west to 192,[4] where they faced 159 French and British divisions.[5] This advantage would be steadily reduced as the American troops arrived during 1918. The Entente Powers could therefore expect vigorous offensive action by the Germans at an early date. Haig accordingly assembled his four army commanders on 3 December 1917 and instructed them to 'give their immediate and personal attention to the organisation of the zones for defensive purposes and to the rest and training of their troops'.[6]

## The Existing Defences

The *Official History* noted the scale of the task:

> There was much to be done before the British front could be considered adequately prepared to meet a serious enemy offensive. During the previous two years and more all the thoughts and energies of the British Armies in France had been concentrated on attack and in consequence defensive arrangements had to some extent been neglected. Troops and labour had been massed on the offensive fronts, whereas the garrisons on the rest of the line had been reduced to the strength necessary to deal with local operations. Since these were unlikely to be of an important character as long as a British offensive was being seriously pressed elsewhere, the garrisons had been usually too weak in numbers to do more than keep in repair those defences which were actually in occupation.[7]

The state of the British defensive doctrine may be illustrated by an examination of the German attack at Vimy Ridge on 21 May 1916.

After the battle of the Marne, the Germans occupied strong defensive positions along the Vimy Ridge. The French made repeated efforts to seize the ridge but met with little success. The last attack, which ended in October 1915, reached the crest line at one point, only for it to be lost to a German counterattack in February 1916. After this, the Germans held the entire crest of the ridge, except for a short stretch in no-man's-land.[8] When the British took over responsibility for the sector in March, they were concerned at the excellent observation over the entire defensive system enjoyed by the Germans, although this advantage was partly offset by the fact that the maze of old works behind the British lines allowed the reserves and artillery to conceal their locations and to draw the German artillery fire against empty positions by making them appear occupied. Further forward, the infantry works were very weak and consisted of a line of posts only. The British tended to see this as a sign of French carelessness, whereas it was in fact a consequence of the French doctrine of defence primarily by artillery fire not manpower.[9] The weakness of the defences was increased further by the extent of German mining operations, which threatened to obliterate the British positions at a single stroke.

Once the state of the defence became clear, Haig ordered Allenby, whose Third Army held the Vimy sector, to adopt a system of outposts supported by strongpoints and to select a better position to the rear.[10] Such a position already existed, 3,500 yards behind the current front line. It appears that Haig intended that this should become the new front line and that the area in front should be abandoned to the enemy. The new line would then be held by the doctrine of rigid linear defence. It is of interest that Haig does not appear to have considered the possibility of holding the existing front line and the area behind it as an outpost zone with the main line of resistance on the more favourable ground 3,500 yards behind. Such a system would have had similarities to that adopted by the German Third Army in Champagne during 1915 and which was fully described in pamphlets captured and translated by the British.[11] Such a system would have enjoyed considerable defensive strength. First, there were great possibilities for camouflage among the numerous old positions in the outpost zone. Second, the main defences would have been at the limit of range of German field guns deployed behind the Vimy Ridge, making a heavy barrage difficult to achieve and keeping British guns relatively free from counterbattery fire. Third, any German advance would be in full view of the British gunners, allowing them to engage the attackers long before they reached the main defences. As in the French system, the outpost zone could be held lightly with most of the defensive strength being supplied by artillery fire. The sector could therefore have been garrisoned by a relatively small force yet with considerable security, releasing forces for use in counterthrusts or for offensive operations elsewhere.

Not only did Haig not consider adopting such a defensive system, he almost immediately rescinded the order to retire to stronger positions in the rear and instructed Allenby to maintain the existing line. To withdraw was considered unacceptable because it would involve abandoning ground the French had suffered considerable losses to capture. Haig also wished to deceive the Germans into thinking that the British were about to launch an offensive on the Vimy sector, as a cover for the preparations for the actual attack on the Somme. Finally, he desired 'that the principle of aggression should be instilled into the troops'. The British therefore did not prepare a defensive line to the rear but remained in their exposed positions and adopted a vigorous programme of mining and raiding. The strain on the troops was considerable and was reflected in the 1,200 casualties suffered in this sector in the following five weeks.[12]

Despite these casualties, the British miners enjoyed considerable success and caused the Germans some anxiety. The temporary commander of this sector, General von Freytag-Loringhoven, otherwise Deputy CGS, decided to resolve the situation by driving the British off the ridge by means of a limited attack. Freytag-Loringhoven's considerable influence allowed him to build up a powerful force of artillery and a large supply of ammunition for this attack.[13] The troops holding the British front line suspected an attack was imminent because of the systematic destruction of their positions by the German artillery, but no action was taken by senior commanders on the grounds that aerial photographs did not show any preparations.[14]

The Germans attacked on the evening of 21 May. The co-ordination of the British defence was hindered by the coincidental fact that a minor adjustment of boundaries within the BEF on the previous day meant that the sector assaulted was transferred from one army to another, resulting in a total change of garrison and chain of command. The new garrison was provided by 140th and 141st Brigades of 47th Division, which held the 2,000-yard-wide divisional sector with five battalions. Because the Germans had excellent observation over the British forward positions, it had been found necessary to hold the front line with outposts only and keep the bulk of the defenders in the support line well down the slope to the rear.[15] Even here, movement was dangerous and communication with the outpost line was possible only under cover of darkness.[16] Despite the weakness of the defences, the entire garrison was deployed here. The local reserves were billeted several miles to the rear and were not immediately available.

The Germans prepared the attack with a four-hour bombardment with 70,000 shells. The front defences were obliterated, the British field guns were suppressed and the villages in which the reserves were billeted were demolished. When the German infantry attacked at 7.45 p.m., they found the defences of 140th Brigade shattered. The British mine heads were seized with little difficulty and a new line consolidated along the British support trench. Resistance was greater on the flanks, where the bombardment had been less effective, but the objectives were taken.[17] The British rigid defence had proved unable to prevent the Germans seizing most of the defences on the 140th Brigade front at little cost, the dense garrison having been largely eliminated by the preparatory bombardment.

Minor counterthrusts were made by the front battalion reserves, but these were too weak to delay the German attack.[18] A few companies from brigade reserve were committed at 2.00 p.m. on 22 May, over six hours after the initial German attack, but found the enemy already dug in. The British made no further counterattacks until the evening of 23 May, almost 48 hours after the German assault. An attack by three brigades planned for 1.30 a.m. on 23 May was postponed until 8.25 p.m., because the preparations were considered insufficient. Surprise was not achieved: the German artillery bombarded the British infantry as it formed up and the German infantry repulsed most of the assaults and soon ejected those few enemy soldiers who succeeded in entering their positions. After this failure, the British decided that the forces required to recapture the lost ground were needed more urgently elsewhere and so the sector became quiet. Total casualties were 2,475 British and 1,344 German.[19]

This operation showed the nature of British defence doctrine and revealed some of its faults. The British generally relied on a rigid defence of the foremost line, although the main line of defence might be the support trench if the front trench was particularly unfavourably placed, as at Vimy. This line was held by the majority of the defenders as a continuous position, relying on the firepower of rifles rather than of machine guns. No flexibility of movement was allowed to the defenders, most of whom were required to hold their positions rigidly. The vulnerability of these troops to artillery fire was not appreciated even though it greatly reduced the strength of the linear defence.

The location of positions was determined primarily by considerations other than that of defence. The suitability of a position for possible offensive action in the future and a belief that the voluntary abandonment of ground was an admission of failure were often factors of greater importance in the placing of positions than whether a line was suitable for defence. One consequence was that the British trenches were usually overlooked by the Germans, who had deliberately placed their positions on commanding ground. When coupled with the doctrine of rigid forward defence this resulted in the British suffering heavy casualties, which reduced morale and constituted a constant drain on the physical and mental strength of the BEF, so reducing its offensive capability.

A second characteristic of the British doctrine was that there was little capability to respond to an enemy attack that overcame the rigid resistance of the front-line garrison. At Vimy, the only reserves immediately available were a few companies in brigade reserve and even these could not be committed until more than six hours after the German attack. Even where reserves were available, commanders were often unwilling to commit them without explicit permission from above.[20] At Vimy, the British required more than two days to mount a co-ordinated counterattack and even this was largely unsuccessful.

## The Jeudwine Committee

Once the British realised that they would have to spend much of 1918 on the defensive, it became a matter of vital urgency for an up-to-date doctrine for defence to be adopted and put into practice, since it was clear that the existing system of rigid linear defence was inadequate to cope with the major German attacks that could be expected. It has been said that imitation is the sincerest form of flattery: having spent three years in unsuccessful attempts to penetrate the German lines, the British concluded that there must be some value in the enemy's doctrine of defence. Accordingly, Haig decided that the BEF would use the German doctrine against the Germans themselves.

Haig set up a committee of three senior officers to examine the German doctrine and to adapt it to British use. The *Official History* mentions this committee only briefly and gives no indication as to the officers' identities.[21] Fortunately, the unpublished memoirs of Brigadier-General Sir James Edmonds reveal that the officers were Major-General Jeudwine, Brigadier-General McMullen and Edmonds himself.[22] Major-General Sir Hugh Jeudwine was described by Edmonds as 'the most experienced divisional commander'. An artilleryman, he had experience of staff work at division and corps level and had commanded 55th Division since its formation on the Western Front early in 1916.[23] Brigadier-General C. N. McMullen was chief of staff of XIX Corps.[24] His previous post had been in the Operations Section of Fifth Army, where he had been involved in the planning for Passchendaele.[25] Colonel J. E. Edmonds was one of the most brilliant staff officers in the army. After distinguished service in the General Staff at the War Office and as chief of staff of 4th Division, he had joined the office of the Engineer-in-Chief, GHQ, at the end of 1914.[26] The three officers therefore had experience of command at the divisional level, staff duties at corps and army level, and field engineering.

Edmonds recorded that the committee was required to advise on the best way to defend against a German offensive.[27] It might be expected that the first stage of its work would have been to analyse the probable form of such an offensive. Questions such as the amount of warning of an attack that might be received, the length of front that would be attacked, the depth of the objectives assigned to the German troops and the tactics employed by the enemy infantry and artillery in breaking through the British line were all of vital importance in determining the system of defence that should be adopted. No such analysis appears to have been made. Instead, the committee concentrated solely on adapting the German doctrine for British use. In so doing they ignored the fact that this doctrine had been developed to counter British offensives whose location had often been apparent weeks before the guns opened fire and which had relied on prolonged saturation bombardments to shepherd forward infantry using linear tactics. The recent German attacks at Riga, Caporetto and Cambrai should have made it clear that the enemy would employ an offensive doctrine quite different from that of the BEF. The suitability of the Germans' defensive doctrine to meet their new offensive doctrine was questionable.

Having made one error of omission, the committee compounded their mistake by making a further error. Rather than analyse the substantial body of information available on the German doctrine in order to discover its workings, the committee concentrated on only one manual, *Allgemeines über Stellenbau*, which it considered 'summed up the enemy's experiences after nearly three years' defensive warfare on the Western Front'.[28]

Unfortunately, this manual was in fact not directly concerned with the German defensive doctrine at all and was in any case completely out of date by the time the committee met.

*Allgemeines über Stellenbau* (General Principles of the Construction of Field Positions, hereafter *Construction*) was, as its title suggests, a field engineers' manual. It therefore dealt only with the layout of the defensive zone, the design and positioning of field works within that zone, and the execution of construction plans. The manual did not discuss such vital factors as the deployment of the garrison, the tactics it was to employ nor the means by which the battle should be directed. Curiously, the Jeudwine committee was aware of the German manual covering the actual conduct of the defence, *Die Führung der Abwehr im Stellungskrieg* (The Principles of Command in the Defensive Battle in Position Warfare, hereafter *Command*) and indeed drew attention to it in its report.[29] Despite this, the committee acted as if *Command* was merely a supplement to *Construction* rather than the reverse.

The committee may have been misled by the designations given to the two manuals by the Germans. Both documents were part of the *Sammelheft der Vorschriften für den Stellungskrieg*[30] which took the form of a ring binder into which the various regulations for position war could be inserted. This format had been adopted by the German Army in order to allow individual manuals to be readily up-dated and replaced without the need to republish the entire range of manuals for position war. The numbers assigned to the individual manuals were no guide as to their relative importance. It is possible that the Jeudwine committee did not appreciate this fact. If so, this may account for *Construction*, numbered Part 1a, being considered more important than *Command*, numbered Part 8.

A possible further factor in the decision of the committee to concentrate on *Construction* is the position of Edmonds. Although the most junior in rank of the three officers in 1917, Edmonds had been the most senior in 1914.[31] Ill health had blocked further promotion. Edmonds had spent most of the war at GHQ and was close to many of the army's most senior commanders, including Haig and Allenby, several of whom had been his contemporaries at the Staff College. Added to this, Edmonds had a reputation for great intelligence, reflected in his nickname, Archimedes. As a result, it is likely that he enjoyed an influence over his colleagues far greater than his rank might suggest. Edmonds was an engineer by training and he approached the German doctrine from this perspective. This may account for his considering the physical layout of the defences as central to that doctrine. His unpublished memoirs suggest that, even in the 1950s, he believed that field positions were indeed the basis of the German doctrine,[32] despite the fact that one of his assistants in writing the *Official History*, Captain G. C. Wynne, had demonstrated the true nature of the

German system in his book *If Germany Attacks*, published in 1940. The Jeudwine committee may have been swayed by Edmonds' opinion in its decision to rely mainly on *Construction*.

*Construction* was not only the wrong manual to copy, it was also out of date by December 1917. The edition used by the Jeudwine committee was the third edition, issued on 15 August 1917 and translated by the British on 12 December.[33] This edition had been rendered obsolete almost immediately by the considerable changes made in the German doctrine after the British attack of 16 August.[34] The same error was made with *Command*. The edition used was the second, issued on 1 March 1917 and translated by the British in May,[35] which pre-dated not only Passchendaele but also Arras. It therefore took no account of the major alterations made to the German defensive doctrine during those two battles. These were sufficiently great as to require a third edition of the manual to be issued on 1 September 1917 and even this was amended on 23 October.[36] The edition of 1 March was therefore completely out of date by the time the Jeudwine committee examined it in December 1917.

This reliance on old German material, rather than an analysis of the enemy's current methods, was typical of GHQ. Edmonds himself appears to have appreciated this error when he came to write the *Official History*. In 1939, he noted,

> The secret of the defeat of the enemy methods, acquired by costly experiment in a series of combats . . . might instead have been learnt by a closer study of the changes in the German defensive and offensive battle.
>
> In May 1917, French GQG formed a special (instruction) section . . . which was charged with the study of the enemy's tactics in offence and defence. . . . No attempt was made [by the British] to forecast and provide against possible variations in the enemy's tactics, although in 1915, 1916, 1917 and 1918 they were constantly changed, in fact, after every battle. . . .
>
> The General Staff [at] GHQ was content to translate such out-of-date enemy pamphlets on the defensive battle as fell into its hands and to issue instructions for future action based on them. No pamphlet on the defensive battle, however, was put forth until May 1918, when SS 210: The Division in Defence was published. In SS 135: The Training and Employment of Divisions 1918, published in January 1918, nothing whatever was said about defence except a short section on the 'organisation and strengthening of the captured position'. Although SS 135 dealt with attack, it contained no word about preparations to meet and foil the action of the German reserves (*Eingreifdivisionen*).[37]

The Jeudwine committee and the GHQ Operations Staff had no excuse for relying on out-of-date manuals. The GHQ Intelligence Branch had gathered a mass of information regarding German practice. The quality of much of the branch's work is indicated by the accuracy of the predictions it made regarding the form and location of the German counterattack on the opening day of Passchendaele, 31 July 1917.[38] Captain Wynne, who had access to many of the Intelligence Branch's papers, now secret or destroyed, noted,

> Their intelligence summaries showed perfectly correctly the disposition of the German defence forces in practically every engagement. Captured documents, such as the German 'Instructions for a Counterattack Organised in Depth', translated, printed and circulated by GHQ on 29 July 1917, and 'The Employment of Counterattack Troops', on 30 August 1917, could have left no possible doubt as to the main feature of the new German defensive battle. These and the excellent intelligence summaries and situation maps showed distinctly that its first essential was a weak garrison in the forward and battle zones with the bulk of the defence forces organised in depth behind the battle zone for the immediate counterattack.[39]

Having analysed the two German manuals, the Jeudwine Committee concluded that there was not enough time for the poorly trained British troops to master the German doctrine[40] and a simplified version of the German system was proposed.[41] The existing front line was to be held as an outpost line. It would be thinly garrisoned and would be abandoned in the face of a heavy attack. Behind this was to be a zone 4,000 yards wide over which would be scattered strongpoints and machine-gun posts, which were to be held rigidly even when surrounded. The rear of this zone was marked by the line of resistance. This line, which was usually to be out of enemy field artillery range, was to be held rigidly by the bulk of the garrison. If any part of this line was lost to the enemy, supports and local reserves held under cover to the rear were to recapture it by counterattack.

The committee's recommendations offered little improvement on existing practice. Indeed, the committee noted that the line of resistance might sometimes coincide with the outpost line, making the system no different from the existing doctrine. An examination of the recommendations as regards area defence, invisibility and immediate responsiveness reveals the weakness of the system proposed.

The one concession to area defence in the recommendations was the zone between the outpost and resistance lines and not even this was to be employed universally. The majority of the garrison was still to be concentrated in a linear deployment, making the troops highly vulnerable to enemy artillery fire. Although the line of resistance was to be out of range of the enemy's field guns, the number of heavy guns available to the Germans was sufficient to cause severe casualties to defenders in dense linear formations. The latest German concept of using the outpost zone as an artillery barrage zone, detailed in a document translated by the Intelligence Branch shortly before the Jeudwine Committee sat, was entirely passed over. The presence of numerous strongpoints and machine-gun posts between the two lines prevented the outpost zone being used in this way by the British.

In the German system, invisibility was considered vital to reduce the effectiveness of enemy artillery fire and to allow counterthrusts to be launched unexpectedly. The concept was omitted by Jeudwine's committee except in the recommendation that the supports and local reserves behind the line of resistance be held under cover. No mention was made of the importance of reverse-slope positions, while the strongpoints and machine-gun posts scattered between the two lines would have been clearly visible on aerial photographs.

Finally, the essence of the German system was its emphasis on immediate responsiveness. While ground might be given up temporarily and troops ordered to hold on even if surrounded, the intention was always that the entire position should be back in the defenders' hands at the close of the action. This not only maintained the integrity of the defence but also encouraged the forward defenders to hold out in the confidence that they would soon be relieved. Although the Jeudwine committee also intended that the entire position should be recaptured, few forces were allocated to the counterattack. No mention was made of the *Eingreif* divisions, whose role was so central to the German doctrine. Such was Edmonds' misunderstanding of the German system that, even in the 1950s, he believed the *Eingreif* divisions were introduced only in 1918 as a German development of the Jeudwine Committee's ideas which Jeudwine himself had employed in action in April of that year.[42]

Writing after the war, Captain Wynne derided the committee's recommendations, classing the system proposed as merely a delaying action rather than a true defensive action.[43] Given the system's weaknesses, this harsh judgement was well founded. Had the system been employed in March 1918, it is possible that the Germans might have broken through the British line with incalculable consequences.

## The GHQ Memorandum on Defensive Measures

GHQ rejected the recommendations made by the Jeudwine Committee, 'preferring to adopt the German system undiluted'.[44] Its understanding of that doctrine was published on 14 December 1917 as the GHQ

'Memorandum on Defensive Measures'.[45] In 1937, Wynne claimed that the authors of the memorandum,

> quite frankly adopted almost word for word the field position document [*Construction*], describing the organisation of the zones of defence and the fortified locality system as the basis of the new British defence tactics, and filled in the gaps about the conduct of the actual battle by taking whole sentences intact from General Ludendorff's textbook [*Command*].[46]

Although Wynne's claim that the GHQ Memorandum was an almost verbatim copy of the German pamphlets is exaggerated, a comparison of the British and German documents shows that the former was indeed based on the latter. Despite the great debt owed by the GHQ Memorandum to the German pamphlets, however, the British document omitted large parts of the German doctrine and altered others to such an extent as to make the system laid down by GHQ quite different from the German original. The first point to note is the brevity of the GHQ Memorandum, which fills little more than six pages of type. By comparison, the translation of *Construction* filled six and a half pages of text, while the translation of *Command* filled 17 pages. Even allowing for a degree of overlap between the two German pamphlets, the GHQ Memorandum was less than one-third the length of the German originals. Since the German documents are by no means long-winded, this inevitably meant that the GHQ Memorandum omitted a large proportion of the German material.

After a brief summary of the current strategic situation as a background for the need to stand on the defensive,[47] the GHQ Memorandum listed four main principles of defence. First, the defence must be conducted in an active manner, even in the face of superior numbers.[48] This appears to be a mixture of two quite separate principles given by the German documents. The first principle was given in *Command*[49] and instructed that commanders must not remain passive between enemy assaults but must make every effort to hamper enemy preparations. The GHQ Memorandum echoed this by ordering the use of raids, patrols and bombardments to the same end. The second principle came from *Construction*[50] and laid down that the defending troops must fight an active and mobile battle. This was interpreted in the GHQ Memorandum as calling for counter-attacks to be prepared in advance. The spontaneity of action and freedom of movement in the German pamphlet were omitted.

The second principle in the GHQ Memorandum was that of economy of force[51] and was again copied from *Command*.[52] The meaning given to the concept, however, was quite different. The German doctrine regarded economy of force as the achievement of effective defence with the minimum use of manpower through maximum reliance on firepower and efficient command, tactics and organisation. The British saw economy of force as the result of the construction of strong, well-sited defensive positions, which would require fewer men to hold them.[53] The Germans sought to use fewer men by improving the quality of their formations, while the British sought to achieve the same end by improving the quality of their positions.

The third principle was that of organisation in depth,[54] which applied not only to the infantry and machine guns but also to the artillery and mortars. This accorded fully with the relevant paragraph in *Construction*.[55] The GHQ Memorandum, however, omitted the second part of the German paragraph, which emphasised the importance of the system becoming ever stronger as the enemy penetrated deeper into the defences. The British therefore left out both the main function of defence in depth and also the idea that troops should tend to be deployed towards the rear of the defensive system.

The final principle was the importance of maintaining the confidence and fitness of the troops.[56] This principle, while sound, is so generally applicable that its inclusion as a specific principle of defence is surprising. It is of note that *Command* also listed four principles of defence, of which the British copied three. The fourth principle, omitted by the British, was that ground should be abandoned if it was no longer required by the tactical situation.[57] Since the concept that ground had worth only in so far as it favoured the defence was central to the German doctrine, its omission by the British substantially altered the resulting defensive system.

The GHQ Memorandum next dealt with the vital question of the enemy's probable method of attack.[58] The memorandum noted that the attack might come at any point of the line with little prior warning. The corresponding paragraph in *Command*[59] pointed out that British preparations for their offensives had given weeks and even months of warning of the precise location of an attack. That this difference between British and German practice in the offence might affect the system of defence employed appears not to have been considered by the authors of the GHQ Memorandum. When discussing the tactical form of a German attack, the GHQ Memorandum merely stated, 'We must expect an attack by masses of infantry, offering a very vulnerable target, but preceded by an intense bombardment which may be either of long or short duration'. While this was a fair description of British offensive tactics, it gave no hint of the dynamic nature of current German tactics.

The GHQ Memorandum then turned to the general scheme of defence.[60] Although largely taken from *Construction*,[61] omission and alteration meant that the British scheme bore little resemblance to the German system. The GHQ Memorandum began: 'A careful study of the ground is necessary with a view to the main resistance being made on ground favourable to us.'

However, whereas the German manual emphasised, 'The ruling factor in the choice of the general lie of the positions and lines is consideration of the rearward communications, and of our own and the enemy's artillery',[62] the British memorandum gave no indication as to what made ground favourable to the defender. In particular, the German emphasis on the value of reverse-slope positions, the cornerstone of the system, was entirely omitted.

The absence of guidance from GHQ as to the factors that should determine the best location for the main zone of resistance was compounded by the general location of this zone being determined by GHQ itself on maps issued with the memorandum. Since the BEF held about 100 miles of front, it is unlikely that GHQ officers had been able to visit the lines to make a personal reconnaissance. Rather it is probable that the location of the main zone of resistance was determined by GHQ *on the basis of map studies only*. This may be contrasted with German practice in which defences were located largely on the basis of detailed personal observation of the ground by officers from corps and army headquarters.

The GHQ Memorandum laid down that, as in the German system, there should be three defensive zones: outpost, battle and rearward, of which the battle zone was to be the main area of resistance. Despite the fact that for much of its length the British front line was on ground poorly suited to defence, the GHQ Memorandum stated that an outpost zone was to be employed only 'where the battle zone does not coincide with our present front-line system'. By contrast, although most of the German line had from the first been carefully chosen for its defensive strength, *Construction* stated that the battle zone and the front-line system 'may sometimes coincide'.[63]

The GHQ Memorandum faithfully copied *Construction* in stating that the role of the outpost zone was to guard against surprise and to compel the enemy to launch a full-scale attack in order to capture it. Although neither German nor British documents laid down the exact strength with which the zone was to be garrisoned, the GHQ Memorandum appears to have envisaged a stronger garrison than did *Command*.[64] The GHQ Memorandum again omitted any reference to the denial of enemy observation over the battle zone by the outpost zone, one of its main functions in the German system,[65] where it was employed to control the crest line in front of the reverse-slope battle zone.

The GHQ Memorandum again copied *Construction* in instructing that the battle zone should be 3,000 yards deep and filled with numerous trench systems, switch lines and defended localities.[66] The memorandum instructed that plans for counterattacks were to be drawn up, but gave no indication as to the size or purpose of these attacks.

The final part of the defensive system was the rearward zone. In the

German system, this was a complete second defensive position directly behind the battle zone.[67] It could either block an enemy penetration through the battle zone or become a new battle zone if the loss of the outpost zone forced the conversion of the existing battle zone into a new outpost zone. The GHQ Memorandum stated that the British rearward zone should be between four and eight miles behind the battle zone. This gave the British defence none of the flexibility of the German system and meant that a large area would be lost if the battle zone were penetrated. Further, whereas the German rearward zone was to be built in simple form before the battle began, the British zone was only to be marked out.

Having laid down the physical structure of the defence, though without indicating how the garrison was to be deployed, the GHQ Memorandum gave the method by which the battle was to be fought.[68] The garrison of the outpost zone was to hold its ground. Those troops occupying defensive works were to fight to the last man. If the enemy penetrated the position, local reserves should launch immediate counterattacks. Should these counterattacks fail, higher commanders were to decide whether the zone was worth the employment of units from the general reserve to recapture it. The GHQ Memorandum concluded that such employment of reserves would seldom be justified.

The battle zone was to be held rigidly. Should it be penetrated and local counterattacks fail to halt the enemy, a deliberate counterattack by the general reserve was to be employed. Unless the penetration was narrow, time would be required to prepare such an attack, which would seek not only to block the penetration but also to inflict a reverse on the enemy. The GHQ Memorandum indicated that the forces for these attacks would be allocated from GHQ reserve. This section was clearly adapted from *Command*.[69] In the process, however, the German doctrine suffered a gross distortion. The immediate cause appears to have been a misunderstanding of the German manual. In discussing the new tactics, the manual examines the action of the 'garrisons of the foremost trenches'. In context, it is evident that these trenches are those at the front of the battle zone, but the authors of the GHQ Memorandum believed that the trenches meant were those at the front of the outpost zone.

The result of this misunderstanding was a major alteration of the defensive system. In the German doctrine, the outpost zone was to be held lightly with the sole purpose in battle of compelling the enemy to expend time and material in its capture. The main battle was to be fought within the battle zone.[70] In the GHQ Memorandum, the outpost zone was to be held rigidly even in the face of a major attack. In effect, the British system had no outpost zone in the German sense. This was reflected in GHQ's decision on 3 January 1918 to replace the term 'outpost zone' with 'forward zone', 'on the grounds that the word "outpost" might lead the advanced troops to fall back without serious resistance',[71] precisely what they were supposed to do in the German system.

It is of note that the idea of the outpost garrison falling back to a main line of resistance in the face of a strong attack had been discussed at the General Staff conference of January 1911 and had been firmly rejected. The majority view was that any rearward movement was bad for morale and should be avoided if at all possible. The main line of resistance should therefore be placed along the foremost line of troops, that is, the outpost garrison.[72] The similarities between this doctrine and that laid down in the GHQ Memorandum suggests that the authors of the memorandum were not simply adapting the German doctrine to British use but were in fact adapting it to existing British practice.

The German doctrine emphasised that the function of the new tactics was to 'cause the fighting to take place not *in*, but *for* the front line'.[73] While the defence of strongpoints and the launching of counterthrusts within the position were vital to this doctrine, the key to the German system was the counterthrust by the general reserve from behind the position:[74] by the end of October 1917, two-thirds of the defenders were allocated to this role. The knowledge that substantial forces were available to recover ground temporarily lost gave the garrisons of strongpoints in the battle zone the confidence to fight on even when surrounded. Only if the counterthrusts of the *Eingreif* divisions failed and a counterattack was needed were commanders required to assess whether such an operation was justified.[75] A decision not to make a further attack would not affect the garrison of the outpost zone because the strongpoints in this zone would in any case have fallen by the time a counterattack could be launched. In the GHQ Memorandum, the only immediate counterattacks were to be made by local reserves. The general reserve was available only for deliberate counterattacks. The key element of the German doctrine, the counterthrust from behind the position by the *Eingreif* divisions, was therefore entirely missing from the GHQ Memorandum. As a result the garrisons of strongpoints would know that there was little hope of relief once they were surrounded and their resolve to fight to the last would be accordingly reduced.

After discussing the administrative arrangements for the building of the works,[76] the GHQ Memorandum turned to the actual construction of the defences.[77] One of the factors considered was cover. *Construction* stated that the effectiveness of the artillery of both sides was 'the ruling factor in the choice of the general lie of the positions'.[78] The GHQ Memorandum repeated this with the alteration that this was 'one of the essential considerations'.[79] The emphasis on the vital need for reverse-slope positions for the infantry given in the German manual was once again omitted. It echoed *Construction* in urging that positions be camouflaged both from ground and air observation and noted that this assisted the achievement of surprise.[80] Once again, however, the British toned down the language of the German manual, which stressed 'The inconspicuousness of all works from both ground and air becomes of decisive importance'.[81] In the GHQ Memorandum, it was merely stated that 'particular attention' should be given to camouflage.

The German defensive system as expressed in *Command* and *Construction* consisted of three zones: the outpost zone was lightly garrisoned and was designed to hold the enemy back from the main position and to compel him to expend considerable material in its capture; the battle zone was more strongly held, to delay and disorganise the attackers; the rearward zone was primarily a concentration area in which reserves could be held, out of enemy fire, ready to launch an immediate counterthrust to drive the exhausted attackers back out of the entire defensive system and so relieve the forward garrison. Good artillery observation over the battle zone and the denial of this to the enemy were considered of decisive importance. The majority of the defending troops were held under cover and out of enemy artillery range.

The defensive system laid down in the GHQ Memorandum also had three zones: the forward zone was to be held rigidly in an attempt to halt an attack, if lost it was generally to be abandoned; the battle zone was to be strongly garrisoned and its integrity to be maintained at all costs; several miles behind the battle zone, the rearward zone was to be marked out in case a second position was required. Behind this, divisions in army and GHQ reserve were to stand ready to mount carefully prepared deliberate counterattacks to block penetrations of the battle zone. Apart from the local reserves of the forward divisions, no counterthrust capability was available to recapture the ground lost. Good artillery observation and cover from enemy observation were noted but not stressed. The majority of the defending troops were held within enemy field-artillery range.

In its general remarks on the German March offensive, the *Official History* implied an important influence on the authors of the memorandum. It noted that the defensive system used by the British was not a new theory but had been known before the war, when it was called in derision the 'blob' system.[82] This system was first suggested by Major Ernest Swinton in a lecture to the Royal Artillery Institute at Woolwich in 1908.[83] The idea had been rejected as 'suicidal' on the grounds that it depended on strong counterattack reserves[84] and that the defended localities were vulnerable to artillery fire. The authors of the GHQ Memorandum appear to have believed that the German defensive system was based on Swinton's idea and that the enemy had somehow overcome its deficiencies.[85] It may be suggested that the system laid down in the GHQ Memorandum was in fact influenced more by that idea than by the German defensive system, which was twisted to fit the authors' preconceptions. The doctrine with which the BEF was to face the Germans in 1918 was therefore not so much elastic defence in depth but 'blob' defence.

## Implementation of the GHQ Memorandum

The GHQ Memorandum on Defensive Measures gave only the broad outlines of the doctrine of defence that the BEF was to adopt. It gave few details as to the depth of the defensive system, its layout or the distribution of its garrison. This 'tendency always to stress principles rather than actual methods' was typical of GHQ under Haig[86] and reflects his perception of the role of the commander.[87] An examination of the way in which the principles given in the memorandum were applied in practice may serve to demonstrate the limited extent to which the British Army understood the nature of the German doctrine. The *Official History* account of the German offensive of March 1918 gives considerable information on the defences on the sector of front attacked and reproduces the defence schemes of Third Army,[88] VI Corps[89] and 18th Division.[90]

As in the German doctrine,[91] the depth of the forward zone was not laid down directly but was a consequence of the battle zone being positioned on more favourable ground some distance to the rear. Although the GHQ Memorandum had implied that the forward zone might often be dispensed with and the battle zone cover the area directly behind the front line, the *Official History* shows that this was rarely the case.[92] Since the forward zone was simply the area between the front line and the front of the battle zone,[93] its depth varied considerably, but averaged 2,500 yards. Its defences were usually organised in three lines. The first two lines were generally continuous trench lines, while the third was often a series of redoubts.[94] The first two trench lines were the old front and support lines and the troops continued to refer to them as such,[95] indicating little change in tactical approach among the forces who would have to put the new doctrine into practice. Two systems of defence were used. In some areas, the front and support trenches were linked with new trenches to create fortified localities to be held by one or two companies,[96] the third line of redoubts acting as bases for local reserves. In other areas, the first and second lines were held by individual posts, each garrisoned by between half and one platoon, while the redoubts of the third line were each held by between half and one company.[97]

On the front attacked on 21 March, Third Army held its line with eight divisions (one per 6,250 yards) and Fifth Army with 11 divisions (one per 6,545 yards). Of the 190 battalions in these divisions, 65 were deployed in the forward zone,[98] an average of three and a half battalions from each division. This was approximately the same proportion of strength as laid down in the German doctrine, but the British garrison was more thinly spread owing to the width of the sectors assigned to each division, which were almost double those laid down by the Germans.

Details as to how these troops were deployed within the zone are given in the 18th Division defence scheme.[99] This division had two brigades in line and one in corps reserve. Three battalions were placed in the forward zone, one from 55th Brigade and two from 53rd Brigade. Each of these battalions deployed two companies in the front system of defences, which consisted of posts in the front and support trenches. The remaining two companies held the defended localities distributed chequerwise in depth behind the support trench. One of the companies was earmarked as a local reserve for immediate counterattack. Overall, each battalion in the forward zone held the front defences with about 20 posts, each of section or platoon size, in two rows, with up to 200 yards between each post. The third line consisted of five or six redoubts, most garrisoned by a single platoon, with the counterattack company either in one redoubt or divided between two. These redoubts were an average of 500 yards apart.

The situation of the forward zone was therefore very weak. The majority of the garrison was deployed towards the front of the zone, despite the fact that, as with 18th Division,[100] the greater part of the zone was under enemy observation and therefore vulnerable to artillery bombardment. VI Corps' designating a reverse-slope trench as the main line of resistance[101] was exceptional. In the German doctrine of early 1917, much of the garrison of the outpost zone had been static, but its positions had consisted of concrete shelters (MEBUs), which were capable of withstanding all but a direct hit and permitted the soldiers inside to emerge within seconds of the barrage lifting. The troops were not intended to fight from the shelters but were to deploy to nearby shell holes. Even the MEBUs were found to be inadequate and the final version of the doctrine, in October 1917, relied almost entirely on dispersion and mobility, rather than concrete, to counter the Allied artillery. In March 1918, there was not a single concrete machine-gun post on the sector of the British line attacked by the Germans. Few posts possessed even deep dug-outs, which the Germans in any case considered death traps.[102] Despite this, the garrison of the forward zone was ordered to 'hold their defences at all costs'[103] and 'units had been warned that there could be no retreat'.[104] The troops were therefore compelled to remain in full view of the German artillery observers in positions without effective cover.

Those posts that survived the initial bombardment could expect to be defeated in detail. The posts were intended to be 'inter-supporting'[105] and their location had been selected so that they enjoyed wide fields of fire and could cover the ground between the posts.[106] While this was more feasible towards the front of the zone, where there was a greater density of posts, the wide spacing of redoubts in the third line made these positions generally unable to support each other. The entire system was in any case dependent on clear observation. While the actual attack on 21 March was by chance covered by thick fog, some kind of screen was likely.[107] The guns supporting the defenders were not assigned barrage zones in case of low visibility,[108] suggesting that the British had not fully appreciated the dangers of a covered attack.

The depth of the battle zone was generally 3,000 yards.[109] In the Fifth Army sector, the zone was organised on the same basis as the forward zone,[110] the front defences based on the old reserve line and defended localities behind. In the Third Army sector, the battle zone was organised with existing trench systems at its front and rear[111] (the old corps and army lines)[112] and a new line dug between them.[113] The systems were connected by communication trenches and switch lines. In the Fifth Army sector, the garrison of the zone was similar to that of the forward zone (44 battalions to 37), an average of four battalions per division. The garrison in the Third Army sector was considerably stronger (47½ battalions to 28½), almost six battalions per division.[114] This gave Third Army one battalion per 1,000 yards of front and Fifth Army one per 1,600 yards. In both armies, although the density of troops was similar to that called for by the German doctrine, the proportion of the available forces committed to the battle zone was greater than in that doctrine.

The garrison of the battle zone was deployed in a similar pattern to that of the forward zone: two rows of small posts at the front of the zone with a chequered row of defended localities behind them. As in the forward zone, the majority of the garrison was deployed towards the front of the zone in fixed positions, but these were generally less well constructed than were those of the forward zone.[115] The zone was therefore stronger than the forward zone in only two respects: first, the greater density of troops in the Third Army sector meant that positions were closer together and so better able to provide mutual support; second, the zone lay 2,500 yards from the German lines and so was less exposed to enemy artillery fire and could also expect more warning of an attack than the forward zone.

The rear zone existed mainly on paper. In the German system, the zone was to provide sheltered concentration areas for the *Eingreif* divisions. In the British version, the rear zone was a single trench system[116] intended as a fall-back position. An inspection on 14 March 1918 of the zone in the Fifth Army sector revealed little more than rows of notice boards marking the sites of fieldworks still to be constructed.[117] The absence of physical defences was matched by an absence of troops. Third Army deployed only four battalions in the zone (half a battalion per division), while Fifth Army had 29 battalions (two and a half per division).[118] These were the only units immediately available to counterattack enemy penetrations of the battle zone. The British defensive system included no *Eingreif* divisions.

If the defensive system is examined with regard to the concepts of area defence, invisibility and immediate responsiveness its differences from the German doctrine become most apparent.

Area defence was based on the recognition that dense bodies of troops were both highly vulnerable to artillery fire and also poorly suited to the development of maximum firepower from automatic weapons. Distribution of the garrison over a wide area diluted the enemy's artillery fire and enabled the defenders to enfilade attacking troops. An integral part of the concept was that soldiers should enjoy at least a limited amount of freedom of movement, in order to avoid particular concentrations of hostile fire. By the end of 1917, the Germans had extended this concept to create an outpost zone 1,500 metres deep from which troops would withdraw in the event of a major attack, while the garrison of the battle zone was almost entirely mobile.

In the British system, the garrisons of both the forward and battle zones were distributed in a series of lines towards the front of each zone. Of the 190 battalions holding the sector of front attacked on 21 March 1918, 160 (84 per cent) were within 3,000 yards of the front line,[119] compared to a maximum of 50 per cent of the strength of the forward divisions in the German system. The British garrison was also locked into static positions with no flexibility to move to areas of less dense artillery fire, reflected in the troops calling the defended localities 'bird cages':[120] they considered that they had as much hope of surviving a German attack as would a bird in a cage. Rather than occupying one continuous defended zone 10,000 metres deep, as in the German system, the British troops were largely concentrated into two zones each no more than 1,000 yards deep.

The second German concept was that of invisibility. By making full use of camouflage and deception, the Germans sought to divert enemy fire on to empty positions and to disguise the true form of the defence. In this way, the British superiority in artillery was made less effective and the attackers were constantly surprised by fire and counterthrusts from unexpected directions. The British defence schemes recognised that positions should be 'as invisible as possible'. The GHQ Memorandum pointed out that 'concealment of machine-gun posts must be one of the first considerations'[121] and 'particular attention should be paid to adapting defences from air and ground observation'.[122] Nevertheless, hundreds of miles of trenches and thousands of posts and fortified localities were built within the defensive zone, often with little attempt being made to conceal their location. Whereas the Germans considered invisibility to be the prime factor, considering a position known to the enemy to be of little value, the British appear to have preferred the comfort given by earthworks.

The third German concept was that of immediate responsiveness. The Germans considered the immediate counterthrust to be the key factor in the successful conduct of the defence. For this reason, the majority of the defending forces were allocated to this role. For the counterthrust within the position by the front divisions, only two companies (50 per cent) of each of the three front battalions and one company (25 per cent) of each of the three support battalions, were *not* assigned a mobile role: two-thirds of the front division's troops were intended for the counterthrust. By October 1917, each front division was supported by an entire fresh *Eingreif* division for the counterthrust from behind the position. Of the 18 battalions assigned to each sector, therefore, the equivalent of almost 16 battalions (88 per cent) were designated to carry out counterthrusts. In the British system, the proportions were reversed, 75 per cent of the troops in both the forward and battle zones were assigned *static* duties. While the battalions deployed in the rear zone were in theory available to launch counter-attacks, they were intended primarily as a static garrison for the rear trench system of the battle zone.[123] Third Army deployed only four of its 80 battalions in the rear zone, suggesting that little weight was given to the idea of a counterthrust from behind the position. In general, of the ten battalions assigned to each sector, only the equivalent of perhaps three were designated counterattack troops.

The concept of the *Eingreif* divisions, by which the attackers were to be driven back, was severely distorted in the British system, although the British did hold a number of divisions behind the lines. Third and Fifth Armies each had four divisions in corps and army reserve (three of the Fifth Army divisions were cavalry, each with only the strength of an infantry brigade when dismounted) with a further two divisions of the GHQ reserve behind each army. This gave Third Army one reserve division to 8,100 yards of front and Fifth Army one to 18,000.[124] While the forces assigned to Fifth Army were clearly deficient, those assigned to Third Army were approximately equal to those given in the German doctrine in March 1917, although the final version of the doctrine required twice as many *Eingreif* divisions.

The error was not so much in the number of divisions kept in reserve as in their positioning. The division in Third Army reserve nearest to the front was ten miles behind the lines,[125] too far for an immediate response to an enemy attack. The German doctrine required that the *Eingreif* divisions be sufficiently close behind the battle lines to be able to reach the rear of the battle zone before the enemy penetrated to that depth.[126] Taking into account the amount of time the attacker would require to advance this far, the Germans considered that the *Eingreif* divisions should be no more than 10,000 metres behind the front line. The divisions held in reserve under the British system were at least twice this distance behind the front line.

Even if the reserve divisions had been closer to the front, their effectiveness as *Eingreif* divisions would have been severely limited. The key to the function of the *Eingreif* divisions in the German doctrine was that they should meet the enemy at a time when the latter were exhausted and disorganised and so unable to withstand a determined counterthrust. The early arrival of the divisions was therefore of central importance. Although the VI Corps defence scheme stated, 'It must be thoroughly impressed on all leaders that the counterattack, in order to be successful, must be delivered whilst the enemy is still disorganised and before he has had time to consolidate his position',[127] it defined an 'immediate' counterattack as one which took place within *24 hours* of the original attack.[128] The implication of this definition is that 'immediate' counterattacks would rarely be launched before a number of hours had passed since the initial enemy attack. This may be contrasted with the German insistence on immediate counterthrusts being made to take advantage of fleeting opportunities, that is within minutes or at most an hour or two. Such immediate responsiveness appears to have been alien to the British approach. The divisions held in reserve behind the British lines in readiness for a counterattack were not held on alert for immediate action: divisions in army reserve were under six hours notice to move, while those in GHQ reserve were allowed a full 24 hours warning before being expected to move.[129]

Had the British assigned narrow sectors to each of the front divisions, these would have been able to hold back one brigade as a divisional *Eingreif* formation and so not have been dependent on the presence of *Eingreif* divisions behind the lines. The German regulations laid down that a division holding a 5,000-metre sector of front required a supporting *Eingreif* division but that a sector of 3,000 metres might be held by one division unsupported.[130] When the British copied the system, they omitted the *Eingreif* divisions but did not adopt the narrower frontages that this required. British divisions were therefore usually allocated frontages of some 5,000 yards[131] (although 18th Division was allocated 9,500 yards)[132] without any support. The cause of this error may have been the reliance of the GHQ Memorandum on *Construction*. This engineering manual laid down the width of front that should be assigned to each front division but was not concerned with the *Eingreif* divisions, since these needed no fieldworks, and therefore made no mention of them.

The divisions garrisoning the front line could expect little immediate help from the formations held in reserve. The only forces immediately available to counterattack were the counterattack companies in the forward and battle zones and the battalions in the rear zone. Even these were severely regulated. The GHQ Memorandum instructed,

> Plans and preparations for the employment of troops . . . in the counterattack must be carefully worked out. . . . Frequent practice of

> counterattacks by reserves, large and small, should be carried out. The form of these attacks should be laid down in the defence schemes of formations and units, and practised on the ground for which they are planned.[133]

The level of detail to which these attacks were planned is indicated by the 18th Division defence scheme: 'The exact localities against which counterattacks will be delivered will be notified by divisional headquarters. This will limit the responsibility resting on those commanders who are empowered to order a counterattack.'[134] Although careful planning and practice was essential to the success of counterattacks, the definite sense of regulation given by the defence schemes suggests that the British had converted the free creativity of the German system, with local initiative conforming actions to circumstances, into a drill, with actions laid down from above and in advance. Little provision was made for response to a sudden unexpected opportunity, a capability central to the German doctrine.

Although the concept of the counterattack was included in the GHQ Memorandum, it is doubtful whether it was accepted by more than a small minority of officers. The previous doctrine of rigid defence, with counterattacks being carefully organised over a period of days by senior commanders, appears to have remained ingrained. The 18th Division defence scheme argued,

> Although it is sound in principle to earmark in each battalion a company for counterattack, it does not always follow that it is necessary for that company to counterattack. In the event of a very heavy attack, a local counterattack by a company or smaller body of men may not be of much assistance to the defence, whereas the addition of these men as a garrison to the defensive line may hinder very considerably or arrest the enemy's advance.[135]

In those divisions in which the existing doctrine of rigid defence was maintained, which was probably the majority, it is probable that even those counterattack forces that were available were unlikely to be employed in that role.

The consequence of there being no provision for *Eingreif* divisions behind the lines nor for front divisions to assign their own *Eingreif* brigades was made clear in the defence scheme of 18th Division:

> Brigade and battalion commanders are to realise that they must be self-supporting in the areas entrusted to them. They must not expect reinforcements, for these will not be forthcoming. The only help that they can expect will be that afforded by a deliberate counterattack with all available reserves organised by the higher commanders.[136]

Since any deliberate counterattack would take place a minimum of 24 hours after an initial enemy attack, it was clear that, in reality, no help would be forthcoming. Captain Wynne wrote that Ludendorff

> never intended his zone of fortified localities . . . to stop a determined offensive by itself. . . . The counterattack divisions were meant and had proved themselves to be the crux of the system, and yet the British Fifth Army attempted to hold its long line with the 'bird cages' only. It had no counterattack divisions, not even within 24 hours by rail or road.[137]

## Could the British have Adopted the German Doctrine?

The British *Official History* argued that perhaps the most important cause of the disasters of March 1918 was that, 'As so often in its history, the British Army had been called upon to undertake a task beyond the power of its numbers'.[138] This argument seeks to demonstrate that defeat was caused by the politicians in London starving the BEF of men rather than by flaws in the defensive doctrine or its implementation. While it is beyond the scope of this study to examine to what extent the supply of replacements to the BEF was in fact restricted,[139] it is possible to analyse the forces available to determine whether they were sufficient to implement the German doctrine.

The March 1917 edition of *Command* laid down that the width of divisional sectors on a battle front should generally be between 2,750 and 3,500 yards.[140] On the eve of the German offensive in March 1918, the BEF held a front of 126 miles.[141] Allowing for sections of the front being unfavourable to the attack and so permitting a light garrison, it may be calculated that the British would have required about 55 divisions to hold the line in accordance with the German doctrine. In addition, about 30 more divisions would have been required as *Eingreif* formations.[142] The total number of divisions theoretically required was therefore 85. In March 1918, the BEF consisted of 60 infantry divisions and three cavalry divisions[143] (each of which was equivalent to one infantry brigade[144]), 24 divisions short of the number required by the new doctrine. The *Official History*'s argument that defeat was caused by a serious shortage of troops therefore appears at first sight convincing. Further investigation shows this argument to be somewhat superficial.

Shortly before the March offensive, the British divisions in the BEF changed from 12-battalion organisations to nine-battalion structures. Over a period of six weeks, 115 battalions were disbanded, 38 were amalgamated into 19 and seven were converted to pioneers. The men from the 141 battalions that disappeared from the order of battle were used to bring the remainder up to full strength[145] (950 men), of whom 800 were directly combatant.[146] Divisions also included a pioneer battalion with a combat strength of about 600 men, which could be used as infantry if necessary. Each division therefore had 7,800 combat infantrymen. At this time, a German battalion contained only 750 men,[147] of whom 650 were combatant.[148] Since German divisions had no pioneer battalions, their total combat infantry strength was about 5,850 men. Each British division was therefore equivalent in numbers of infantry to one and a third German divisions. Canada, Australia and New Zealand were not suffering the same manpower shortages as was Britain and had not reduced the number of battalions in their ten divisions in France.[149] The strength of the 12 infantry battalions and one pioneer battalion in each of these divisions was 10,400 men, equivalent to one and three-quarters German divisions. If the greater strength of the British and Empire divisions is taken into account, the 60 divisions of the BEF were equivalent in combat infantry manpower to about 84 German divisions. This is almost exactly the number of divisions that the German doctrine required for the length of front held by the BEF in March 1918, suggesting that sufficient manpower was available to implement that doctrine.

The figure of 85 German-strength divisions required to defend the front of the BEF assumes a battle-strength defence along almost the entire front. Such a defence was never achieved by the Germans themselves. For most of 1917, there were 137 German divisions on the 450-mile-long Western Front.[150] The 150 miles of front from east of St Mihiel to the Swiss border were quiet, largely owing to the difficulty of the terrain, and were held by no more than 20 divisions.[151] This left 117 divisions to hold the 300 miles of front from St Mihiel to the North Sea, an average of 4,500 yards per division, whereas the March 1917 edition of *Command* would have required 200 divisions. The Germans therefore held most of the line lightly and concentrated their forces on those sectors where the enemy was attempting to break through. This practice was dependent on early identification of the location of enemy offensives.

The BEF enjoyed a substantially more favourable ratio of troops to length of front in March 1918 than had the Germans in 1917. So long as the German focus could be identified at least a few days before an offensive began, Haig had the resources of manpower necessary to strengthen the threatened sector of front to the extent required by the German doctrine before the attack took place. Haig considered his manpower fully adequate for the defence of the front assigned to the BEF: Henry Wilson reported, 'Haig told the War Cabinet [on 7 January 1918] that he was quite confident he could hold his own and never insisted on the necessity of being supplied with men', and on 12 March, only nine days before the German attack,

Haig wrote that he expected no shortages of manpower 'before the autumn'.[152] It appears reasonable to conclude, therefore, that the post-war argument that the BEF did not have sufficient manpower to implement the German doctrine has little basis.

The second reason given by the *Official History* to explain defeat was that insufficient time and labour were available to construct the defences required by the new doctrine.[153] To support this, the *Official History* provides figures for the number of men working on the defences in the Fifth Army sector from 5 January to 16 March 1918.[154] These rise from four men (sic) in the first week to 8,830 men in the last week, with an average of 2,488 men per week. Since Fifth Army held 42 miles of front,[155] 2,488 men per week was clearly inadequate to build the defences required. In a footnote to its discussion of labour, however, the *Official History* points out that there were available to Fifth Army, in addition to the numbers quoted above, 14 entrenching battalions and the engineers and pioneers of the infantry divisions.[156] Furthermore, since normally only the forward zone was kept fully manned, most of the troops assigned to the two rear zones were also available for work on the defences.[157] From these sources, a total of perhaps 66,000 men would have been available for the construction of defences.[158] In addition, artillery units could be expected to build their own positions.

The question of labour available to Fifth Army is of particular importance, since 25 miles of its front were taken over from the French only in January 1918 and were, according to the *Official History*,[159] in very poor repair. Yet, on 20 November 1917, General Gough, reporting the results of his initial inspection of this sector, noted that the construction of defences by the French was well advanced and that the sector included '230 kilometres of light rail which makes an excellent system together with the excellent roads'.[160]

Since it appears that sufficient labour was available, although vital materials such as reinforced concrete were in short supply, and that the defences were in a reasonable state when the British took over the sector, the weakness of the defences in March 1918 must be explained by other means. The *Official History* gives a clue to one factor when it states that the intention had been to elaborate the defensive zones by 'a labyrinth of trenches and switches, tiers of wire and hundreds of "pill-boxes", machine-gun nests and deep dug-outs'.[161] While the Germans had sought to produce such a system of defences earlier in the war, the elaboration of works to the extent envisaged by the *Official History* was no longer intended even in the August 1917 edition of *Construction* copied by the British. This specifically urged caution in the construction of defended localities that required large garrisons and rejected an exaggerated desire for strong works as this reduced the total number of works that could be built.[162]

A similar policy was adopted by the French when they held the sector. The British, however, locked their troops in a mass of positions which there had not been enough time to complete.

It appears that the main factors that made the British Army unable to adopt the German doctrine of elastic defence in depth successfully were that the doctrine was based on a higher standard of training than was achieved by British troops and on a more decentralised system of command than that used by the British Army.

The German doctrine officially made the *Gruppe* of nine men under an NCO the basic tactical unit.[163] The new tactics were dependent on the effectiveness with which junior NCOs could lead their men within the context of the regimental operation. Owing to the dispersed formations required by the doctrine, officers at platoon and company level could direct the actions of their sub-units only through the use of directive command. These tactics made enormous demands on both men and NCOs. A high degree of cohesion within units was required such that the mutual trust vital to co-ordination between sub-units might be achieved. It was also necessary for NCOs to be skilled in command and to enjoy the confidence of the men whom they led. This became all the more essential as increasing numbers of platoons and even companies came to be commanded by NCOs.

A key aspect of low-level effectiveness is primary group cohesion, the sense in which soldiers feel they 'belong' to a particular unit and have a trust in, and a loyalty to, it and its members. The German Army took considerable care to promote such feelings. Units and formations were recruited from defined geographical areas and soldiers returned to their original units after recovering from their wounds.[164] While the system could not be fully maintained throughout the war, examination of the rolls of honour in a number of German regimental histories suggests that most men died while serving in their original units.

The British Army entered the First World War with a system similar to the German. Most men joined their local county regiment and served in its two Regular battalions throughout their careers. The system continued, with growing difficulty, during the first two years of war but increasingly broke down thereafter.[165] From the middle of 1915 it became more and more common for recruits trained in one regiment to be drafted to another regiment at the front[166] and to be posted to yet another regiment after being wounded. This reached a peak during the confusion of late March 1918, when units might receive replacements from any regiment in the army.[167] In general, only officers could expect to remain within one regiment and to return to their old battalion after being wounded and even here the system became increasingly inefficient.[168]

The practical workings of the replacement system have been examined in a study[169] of the reconstitution from July to October 1916 of 169th Brigade of 56th Division, after it lost 1,889 men at Gommecourt on 1 July. The process indicates that the mixing of men from different units was not the result of insufficient drafts from individual regiments being available, but of either administrative incompetence or deliberate policy.

169th Brigade consisted of four Territorial Force battalions of the London Regiment, created in 1908 from the former Volunteer battalions of several Regular regiments. The new regiment was not a success and achieved little regimental standardisation, reflected by most of the battalions retaining their former titles. 'In fact each battalion was virtually a regiment in itself and if the men had any loyalty outside their own unit, it was probably to their old Regular regiment rather than to the London Regiment.'[170] This was recognised by the abolition of the regiment after the war. The various battalions had worked hard to create a strong spirit of unit loyalty and had attempted to develop altruism amongst the men, the basis of primary group cohesion. Despite heavy casualties before the Somme, the battalions of 169th Brigade had largely received replacements from their own third-line training battalions and so had retained much of their pre-war character. This changed dramatically after Gommecourt.

During July 1916, the 5th (London Rifle Brigade) received 626 replacements. Only 16 were LRB men and 15 of these had originally been detailed for another battalion in the brigade. Of the remainder, 121 came from four other battalions of the London Regiment and 494 from 1/8th Middlesex Regiment. Men from two other battalions had been detailed but were then sent to other units. In the reconstituted battalion, therefore, fewer than half of the men were 'genuine' LRB. The sense of betrayal felt by the LRB men was all the greater because a draft of 590 men from the battalion's training unit was available at Rouen. The dilution of the battalion with men from other units was therefore almost totally unnecessary. The picture in the 9th (Queen Victoria's Rifles) was similar. During July the battalion received 414 men from seven different battalions of the London Regiment, and from two Middlesex battalions, the Border Regiment and the Norfolk Regiment. Its commander complained that the battalion now contained men from 17 different regiments.

So common was the drafting of men from one regiment to another at this time that, 'The whole of the 56th Division was in fact full of men busily changing buttons, shoulder flashes and cap badges, while others were trying on kilts or swopping kilts for trousers'. Attempts by battalions to recover their own men by exchanging replacements were blocked by divisional headquarters. This was presumably on the orders of the Army Council, which appears to have regarded the soldiers' loyalty to their original battalions to be more an inconvenience than a vital part of combat effectiveness.

The complaints made by the battalions at the way in which the War Office abandoned its promise that Territorials would not be transferred between units concerned not the quality of the men brought in from outside but the effect that this had on the character of units. The London Rifle Brigade considered itself an elite. Most of its pre-war personnel had been artisans or office workers. As befitted a unit of intelligent and highly motivated men, the battalion had operated a relaxed system of command in which relations between officers and men were close and discipline internal. As the battalion received drafts of men from working-class areas, the relationships became more rigid as the officers were forced to adopt a stricter system of discipline. Although the 'genuine' LRB men[171] understood the need for the change, it nevertheless tended to alienate them. They were further alienated by the fact that the replacements tended to retain a definite loyalty to their former regiments, regarding themselves as merely 'attached' rather than 'transferred' to their new units. They also came from a different part of the country and were of a different social class to the traditional LRB men. In general, the LRB men seem to have felt resentful that their battalion had been taken from them. In such circumstances, the development of strong low-level cohesion was all but impossible.

The position of the NCO was of equally great importance in the German doctrine. The high standard of NCOs in the German Army has been discussed in Chapter 3. The quality of the NCO corps meant that officers trusted them to carry out tasks independently and to command platoons, and even companies, in the place of officers, while the troops were ready to follow them even in the confusion of defence in depth. The British Army could not so rely on its NCOs. The pre-war training of NCOs was not of a high level, as has been argued in Chapter 4. In the early stages of the war, a large proportion of the Regular NCO corps was either commissioned or killed in action. Thereafter, NCOs were a weak link in the chain of command and remained so throughout the war. In a paper written late in 1918, Maxse complained that the best NCOs were quickly commissioned, while the remainder were mainly 'privates with stripes'. He noted that potential NCOs received little training in leadership and he therefore called for a central school to train platoon sergeants.[172] The extent to which NCOs were taken for commissioning is shown by each division being required to send ten NCOs for officer training each month.[173]

The limited quality of NCOs was both reflected in and caused by the large number of officers assigned to battalions. British battalions typically had three times as many officers as did German units[174] and the number grew steadily during the war, reaching 43 per battalion, with more surplus, by August 1918.[175] The *Official History* noted the effect that this glut of officers had on the troops:

> When British troops lost their officers, they were . . . apt to fall back, not because they were beaten but because they did not know what to do and expected to receive fresh orders. Perhaps the large number of officers commissioned and the fact that a sergeant rarely held command of a platoon for more than a few days lessened the prestige of the noncommissioned officer.[176]

One consequence was that subalterns often had to carry out tasks better left to NCOs[177] and so suffered even more heavily than otherwise.

The high turnover of officers in the British Army was one factor that prevented the officer corps achieving the high standards demanded by the German doctrine. The most important factor, however, was that almost half of all wartime commissions had been granted in the first months of the war to men with little or no prior training or means of acquiring it.[178] Most of these subalterns, despite their undoubted zeal and potential, remained novices when compared with the combat skill of the German NCOs. The practice of commissioning men lacking in military training, solely on the grounds of their background, had a long history in the British Army. Fully 80 per cent of replacement officers commissioned during the Crimean War were similarly appointed straight from civilian life, and were usually posted to the front without having undergone any form of military training.[179] As Gwyn Harries-Jenkins has pointed out,

> It is apparent that for many commentators [even after the War], it was far preferable for the officer to be a gentleman, notwithstanding his many failings, than for him to be a cad whose professionalism would be matched by his mercenary attitudes. . . . [They argued] that the average Englishman would not accept as an officer anyone who was not his social superior, a thesis which specifically precluded considering the professional ability of the military officer.[180]

The German doctrine depended as much on the decentralisation of command as on a high standard of training. If fleeting opportunities were to be seized in which to launch counterthrusts within the position in order to exhaust and confuse the attackers, the *Kampftruppenkommandeure* (KTKs) (combat troops commanders) needed to have direct command over the three battalions in their regimental sector. If the counterthrust from behind the position was to meet the enemy at his moment of greatest vulnerability, the front division commander had to have direct command over the *Eingreif* division assigned to him. The essence of the system was that officers commanded sectors of front and enjoyed full command over all units within their sectors, regardless of seniority.

Such decentralisation of command was inconceivable to the British. This was reflected in two ways. First, the German system required that regiments be deployed in depth, with one battalion in each zone. This gave the KTK command over the whole depth of the defence and allowed him to control the entire course of the battle without transferring responsibility to another commander. When the British adopted the German system, this deployment was not demanded by GHQ. While many brigades were deployed in the German way, some arranged their battalions in depth and others were placed wholly within a single zone by their divisions.[181] Although the commander of each front battalion was designated 'Officer Commanding Front-Line System', a clear copy of the German system of KTKs, these officers were nowhere given command over the entire brigade zone, nor indeed could they manoeuvre even their own battalion without permission from the brigade commander.[182]

A similar situation existed at higher level. British practice was for commanders at each level to retain a reserve under their direct command, usually a formation two levels down. Thus a corps commander's reserve would be a brigade detached from one of his divisions, while a divisional commander would take a battalion from one of his brigades.[183] These units would come under the direct command of their parent formations only on the order of the higher commander. The effect was to increase the centralisation of command. Since a divisional commander might have only two of his three brigades under his direct command, he did not have the reserve necessary to exploit a sudden opportunity or to save a sudden crisis. As a result, his formation was condemned to a largely static role by an insufficiency of forces. His only direct means of affecting the battle in an active way was through the use of his single reserve battalion. For any larger scale action, he was forced first to request that his third brigade be returned to him. This process took time, in which an opportunity might pass. Brigade commanders were placed in the same position as the divisional commander, since the latter removed part of their force to form his own reserve. Thus they too had to ask permission to use parts of their own formations. This system was incompatible with a doctrine that placed a premium on the rapid response of commanders at all levels to fleeting opportunities.

The conclusion from this examination of training and command is that the British Army would probably not have been able to implement effectively the German doctrine of elastic defence in depth even had it been correctly understood. The quality of training and cohesion of the British troops was generally below that to which the Germans had declined in late 1916. This itself had been considered by OHL to be too low for the new doctrine and a major training programme had been required to bring the troops up to the standard needed to implement that doctrine in 1917. Despite the greater density of forces enjoyed by the BEF and the fact that almost one-third of its divisions were in reserve, the *Official History* claimed that 'it was impossible to pull out even a small proportion of the divisions for even a fortnight's training',[184] thereby highlighting the differences in attitude towards training in the two armies. Equally, the decentralisation of command that had been developed in the German Army over the previous century was beyond the capabilities of most British officers and NCOs, and contrary to the British Army's philosophy of combat as structured and following a course that could be predicted.

Perhaps the greatest error made by GHQ in seeking to adopt the German doctrine of elastic defence in depth was the failure to discern that that doctrine was based on a quite different approach to military operations from that held by the British Army. Despite this, Haig wrote in his diary on 2 March 1918,

> I told Army Commanders that I was very pleased at all I had seen in the fronts of the three Armies which I had recently visited. Plans were sound and thorough and much work had already been done. I was only afraid that the enemy would find our front so very strong that he will hesitate to commit his army to the attack with the almost certainty of losing very heavily.[185]

# 8
# The Battle of St Quentin, 21 March 1918

> The attack, just as does the defence, demands *strict command, careful and thorough directives [Weisungen] for the combined action on all arms* within the combat sectors and with the neighbouring sectors and also clear designation of attack objectives. On the other hand, every attack offers *opportunity for free activity and joyfully decisive [entschlussfreudigen] action* even for the individual soldier.
>
> *Der Angriff im Stellungskrieg*

The German offensive that began on 21 March 1918 was one of the most stunning operations of the First World War. After more than three years of stalemate on the Western Front, the German Army punched through the British lines and came close to winning the war. Eighteenth Army alone advanced 38 kilometres and took 50,000 prisoners.[1] That victory slipped through Ludendorff's grasp appears to have been as much the consequence of technical factors affecting logistics[2] as of British and French actions. As soon as the scale of the disaster became clear, British soldiers and politicians began to look for a convenient explanation. The first casualty was General Hubert Gough, replaced as commander of Fifth Army on 28 March.[3] At the time, Lloyd George and other members of the war council made it clear that they considered Gough entirely responsible for the defeat.[4] The government was soon compelled to acknowledge the injustice of its action, although only in private.[5]

After the war, a different explanation was proposed: 'one officer wrote that the *Official History* draft read as if "Mist and Masses" overcame Fifth Army.'[6] It will be argued that neither of these factors is adequate to account for the British defeat. It is sufficient here to note that, first, whether the fog actually assisted the German attack is questionable. In any case such weather is not unusual and the defence schemes should have taken this into account. Second, the argument of overwhelming numbers appears persuasive only at first. Fifty German divisions were in action against 21 British divisions on 21 March 1918,[7] odds of five to two. A glance at the first day of the Somme, 1 July 1916, shows 14 British divisions in action against only three German divisions, odds of almost five to one, double the numerical superiority enjoyed by the Germans in 1918.

A third explanation was developed by the French and taken up by the British and Americans. It was noted that the greatest advance had been made by Eighteenth Army under General Oskar von Hutier and that he had been brought to the Western Front after his skilful capture of Riga in September 1917. The new tactics employed by the German troops were therefore ascribed to his genius and dubbed 'Hutier tactics'. Any army could be excused defeat at the hands of a new Napoleon.[8] The persistence of the 'Hutier legend' may in part be because of the grain of truth on which it is based. The tactics employed by the German troops were indeed in advance of Allied practice and played a major part in the successes of early 1918. What was not true was that the tactics had been developed by Hutier in the late summer of 1917. The story of the tactics begins almost three years earlier.

## The Development of German Offensive Tactics

German sources regard the action at Soissons on 13 January 1915 as marking the start of the development of the tactics employed in 1918.[9] This was a minor operation by III Corps of First Army, designed to seize the Uregny Plateau, an area of high ground overlooking the German positions. The chief of staff of III Corps, Major Hans von Seeckt, realised that the tactics used up to that time were no longer effective in the context of position war. The subordination of the artillery to the infantry battle, as laid down in the pre-war regulations,[10] had led many officers to believe that the infantry could operate virtually independently, without waiting for artillery support.[11] The consequence was often a bloody repulse. Seeckt saw that the pre-war regulations had been wrong to subordinate the artillery to the infantry battle. Instead, the two arms must be mutually supportive. His plan of operations was therefore new in that it made the infantry and the artillery equal partners in the attack.

The German artillery bombardment began at dawn on 13 January 1915 and continued for five hours.[12] The French positions consisted of three lines of trenches, which were not dug very deeply and had no shell-proof cover. Seeckt was well aware that, even in these favourable circumstances, it was not possible to kill all of the defenders, given the limited amount of time and ammunition available. His intention was instead temporarily to eliminate the defensive power of the sector to be attacked, by shattering the morale of the forward garrison and of the supporting artillery, and by hindering the movement of enemy reserves. The bombardment produced the desired effect, many of the French troops fleeing as soon as the German infantry attacked.

The importance of Soissons was that it demonstrated the interdependence of artillery and infantry and also confirmed the validity of the pre-war doctrine that fire was best used to suppress the defenders' morale preparatory for the assault. Seeckt's innovation was to achieve this suppression by means of artillery fire rather than by rifle fire.

Interestingly, the Germans and the French drew precisely opposite conclusions from the action. The French, impressed by the effectiveness of the preparatory bombardment, concluded that the artillery was now the main arm and that the infantry should be subordinated to it.[13] From here it was but a short step to the doctrine of '*l'artillerie conquiert, l'infanterie occupe*', in which the infantry was reduced to 'mopping up'. Seeckt, by contrast, concluded that major modifications were required in German infantry tactics. The infantry, using the pre-war linear formations, had advanced rapidly over the area prepared by the artillery, easily breaking into the enemy positions. Once the troops moved beyond this area, however, and attempted to break through the French positions, the advance slowed dramatically and losses mounted.[14] Without artillery support, the infantry was largely ineffective. Seeckt realised that the infantry could not rely on the artillery to produce a breakthrough and still less to produce a break-out. If a war of movement was to be resumed, tactics would have to be changed to enable the infantry to achieve victory through its own integral firepower. The formation on 2 March 1915, six weeks after Soissons, of Sturmabteilung Kalsow to test assault cannon was an attempt to solve precisely this problem and indicates that Seeckt was not alone in identifying deficiencies in German infantry tactics.

The next stage in the development of German offensive doctrine was marked by a report prepared by Third Army in April 1915, in which the errors made by the French in their recent Champagne offensive were analysed.[15] The report concluded that the French had made only two major errors: they had attacked on too narrow a front and they had failed to suppress the German artillery. Perhaps reacting to their experience at Soissons, the French showed a tendency to rely too much on their artillery to clear positions and did not press their infantry attacks quickly enough or with sufficient force.[16] The report drew a sharp distinction between purely tactical operations designed to seize a particular enemy position (a break-in) and operations intended to pierce the enemy line (a breakthrough). The vital difference between the two types of operation was that whereas a detailed plan could be drawn up for the former, only probabilities could be foreseen for the latter: 'other decisions must be made according to the exigencies of the moment.'[17]

The front of an attack should be at least 20 kilometres. The assault should not be uniform but should seek to penetrate the defences only in the most favourable sectors and to pin the defenders elsewhere. The latter sectors should be attacked from the flanks and rear by reserves passed through the penetrations for this purpose.[18] In this way, von Schlieffen's insistence upon envelopment and the avoidance of frontal attacks was maintained and extended down into the realm of tactics. Reserves were to be ready to exploit unexpected success by the pinning attacks: 'In spite of the most carefully organised preparations, success in war can never be counted upon with certainty at the desired spot. Many of the greatest victories have been gained by following up an advantage which at first sight appeared of secondary importance.'[19] The role of the artillery was vital to the success of an attack. No attempt would be made to eliminate the defending garrison or its fieldworks physically. The attacking artillery was to damage the enemy wire and flanking positions, to suppress the defenders' guns and hinder the bringing forward of reserves. The neutralisation of the enemy artillery was considered of the greatest importance.[20]

The infantry were still to employ standard linear tactics, companies attacking in up to six lines. It was, however, noted that 'the grenade is the principal weapon for use against an enemy in the trenches'. The authors of the report appear to have identified the same deficiency in infantry tactics as had von Seeckt: the infantry was unable to operate effectively once it advanced beyond artillery support. In an attempt to solve this problem, the report urged that reserves accompanied by machine guns and horse-drawn cannon follow close behind the attacking troops, in order to deal with enemy positions hindering the attack and to repulse counterattacks.[21]

The essence of the offensive system proposed by the Third Army report was speed and flexibility. As at Soissons, the artillery preparation was to neutralise the firepower of the defence just long enough for the infantry to assault the enemy line. Attacks were to be made only at the most favourable points and the strongest sectors of the enemy position were to be taken by envelopment. The attacking troops were to push on until nightfall and allow the enemy no time to consolidate. The objective for the first day was to be a natural feature beyond the enemy gun line.[22] Great flexibility was required to exploit unexpected opportunities and this was supported by the allocation of artillery pieces to accompany the advancing infantry and so make it less dependent on pre-planned indirect fire. Here in outline was the doctrine employed in 1918.

The opportunity to test these ideas came at the beginning of May 1915. Renewed Russian operations had put Austria-Hungary in a desperate position and compelled a call for German assistance. Rather than merely prop up the line, the Austrian chief of staff, Conrad von Hötzendorff, suggested a counteroffensive (*Gegenschlag*) be launched in Galicia on the Gorlice–Tarnow sector. A breakthrough here would split the Russian front. Falkenhayn agreed and transferred eight divisions of German troops from the Western Front. The main blow was to be struck by the recently formed Eleventh Army under Generaloberst von Mackensen, supported by the Austro-Hungarian Fourth Army (a total of nine German, eight Austro-Hungarian and two cavalry divisions), on a 20-mile front.[23] Such a concentration of forces was not unusual by Western Front standards but represented a crushing novelty in the east, where positions were generally less developed, particularly as regards wire and shell-proof dug-outs. The chief of staff of Eleventh Army was Seeckt, promoted to colonel and given the opportunity to put his ideas into practice.

The first stage of the attack was a larger-scale repeat of Soissons. After a night of harassing fire on the Russian positions, the German guns began an intense four-hour bombardment at 6.00 a.m. on 2 May. The shallow Russian positions were shattered and the already low morale of the defenders collapsed. When the German infantry moved forward at 10.00 a.m., many of the Russians fled. Once again, Seeckt had shown that a short but intense bombardment could successfully suppress the power of the defence in preparation for an assault. As at Soissons, the Germans had achieved a break-in to the enemy position. At Soissons, it had been clear that the German infantry's tactics were inadequate to convert a break-in into a breakthrough. For Gorlice–Tarnow, Seeckt appears to have adopted the recommendations of the Third Army report. He attached some batteries of field guns to the advancing infantry and adopted a more flexible system of command, as was made clear in Eleventh Army's General Instructions.[24]

The attack was to be made at a rapid pace, so denying the enemy time to organise resistance on rearward positions and hampering the launching of counterattacks. The infantry was to be deployed in depth in order to keep up the momentum of the advance and to allow the envelopment of bypassed enemy positions that might hinder neighbouring units. While the danger of envelopment of deeply penetrating forces compelled Seeckt to fix certain linear objectives that were to be reached simultaneously, these objectives were not to hamper the advance: 'Any progress beyond these lines will be thankfully welcomed by the army [headquarters] and made use of.' Army headquarters would provide only general guidance: it was the responsibility of corps and divisions to maintain close lateral as well as rearward communications in order to respond to circumstances as they developed. The key was a dynamic adaptation to changing situations in which every formation sought both to achieve its own objectives and to assist its neighbours. The battle was to be an interlinked whole, not simply a number of adjacent corps assaults. Indeed, the German troops, schooled in von Schlieffen's doctrine of envelopment, proved too eager to wheel to the flanks to assist their neighbours, to the detriment of their own advance.[25]

The offensive was a stunning operational success. By 4 May, the Germans had taken 140,000 prisoners. When the front restabilised at the end of September, they had advanced over 300 miles and had inflicted two million casualties.[26] The subsequent development of the German offensive doctrine may be best examined by analysing changes in artillery and infantry tactics separately.

*Artillery*

Any analysis of the development of German offensive artillery doctrine must focus on the career of Oberstleutnant Georg Bruchmüller. In 1914, Bruchmüller was in early retirement, caused by a nervous breakdown after falling from his horse a year earlier. On mobilisation, he was assigned to command Garde-Landwehr-Artillerie-Bataillon 2 and became foot artillery staff officer of the fortress of Culm. In November 1914, he became artillery commander of the recently formed 86th Infantry Division and in 1915 he combined this post with command of Feldartillerie-Regiment 86.[27]

Bruchmüller was by training a foot artillerist, the branch equivalent to the British Royal Garrison Artillery (RGA). The RGA was generally more proficient at the theoretical aspects of gunnery, including indirect fire, than were either the Royal Horse Artillery or the Royal Field Artillery,[28] and the situation appears to have been similar in the German Army. Bruchmüller's technical knowledge was probably well above average even for the foot artillery, for this last posting before retirement had been as an instructor at the *Fussartillerie-Schiesschule* (Foot-Artillery Firing School). His ability is reflected by his receiving upon retirement letters of commendation from the commander of the school, General von Ziethen, and the Inspector-General of the Foot Artillery, General von Lauter.[29]

As a divisional artillery commander, Bruchmüller enjoyed direct control over all the guns of his formation: he was a 'leader of troops with the power of command'.[30] This was a deliberate response to the often haphazard employment of artillery in 1870,[31] a point clearly made in the pre-war field artillery regulations: 'The larger the force of artillery the more important it is that complete control of its fire should be in the hands of the artillery commander. The idea is that the full firepower of every battery is used to the best advantage.'[32] Although British organisation was similar, its philosophy, and therefore its function, was quite different. In 1914, the staff of a British divisional Commander Royal Artillery (CRA) consisted of a brigade major (added in 1913),[33] a staff captain and an ADC. Not only was this staff too small to exercise effective control over the division's four artillery brigades (each equivalent in size to a German artillery battalion), no communication equipment was provided for it so to do: 'Our prewar conception of this appointment [the CRA] seems to have visualised primarily the role of an artillery adviser to the general officer commanding the division and to have considered the occasions on which he would exercise direct command of the artillery of the division as exceptional.'[34] Since no guidelines were given as to how the guns were to be deployed, this varied between divisions according to the whim of the divisional commander. Not a few of these officers bypassed their CRA and assigned artillery brigades (that is, battalions) directly to the infantry brigade commanders,[35] making impossible the central control of artillery that the Germans considered so important.

Above divisional level, German and British practice was similar. In neither army did formations above division have a permanent artillery component. Instead, guns were attached from a general reserve according to requirements and were commanded directly by the headquarters of the formations to which they were attached. In both armies, formations above division maintained artillery advisers, who were to assist in the proper use of attached artillery but who had no power of command.[36] Given that the artillery advisers in both armies occupied similar positions, it is not surprising that they faced similar difficulties. Alan Brooke recorded, 'An energetic performance of their duties infringed on the prerogatives of subordinate commanders and staffs, whilst a more retiring attitude resulted in their advice being either not sought for or ignored when tendered.'[37] Bruchmüller expressed similar views, although he appears to have been less concerned with infringing the rights of subordinates,[38] perhaps because of the German doctrine that artillery should be centralised.

The system of centralisation of artillery at divisional level was consistently employed by the Germans until the spring of 1916 and was the basis of the plan developed by the artillery adviser of Tenth Army for the attack at Lake Narotsch, on the Eastern Front, in March of that year. This officer intended simply to divide that army's artillery assets among the various divisions and to allow each division to draw up its own fire plan. One of the divisions involved was 86th Division, and Bruchmüller, who had by now taken part in three important battles in the east, believed that the proposal of the Tenth Army artillery adviser did not make best use of the available assets. Accordingly, he drew up counter-proposals of his own, that involved the co-ordinated fire of all the army's guns, and forwarded them to the artillery adviser. Despite the implied criticism of his own proposals, the artillery adviser accepted the advantages of Bruchmüller's proposals and passed them on to Oberst Hell, Tenth Army chief of staff. Hell was convinced by Bruchmüller's arguments, and when Tenth Army attacked on 18 March it employed a unified fire plan to which all divisions had to comply. The result was a brilliant success.[39] This incident may be contrasted with British practice. Shelford Bidwell and Dominic Graham identified

> the long struggle [of the Artillery Staff] with the General Staff to ensure that the artillery was consulted before a plan was made [and]

> that all the artillery in a battle was controlled, initially, by a single commander who had the right to issue orders down the artillery chain of command ... Matters improved but the battle with the General Staff was never won. The General Staff, quoting the Staff Manual [written by the General Staff], insisted that orders could only be issued through army, corps or divisional commanders. An artillery officer could only issue orders to the units that were directly under his command. Consequently, on the Somme, Major-General Budworth, Rawlinson's Major-General, Royal Artillery, could not compel the corps artillery to comply with his plan for 1 July 1916, and only XIII Corps actually did so, almost to the letter and with success.[40]

Here was a further example of the differences in outlook between the German and British armies. The Germans saw operational effectiveness as the overriding objective of all command systems. In general, it was considered that this was best achieved through extensive decentralisation, enabling commanders on the spot to react rapidly to local circumstances. This doctrine, however, was not written in tablets of stone. If centralised command promised greater operational effectiveness then command would unhesitatingly be centralised. The development of a fire plan in advance for an attack by known forces from known locations at a known time against known enemy positions and forces was such a circumstance. Thereafter, command would be progressively decentralised as the situation became ever less certain. British practice was to adopt the German concept of decentralised command as a rigid dogma, to be applied regardless of the situation. This led to considerable resistance against artillery advisers at corps level and above being given executive authority, despite the fact that most CsRA at divisional level were from the RHA or the RFA and had little knowledge of detailed fire plans.[41]

The success of Bruchmüller's system of artillery command was such that when Oberst Hell was appointed chief of staff of Army Group von Linsingen in the summer of 1916 he brought Bruchmüller with him as his artillery adviser,[42] a major promotion. Soon after, the army group was attacked by General Brusilov's South-West Army Group. The Russian offensive made rapid progress against von Linsingen's largely Austrian command, taking 450,000 prisoners, but ground to a halt owing to a lack of reserves.[43] On 19 July, in the midst of the battle, the Germans attempted a counterstroke (*Gegenschlag*) at Tarnopol, for which Bruchmüller drew up the artillery plan. Following the doctrine developed by Seeckt at Soissons and Gorlice–Tarnow, the bombardment was to be brief but intense, designed to suppress the defending artillery and demoralise the enemy infantry. Surprise was essential, in order to deny the enemy time to reinforce his defences. Apart from laying down a centralised fire plan, Bruchmüller for the first time employed the system of predicted shooting: 'For the purpose of this crushing artillery blow he had organised a special artillery battering-train, each gun of which had a chart of its idiosyncrasies, so that ranging shots were unnecessary and each battery was expert in its allotted task.'[44] The attack was highly successful, the Germans advancing 80 miles and capturing 42,000 prisoners.

The Eastern Front remained relatively quiet for much of 1917 and Bruchmüller's next major action was at Riga in September with General von Hutier's Eighth Army. The initial attack was to be made by three divisions on a front of nine kilometres and was intended to seize a bridgehead across the River Dvina, some 300 metres wide at this point. The 750 guns and 550 mortars were collected with great secrecy for the attack in order to achieve surprise. By this stage in the war, the Germans had developed an artillery organisation based on tasking. The guns were divided into four categories: *Infanterie-Kampf-Artillerie* (IKA) (infantry support artillery), under divisional command; *Artillerie-Kampf-Artillerie* (AKA) (counterbattery artillery), under corps command; *Fern-Kampf-Artillerie* (FEKA) (harassing artillery), also under corps command; and *Schwerste-Flachfeuer-Artillerie* (SCHWEFLA) (distant bombardment artillery), under army command.[45]

The bombardment at Riga began at 4.00 a.m. on 1 September. For the first two hours, all IKA and AKA batteries were used to fire gas to suppress the Russian guns, while three batteries of field howitzers gassed command posts, observation posts and other key elements of the enemy command system. All this was done in darkness, without prior registration. At 6.00 a.m., the IKA batteries shifted their fire and engaged the Russian infantry positions with high explosive, while the AKA continued to gas the enemy guns. At 9.00 a.m., three-quarters of the AKA shifted to the front defences for ten minutes of intense bombardment before the infantry attacked at 9.10 a.m.[46] Once the infantry assault began, control of the guns was given to the divisions and a form of creeping barrage was laid down ahead of the infantry. Unlike similar British barrages, the German guns did not simply make lifts at predetermined intervals: observers kept track of the advance of the infantry by means of flares and the fire of the guns was adjusted accordingly.[47] The attack was a complete success. Defensive fire was negligible, many batteries of guns having been abandoned by their panic-stricken crews.[48] Much of the Russian front-line defensive system had been similarly abandoned.[49]

The essence of Bruchmüller's system was that artillery should be used to neutralise the defence immediately before an attack. A prolonged bombardment that gave the defender time to bring up reserves and churned up the ground over which the troops were to advance was considered counter-productive. Preliminary bombardments were to be brief but intense, and relied heavily on gas. Rather than spread fire over wide areas, fire was to be concentrated on individual enemy positions, particularly gun positions, and key parts of the command system, such as command posts and telephone exchanges. Best use of the available firepower was to be achieved through centralised planning, but control was to be decentralised as soon as the assault began. Surprise was of the greatest importance. Guns were to be concealed until the beginning of the operation and were to fire without previous registration. The accuracy of this fire was greatly improved by the system of predicted shooting developed by Hauptmann Pulkowsky towards the end of 1917.[50]

### *Infantry*

Seeckt's attack at Soissons in January 1915 had revealed that the German infantry no longer possessed the fighting power needed to overcome resistance by its own efforts. The central problem was that the post-1870 fire tactics, based on the fire of linear formations of riflemen, were no longer effective in the face of quick-firing cannon and machine guns. The answer was the development of the *Stosstrupptaktik* (assault squad tactics) by Rohr and Reddemann, discussed in Chapter 3. The new tactics were based on small assault squads (*Stosstrupps*), supported by infantry-controlled heavy weapons (*Truppwaffen*).

From the start, the assault detachment set up by OHL to develop new tactics was intended to become a training unit to disseminate its techiques to the whole of the infantry.[51] This proved to be particularly necessary because assault squad tactics were much more difficult than the old fire tactics, while the quality of training of the infantry had declined owing to casualties and the use of the best men as cadres for new divisions.[52]

Rohr took command of the assault detachment on 8 September 1915.[53] By December, he had developed and tested assault squad tactics sufficiently to run a short one-week course, for 43 officers and 351 men of 12th *Landwehr* Division, which included a demonstration assault by Rohr's men.[54] A second course was run for the cyclist company of 8th Bavarian Reserve Division from 29 January to 11 February 1916. It included training in the use of grenades and steel shields, the crossing of obstacles, the preparation and organisation of an attack, reconnaissance and combination with heavy weapons. The finale was again a full-scale practice attack on a dummy position.[55] The result of this course was that 8th Bavarian Reserve Division possessed its own assault company, which could be used both to undertake particularly difficult operations and to disseminate assault squad tactics through the division. Sturmabteilung Rohr fought at Verdun for the first three weeks of that offensive and suffered heavy casualties. Until these had been replaced, no more training courses could be organised.

To avoid this situation recurring, OHL expanded the unit to battalion size on 1 April.[56]

The next stage in the planned dissemination of assault squad tactics throughout the army occurred on 15 May, when Falkenhayn ordered each army on the Western Front to send two officers and four NCOs to Rohr for two weeks' training. On returning to their parent armies, these men were to begin the creation of assault detachments in every formation in those armies.[57] In a number of cases, units and formations had already formed specialist assault squads, whether independently or in imitation of Rohr, making the task of the men trained by Rohr easier.[58] By this means, Sturmbataillon Rohr began to have a definite influence on the training and tactics of the whole army.[59]

On 4 June, Falkenhayn ordered the conversion of four battalions of *Jäger* to assault battalions.[60] This marked the start of a twin-track policy for the dissemination of assault squad tactics. The first track was that the assault detachments set up by individual formations would use the new tactics in local operations, increasing the fighting power of their units and demonstrating the effectiveness of the tactics to the infantry as a whole. Their use in combat, however, meant that these detachments had little opportunity to run training courses. Their main function was to act as an example of good practice. The second track was the creation of a number of assault battalions which would concentrate on training. The men sent on courses run by these units would already have some experience of the new tactics, through joint operations with their formations' assault detachments, and would generally be convinced of the tactics' value before coming on the course, making them keener students. The training provided by the assault battalions could therefore be more intensive.

The formation of the new assault battalions was interrupted in July by the Brusilov offensive. So desperate was the need for troops that three of the four *Jäger* battalions were withdrawn from the conversion process and sent to the Carpathians. Only one, redesignated Jäger-(Sturm)-Bataillon 3, completed the change-over. On 20 August, it became the assault battalion of Second Army.

There seems little question that Falkenhayn would have taken steps to provide more assault battalions, as had been intended, once the crisis in the east was past, had he not been replaced by Hindenburg and Ludendorff on 29 August. Although Ludendorff inspected a company of Rohr's battalion on his visit to the German Crown Prince's headquarters on 7 September, his first contact with the assault battalions,[61] OHL issued no orders regarding these units for a further six weeks. The change at OHL meant that the spread of assault squad tactics continued only at a slow pace. Although each of the two existing assault battalions could train 400 officers and men per month,[62] this was inadequate if the tactics were to become universal. Even so, by the end of October, most formations on the Western Front had established assault detachments and training units, although the size and nature of these varied considerably.[63]

Once Ludendorff turned to the question of infantry tactics, he soon recognised the value of the assault battalions as training units and the need for a standard organisation.[64] On 23 October, he ordered that the creation of more assault battalions, begun by Falkenhayn in June, be completed. Owing to the number of assault detachments already formed, most of the new units were created by merging formation detachments into army assault battalions rather than by converting existing units. In December, assault battalions were approved for each army on the Western Front and for each army and army group in the east.[65] By the end of 1916, therefore, the two tracks of Falkenhayn's policy were in place. Each army had its own permanent assault battalion and many formations had temporary assault detachments. The effectiveness of this system is indicated by the successive editions of von Lossberg's *Ausbildungs-vorschrift der Fusstruppen* (AVF) (Training Manual of the Foot Troops).

The initial draft of the AVF, written in December 1916, laid down that the main tasks of the assault battalions were the training of the maximum number of officers and NCOs as instructors in the new tactics and the perfection of those tactics.[66] By the time the AVF was issued, in January 1917, a number of changes had been made, although the published version dealt with the assault battalions, under the heading of *Kampfschule* (combat schools), in much the same way as had the initial draft. The main changes were in the discussion of the organisation of the infantry company and revealed the extent to which assault squad tactics had been adopted by the infantry in general. The manual suggested the formation of a fourth platoon, to consist of the company's specialists: storm troopers, light machine-gun crews and grenade-firer crews.[67] The storm troopers were to be the best men in the company, trained by the assault battalions to form assault squads that would lead attacks.[68]

The second edition of the AVF, issued in January 1918, abolished the fourth platoon of specialists.[69] In a section headed *Stosstruppausbildung* (assault squad training), the manual laid down that all soliders were to be trained in the assault squad tactics, including combination with support weapons.[70] Troops were now to be trained equally in the rifle tactics of open war and the assault squad tactics of position war.[71] This change may have been influenced by the success of the German counterattack at Cambrai, at the end of November 1917. Although the divisions involved had received no special training in the techniques of the offensive, the troops employed assault squad tactics with great skill.[72] The January 1918 edition of the AVF recognised that the new tactics were no longer the preserve of specialists. Ony 18 months after Falkenhayn ordered the first training courses, assault squad tactics had become the standard doctrine for position war.

The nature of assault squad tactics was expressed in the pamphlet *Anweisung für die Verwendung eines Sturmbataillones* (Instructions for the Employment of an Assault Battalion), issued by Rohr on 27 May 1916, and subsequently incorporated into the AVF.[73]

The assault battalion would normally be used to lead particularly difficult attacks. It would not be used as a complete unit but would assign individual assault squads to the infantry. This made the best use of the individual training of the storm troopers and reduced casualties. The storm troopers were to make a personal reconnaissance of the ground one or two days before the attack and were to discuss the operation with the infantry who were to assist them. The officers of the assault detachment had a particular responsibility to ensure that their men were employed correctly.

Attacks were not to be made in skirmish lines, which were vulnerable to the defenders' wire obstacles and machine guns, but in a number of small assault columns, each attacking at a favourable point. The assault was to be led by the assault squads, who were to reach the enemy position at the same moment that the artillery barrage lifted. Here they were to break into the enemy position, roll up (*aufrollen*) the trenches and capture any strong-points. Close behind the assault squads were to follow squads of infantry, who were to clear and consolidate the position. A basic principle was that the assault should be made by the minimum number of men consistent with the achievement of the objective.

Support weapons were to be allocated to the assault squads as required. Machine guns were to provide flanking fire and support against unexpected targets. Flamethrowers were highly effective for rolling-up trenches but were vulnerable to enemy fire and so should not be used in the first wave. Infantry guns could be used to engage machine-gun posts and strongpoints, but had to be carefully hidden before the attack. Light mortars and grenade-firers should be employed to suppress the defence before the assault and then follow behind the assault squads as a mobile reserve of fire. Finally, after the attack, the men of the assault battalion were to be withdrawn at once in order to prepare for other operations.

### *Der Angriff im Stellungskrieg*

Despite these considerable developments in the tactics of both artillery and infantry, the German Army had as yet produced no manual specifically concerned with the attack in position war. This deficiency was rectified on 1 January 1918 with the publication of the manual *Der Angriff im Stellungskrieg* (The Attack in Position Warfare). As with *Die Abwehr im Stellungskrieg*, the new manual was largely written by Hauptmann Geyer. The importance attached to the doctrine laid down in the manual may be gauged by its issue to every officer down to and including battalion commanders.[74]

The manual opened with a number of principles considered basic to successful offensive action. The first of these was a high standard of training among the troops, including not only technical knowledge about weapon capabilities and formations, but also the maintenance of an offensive spirit. The second was the need for a high standard of command: 'The attack . . . demands strict command, [and] careful and thorough directives for the combined action of all arms . . . On the other hand, every attack offers opportunity for free activity and joyfully decisive action even for the individual soldier.' This balance between careful planning and dynamic responsiveness was central to the German philosophy of combat. Third, all arms and all leaders should be closely linked, from front to rear, rear to front and to both sides. This preserved order and allowed rapid and appropriate reaction to events. Fourth, 'every attack must have its *Schwerpunkt* [focus of energy]'. The entire disposition of forces and allocation of resources was based upon this. Fifth, the attacking troops must maintain the momentum of the assault and must advance quickly and deeply. Flank and rear protection, as well as fire support, were the responsibility of supporting troops. The key to success was not mass but the firepower of the artillery and infantry. Indeed, excessive mass could hinder the attack. The manual emphasised, 'Everything depends on quick and independent action by all ranks within the context of the whole'. The final principles were the decisive importance of surprise, the effectiveness of flank attacks[74] and the need for skill in the use of ground.[75]

The emphasis on the need for dynamic reaction to circumstances was repeated in the section on command. Regardless of the overall size of an attack, the basic combat unit (*Kampfeinheit*) was the division, for it alone combined the action of all arms into a single operation. Although the initial stage of an attack had to be co-ordinated centrally, divisional commanders were to have their freedom of action restricted as little as possible and were to make their own plans according to local circumstances within the framework of the whole.[76] Divisions should be assigned sufficiently narrow sectors, generally no wider than two kilometres, to allow them to penetrate through the entire depth of the enemy defences. To avoid unnecessary delays, divisions were to advance to the limit of their ability and have a second-line division already under command to renew the attack as soon as the front division faltered.[77] The system was in effect the same as that of front divisions and *Eingreif* divisions in the defensive doctrine.

Reserves were to be employed early in order to maintain momentum. It was recognised that, even in the best-planned battles, the decision where to commit reserves would have to be made on the basis of imperfect information. As a general guide, reserves should be directed against points where the enemy was weakening or that promised opportunities. This was the best way to help sectors where the attack was progressing only slowly. Even in the face of enemy counterattacks, reserves might be better employed in reinforcing success than in supporting the threatened sector. The most important consideration was the maintenance of the firepower of the troops already committed. Commanders were therefore to be far forward. In part this was to reduce the number of changes of headquarters' location, with its inevitable confusion, and in part to ensure that commanders had a good view of the battle area. Effective communications were essential. As the battle shifted into mobile war, commanders should be ever further forward, often on horseback, in order to counteract the greater confusion and uncertainty of such operations.[78]

Reconnaissance was considered essential both before and during the battle.[79] Information on friendly troops was of great importance and units were to make regular reports on their situation, at set times and when reaching certain locations. Nevertheless, staffs were not to rely solely on such reports but were to use their own means to clarify the situation in both their own and neighbouring sectors. Of equal importance were close communications between artillery, mortars and infantry.[80]

The manual next turned to the individual arms, beginning with artillery and mortars. While preparatory bombardments might last only minutes, or even be dispensed with entirely, large-scale attacks usually required several hours of preparatory fire.[81] No mention was made of bombardments lasting more than a few hours. The various tasks assigned to the guns were similar to those developed since the Soissons attack. It is of note, however, that the accompaniment of the infantry with infantry guns and some field guns as support batteries was now officially approved and considered of exceptional effectiveness.[82] At the start of an operation, artillery was to be centrally controlled.[83] Its most important task was the suppression of the enemy guns during the assault: a complete defeat of the defender's artillery was considered impossible. Gas, as Bruchmüller had found at Riga, was very effective for this task. In the preparation of the enemy trenches for attack (*Sturmreifschiessen*), the moral effect of the preparatory fire was considered as important as its physical effect. The moral effect was to be increased by directing particularly dense and heavy-calibre fibre against break-in points, the use of mortars and flanking fire and reliance on short but very intense bombardments.[84]

Turning to the infantry, the manual laid down a single principle that may be considered the basis of assault squad tactics:

> For success in the infantry assault, the number of infantrymen committed is not the decisive factor. Rather, the decisive factors are the combat power of the infantry, produced by rest, training and

> equipment, the care taken in the preparations, the cleverness of command and troops, and also the speed and decisiveness of their actions.[85]

The infantry's combat power consisted not merely of the number of riflemen and grenadiers but included equally its firepower, produced by supporting heavy weapons.[86]

Within the sector assigned to each division, attacks were not to be uniform. Centres of resistance should be avoided and passed by, to be enveloped by reserves, consisting of all-arms combat teams, able rapidly to overcome the resistance of isolated strongpoints. The leading troops should avoid every unnecessary delay and advance as quickly as possible. For this reason, particular care had to be taken to ensure that seized areas were cleared by reserves. The larger the attack, the greater the opportunity there was for individual assault squads to act independently within the context of the whole. Small advantages won in this way should be exploited. This made effective low-level leadership essential. 'The forward pressure of the troops cannot therefore be emphasised too strongly. Particularly in a major breakthrough, the bravest decision is generally the best.' As the depth of the advance grew, senior commanders would find it ever more difficult to react quickly enough. 'In such circumstances, independent and cheerfully responsible [*verantwortungsfreudigen*] action by junior commanders is important.'[87]

## German Preparations for the Offensive

After long and careful deliberations, the Germans decided in January 1918 to attack on a 50-mile front between Arras and the River Oise, opposite Amiens, an operation code-named Michael. The attack was to be made by three armies: Seventeenth, Second and Eighteenth.

Seventeenth Army was created at the end of January 1918, when its commander, General Otto von Below, arrived on the Western Front.[88] Below had begun the war as commander of I Reserve Corps and had fought at Tannenberg. In November 1914, he succeeded Hindenburg as commander of Eighth Army, which he led until October 1916. After six months as theatre commander in Macedonia, Below was called to the Western Front in April 1917, where he took over Sixth Army from Falkenhausen and fought against the British offensive at Arras. In September he was again moved, to command Fourteenth Army on the Italian Front in the highly successful Caporetto offensive.[89] In January 1918, he returned to the Western Front with his staff, redesignated Seventeenth Army.[90] General Otto von Below was a highly experienced commander. He had served on every front on which German troops were engaged and had been intimately involved in the battles of Tannenberg and Caporetto, two of the most spectacular victories of the war. He brought with him an existing staff, that had proved its worth in the recent operations in Italy.

Second Army was commanded by General von der Marwitz. Commander of II Cavalry Corps in 1914, Marwitz moved to the Eastern Front in October 1914, where he led XXXVIII Reserve Corps and later VI Corps. He returned to the West in 1917 as commander of Second Army and masterminded the successful counterattack (*Gegenangriff*) at Cambrai.[91] Marwitz therefore had experience of fighting the British and knew the ground over which his troops would fight.

Eighteenth Army was created in December 1917 and was commanded by General Oskar von Hutier. Hutier had commanded 2nd Guard Division in 1914. He was promoted in April 1915, to command XXI Corps on the Eastern Front, and again in April 1917, to command Eighth Army, which he led in the capture of Riga in September of that year.[92] The staff for Eighteenth Army was the redesignated headquarters of Army Group Woyrsch, transferred from the east.[93] As has been noted, Hutier was in no way the inventor of the new German tactics. His choice to command Eighteenth Army was probably because of his recent success at Riga. Each of the three army commanders selected had won an important victory towards the end of 1917 by using the methods that were incorporated into *Der Angriff im Stellungskrieg.*

The three armies that were to carry out the attack were assigned 74 divisions, of which 11 were *Stellungsdivisionen* (low-quality position divisions) that were merely to hold sectors of the line where no attack was to be made. Three divisions were held in OHL reserve. Of the remaining 60 divisions, 42 were to attack Gough's Fifth Army and 18 were to attack Byng's Third Army.[94] Since only part of Byng's army was to be attacked, the initial odds were similar along the entire front, at about two to one.[95] The collection of large forces, however, was of itself no guarantee of success. As the new German offensive doctrine stressed, the quality of the troops was at least as important as their quantity. The first stage of achieving a high standard among the attacking troops was the withdrawal of all men over the age of 35 from those units assigned to the attack and their replacement by younger men from the formations left on the Eastern Front.[96]

Having concentrated the best of Germany's soldiers into the attacking divisions, resulting in up to half the strength of each unit being made up of pre-war troops,[97] Ludendorff put them through a rigorous programme of training. Special importance was placed on individual training, as had been the case before the war. The courses for senior officers and their staffs were revised in accordance with the offensive doctrine and new courses established for junior officers and NCOs.[98] Fifty-six divisions (equivalent to the entire BEF) were pulled out of the line and given three weeks' intensive training.[99] The care with which these courses were organised was revealed by Ernst Jünger, a company commander in Fusilier-Regiment 73. Jünger recorded that when his division (111th) went through the programme in January 1918, a detailed training scheme was issued down to company level. The troops practised the skirmish tactics to be used in open warfare and assault squad tactics for attacks on trenches. Long hours were also spent on firing ranges, honing the troops' marksmanship skills.[100]

The programme followed by Jünger's division, which ended with a 24-hour exercise by the entire division,[101] was conducted under as realistic conditions as was possible and with ample supplies of live ammunition.[102] Accidents happened and were accepted as an unavoidable consequence of the realistic training essential if the required standard of training was to be achieved. Jünger reported that one of his machine-gunners accidentally shot an officer off his horse and not a few artillerymen lost fingers while manhandling their guns across broken ground.[103] Not only did existing skills have to be refined, the troops had to learn new skills also. Chief amongst these was the ability to operate as part of a combined-arms team. Every exercise was therefore carried out with units of both infantry and artillery acting together.[104] With the increased chaos of the anticipated battle, the artillery could no longer expect to be protected by the infantry as it advanced over recently seized ground. Every battery was therefore issued two machine guns for self-defence and sent one officer on a machine-gun course.[105]

## The Battle

The 50-mile stretch of front attacked by the Germans on 21 March 1918 was defended by 19 British divisions, with several more in reserve. A detailed examination of the entire sector is impossible in the limited space available. Even the brief account of the events of that day given by the *Official History* fills more than 100 pages of text.[106] This study, therefore, will focus on the action on the front of 30th and 36th (Ulster) Divisions of XVIII Corps, commanded by Lieutenant-General Sir Ivor Maxse. The third division of XVIII Corps, 61st Division, will not be covered, since the events on its front were similar to those experienced by 30th Division. This sector is of interest because of the variation in the course of the battle in the zones of the two divisions and to its witnessing the very first use of tanks by the German Army.

MAP 4
St Quentin, 21 March 1918: The Battlefield

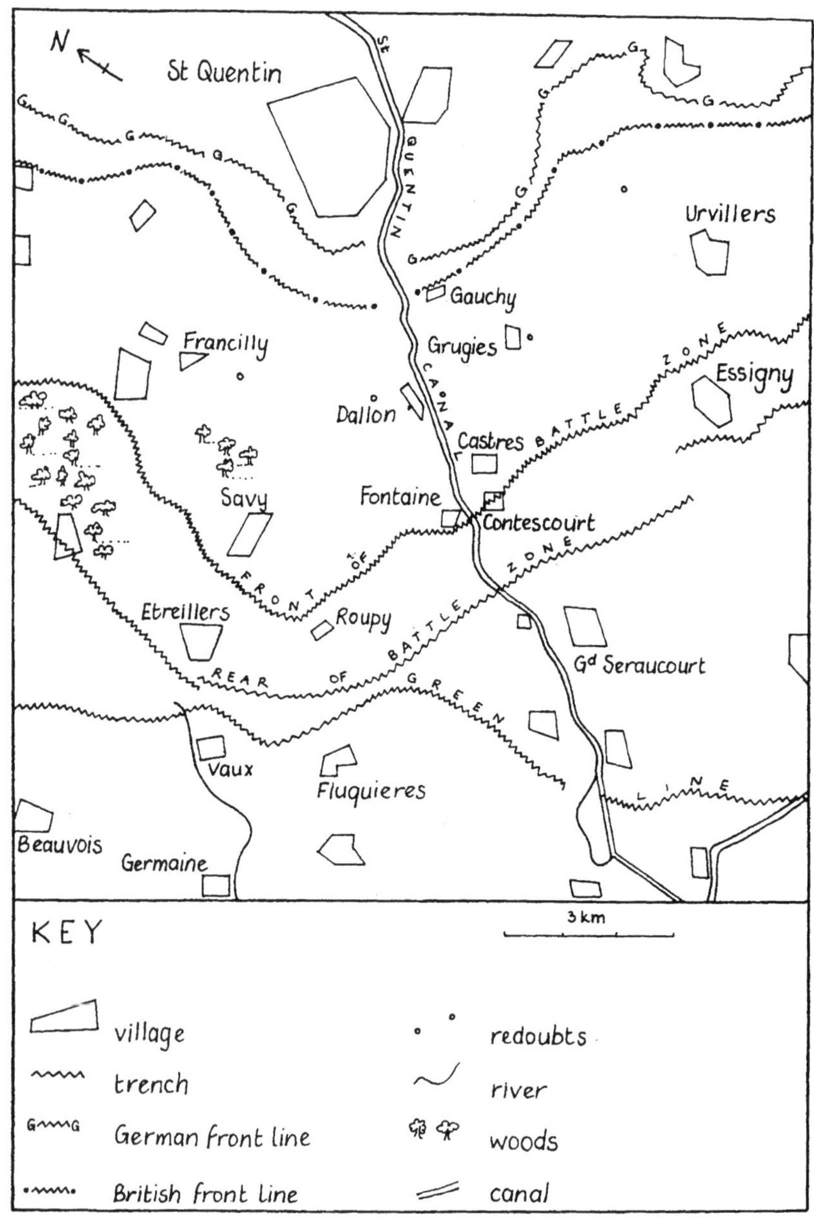

The sector held by XVIII Corps was a little over nine miles wide and lay opposite the German-held town of St Quentin (Map 4). The whole of the forward zone was exposed to German observation, but most of the battle zone was on reverse slopes. The defence of the sector was rendered more difficult by a number of valleys, including that of the River Somme, that penetrated the position from the north-east to the south-west. As on much of the Fifth Army front, the fieldworks on this sector consisted of a line of posts, 300 yards apart, along the front line; a row of 14 large defended localities, called the Line of Redoubts, at one-mile intervals 1,500 yards behind the front line; and a few trenches and machine-gun posts protected by wire at the front of the battle zone, which had little depth.[107] The deployment of 30th and 36th Divisions was typical of the British defensive doctrine (Map 5). Of the six brigades in the two divisions, five were deployed in the defensive system, each with one battalion in each of the three zones. The sixth brigade, 89th of 30th Division, was held in corps reserve.[108]

A comparison of the order of battle of the two divisions before[109] and after[110] the recent reorganisation of divisions from 12 to nine battalions shows the extent of the upheaval. In 30th Division, each brigade disbanded one battalion and transferred another to one of the other two brigades. Since only New Army battalions were disbanded, this effectively changed the division from a New Army formation largely recruited in Manchester and Liverpool but with a stiffening of Regular battalions into one with two largely Regular brigades and one Liverpool brigade. The extra upheaval caused by the transfer of battalions between brigades appears to have been motivated by a desire to disband the highest numbered (and therefore junior) battalions of the Manchester and King's (Liverpool) regiments. Had this urge for administrative neatness not been followed, no transfers between brigades would have been necessary and the upheaval caused by the reorganisation would have been halved. The situation in 36th (Ulster) Division was still more dramatic. Fully eight of its 12 battalions were disbanded and five Regular battalions were brought into the division. While its character as an Ulster formation was largely preserved, its uniqueness as a division raised by the Ulster Volunteer Force was shattered. This virtual disbandment of their old division must have affected the morale of the remaining UVF men. Since the reorganisation was completed only a few weeks before the German offensive, the British formations had little time to settle down to the new organisation and adapt to the changes in tactics and assignment of battalions.

### *The Artillery Bombardment*

For the preparatory artillery bombardment for the attack, the Germans concentrated 6,473 cannon, out of a total of 13,832 guns on the Western

MAP 5
St Quentin, 21 March 1918: British Defences

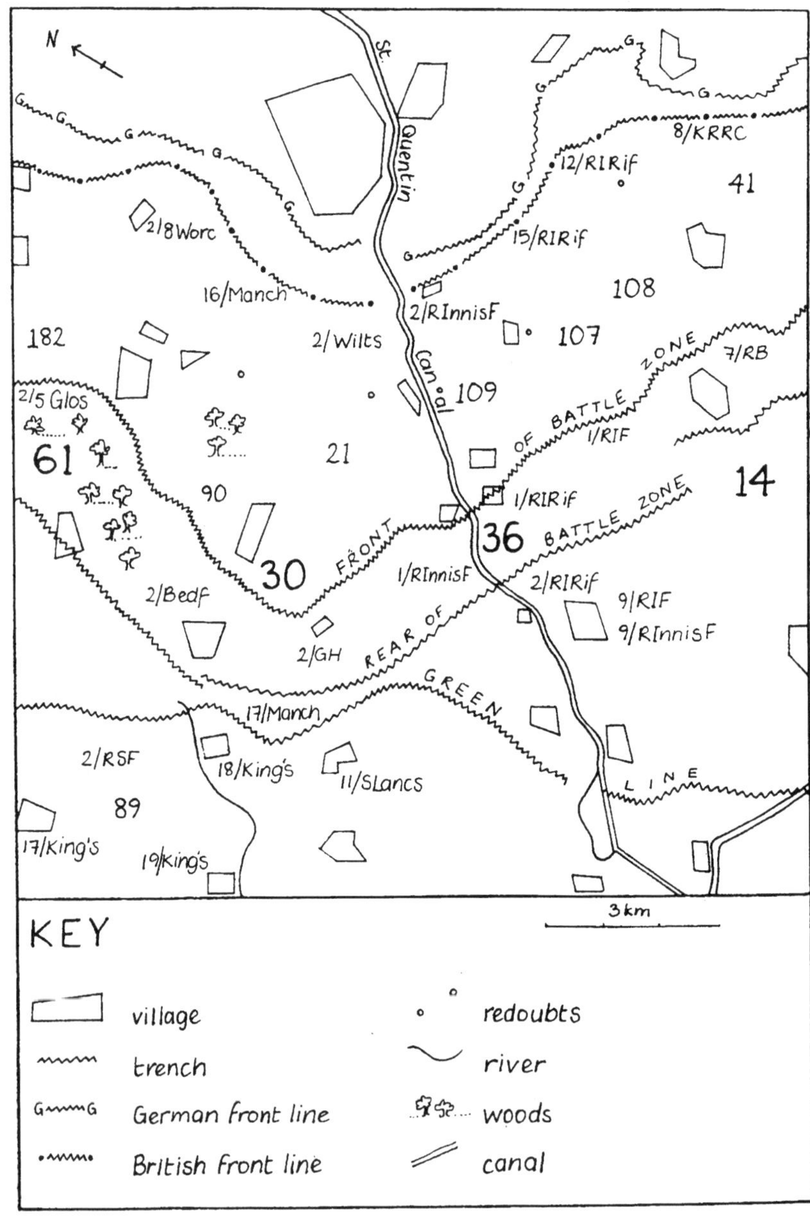

Front. There were also 3,532 mortars, out of 8,845 in the west.[111] The guns alone were to fire 1,160,000 shells in the preparatory bombardment.[112] Although the number of guns was impressive even by First World War standards, they were spread over a very long front, giving only 50.16 heavy guns per mile. This was only one and a half times the density used by the British at the start of the Somme and less than that achieved by the British by the end of that battle.[113] The density of guns was therefore by no means exceptional.

What was exceptional was that the entire preparatory bombardment was to last only five hours and 40 minutes and was to be made without prior registration. This system owed much to the methods developed by Bruchmüller, but was modified to suit the particular circumstances of the Western Front. Although Bruchmüller probably played an important role in the planning of the artillery barrage for the offensive, he had executive authority over the guns of Eighteenth Army only. The other two armies had their own artillery commanders, who were themselves prominent artillerists, and a number of other leading gunnery experts were attached to the three armies. The overall plan was therefore a joint product.[114] Thanks to Bruchmüller's talents as a self-publicist after the war, however, more is known about the artillery preparation on the front of Eighteenth Army than on the rest of the front attacked. The programme given here is therefore that drawn up by Bruchmüller. Those of Second and Seventeenth Armies will have been similar.[115]

The first phase of the bombardment was to begin at 4.40 a.m. on 21 March. For the first 20 minutes, until 5.00 a.m., every gun and mortar was to fire an intense bombardment on the British artillery and mortar positions, command posts, telephone exchanges and the billets behind the lines. The British guns were to be bombarded with nine gas shells to every two shells of high explosive, the other targets received gas and high explosive in equal quantities.[116] The mortars were to cease fire at 5.00 a.m, but the guns were to continue to fire on these targets, except for a ten-minute period from 5.30 a.m., until 6.40 a.m., the end of the first phase.

As at Riga, the intention was not to achieve complete destruction of the enemy position, impossible in the few hours available, but to shatter the morale of the enemy troops.[117] The weight of the initial phase of the bombardment and the suddenness of its beginning[118] were important factors in the moral effect of the artillery preparation. The bombardment was also intended to cause confusion behind the British lines. The shelling of command posts and telephone exchanges struck at the nodal points of the British command system, disabling the army's 'brain' and cutting its 'nerves'. If the bombardment was effective, many British headquarters would be crippled or left unable to communicate with their units. The cutting of communications with headquarters would have caused confusion among the troops holding the forward defences, who were conditioned to rely on detailed orders from above. The unexpected shelling of billets far behind the lines was intended to extend this paralysis to the reserves.

In the middle of the first phase, from 5.30 a.m. to 5.40 a.m., all but the heaviest guns were to shift their fire to the British infantry defences. The British forward zone and the front of the battle zone were to be engaged with high explosives only, the rear of the battle zone with a mixture of gas and high explosive. This sudden bombardment was probably intended to deceive the defenders into leaving their dug-outs and manning the defences in anticipation of an assault, making themselves vulnerable to the main bombardment when it resumed after this sub-phase.

The second phase lasted 30 minutes, from 6.40 a.m. to 7.10 a.m., and was divided into three periods, each of ten minutes, in which particular groups of guns were to check the accuracy of their fire and detect any errors in the table for predicted fire drawn up for each gun.

During the third phase, from 7.10 a.m. until 8.20 a.m., the AKA (counterbattery artillery) and FEKA (harassing artillery) were to continue to bombard their previous targets while the IKA (infantry support artillery) engaged the enemy defensive positions. On the Eighteenth Army front, the IKA had been divided into 13 sectors, two or three to each corps. In each sector, the guns were divided into four groups: group 'a' consisted of howitzers, group 'b' of howitzers and super-heavy howitzers, and group 'c' and 'd' of field guns.[119] From 7.40 a.m., IKA 'a' was to sweep the ground between the trenches of the front part of the forward zone for 15 minutes, IKA 'b' was to shell certain key strongpoints for ten minutes and then sweep backwards over the forward zone, and IKA 'c' was to sweep the battle zone with tear gas and high explosive for ten minutes.

The fourth phase, from 8.20 a.m. until 9.35 a.m., was very similar to the third phase, the various sweeps commencing at 8.50 a.m. The targets were to be the same, except for certain FEKA batteries.

For the fifth phase, covering the final five minutes of the bombardment, from 9.35 a.m. to 9.40 a.m., most guns were to engage the British forward zone, covering it entirely with fire, while others were to shell the front part of the battle zone. All were to fire high explosive only. Counterbattery work was to continue. In an attempt to achieve surprise, there was to be no immediate change in the bombardment when the infantry attacked 'without hurrahs' at 9.40 a.m.

Despite thick fog on the morning of 21 March, the German guns opened fire precisely on schedule at 4.40 a.m.[120] The bombardment was generally accurate, despite the lack of previous registration. Headquarters, telephone exchanges and transport centres were all hit. Most of the telephone cables to the forward zone were quickly cut, despite their being buried six feet deep: the Germans had located them on aerial photographs and shelled the junctions.[121] The overall effect was to shake the morale of the rear area troops and temporarily to paralyse the British command system. The order to man the battle zone, however, was successfully communicated to the troops within minutes of the bombardment beginning.

Comparatively few men were killed by the bombardment in the forward and battle zones, although a number of posts were wiped out by direct hits and many of the defenders of other posts were wounded. The main effect of the shelling was that it cut communications to the forward zone, often within minutes of the guns opening fire.[122] The fate of the battalions deployed here often remained a mystery until after the war, many disappearing virtually without trace.[123] This cutting of communications, coupled with the thick fog, prevented information being passed back to the British artillery as to the moment of the attack. The guns could only fire on their pre-set counter-preparation lines.[124] Although this fire was not observed, it had been carefully planned in advance and was probably not much less effective than if it had been observed. Conversely, the German gunners were unable to observe their own fire, which resulted in a number of British defended localities being almost untouched by the bombardment.[125]

### *The Assaulting Troops*

The manual *Der Angriff im Stellungskrieg* was primarily concerned with the conduct of the offensive at battalion level and above, as had been its defensive predecessor, *Die Abwehr im Stellungskreig*. In part, the omission of detailed regulations for the minor tactical level was caused by the continuing development of ideas in that field. Throughout most of 1917, whenever assault battalions were used in the combat role they were employed for particularly difficult raids and they did not play a significant role in the various defensive battles of the year. Although assault squad tactics were increasingly used by the line infantry, there was little work done on linking the new tactics into the larger context at battalion and regimental level.

For the counterattack at Cambrai, Second Army committed one company of Jäger-(Sturm)-Bataillon 3 to support 28th Infantry Division. On the right, the division placed its own infantry in the first and third waves and the storm troopers in the second wave. On the left, the storm troopers were placed in the first wave with two waves of infantry behind. In both cases, the leading wave of infantry formed a skirmish line, while the storm troopers and the rear wave of infantry formed assault squads. In the battle, the Germans found that the skirmish lines quickly broke down into assault squads and that attacks soon came to be led by the storm troopers, with the infantry following behind to mop up and widen the gaps that they had created.[126]

The German high command decided that the assault battalions of the three armies attacking in Operation Michael should be used in their entirety to aid the assault. Jäger-(Sturm)-Bataillon 3, which had now become the leader of the assault battalions in the tactical development of assault squad tactics, used the course that it ran for the divisions pulled out of the line in preparation for the offensive to test various ways in which assault battalions could be committed. The conclusion drawn was that every attack needed to be spearheaded by an assault squad from one of the assault battalions. The calculation as to how many squads would be required was based on the assumption that each assault division would attack with two of its three regiments, each regiment with two of its three battalions and each battalion with three of its four companies, making a total of 12 companies on the divisional front. Each company would concentrate its assault on a single break-in point and so would require the assistance of one assault squad. Certain attacks would be particularly difficult and so require more than one squad, making a divisional allocation of about 20 squads necessary. Each company of the assault battalion could provide ten assault squads; the unit as a whole could therefore supply enough for two divisions.[127] Since there was only one assault battalion in each army, assault squads could thus be assigned to only those divisions that were the army's *Schwerpunkt* (focus).

The formation adopted by the leading troops was to consist of three waves. The first wave was made up of small patrols, about one section from each assaulting infantry company, that would reconnoitre the enemy position and identify hostile strongpoints. About 200 metres behind these patrols came the attached assault squads, supported by a few infantry sections, each with a light machine-gun squad and about half with a flame-thrower team. This wave would envelop any strongpoints that threatened to delay the advance. 150 metres behind the storm troopers came stronger forces of infantry and heavy machine guns, to provide fire support for the assault squads. These troops protected the rear of the storm troopers and widened the gaps that they created.

The attacks were supplied with large numbers of heavy weapons. One assaulting regiment in Second Army, the focus of its division, was assigned: a number of assault squads (probably ten) from Jäger-(Sturm)-Bataillon 3, each with its own light machine gun; several heavy weapons from the assault battalion (probably two infantry guns, two light mortars and two manportable flamethrowers);[128] one 12-gun company from a *Maschinengewehr-Scharfschützen-Abteilung* (MGSSAbt) (machine-gun sharpshooter detachment); one 12-gun *Gebirgs-MGSSAbt* (mountain machine guns); the divisional mortar company, of four heavy and eight medium mortars; a battery of four field guns; a battery of six infantry guns; and half a platoon of combat engineers. The regiment already possessed three 12-gun machine-gun companies and a detachment of six light mortars.[129] The total number of support weapons in this regimental sector on 21 March 1918 was 104, about 17 for each break-in point. In addition, each company had six organic light machine guns.

*The First Phase*

The front held by 30th and 36th (Ulster) Divisions coincided approximately with the attack sectors assigned to the German IX (Generalleutnant Ritter und Edler von Oetinger) and XVII (Generalleutnant von Werern) Corps (Map 6). These two corps attacked with five divisions in the first line and seven in the second and third lines. Conveniently, the attack sectors of each division accorded roughly with the front held by each of the British brigades.

1st Bavarian Division was the left-hand formation of XVII Corps.[130] It attacked with two regiments up, Bayerisches-Infanterie-Regiment (BIR) 1 on the left and BIR 24 on the right, with BIR 2 in reserve. The division appears to have adopted the recommended deployment, with each attacking regiment having two battalions up and each battalion three companies up, a total of 12 assault points on the divisional frontage. The regimental histories do not record the presence of any attached storm troopers, so the division probably relied on its own assault detachment to spearhead the assault.

The Bavarians moved forward at 9.15 a.m., before the preparatory bombardment ended, in order to reach the British front line at precisely 9.40 a.m. The thick fog reduced visibility to only ten metres, causing several units to become disorientated. Little resistance was faced from the British front line and there was little defensive artillery fire. Deeper into the British defences, the fog allowed several machine-gun posts to escape detection until they opened fire, causing heavy casualties. By the time the fog began to lift, at about 11.00 a.m., 1st Bavarian Division had penetrated deep into the British forward zone.[131] BIR 1 had captured most of Urvillers and had overrun most of the garrison of this sector, 8/King's Royal Rifle Corps (KRRC) of 14th (Light) Division: the battalion commander surrendered and only two men reached the battle zone. BIR 24 had been almost as successful. In co-operation with 36th Division on the right, it had overrun 12/Royal Irish Rifles (RIRif), only the defended locality at Le Pontchu and a few isolated posts still holding out.

To the right of 1st Bavarian Division was 36th Division, coincidentally attacking its British numerical counterpart. The division assaulted with Grenadier-Regiment 5 on the left and IR 175 on the right. IR 128 was in divisional reserve, except for one battalion linking the division to the Bavarians on the left. This battalion, I/128, formed the core of a battle group under Hauptmann Grote that also included 4/ and 5/Rohr, 2 MGK/Rohr, 1MWK/Rohr, a battalion of field guns and the four A7V

MAP 6
St Quentin, 21 March 1918: First Phase

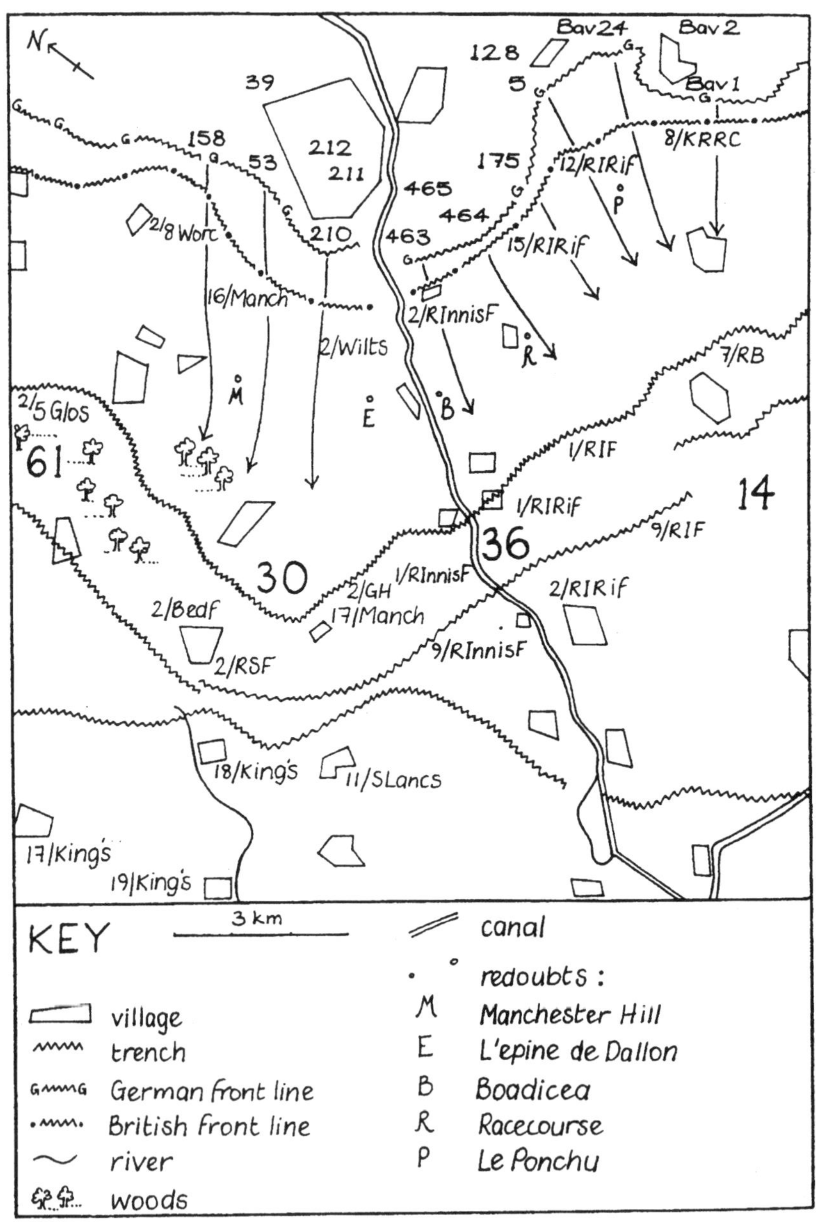

tanks of schwere-Sturmpanzerkampfwagen-Abteilung (sStPKWAbt) (heavy assault armoured combat-vehicle detachment) 1.[132] Moving forward at 9.40 a.m., Abteilung Grote took the British front line with ease. Soon, however, British machine guns engaged the tanks and this, combined with the thick fog and gas blown from the south-west, delayed and confused the advance. Even so, by 11.00 a.m. the battle group had pushed well into the positions of 12/RIRif. Apart from assisting in the capture of one stretch of front line where the German infantry was held up, the British garrison fleeing at the sight of the tanks, Abteilung Grote was outpaced by the speed of the advance.

GrenRegt 5 passed over the British front line almost without noticing it, the garrison being dead or trying to surrender.[133] Here too the confusion caused by the fog was the greatest obstacle to the advance. Units stumbled on British posts, many of which surrendered, but others caused heavy casualties. Those that resisted were mostly overrun by the second or third wave of the attack. Even the regimental headquarters was involved in the capture of one post of 40 men from 15/RIRif. At about 10.40 a.m., 6/5 came across a battery of field guns still firing on their counter-preparation targets, unaware that the German infantry was so close. The company had soon put its regiment's mark on eight brand-new British guns. 8/5 captured two more guns a few minutes later. By 11.00 a.m., the whole of the forward zone of 15/RIRif had been overrun. Only a few small posts, notably Racecourse Redoubt, still remained in British hands.

238th Division was one of 13 divisions formed during the winter of 1916–17. As was German practice, the officers were taken directly from the front or from recovered wounded, as were half the rankers. The remainder were recruits from the class of 1898.[134] At St Quentin, the division appears to have attacked with all three regiments in line.

IR 464 was the left-hand unit of the division.[135] Although it suffered a number of casualties while forming up, particularly among the accompanying battery from Feld-Artillerie-Regiment (FdAR) 62, when the British artillery responded to the German bombardment, the regiment was able to move off at the moment the barrage lifted. The main attack started at 9.40 a.m., but on some sectors patrols appear to have been sent forward at 8.30 a.m. The lead troops found the British front-line garrison dead or stunned and the position was overrun within minutes. A few machine-gun nests had survived the bombardment, but they were blinded by the fog and were left to the following waves. The first heavy fighting took place in the British line of redoubts. Most posts were soon overcome by the flamethrowers, though some fought on desperately even after they had been surrounded. By 11.00 a.m., the line had fallen, only one large post, probably Racecourse Redoubt, remaining.

The right-hand unit of 238th Division was IR 463.[136] Assaulting at

9.40 a.m., the Germans quickly crossed the British front line, which they found already evacuated, and had seized Gauchy by 10.15 a.m. As the advance continued, the Germans again came across isolated machine-gun posts, the battle becoming a number of individual skirmishes as these posts were overrun or left to the following waves. The fiercest skirmish was around Grugies, starting at 10.20 a.m. Here the flamethrowers again proved their worth: one burst of flame was usually enough to persuade the defenders of a post to surrender. Shortly before 11.00 a.m., III/463 captured a British battalion headquarters, probably that of 15/RIRif. By this time, the only post holding out in the neighbouring zone of 2/Royal Inniskilling Fusiliers (RInnisF) was Boadicea Redoubt, defended by one company under the battalion commander, Lord Farnham.[137]

To the north of 238th Division, IX Corps attacked with two divisions, 45th Reserve on the left and 50th on the right. The sector of 45th Reserve Division was only 1,500 metres wide at the front line, broadening to 3,000 metres by the line Roupy–Fontaine.[138] Owing to the limited space available, the division initially attacked with only RIR 210. RIR 211 was to move up on the left once L'Epine de Dallon was reached and RIR 212 was to be inserted between the first two regiments when the advance reached Roupy. To support its attack, 45th Reserve Division was allocated elements of Garde-Grenadier-Regiment 3 of 5th Guard Division, a number of mortars (giving it a total of 44), 12 assault squads and a number of flame-throwers (probably from Eighteenth Army's Sturmabataillon 12), the 12 machine guns of Gebirgs-MGSSAbt 215 and the guns of one battalion of ResFdAR 45 and of InfGeschBatt 27.

The division moved forward promptly at 9.40 a.m. and quickly crossed the British front line. The garrison of this position appears to have been virtually annihilated by the preparatory bombardment, for the regimental history of 2/Wiltshire gives the time of the first attack as 10.00 a.m.,[139] by which time the Germans were actually approaching the line of redoubts. The first real resistance was at Oestres, where elements of II/210 and I/211 captured 250 British troops after a fierce close-quarters battle. Apart from this incident, the main obstacles to the German advance were the fog, which again caused much confusion, and the British artillery. 10/212 was hit by a single shell that killed 26 men and wounded many more, virtually eliminating the company, while InfGeschBatt 27 was rendered immobile by a direct hit that killed most of its horses.[140] By 11.00 a.m., the Germans had penetrated the line of redoubts. Apart from a few machine-gun nests that were blinded by the fog and easily enveloped, the only resistance left in the forward zone was from the redoubt at L'Epine de Dallon, held by Lieutenant-Colonel A. V. P. Martin, commander of 2/Wiltshire.

North of 45th Reserve Division, 50th Division attacked with IR 53 on the left and IR 158 on the right. Fusilier-Regiment (FusRegt) 39,

Ludendorff's old regiment, was in reserve. The division was the focus of IX Corps and had received a substantial allocation of supporting forces. The lead regiments were assigned: half of Sturmbataillon 5 (Rohr), including flamethrowers, two pioneer companies, a machine-gun company and an infantry-gun battery; two 12-gun companies of MGSSAbt 36; two batteries of FdAR 99; a battery of InfGeschAbt 7; a pioneer company; and the divisional mortar company, a total of over 80 heavy weapons, in addition to the regiments' own integral weapons. The division also received sStPzKWAbt II, of five captured British tanks, and Abteilung Maillard, of two Guard light-infantry cyclist companies and Sturmkompagnie 13.[141]

The attack began smoothly. The British front line was found to be largely empty and was captured without loss.[142] With visibility reduced to only 15 metres by the fog, confusion resulted immediately. As units became lost and men became separated from their platoons, officers simply took over command of whatever troops were near them. After the war, the survivors of 16/Manchester claimed that their front was never attacked and that their positions were taken by envelopment.[143] The German regimental histories make it clear that the front was in fact attacked. The reason for the difference in the accounts is probably that individual posts were bypassed as the attackers moved through the gaps between them and were then enveloped from behind by the second wave of German troops. This was the situation along most of the front. Resistance grew as the Germans advanced into the forward zone. Again, the battle took the form of many isolated skirmishes in which British posts seem generally to have been overcome after only a brief struggle. All three German regimental histories emphasise the speed with which the British were defeated and, unlike several other histories, make no reference to casualties. By about 11.00 a.m. all that remained of 16/Manchester was the 200-man garrison of Manchester Hill, under Lieutenant-Colonel W. Elstob.[144]

Overall, the first 80 minutes of Operation Michael had been an astounding success: the German infantry had advanced 1,500 metres and had breached the British line of redoubts. Although this line had been expected to hold the German attack without support for a full 48 hours, it had disintegrated in less than 90 minutes. In most sectors, only one redoubt still held out, usually that containing the battalion headquarters. Of the eight battalions holding the forward zone in XVIII Corps, about 6,500 men, only 50 escaped.[145] German casualties were probably no more than a few hundred. The picture was similar along the whole 50-mile front:

> Of the [37] battalions posted in the forward zone [of Fifth Army], many had entirely ceased to exist as units, whilst in the majority of the

> others, only few officers and men remained . . . [In Third Army,] the [28½ battalions of] troops occupying the forward zone had been mostly killed, buried by the bombardment, or taken prisoner; the few survivors were not capable of much resistance, and none returned to tell the tale.[146]

### *The Second Phase*

In order to allow mutual support between the attacking formations and to encourage envelopment rather than frontal attack, the Germans had assigned sectors to their divisions that ran diagonally to the British front, not perpendicularly as was more standard practice.[147] As the troops advanced, they therefore shifted to their left. One consequence of this was that 1st Bavarian Division moved out of the sector defended by 36th (Ulster) Division and into that of 14th (Light) Division, outside the scope of this study.

36th (Ulster) Division had issued the order to man the battle zone, 'Bustle', within minutes of the German bombardment beginning and the troops were in position by 7.30 a.m.[148] Since communication with the garrison of the forward zone was lost within minutes of the guns opening fire, the battalions in the battle zone could do little more than wait for the enemy to arrive, which they began to do from about midday. An hour later, as the fog cleared, the Germans attacked the zone. GrenRegt 5 of 36th Division pushed on to Essigny, to the right of 1/RIF, and captured the village shortly after 1.00 p.m. (Map 7). The Germans had now reached the rear of the battle zone in this sector. While IR 175 covered the front of 1/RIF, GrenRegt 5 pushed past Essigny and attempted to envelop the flank of 108th Brigade, but this move was blocked by 9/RIF. The position was stabilised until dusk, when the Irishmen withdrew to behind the Crozat Canal, in order to avoid envelopment after the defeat of 14th (Light) Division on their right.[149]

In the forward zone, elements of 12/RIRif had been bypassed at Le Ponchu and a nearby quarry. The desperate resistance of the garrison, reinforced by stragglers from other posts, had caused some delay to the German advance. At about 12.30 p.m. the four A7Vs of sStPzKWAbt I, supported by two companies of Rohr's storm troopers and I/128, caught up with the advance. A fierce fight ensued, in which the German tanks played a vital role, overrunning several machine-gun posts and engaging the British positions at close range from the rear. When the redoubt finally fell, at about 2.15 p.m., the Germans took several hundred men prisoner. 12/RIRif had lost its entire battle strength of 22 officers and 566 men.[150]

On the sectors held by 107th and 108th Brigades, the lifting of the fog from about midday gave the advantage to the defenders.[151] Finally able to see their targets, the British machine guns did considerable

MAP 7
St Quentin, 21 March 1918: Second Phase

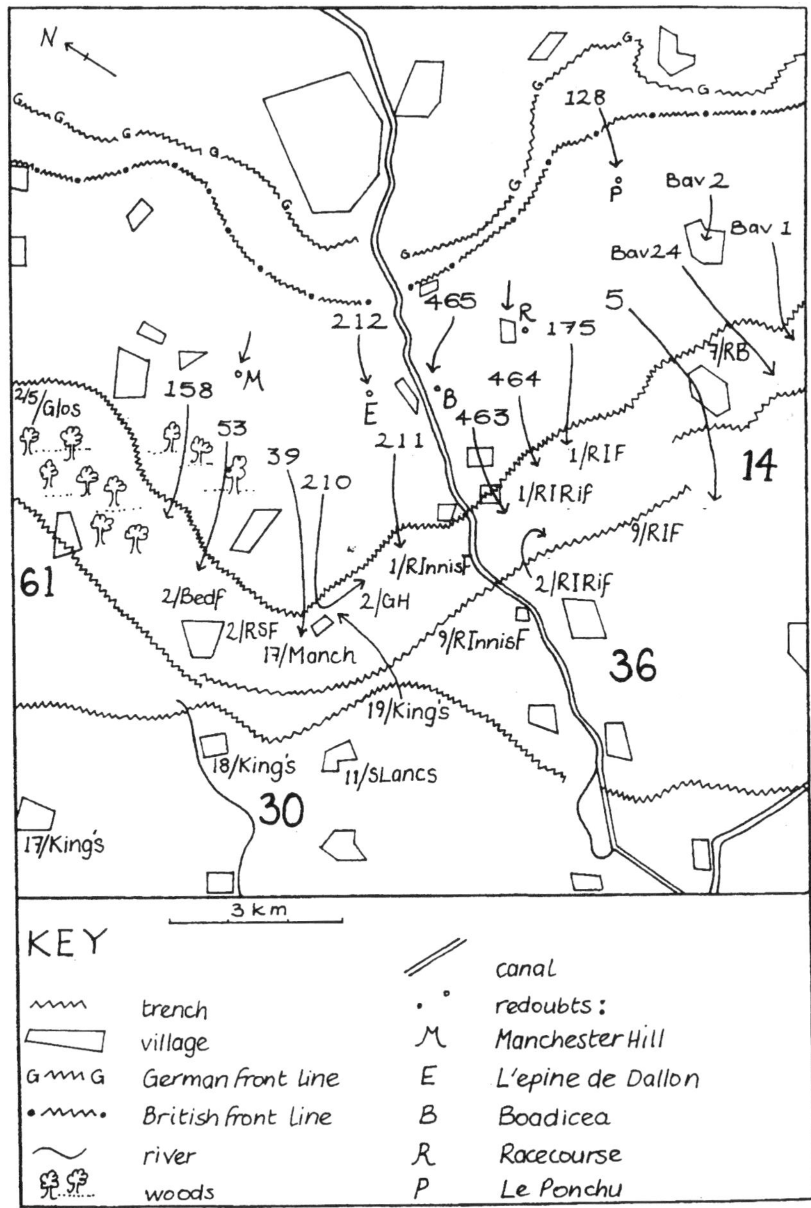

execution. Disordered by the fog and delayed by this fire, the German infantry lost touch with their artillery barrage. No signals had been arranged to call back the barrage. Nor could the infantry rely on the accompanying batteries for support, as these had fallen behind because of the loss of many of their horses. Only at Contescourt could IR 463 break into the battle zone. The garrison here was weak because the platoon assigned to defend the village had been wiped out by a single shell as it moved up to its position. Determined counterattacks by C coy 1/RIRif were repulsed, with heavy casualties. The position stabilised during the afternoon, but IR 463 was gradually able to expand its toe-hold in the British position. Renewed counterattacks after dusk by part of 2/RIRif were again bloodily defeated.

While the attack was largely stalled in front of the battle zone, the Germans dealt with those few posts still holding out in the forward zones. Racecourse Redoubt, held by men of 15/RIRif, survived until after 6.00 p.m., when it surrendered after the death of its commander, Second Lieutenant Edmund de Wind, who was posthumously awarded the Victoria Cross for this action.[152] The other defended locality was Boadicea Redoubt, held by two companies of 2/RInnisF. The account in the regiment's history states that the redoubt was surrounded, smothered with shells and under constant grenade and flame attacks, and that it finally surrendered only when resistance was no longer possible. The history of IR 463 gives a rather different picture. The redoubt had escaped serious damage during the preparatory bombardment and so was treated with caution by II/463 when it surrounded the locality. An attack was planned for 2.15 p.m., when substantial artillery support would be available. At 1.15 p.m. Leutnant Flotz, with two NCOs and two English-speaking officer cadets, requested permission to parley with the British. Shortly after they approached the redoubt, the garrison of 11 officers and 241 men surrendered. Colonel Farnham requested, and was given, a letter stating that he had resisted bravely before surrendering. Elsewhere in the battalion's sector, a post defended by a captain and 30 men surrendered to a single German NCO.

On the front of 21st Brigade also, the fog began to lift at about midday.[153] 45th Reserve Division had been delayed by the defended locality at L'Epine de Dallon and the German troops did not reach the front of the battle zone until about 1.00 p.m., by which time it was held by both 2/Green Howards and 17/Manchester. After an exploratory attack against Roupy at about 1.30 p.m., the Germans halted for almost two hours to reorganise under the cover of the rapidly lifting fog, an indication of how disorganised they had become in the conditions of poor visibility. The battle was resumed at 3.30 p.m. The Germans, now in full view of the defenders, suffered heavily from the British artillery and from 'shorts' from their own guns.

The attack was concentrated on the front of 2/Green Howards. After over an hour of fierce fighting, IR 210 and elements of III/FusRegt 39[154] broke into the British positions on the outskirts of Roupy. A counterattack by C coy 2/Green Howards was wiped out by heavy machine-gun fire. Although no deeper penetration could be made, men of IR 210, supported by two flamethrowers, were able to roll up the British front line southwards. The defended localities behind the line, however, were still holding out when darkness fell. A counterattack by 19/King's at 1.15 a.m. on 22 March succeeded in recapturing part of the line.[155]

L'Epine de Dallon was held by about 200 men of 2/Wiltshire under Lieutenant-Colonel A. V. P. Martin. Although bypassed by the leading German troops, the redoubt caused considerable delay to the advance. A frontal attack shortly after noon by II/212 and III/210, supported by several accompanying batteries, was repulsed. The attack was renewed at about 2.00 p.m., with support from 6/212 and some elite storm troopers, who attacked from the rear. Colonel Martin was wounded[156] and the garrison surrendered.

The attack of 50th Division had also stalled in front of the battle zone.[157] The leading troops reached Savy shortly after 11.30 a.m. and had soon overwhelmed its garrison, although not without a fierce struggle. Thirty prisoners were taken in the village and a further 100 were caught as they fled. The Germans reached the front of the battle zone at about midday and were pinned at once by the machine guns of 2/Bedford. Repeated attacks suffered heavy casualties and won only a small foothold in the British position. The artillery barrage had moved on by now and it was not possible to call it back before dusk. The situation therefore became stable.

A fierce battle was raging meanwhile around Manchester Hill, an action that has become the most famous incident of the day's fighting.[158] The redoubt was held by 168 men of 16/Manchester and was surrounded shortly after 11.30 a.m. There were a number of skirmishes, but no determined assault was made by the Germans until 3.00 p.m. A total of five infantry companies were involved in this attack and their regimental histories note the determination of the defenders and the heavy casualties suffered. After about an hour, Colonel Elstob was killed and the defenders surrendered. Elstob was awarded the Victoria Cross. The action around Manchester Hill was probably the most successful defence of any defended locality in the forward zone and deserves recognition. Unfortunately, the regimental history spoilt its case when it claimed, 'Of the original garrison of eight officers and 160 other ranks, only two officers and 15 other ranks survived'.[159] In fact, the roll of honour given at the rear of that same history lists a total of only 76 men killed from the entire battalion on 21 March. Probably no more than 40 men actually died on Manchester Hill.

*Casualties*

In 1978, Martin Middlebrook attempted to produce the first detailed estimate of casualties for 21 March 1918. His calculations produced totals of 39,929 German casualties and 38,512 British casualties, including 21,000 prisoners.[160] Because of the incomplete nature of the data available, he did not attempt to give a breakdown by formation of the casualties.

In the four German divisions principally engaged against 30th and 36th (Ulster) Divisions, eight of the 12 regiments recorded casualty figures for 21 March 1918 in their post-war histories. Of these eight, three gave figures for killed and missing only. Middlebrook assumed that the category of 'missing' covered both men killed but whose bodies were never identified and men taken prisoner.[161] Several histories, however, record the deaths of men who died in captivity, suggesting that men who were taken prisoner but survived the war were not listed. The category of 'missing' would therefore cover only those men killed but whose bodies were never identified. The average number of dead (including missing) in the eight regiments that give figures was 71.9, and the average number of wounded in the five regiments that gave figures was 314.4. From this, it may be estimated that the 12 regiments suffered a total of 863 killed and 3,773 wounded. In addition, there would have been a small number of men taken prisoner, perhaps 20. Middlebrook calculated that infantry casualties represented 87.5 per cent of the total.[162] Applying this to the figures above, it appears likely that the four German divisions examined suffered a total of 5,318 casualties on 21 March 1918, of whom 986 were killed, 4,312 wounded and 20 prisoners.

For the British, Middlebrook was able to trace almost every individual killed.[163] The totals for 30th and 36th (Ulster) Divisions were 245 and 267 respectively, but these figures appear to be for infantry only, which represented 81 per cent of the total. The total dead for the two divisions was therefore 632 men. For the wounded, Middlebrook calculated a total of about 10,000, the share of the two divisions was probably about 1,050. As regards prisoners, Middlebrook estimated a total of 19,544 infantrymen, of whom 2,392 were from 36th (Ulster) Division. An estimate of 1,708 men captured from 30th Division, which lost less ground, seems fair. A further 7.7 per cent should be added to cover non-infantry prisoners, giving a total of 4,416, which is probably a minimum. The British therefore suffered 6,098 casualties, of whom 632 were killed, 1,050 wounded and 4,416 prisoners. The figures may therefore be compared:

| | *Killed* | *Wounded* | *Captured* | *Total* |
|---|---|---|---|---|
| Germans | 986 | 4,312 | 20 | 5,318 |
| British | 632 | 1,050 | 4,416 | 6,098 |

## Conclusions

The presence of thick fog over much of the battlefield during the morning of 21 March 1918 has done as much after the event to obscure what actually happened as it did at the time. Writing in 1931, General Gough claimed that the fog greatly assisted the Germans. He argued that the British defensive system was dependent on a minimum visibility of 1,000 yards and that with the fog reducing visibility to 20 yards, posts could only wait until the enemy was almost on top of them and could give no mutual support. Gough believed that had there been no fog the German losses would have been doubled.[164] His views were echoed by the *Official History*.[165]

Conversely, Ludendorff claimed that 'the fog impeded and retarded our movements and prevented our superior training and leadership from reaping its true reward'.[166] At least one British historian, W. Shaw Sparrow, agreed with this verdict. In an analysis of the battle of St Quentin published in 1922, he concluded that the fog had been of increasing advantage to the British.[167] Finally, the *Official History* suggests that the British commanders at the time were not unduly concerned by the fog:

> In the defence schemes, no provision had been made for weather conditions, and when on the evening of 20 March, the mist and fog began to form, no special instructions were issued as to the attitude to be adopted. The matter was not overlooked: special precautions were not considered necessary in the circumstances.[168]

If the entire defensive system had indeed been dependent on a minimum visibility of 1,000 yards, the failure to react to the presence of fog would have been criminally negligent. The fact that no extra precautions were taken suggests that the British commanders did not consider that the fog would seriously hamper the defence.

In general, the fog was a definite benefit to the British. Few troops needed to move once they were in their positions, which were reached by familiar and well-signposted routes. The forward observers were blinded and signal flares could not be seen, but the gunners could still fire on their pre-planned counter-preparation targets and caused considerable damage to the German troops in this way. Whether this fire would have been much more effective had it been observed is questionable. In the forward zone, most posts were neutralised by the preparatory bombardment. In most sectors, the German infantry were able to cross the British front line almost unopposed. Even when the fog lifted, those posts that still held out caused few casualties to the passing Germans. Although the garrison of Manchester Hill defended itself vigorously for several hours, it had little delaying effect on the Germans, who could be seen marching past on all sides.[169] There seems little reason to think that these posts would have been much more effective had there been no fog. As for the battle zone, the fog was certainly no disadvantage to the defenders of that zone, since it lifted before the Germans penetrated to this position.

Moving on to the Germans, every one of the regimental histories emphasises the confusion caused by the fog. In every unit, sub-units and individuals became detached: much of the fighting was done by *ad hoc* groups of men, often from a number of different regiments, led by whatever officers were present. Many units also became disorientated and strayed from their assigned paths, so that some British positions were overlooked by the leading waves and subsequently caused heavy casualties to the supporting waves. The fog also hindered the German tactics, which were based on the identification and exploitation of weak points in the defence. Unable to see the British positions, many German units stumbled on to untouched defensive posts. In the ensuing mêlées, the Germans were generally unable to make use of their support weapons, a key element in assault squad tactics. The problem was compounded by too many troops being committed in the initial attacks, with the result that units' sectors were very narrow and therefore room for manoeuvre was limited. This problem was quickly identified and later attacks were made with the troops much less densely packed, allowing better use of ground and reliance on envelopment rather than frontal attack.[170] When the fog lifted, the German formations were already badly disordered and much of the infantry had become separated from the supporting heavy weapons. The entire advance had been delayed and consequently the protective artillery barrage had moved too far ahead from the attacking troops. In this state, the Germans were suddenly faced with the comparatively untouched and strongly manned battle zone. The benefit of the fog to the British was far greater here than it had been in the forward zone.

The fighting on 21 March was extremely confused. This can obscure the fact that in a single day the Germans had broken into a heavily defended position to an average depth of over two miles and on a front of 50 miles, capturing an area of 100 square miles, three times as great an area as that captured by the British during the entire Passchendaele offensive: by First World War standards, it was a major victory. Nor was this the end of the advance. Whereas the British tended to fight individual set-piece battles within a campaign, with up to two weeks between each attack, the Germans maintained the momentum of the offensive with fresh troops, who renewed the attack on the following day.

The success of the German attacks was a result of the high standard of training of the troops and the extensive decentralisation of command. The troops could implement assault squad tactics effectively, could co-operate with heavy weapons and were ready to act on their own responsibility within the context of the whole. The decentralisation of command, coupled with commanders being well forward, meant that operations could continue effectively despite the limited amount of information reaching senior commanders.[171] Commanders on the spot had a clear idea of what was required overall and had the resources under their immediate command to carry it out. The fact that powerful attacks could be launched against the battle zone by disordered troops almost as soon as the position was reached, without long delays to co-ordinate plans, demonstrates the dynamic responsiveness of the German command system.

For much of the day, the British command system was largely inactive. Once the order to man the battle zone was given, most battalions fought in their positions without further guidance. The most important element of this relative inactivity by commanders, particularly at division and corps level, was with regard to reserves. Throughout the day, a number of British battalions waited passively behind the battle zone: 11/S.Lancs stayed around Fluquieres, and the three battalions of 89th Brigade remained in their alert positions nearby.[172] 2/RIRif and 9/RInnisF[173] were also left idle for much of the day. Had these six battalions been committed shortly after noon, they and the eight other battalions defending the battle zone could have launched a powerful counterthrust precisely when the Germans were at their most disordered and so least able to resist such an attack. Such a counterthrust might well have had success similar to that enjoyed by so many *Eingreif* divisions against British attacks.

Had such a counterthrust been integral to the British defence schemes, those fortified localities in the forward zone that had not fallen to the initial German attacks might have held out longer. The surrender of these localities, usually after only limited resistance and as soon as their commanders were disabled, was in large part because they knew that no attempt would be made to relieve them for at least 24 hours, by which time it was obvious that they would have been overwhelmed. Since defeat was inevitable, the troops saw little reason to risk death. Had swift relief been promised, their attitude would have been different and several localities might have held out longer, to the considerable assistance of any counter-thrust from the battle zone. However, such a counterthrust appears not to have been considered by the British commanders. Perhaps the decentralisation of command on which it depended and the relative chaos of the resulting battle were unacceptable to the army's philosophy. The opportunity was not to recur.

Haig's plans, however, were by no means passive, as Denis Winter has recently uncovered. By the beginning of March, Haig had correctly identified both the location and probable date of the German offensive.[174] Why, then, did he not send more troops to reinforce Third and Fifth Armies? Plans for the redeployment of several divisions from the north had already been drawn up.[175] The answer appears to be that Haig intended to launch a counterstroke (*Gegenschlag*) against the flank of the German thrust. Gough was ordered to fall back to the Crozat Canal if heavily attacked, drawing the Germans forward into a salient. Preparations were made to enable this complex manoeuvre to be carried out with the minimum of confusion, while exhausting and dislocating the German advance.[176] Having rendered the enemy off balance, Haig planned to deliver a counterstroke from the Third Army sector, after rapidly re-deploying six divisions southwards from his reserve by using an extensive light railway system, designed for precisely this purpose, whose construction had absorbed much of the BEF's labour during the previous winter.[177] It was a daring plan and first reports of the German offensive suggested that it might succeed, since the enemy had attacked at the exact location and time predicted. The reaction of those who knew of Haig's plan was one of near jubilation: John Buchan, a key figure in the Ministry of Information, exclaimed to Charles Bean, the Australian Official Historian, 'Good news! The Germans have fallen into every trap we have laid'. Haig himself wrote, 'I am glad the attack has come'.[178]

In fact, the plan proved a total failure. Far from delivering a decisive counterstroke against an exhausted enemy, the BEF soon found itself fighting for its very survival. There seem to have been two main causes for this reversal. First, a number of senior commanders appear to have been unconvinced of the merits of Haig's plan, preferring to rely on a more traditional rigid defence. The *Official History* noted,

> No warning seems to have been given to any brigade or battalion commanders, and therefore none to the lower ranks, that in certain circumstances there might be an ordered retreat; divisional routes had been reconnoitred for this, but information of such nature was certainly withheld from regimental officers.[179]

The ordered withdrawal intended by Haig to draw the Germans into the trap was therefore rendered impossible. The second, and more important, cause was the sheer speed of the German advance. The line of redoubts in the British forward zone had been expected to hold the German attack for a full 48 hours.[180] In the event, it disintegrated in less than 90 minutes. Haig's plans, based on the slow pace of his own offensives, appear to have been for the counterstroke to be launched on the eleventh day after the German attack, and his schemes for bringing up reserves were calculated accordingly. Such was the pace of the German advance that these reserves had to be committed piecemeal after only three days, in order to prevent a German break-out.[181]

The inability of the British commanders to cope with the tempo of the German offensive was again repeatedly demonstrated during the retreat that followed 21 March. John Keegan has claimed that, 'In March 1918, the British Fifth Army collapsed, as much morally as physically',[182] by which he appears to mean that the troops lost the will to fight. As a judgement on the fighting soldiers of Fifth Army, this is unfair. Although a number of troops in the forward zone surrendered with little struggle, this was a consequence of the hopeless situation in which they had been placed and was not typical of the spirit of the BEF as a whole. Military Police sources note that most combatant stragglers were eager to return to their units and continue the fight, and that the majority of stragglers were non-combatant labourers, many of whom were not even British.[183] As a judgement of the command system, however, Keegan's words are far more justified, though again his concentration on Fifth Army alone is not. As Tim Travers has shown, that command system all but collapsed, with commanders at every level, from brigade to GHQ, unable to contend with the stress of a fast-moving mobile battle.[184] After the Germans had advanced 40 miles and reached the gates of the vital rail centre at Amiens, the offensive ground to a halt, as much because of German inability to solve the problems of the break-out as because of British resistance efforts.

# 9
# Conclusion

> The study of war had done more for Prussia than educating its soldiers and producing a sound system of organisation. It had led to the establishment of a sound system of command; and this system proved a marvellous instrument in the hands of a great leader. It was based on the recognition of three facts: first, that an army cannot be effectively controlled by direct orders from headquarters; second, that the man on the spot is the best judge of the situation; and third, that intelligent cooperation is of infinitely more value than mechanical obedience.
>
> Colonel G. F. R. Henderson, 'War', *Encyclopaedia Brittanica*

Once hostilities ceased in 1918, the British and German armies began the mammoth task of analysing what had happened over the previous four years and assessing the lessons to be learned. In this task, the historical sections of the respective armies were of vital importance, since these held the raw material, such as unit war diaries and orders, from which any sound conclusions must be drawn. A brief examination of the very different responses of the two armies to this challenge may serve to conclude this study.

In Germany, the analysis of military operations had been one of the more important tasks of the General Staff in Berlin. Under von Moltke, it had originated the practice of studying recent wars, both those involving German forces and others of particular interest, and publishing the results in a didactic form. The aims of this practice may be seen clearly in the history produced of the Boer War of 1899 to 1902.[1] The work was published very soon after the war ended and sought to present the narrative in a form that brought out those lessons that were relevant to the German Army, primarily those appropriate to a major war in Europe. Differences were frequently noted between the tactical practices of the British and Boer armies on the one hand and the German and the Continental armies on the other. Phases of a war considered irrelevant to German operations were treated only briefly, the entire guerrilla phase of the Boer War being dismissed in a single paragraph. Although the accounts of Germany's own wars were sometimes affected by concern to protect the reputations of certain individuals,[2] the German official histories were generally works of considerable objectivity and critical analysis, aiming to provide a sound foundation for tactical development. A heavy reliance upon historical precedent was, as we have argued, a constant hallmark of German military thought.

One of the most important terms of the Treaty of Versailles was that the General Staff, including its historical section, be dissolved. The Germans attempted to circumvent the treaty's provisions in numerous ways and succeeded in so doing with regard to the historical section. The section, complete with its archives, was transferred *en bloc* to the Ministry of the Interior and renamed the *Reichsarchiv* (national archive). The change of name and of supervising ministry made little difference to the section, which operated much as before and produced a monumental official account of the First World War.[3] The importance attached to this work is indicated by the size of its staff: over 100 officers were employed in the section, although all but 40 of these were in fact members of the General Staff's intelligence branch, which used the historical branch as a cover. Even so, the Germans had three times as many researchers as did the British.[4]

The fruits of this historical process may be seen in the first manuals published by the German Army after 1919: *Führung und Gefecht der verbundene Waffen* (FüG) (Command and Combat of the Combined Arms) in September 1921[5] and the *Ausbildungsvorschirft für die Infanterie* (AVI) (Training Manual for the Infantry) in 1922.[6] Both manuals show a striking continuity with pre-war doctrine, although with numerous alterations and changes in emphasis as a consequence of the considerable developments in tactics and equipment made during the war.

The AVI shows that the process of replacing the firepower of rifles with that of heavy weapons, begun in 1908 with the first introduction of machine guns, was continued. The new regimental organisation included 81 light machine guns (LMG), 36 heavy machine guns (eight times the ratio of guns to infantry of 1914) and six mortars, as well as a battery of infantry guns for close support. By 1939, these guns, supplemented by a number of anti-tank guns, had become an integral part of the infantry regiment and were no longer part of the artillery. In short, the new infantry organisation was based upon that of the wartime assault battalions. The assault squad tactics were adapted and became standard for both mobile and position warfare. The section, now of nine men, equipped with rifles and grenades, and an LMG team, was retained as the basic tactic unit, including within itself as it did both firepower and assault power. Troops were to be deployed in dispersed formations, allowing fire support from rearward elements, and there was a great emphasis on envelopment, even at the lowest tactical levels, and penetration in depth.

FüG, which was based upon the operations of a mass army rather than the 100,000-man army enforced by the Treaty of Versailles, encapsulated current German military thought. Schlieffen's obsession with envelopment, the *Vernichtungsgedanke* (concept of annihilation), was retained as the central goal of operations. To this end, commanders should always strive to achieve a decisive solution to situations. Strict obedience to superiors' *Entschlüsse* (resolutions), as expressed in their *Absichte* (intents), was to be linked with the greatest flexibility in the solutions adopted. Firmness of will was to be linked with freedom in the choice of means.

The concept of the *Schwerpunkt* (focus of energy) became if anything still more important. Commanders were to analyse situations as an organic whole, seeking to identify the decisive point. Concentration upon this point, a process now termed *Schwerpunktbildung* (the development of a focus of energy), was based upon a conviction that the whole was more important than the parts. As before, there was a tendency to favour the operational level, long considered the General Staff's particular area of skill. In the search for a decisive result, attrition and position warfare were to be avoided. The focus was on mobile operations, in which a decision was more easily and quickly achieved. The offensive spirit of both commanders and troops was held to be of the highest importance, but it was not to be permitted to degenerate into the blind frenzy favoured by much of the line infantry before 1914.

On the whole, therefore, the post-war German Army retained much of its pre-war philosophy and doctrine, which it felt the experience of war had shown to be fundamentally sound, but used historical analysis of that war to discern the lessons to be drawn, and adapted its systems of tactics and command accordingly to suit the new circumstances of the battlefield. The retention of assault squad tactics, and the organisation of weapons and forces that went with them, and their extension into the realm of mobile warfare indicate that the German Army believed that the first two problems of the attack under modern conditions, that is, the achievement of a break-in and its extension to a breakthrough, had been largely solved during the war. The third problem, converting the breakthrough into a break-out, remained.

During the spring and early summer of 1918, the Germans had been able, almost at will, to punch a hole through the Allied positions and to threaten a break-out. Despite having solved the problem of achieving a breakthrough, however, the Germans were unable to secure any decisive success. The net result of the offensives, notwithstanding the great depths of the penetrations and the enormous casualties inflicted, was in fact to wear down the German Army to such an extent that it finally had to ask for an armistice in November 1918. The keys to German success in achieving repeated breakthroughs were, as we have argued, a decentralised command system, a flexible system of tactics and a high standard of training. These factors combined to allow German troops to operate with great effectiveness and at a high tempo even in the kaleidoscopic chaos of a breakthrough battle. Expressed in terms of the Boyd Loop, German success was because of the army's ability to go through the cycle more quickly and make more appropriate decisions than could its opponents. The flaw in the German system, which ultimately turned the early victories into but the prelude of defeat, was that, as we have noted, the third problem of attack, the conversion of a breakthrough into a break-out, had not been solved.

John Terraine, although he does not use the term 'break-out', has argued that the Germans were unable to achieve a break-out owing to two mistakes by Ludendorff: first, that the offensives had no strategic objective; and, second, that no arm of exploitation was employed.[7]

Terraine's first point, that the offensives had no strategic objective, suggests a misunderstanding of the purpose of the offensives and a failure to appreciate the importance of a break-out. Terraine criticises Ludendorff for not having a key city or the attrition of Allied forces as his objective and considers this lack of direction to be central to the ultimate futility of the German offensives. However, both the capture of a key city and the attrition of the enemy army had been tried by von Falkenhayn at Verdun and had been found to be inappropriate for Germany's situation.

Ludendorff's actual purpose was expressed clearly when he told Crown Prince Rupprecht, 'I forbid myself to use the word "strategy". We chop a hole. The rest follows. We did it that way in Russia.'[8] Although Terraine regards this statement as demonstrating Ludendorff's folly, it is in fact a thoroughly sound appreciation of military reality. As Ludendorff himself pointed out, lofty strategic goals were valueless if a break-out was not achieved.[9] Conversely, if a break-out was indeed achieved, the strategic goals would be gained with ease. The traumatic shock inflicted on the enemy army by the very achievement of the break-out was generally sufficient to place it in a state of high stress, unable to react effectively to the further operations of the attacker. Precisely this situation had arisen during the Gorlice–Tarnow offensive in 1915, an operation in which Ludendorff was intimately involved. No strategic objective had been close to the point of attack, which had been chosen purely for its suitability for operations to penetrate the enemy line and achieve a break-out. Once this had been achieved, the Russian Army collapsed with stunning speed. The offensive finally ground to a halt more because of the exhaustion of the German troops, a consequence of the sheer extent of the advance, than because of the resistance of the Russian Army. The experience was to be repeated in 1941. Terraine's argument that lack of a strategic objective close behind the point of attack was central to the failure of the German offensives may therefore be discounted as irrelevant to the achievement of a break-out, the decisive requirement.

On several occasions in 1918, the British and French armies were on the brink of collapse and were barely able to prevent a German break-out, with its incalculable consequences. Terraine's second point, that a break-out might have been achieved had the Germans employed cavalry or armoured vehicles, therefore deserves some attention.

The effectiveness of cavalry in achieving a break-out was minimal. Mounted troops were utterly vulnerable to enemy fire, as had been repeatedly demonstrated in the early years of the war and was to be proved once more in 1918. While even a single enemy machine gun remained in action, no cavalry advance was possible. Armoured vehicles could be divided into three types: heavy tanks, armoured cars and light tanks. The heavy tanks of 1918 had been designed for use in the break-in and break-through phases of position warfare. The British Mark V tank had a maximum (road) speed of 4.6 miles per hour, a range of only 35 miles and was notorious for its mechanical unreliability. Of 414 tanks (mostly Mark Vs) in action on 8 August 1918, the first day of the battle of Amiens, only six were still running four days later.[10] While highly effective for the purposes for which they were designed, the heavy tanks could not solve the problem of the break-out, which demanded rapid movement over considerable distances and several days. Armoured cars offered a better prospect as regards the break-out, and indeed performed well at Amiens.[11] Their main failing was that they were restricted to moving by road and were therefore limited in their flexibility of use and were vulnerable to ambush or demolition.

The greatest potential lay with the light tank. The German Army produced no light tanks during the First World War, one of the General Staff's most serious errors of tactical judgement. Evaluation of the effectiveness of light tanks had to focus on the British Whippet. This had a range of 80 miles, allowing it to operate beyond an initial penetration, but its maximum (road) speed was only 8.3 miles per hour and its armament was limited to four machine guns.[12] While more mobile than an armoured car, its low speed, light armament and poor reliability made the Whippet more an indicator of things to come than an actual solution to the problem of the break-out. Despite some success at Amiens, no break-out was achieved, although Colonel J. F. C. Fuller, chief of staff of the Tank Corps, drew up his Plan 1919 on the basis that one would be achieved by the more advanced Whippet Mark D.

Terraine appears, therefore, to be overstating the case when he criticises Ludendorff for not using cavalry or tanks, although there can be little doubt that the German offensive would have been assisted by the presence of light tanks. This narrow focus on tanks, however, appears to be something of a blind alley.

The key factor that prevented the Germans achieving a break-out in

1918 was that of logistics. As Martin Van Creveld has shown,[13] the supply system of First World War armies was largely dependent upon railways, with horse-drawn or motor transport linking the troops to the nearest railhead. Even when railheads had been established close behind the front, the intermediate transport system was simply unable to keep the troops effectively supplied if the gap between the front and the railhead became wider than about 40 miles, less if the transport had to cross the wilderness of the battlefield. If this gap could not be reduced, by moving railheads forward, the advance would come to a premature halt, regardless of enemy resistance.[14] Conversely, as the defender retreated, he fell back on his railheads and thereby made his supply situation easier.

The importance of the logistic factor was perceived, although unclearly, by the German Army immediately after the war ended. When von Seeckt reformed the army in 1919, he formed a number of inspectorates to control and develop areas deemed vital for future development. One of these inspectorates, under General von Tschischwitz, was given responsibility for motor transport, for both supply and combat.[15] This linking of these two areas, equivalent to the British handing the development of armoured warfare to the Army Service Corps, was probably made more feasible by Germany having been forbidden to possess tanks by the Treaty of Versailles.

In 1922, a certain Hauptmann Heinz Guderian was posted to the Inspectorate of Transport Troops. His initial concern was with logistics and the protection of transport columns. Only gradually did he come to see the potential of motorisation for combat purposes, a view that met with some considerable opposition, even from his own inspector.[16] One of the values of Guderian's approach, which was firmly based on practical experiment and historical research, was that it emphasised the logistic aspects of motorised combat and avoided splitting tanks from the other arms, as was happening in Britain.[17] Guderian's sound grasp of logistics, unusual in a member of the General Staff, and the army's concern for the combined action of all arms meant that when the first *Panzer* divisions were formed in 1934 they consisted of a mixed force of tanks, infantry, artillery and engineers, with fully motorised support services. It was this linkage of a motorised supply system with an all-arms motorised striking force that was to allow the German Army to solve the problem of achieving a break-out and was to result in the spectacular victories of 1939 to 1941.

The course of development was very different in Britain. Perhaps the most important difference was that, whereas the Germans regarded the central problem to be the achievement of a break-out, the British remained focused on the breakthrough. By late 1917, as Tim Travers has demonstrated, opinion in the British Army as to the best means by which to achieve a breakthrough had crystallised into two main camps.[18] Those in the first camp argued that the emphasis should be on technical means, primarily tanks and aircraft, with the infantry and artillery playing a secondary role. Supporters of the second camp believed that the traditional system of tactics, based on infantry and artillery, remained valid and that the new mechanical means should be used to support it rather than to supplant it. It is of note that the 'structural' approach employed by the British led them to assume that there must inevitably be competition between the existing arms and the new arms and that there must therefore be a choice between them. By contrast, the German 'functional' approach was more concerned with how problems could best be solved rather than with which arm solved them, although the structural approach was not unknown in that army.

Haig and GHQ supported the traditionalist view and sought to keep the new technical arms subordinate to the infantry and artillery, even going so far as to attempt to reduce the size of the Tank Corps early in 1918. The Cabinet and the new CIGS, Henry Wilson, favoured the mechanical approach and began to impose it on Haig. This camp convinced an increasing number of senior officers in the field, including Rawlinson and Maxse, of the validity of its arguments and this process culminated in the use of massed tanks and aircraft at the battle of Amiens in August 1918.

Despite the considerable success achieved, however, this battle marked the peak of the mechanical school's influence. Although tanks could have been massed for a second attack, they were not so massed again. For the remaining months of the war, tanks were used as and when they were available and the army reverted to a more traditional system of tactics. This change may in part have been because of the high rate of loss among the tanks at Amiens and the fact that even this mass of tanks failed to achieve a break-out. Although the British attack gave the Germans a shock and inflicted a serious reverse on them, it never came near achieving a break-out.[19] With regard to aircraft, the newly created Royal Air Force was keen to demonstrate its independence and the separateness of its function from that of the army, and it is possible that its post-war distaste for the ground-attack role may have already found some expression in 1918.

The shift back to a more traditional system of tactics was, however, probably more because of improvements in the effectiveness of the traditional arms, most notably the artillery. The central development in artillery tactics was the belated realisation that the main task of a bombardment was not to obliterate the enemy defensive position but to neutralise the enemy garrison, and its artillery in particular, immediately before the assault.[20] It appears likely that the impetus for the shift in approach was the experience of similar tactics employed by the Germans in their offensives, although the idea had been experimented with at Cambrai. The abandonment of prolonged preparatory bombardments and the introduction of predicted shooting allowed fire to be concentrated over time, resulting in dramatic increases in the number of shells fired during the key phases of battles. The infantry's tactics also became more flexible. Partly as a response to Maxse's efforts as Inspector-General of Training, linear formations were abandoned in favour of 'worms' of men in single file, and greater use was made of heavy weapons and low-level manoeuvre.

Since the artillery could now produce an overwhelming weight of fire at the critical moment, yet still retain surprise, and the infantry's combat power had been similarly increased, the need for mechanical aids became less clear. As the German Army grew increasingly exhausted, the progress achieved by the British while relying primarily on the infantry and artillery seemed to vindicate the traditionalist approach and suggested that the stalemate of 1915 to 1917 had been an aberration caused by insufficient resources. Despite the weakened state of the German Army, however, the final Allied offensives did not inflict a clear-cut tactical defeat on the enemy.[21] This suggested that the problem of the break-out had not been solved.

At the end of the First World War, the British Army was in a similar position to the German Army as regards the potential for further tactical development, in that both armies possessed a wide experience of battle and of different techniques and equipment. The British, indeed, were better placed for analysis of the war's lessons, since not only had they made extensive use of tanks, which the German Army had not, but they had access to fuller documentation, including much German material captured during the final phases of the war. The Germans, by contrast, had little access to their enemies' archives and had lost much of their own documentation during the upheavals of 1918 and the near civil war of 1919. We have seen, however, that one of the German Army's first steps after hostilities ceased was to begin an examination of the tactical lessons of the war. What of the British?

The British equivalent of the historical branch of the German General Staff was the Historical Section (Military) of the Committee of Imperial Defence, formed in 1904. Its main task initially was to gather sensitive material for safe-keeping, rather than the preparation of a history of the war.[22] The decision to publish an account was taken in 1915, in response to narratives produced by French GQG that portrayed the British in a poor light. The plan was to produce two separate accounts: a 'popular' history, patriotic in tone and copiously illustrated, to appear at an early date, and a 'detailed staff history', that was to be kept confidential for 40 years, in order to withhold information from the French and Germans.

The plan was not without its merits. From a military perspective, the chief of these was that a proper analysis was to be made of the war and its lessons. That this should remain a confidential document was appropriate, since its findings would give a strong indication as to the army's future procedures. It was upset by two factors. First, the man chosen to write the popular history, the eminent military historian Sir John Fortescue, proved to be rather more outspoken than had been appreciated by those who appointed him. His initial draft chapters were very critical of both politicians and soldiers, quite the opposite of what had been intended for this 'patriotic' work. Fortescue was rapidly removed and the idea of a popular history shelved. The second factor appears to have been that work on the staff history began to reveal material highly damaging to the reputations of a number of senior officers, particularly Haig, and members of the government. In what seems to have been an attempt to protect these reputations, the detailed staff history was also shelved.[23]

Since the Historical Section could hardly produce no history at all, particularly given the flood of often highly critical memoirs and other personal accounts being published, a compromise was reached, probably at the instigation of Brigadier-General Sir James Edmonds, head of the staff-history team. Edmonds' idea was to merge the two projects: 'The public was to be given a "Popular" history which was unreadable; the staff were to get a history propagandist to the point of uselessness.'[24] Whatever the wider implications of the decision to suppress the popular history, the parallel decision to emasculate the staff history was of the greatest importance for British post-war military development. In effect, this decision deprived the British Army of the opportunity of learning not only from its mistakes but also from its hard-won successes. Furthermore, the Army Council instructed Edmonds to delay publication of the work as a whole and to keep brief the volumes covering 1915 to 1917. Despite this deferral of publication, work on the history appears to have proceeded at a fast rate; Edmonds later stated that each volume took only two years to write. By 1930, it appears that all the volumes had been completed,[25] at least as regards their factual material. The delay in publication permitted fine-tuning of the editorial slant, particularly as regards the relationship of Haig and GHQ with the army commanders. The last volumes, covering Passchendaele and Cambrai, were finally published in 1949.

Despite the care taken to omit or play down errors, the *Official History* rarely falsified the record and could not disguise the failures and casualties that resulted from those mistakes. The public concern that greeted the appearance of each successive volume in the bookshops served to underline the Army Council's worries as to the effects of publication. The revelation of the errors made by commanders and troops during the war resulted in enormous pressure on the army to make some formal analysis of the lessons to be learned from those events. This pressure was to lead to the writing of the Kirke Report.

The Kirke Report, issued as a numbered security document in October 1932,[26] represents a peculiarly British response to a problem. Liddell Hart claimed that the report was commissioned early in 1932 as a response to the public outcry that greeted the publication in January of that year of the volume of the *Official History* covering the first half of 1916, including the first day of the Somme.[27] The report itself is actually dated 13 October *1931*, but several pieces of evidence suggest that the year was in fact 1932. First, the report makes several references to Army Training Memorandum No. 4A of 1932,[28] which laid down that the army's first priority was imperial defence. Second, Liddell Hart recorded that he was approached for advice by the report's writers during 1932.[29] Finally, a War Office memorandum concerning the number of copies of the report to be printed (500) is dated 14 October 1932.[30] The date of 1931 given in the report itself is presumably a typing error.

The Kirke Committee consisted of one lieutenant-general (Kirke), five major-generals (including the commanders of two Territorial Army divisions) and two temporary brigadiers. Its terms of reference were as follows:

> (a) What are the principal lessons to be derived from our experiences in the several theatres of the Great War as disclosed by the official histories and reports?
> (b) Have these lessons been correctly and adequately applied in Field Service Regulations and other training manuals, and our system of training generally?[31]

The propagandist nature of the *Official History* has already been noted, as has the fact that only the volumes covering the period up to 1 July 1916 had been published, yet it was on this foundation that the Kirke Committee was instructed to base its report. Liddell Hart later claimed that the CIGS, Field Marshal Sir George Milne, established the committee because he was shocked by the incompetence that the *Official History* was revealing.[32] The terms of reference that Milne gave to the Kirke committee, however, suggest that he was acting more to quell unease within the army than from the intention of instigating a serious investigation of the lessons to be learned from the war. This impression is further reinforced by points made in General Kirke's foreword to the report:

> That a Committee of this nature, convened for a few months, would be able to indicate a clear-cut answer to problems which have formed the subject of close study by every [foreign] General Staff for 14 years was doubtless not expected. Should we have succeeded in giving any slight forward impulse towards the solution of any of them we shall not have laboured in vain.[33]

Kirke's hope that his committee's report would be but the first step in a proper analysis of the war was to be unfulfilled, with bitter consequences for the British Army in 1940. Nevertheless, the report, despite the limitations already noted, was remarkably sound and critical. One factor in this achievement may have been the covert consultation by several members of the committee of Liddell Hart. Liddell Hart's papers include extracts from the report and note constant and repeated use of his ideas, often even unacknowledged quotes from his books.[34]

Liddell Hart believed that Milne wanted to publish the report but had been replaced by Sir Archibald Montgomery-Massingberd by the time it was ready. As the former chief of staff of Fourth Army on the Somme, Montgomery-Massingberd had much to fear from a critical analysis of the war. Liddell Hart claimed that for this reason he attempted to suppress the report.[35] In fact, the next stage in the story of the Kirke Report began on 9 January 1933, before Milne retired, when a number of officers gathered at the Staff College to discuss the report. The list of those attending, given in the official report of the conference,[36] shows that all the army's senior figures were present, down to and including every divisional commander and the colonels on the General Staff at the War Office.

Milne opened the conference with a few remarks that throw further light on his attitude to the need to determine the lessons of the First World War:

> As sufficient time appears to me to have elapsed since the War . . . it seems that the time has now arrived for us to try and endeavour to find out what the lessons of the war were and what advantages we can derive from what has been written [in the *Official History*]. . . . The [Kirke] report will shortly be in your hands. . . . I would also like you to remember that naturally the war in France loomed greater in our imagination than other campaigns, but it is very unlikely that in your lifetime, or even in the lifetime of younger officers, we shall be engaged in a national campaign on the continent of Europe. . . . We must not put too much stress on what was for the British Empire an abnormal situation – war in a European country.[37]

The reference to 'sufficient time having elapsed since the war' may have been an allusion to the death of Douglas Haig in 1928, any serious analysis of the war inevitably bringing his conduct of operations into question. With the CIGS himself so dismissive of the probability of another 'national campaign on the continent of Europe', in fact little more than six years away, it seems likely that the learning of lessons for such a campaign was not considered an overriding priority by the officers assembled before him. Even so, it is remarkable that copies of the report itself were not distributed to those officers until after the conference had started, giving them very little time to consider their response to it.

The discussion on the following two days revealed a number of points of interest, of which two are relevant here. First, no distinction was made between the breakthrough and the break-out, even though, as we have argued, the problems of the latter were very different from those of the former. The term 'breakthrough' appears to have been understood to cover operations after the initial break-in to the enemy position up to a deep penetration of that position. The exploitation of that penetration, central to what we have termed the 'break-out', was barely mentioned. Second, although several officers[38] favoured an expansion of tank forces and the inclusion of infantry and artillery units in armoured formations, to be used to launch a deeply penetrating attack, this was not the majority view.

Most officers appear to have doubted the feasibility of achieving even a deep penetration, the first stage of a break-out. Some went as far as to suggest that even a breakthrough was unlikely and that a frontal, wearing-out offensive gave the best hope of success.[39] More common, however, was the view that once a breakthrough had been achieved the emphasis should be on making the breach in the enemy position broader rather than deeper.[40] In effect, the majority view expressed by the most senior officers in the British Army was that the break-out was not possible and should not be attempted. This may be contrasted with the attitude of the German Army, which believed that the break-out was the most decisive solution to the problem of attack. Owing to their continual emphasis upon achieving a rapid decision, the Germans sought to overcome the challenge of solving the problems of creating a break-out, rather than accept that challenge as impossible.

Milne was succeeded as CIGS by Montgomery-Massingberd in February 1933. For over a year, nothing further was done concerning the Kirke Report. Finally, on 30 April 1934, a revised version of the report was issued down to company level of the Regular Army.[41] Whether copies were issued to the Territorial Army is uncertain. Although most of the points raised in the original report were included in the new pamphlet, a number of comments critical of the high command and in favour of the use of tanks were left out. Perhaps more damaging was the fact, revealed in a secret War Office memorandum, that the pamphlet also omitted 'any matter which might engender in the regimental officer a lack of confidence in the equipment with which the army is at present supplied'.[42]

In short, whereas the German Army made every effort to glean the maximum from its experience in the First World War and identified the break-out as the vital problem to be solved, the British Army all but turned its back on the great campaigns of 1914 to 1918. The *Official History* was distorted and delayed, the Kirke Report belated, hurried and based on insufficient evidence, the discussion of that report made after only a brief period of analysis, and the points raised dismissed as largely irrelevant to the army's main task of imperial policing. The determination on the part of much of the army to forget the experience of war was again demonstrated in the late-1930s, when Captain G. C. Wynne's critical articles, revealing incompetence throughout that war, were met with a barrage of protest and rejection.

The above discussion has necessarily been only preliminary, yet it may serve to indicate the continuity of approach on the part of both the German and British armies before and after the First World War and leads to the conclusion that it was perhaps predictable that the British should suffer repeated defeats at the hands of the German Army at the start of the Second World War.

At the beginning of this study, we put forward a number of hypotheses, the testing of which might serve as a guide to give a better understanding of the German and British armies. It is appropriate here to examine briefly whether these hypotheses have been supported by the findings of the several case-studies.

The first hypothesis was that the difference between the combat effectiveness of the German and British armies owed as much to failings in British performance as to German superiority. We have argued that, although the German Army was often highly efficient in developing and implementing solutions to the problems posed by combat, the introduction of assault squad tactics being a prime example, it was by no means efficient in every case. The increasing narrowness of the training of General Staff officers, the conservative resistance to the replacement of assault tactics with fire tactics and the opposition of even officers such as Fritz von Lossberg to the use of elastic defence in depth, all serve to demonstrate that the German Army was by no means wholly effective in analysing developments and in determining its focus. One of the advantages of employing a comparative approach to the study of armies is that it highlights the fact that success goes not to the most efficient army but rather to the least inefficient.

While the German Army was by no means efficient, the British Army was considerably more inefficient in determining the decisive point. The British Army, in common with much of British society, tended to be highly conservative in outlook and displayed a marked distaste for professional thought and training. The low point of this trend was probably reached in 1900: 50 per cent of the total amount of military literature published in that year was German, only one per cent was British.[43] Although the situation improved considerably after the Boer War, a contempt for theory and a distrust of technical experts appears to have remained strong.

> Cyril Falls revealed a remark of 'a general who gained distinction in the Second World War, Sir Brian Horrocks . . . that he had never been able to understand any military theory.' Falls regarded this as 'a polite way of saying that he thought it worthless and wondered why anybody took the trouble to compose or discuss it.'[44]

The second hypothesis was that these differences in effectiveness were in large measure because the two armies held quite different philosophies of combat. In the German Army, it was generally accepted that the infinite variety of combat made chaos inevitable and unavoidable. The driving force behind most of the developments in command and tactics during the period under investigation was the search for a system by which effective military action could be taken in such uncertain circumstances. Although officers might resist the direction in which these developments took the army, the general acceptance that adaptation to circumstances was essential meant that most of these officers conceded that the changes and challenges resulting from such developments were an unavoidable part of a necessary process.

In the British Army, combat was seen as being inherently structured and the key requirement for success as being order. British systems of combat, as a consequence, sought to minimise chaos and preserve a sequential process of action. Since the maintenance of order and symmetry was considered of central importance, effort was directed towards solving the problems of combat through greater emphasis upon these factors, with pressures to decentralisation and dispersion accordingly resisted. Further, since combat was so ordered, there was little need for deep theoretical analysis of its conduct.

The third hypothesis was that these different philosophies of combat would be expressed most clearly in the command systems employed by the two armies. The German Army's response to the need to achieve a high level of combat effectiveness in an environment of chaos was to instigate a progressive process of decentralisation of command. This system, best termed 'directive command', was based on the assumption that the man on the spot was the best judge of his immediate circumstances. German officers, most notably von Moltke, recognised that it was impossible to maintain communications between the front line and senior commanders to the rear and still achieve tempo. The solution adopted was to provide commanders on the spot with all the information as to the general situation that they could not find out for themselves and to guide them with directives in the form of their superior's intent. Senior commanders then allowed their subordinates considerable room for action, trusting that they would in this way be able to make best use of each and every opportunity to further that intent. The key elements of this system were that free rein was given to the individual creativity of subordinate commanders, while superiors sought to identify the decisive point, direct their subordinates towards it and to reinforce success, even if other than at the chosen point, if it offered to bring about a decision.

The British Army's philosophy of combat as structured led it to develop two distinct systems of command. The first, 'umpiring', was employed primarily at division level and above. Largely based on the system of directive command, umpiring too allowed the commander on the spot complete freedom of action. Unlike the German system, however, the umpire made little attempt to identify the decisive point nor to direct his subordinates to it, other than in a general sense before the action commenced. Further direction during combat was deemed an invasion into the sphere of the subordinate and was in any case considered unnecessary, owing to the predictable nature of combat.

The second and more widely used system of command was 'restrictive control'. Since combat was seen as structured and its vital characteristic as order, commanders sought to retain close personal control of their formations by means of detailed orders. Under this system, subordinate commanders became mere cyphers, simply transmitting instructions from above. The system reached its extreme during 1916, when senior commanders sought to preordain the future by laying down in advance the actions of troops in detail, depriving regimental officers of the opportunity to fulfil their function of leadership. The central characteristics of restrictive control were heavy centralisation of decision making and severe curtailment of individual initiative.

The final hypothesis was that each army's philosophy of combat, and therefore its command system, would have a considerable influence on the systems of training and tactics employed by that army. The German Army's system of directive command demanded that officers and troops be able to operate effectively even when out of communication with their superiors and in a chaotic environment. The achievement of this ability demanded a very high standard of training, not just of weapons skills but of the ability to appreciate tactical and operational situations. Having developed this ability, the army was able to adopt tactics that depended heavily upon decentralised command and low-level initiative and combat skills.

The British Army's system of restrictive control was based primarily on the rigid obedience of orders and the carrying out of a limited number of basic drills. Since these characteristics could be developed with comparatively little difficulty, with much emphasis on parade drill in order to inculcate an attitude of unthinking obedience, there was limited pressure for an intensive programme of training and still less for the development of soldiers capable of a thoughtful appreciation of combat situations. This comparatively low level of training meant that the advanced tactics adopted by the German Army were beyond the capability of most British troops and meant that standard solutions and detailed planning were essential.

In conclusion, the superior combat effectiveness of the German Army compared to that of the British Army in the period 1888 to 1918 was based ultimately on the Germans' philosophy of combat, as inherently chaotic, being better suited to actual fighting than was the British philosophy of combat as inherently ordered. This being the case, the answer to the question posed in the title of this study, 'Command or Control?', must be 'command', although its essential foundations of a very high level of training, in both independent command and tactical skills, and of flexible tactics, as well as the danger of degeneration into umpiring, must not be forgotten.

# Notes

(Full details of books and documents cited below will be found in the Bibliography.)

## Introduction, pp. 1–6

1. Wynne, 'Pattern for Limited (Nuclear) War', p. 488.
2. *The Official History 1915* (1).
3. Liddell Hart papers, 11/1936/42, 11/1957/19.
4. For example, 'Infantryman', pp. 88–101.
5. Editorial, 'British Tactical Doctrine', pp. 365, 369.
6. Letter to author from Denis Winter, 28 September 1991.
7. Dupuy, *A Genius for War*, p. 3.
8. Ibid., p. 4.
9. Ibid., p. 254.
10. Ibid., p. 5.
11. Van Creveld, *Fighting Power*.
12. Elliott-Bateman *et al.*, 'Vocabulary', p. 267.
13. Wallach, *The Dogma of Annihilation*, p. 48.
14. Elliott-Bateman, op. cit., p. 268.
15. E. Wilde in Elliott-Bateman, 'Vocabulary', p. 271.
16. Quoted by Wallach, op. cit., p. 189.
17. A. R. Millett *et al.*, 'The Effectiveness of Military Organisations', p. 22.
18. 'Schlieffen's Tactical-Strategic Problems', p. 71.
19. Quoted by Mountcastle, 'On the Move', p. 17.

## Chapter One, pp. 7–33

1. Showalter, 'Goltz and Bernhardi', p. 310.
2. Wallach, op. cit., p. 22.
3. Letter to the author from Militärgeschichtliches Forschungsamt, December 1990.
4. Quoted by Wallach, op. cit., p. 22.
5. Van Creveld, op. cit., p. 164.
6. Quoted by Wallach, op. cit., p. 22.
7. 'The Other Side of the Hill', No. 2, pp. 73, 75.
8. 'The Other Side of the Hill', No. 17, p. 40.
9. German General Staff, 'Die Entwicklung der deutschen Infanterie', p. 395.
10. Quoted in SS 201/3, Machine-Gun Notes. Emphasis in original.
11. Hughes, 'Abuses of German Military History', pp. 67–8.
12. Ose, 'Der Auftrag', p. 264.
13. Von Regling, 'Grundzüge der militärischen Kriegführung', p. 296.
14. Prince Frederick Charles of Prussia, 'The Spirit of the Prussian Officer', pp. 260–1. Emphasis in original.
15. Goerlitz, *History of the German General Staff*, pp. 83–4.

16. Meyer, 'Operational Art and the German Command System', p. 70.
17. Goerlitz, op. cit., p. 86.
18. Militärgeschichtliches Forschungsamt, ed., 'Die Generalstäbe in Deutschland 1871–1945', p. 18.
19. Ibid., pp. 24–5.
20. See Goerlitz, op. cit., p. 91.
21. Quoted in Rothenberg, 'Moltke, Schlieffen and the Doctrine of Strategic Envelopment', p. 300.
22. Quoted by Goerlitz, op. cit., p. 76.
23. Lind, *Maneuver War Handbook*, p. 5.
24. Holborn, 'Moltke and Schlieffen', p. 180.
25. Meyer, Operational Art, p. 109. Meyer uses the term *Weisungführung* to describe this system of command, but this appears to be a retranslation into German of Moltke's concept of *Führen durch Direktiven*. Letter to author from Militärgeschichtliches Forschungsamt, December 1990.
26. Holborn, op. cit., p. 181.
27. MGFA, 'Generalstäbe', p. 36.
28. Showalter, 'The Retaming of Bellona', p. 60.
29. Ibid., p. 61.
30. MGFA, 'Generalstäbe', p. 18.
31. SS 356 (1918): German Army Handbook, plate 1.
32. Schellendorf, *The Duties of the General Staff*, pp. 248–9.
33. MGFA, 'Generalstäbe', p. 36.
34. Schellendorf, op. cit., pp. 261–2.
35. Ibid., pp. 258–9 and MGFA, 'Generalstäbe', pp. 36–7.
36. H. Rosinski, *The German Army*, p. 107.
37. MGFA, 'Generalstäbe', p. 37.
38. Wilkinson, *The Brain of an Army*, p. 62.
39. Liddell Hart Centre, Edmonds Papers, III/1, 7.
40. Meyer, op. cit., pp. 38, 45.
41. Holborn, op. cit., p. 180.
42. Rosinski, op. cit., p. 169.
43. PRO: WO 33/179; System of Training of Staff Officers, p. 32.
44. Matuschka, 'Organisationsgeschichte des Heeres', p. 197.
45. Ibid., p. 197.
46. PRO: WO 33/179, p. 31.
47. Ibid., p. 32.
48. Rosinski, op. cit., p. 287.
49. Ibid., p. 270.
50. PRO: WO 33/179, p. 32.
51. Rosinski, op. cit., p. 287.
52. Meyer, op. cit., p. 49.
53. Wilkinson, op. cit., p. 80.
54. PRO: WO 33/179, pp. 34–6.
55. Rosinski, op. cit., p. 270.
56. Schellendorf, op. cit., pp. 44–5.
57. Dupuy, *A Genius for War*, p. 30.
58. Schellendorf, op. cit., p. 46.
59. Wilkinson, op. cit., p. 76.
60. Ibid., pp. 77–8.
61. Schellendorf, op. cit., pp. 48–9; and Matuschka, op. cit., p. 197.
62. Wilkinson, op. cit., p. 93.
63. Matuschka, op. cit., p. 196.
64. PRO: WO 33/179, p.33.
65. Ibid., p. 31.
66. Hindenburg, *Out of My Life*, p. 63.
67. Rosinski, op. cit., p. 267.

68. Meyer, op. cit., pp. 51–2.
69. Matuschka, op. cit., p. 197.
70. Model, *Der deutsche Generalstabsoffizier*, p. 15.
71. General Marx (1934), quoted by Rosinski, op. cit., p. 268.
72. Van Creveld, op. cit., pp. 109–41.
73. Quoted by Wilkinson, op. cit., pp. 83, 85.
74. Rosinski, op. cit., p. 270.
75. PRO: WO 33/179, p. 34.
76. Quoted by Wilkinson, op. cit., p. 91.
77. Rosinski, op. cit., pp. 270–1.
78. PRO: WO 33/179, pp. 34–6.
79. Rosinski, op. cit., p. 272.
80. Hindenburg, op. cit., pp. 57, 65.
81. Rosinski, op. cit., pp. 271–2; and MGFA, 'Generalstäbe', p. 19.
82. 'Schlieffen's Tactical-Strategic Problems', p. 69.
83. Hindenburg, op. cit., pp. 59–60.
84. Rosinski, op. cit., p. 272.
85. 'Schlieffen's Tactical-Strategic Problems', pp. 69–70.
86. Hindenburg, op. cit., pp. 56, 58; and MGFA, 'Generalstäbe', p. 36.
87. 'Schlieffen's Tactical-Strategic Problems', p. 70.
88. PRO: WO 33/179, p. 36.
89. Hughes, *The King's Finest*, p. 111, table 26n.
90. Ibid., p. 107, table 25.
91. MGFA, 'Generalstäbe', p. 18n5.
92. Hughes, op. cit., p. 107, table 25.
93. Henderson, *The Science of War*, p. 161.
94. Hughes, op. cit., pp. 120–1, table 30.
95. PRO: WO 33/179, p. 36.
96. Hindenburg, op. cit., pp. 17, 53–67.
97. For example Meyer, op. cit., pp. 296–308.
98. MGFA, 'Generalstäbe', p. 20.
99. Ibid., p.18.
100. Wallach, op. cit., p. 88.
101. Borgert, 'Grundzüge der Landkriegführung von Schlieffen bis Guderian', Vol. IX, pp. 489–90.
102. MGFA, 'Generalstäbe', p. 20.
103. Hindenburg, op. cit., p. 64.
104. Rothenberg, op. cit., p. 314.
105. Wallach, op. cit., p. 53.
106. Rothenberg, op. cit., p. 315.
107. Rosinski, op. cit., p. 95.
108. Holborn, op. cit., p. 194.
109. Quoted in Barnett, *The Swordbearers*, p. 53.
110. *Was bringen Felddienst-Ordnung.*
111. Letter to the author from Militärgeschichtliches Forschungsamt, December 1990.
112. Spohn, 'The Art of Command', p. 1.
113. Ibid., p. 2.
114. Ibid., p. 2.
115. Ibid., p. 7.
116. Ibid., p. 15.
117. Ibid., p. 16.

## Chapter Two, pp. 34–60

1. Bond, *The Victorian Army*, pp. 120–1.
2. Gooch, *The Plans of War*, p. 3.
3. Ibid., p. 4.

4. Quoted by Bond, op. cit., p. 121.
5. Gooch, op. cit., p. 5.
6. Bond, op. cit., p. 121.
7. Ibid., p. 120.
8. Wheeler, *The War Office*, p. 252.
9. Bond, op. cit., p. 120.
10. Ibid., pp. 121–2. Emphasis in original.
11. Gooch, op. cit., p. 7.
12. Hamer, *The British Army*, pp. 110–11.
13. Ibid., p. 112.
14. Gooch, op. cit., p. 8.
15. Hamer, op. cit., p. 60.
16. Ibid., p. 139n4.
17. Ibid., pp. 139–40.
18. Ibid., p. 141.
19. Gooch, op. cit., p. 14.
20. Hamer, op. cit., pp. 145–6.
21. Ibid., p. 152.
22. Ibid., p. 168.
23. Wheeler, op. cit., pp. 251–2.
24. Hamer, op. cit., pp. 167 and 170.
25. Wheeler, op. cit., p.256.
26. Hamer, op. cit., pp. 190–1.
27. Ibid., pp. 190–1.
28. Gooch, op. cit., p. 22.
29. Bond, op. cit., p. 213.
30. Gooch, op. cit., pp. 24–5.
31. Bond, op. cit., p. 214.
32. Hamer, op. cit., p. 201.
33. Ibid., p. 139.
34. Ibid., p. 244.
35. Gooch, op. cit., p. 51.
36. Bond, op. cit., p. 230.
37. Ibid., p. 230.
38. For distribution of duties see ibid., p. 219, table 3.
39. Bidwell and Graham, *Firepower*, p. 47.
40. Bond, op. cit., p. 231, lists the sizes of all three directorates.
41. Ibid., p. 231.
42. Gooch, op. cit., p. 121.
43. Holmes, *The Little Field-Marshal*, p. 136.
44. Quoted by Bond, op. cit., p. 226.
45. Stone, 'The Anglo-Boer War', p. 152.
46. Gooch, op. cit., p. 56.
47. Bond, op. cit., p. 221.
48. Gooch, op. cit., p. 56.
49. Bond, op. cit., p. 226.
50. Gooch, op. cit., p. 67.
51. Bond, op. cit., pp. 226–7.
52. Gooch, op. cit., p. 81.
53. Bond, op. cit., p. 252.
54. Gooch, op. cit., p. 101.
55. Spiers, *Haldane*, p. 122.
56. Gooch, op. cit., p. 102.
57. Ibid., p. 104.
58. Spiers, op. cit., p. 122.
59. Gooch, op. cit., p. 56.
60. Ibid., p. 70.
61. Ibid., p. 73.

62. Ibid., p. 108.
63. Bond, op. cit., p. 231.
64. De Groot, *Douglas Haig*, p. 46.
65. Bond, op. cit., p. 169.
66. Ibid., p. 182.
67. Stone, op. cit., p. 108.
68. Gooch, op. cit., p. 27.
69. Holmes, op. cit., pp. 33–4.
70. Bond, op. cit., p. 195; and Edmonds *et al.*, 'Four Generations of Staff College Students', p. 46.
71. Hamilton, *The Commander*, p. 50.
72. Holmes, op. cit., p. 33.
73. Edmonds, op. cit., p. 42.
74. Liddell Hart Centre: Edmonds Papers, III/2, p. 7.
75. Bond, op. cit., pp. 138–9.
76. De Groot, op. cit., p. 38.
77. Edmonds papers, III/2, 4 and III/5, pp. 14–16.
78. Edmonds, 'Four Generations', p. 42.
79. Bond, op. cit., p. 139.
80. De Groot, op. cit., p. 38.
81. Edmonds, op. cit., p. 42.
82. Bond, op. cit., p. 139.
83. Edmonds, op. cit., p. 46.
84. Ibid., p. 3.
85. Edmonds papers, III/2, p. 23.
86. Quoted by Bond, op. cit., p. 141.
87. Ibid., p. 161.
88. Edmonds, op. cit., p. 45.
89. Ibid., p. 43.
90. Ibid., p. 44.
91. Edmonds papers, III/2, p. 21.
92. Edmonds, op. cit., p. 45.
93. Bond, op. cit., p. 277.
94. De Groot, op. cit., p. 37.
95. Edmonds papers, III/2, p. 1.
96. Ibid., III/2, p. 4.
97. De Groot, op. cit., p. 49.
98. Edmonds, op. cit., p. 44.
99. Godwin-Austen, *The Staff and the Staff College*, pp. 242–3.
100. Ibid., p. 257.
101. Bond, op. cit., p. 154.
102. Gooch, op. cit., pp. 109–110.
103. Bond, op. cit., p. 278.
104. Ibid., p. 278.
105. De Groot, op. cit., pp. 105–6.
106. Ibid., p. 140.
107. This term is used by Elliott-Bateman (*et al.*), 'Vocabulary', p. 265.
108. Stone, op. cit., pp.45–7.
109. Ibid., p. 47.
110. De Groot, pp. 42 and 44.
111. Ibid., p. 46.
112. Ibid., p. 51.
113. Liebmann, 'Die deutschen Gefechtsvorschriften', p. 460.
114. Hamilton, *Commander*, p. 53.
115. Sixsmith, *British Generalship*, pp. 151–3.
116. Ibid., p. 152.
117. Travers, *The Killing Ground*, p. 288.

118. Sixsmith, op. cit., p. 154.
119. Aspinall-Oglander, *The Official History: Gallipoli*, Vol. 2, pp. 383–6.
120. *Exerzier-Reglement für die Infanterie*, para. II.103.
121. Lossow, 'Mission-Type Tactics versus Order-Type Tactics', p. 89.
122. De Groot, op. cit., p. 51.
123. Quoted by Holborn, 'Moltke and Schlieffen', p. 194.
124. Horne, *The Price of Glory*, pp. 48–9.
125. Quoted by De Groot, op. cit., pp. 334–5. Emphasis added.
126. Quoted by Travers, op. cit., p. 211.
127. De Groot, op. cit., p. 248.
128. Wheeler, op. cit., p. 228.
129. Spiers, op. cit., p. 81.
130. Wheeler, op. cit., p. 229.
131. Ibid., pp. 231–2.
132. For example Baynes, *Morale: A Study of Men and Courage*, pp. 20–1.
133. Ascoli, *Companion to the British Army, 1660–1983*, p. 29.
134. Dunn, *The War the Infantry Knew*, p. 105.
135. Perry, *The Commonwealth Armies*, p. 7.
136. Holmes, *Little Field-Marshal*, pp. 124–6.
137. Stone, op. cit., p. 122.
138. Edmonds papers, III/7, pp. 1–2.
139. *Die Armeen unserer Feinde*, p. 19.
140. Edmonds papers, III/7, p. 2.
141. Ibid., III/1, p. 8.
142. Ibid., III/1, p. 5.
143. Stone, op. cit., pp. 14–15.
144. Ibid., p. 15.
145. Amery, *The Problem of the Army*, p. 155.
146. Edmonds papers, III/7, p. 7.
147. Ibid., III/5, p. 25.
148. Stone, op. cit., p. 15.
149. Edmonds papers, III/7, p. 15.
150. Holmes, op. cit., p. 164.
151. Quoted by De Groot, op. cit., p. 51.
152. De Groot, op. cit., p. 182.
153. Travers, op. cit., p. 27.
154. Ibid., p. 112.
155. Ibid., pp. 108–9.
156. Fourth Army Tactical Notes (reprinted in *The Official History, 1916* (1)), Appendix 18.
157. Stone, op. cit., p. 15.
158. Holmes, op. cit., p. 40.
159. Ibid., p. 39.
160. Ibid., p. 53.
161. De Groot, op. cit., p. 64.
162. Ibid., pp. 70–1.
163. Terraine, *Douglas Haig*, p. 29.
164. Ibid., pp. 31–2.
165. Travers, op. cit., p. 286.
166. Ibid., pp. 290–1.
167. Ibid., p. 293.

## Chapter Three, pp. 61–93

1. Balck, *Tactics*, Vol. 1, p. 32.
2. Although the issuing of rifles to cavalry units gave them a limited *Feuerkraft* capability, it was so small compared to that of the infantry as to be of little importance.

3. Griffith, *Forward into Battle*, p. 49.
4. Henderson, 'Military Criticism and Modern Tactics', p. 118.
5. Griffith, op. cit., p. 54.
6. Ibid., p. 48.
7. Showalter, *Railroads and Rifles*, pp. 83–4 and 94.
8. Ibid., p. 101.
9. Griffith, op. cit., p. 53.
10. Lloyd, *History of Infantry*, pp. 239–40.
11. Showalter, op. cit., p. 105.
12. Craig, *The Battle of Königgrätz*, pp. 22–3.
13. Ibid., p. 23.
14. Showalter, op. cit., pp. 106–7.
15. Craig, op. cit., p. 23.
16. Lloyd, op. cit., p. 242.
17. Ibid., pp.249–50.
18. Showalter, op. cit., pp. 112–13.
19. Ibid., p. 241n19.
20. Ibid., p. 113.
21. Lloyd, op. cit., p. 233.
22. Showalter, op. cit., p. 83.
23. Ibid., p. 85.
24. Ibid., p. 102.
25. Ibid., pp. 114–15.
26. Ibid., pp. 115–16.
27. Ibid., p. 94.
28. Craig, op. cit., pp. 67–8, 75 and 77.
29. Showalter, op. cit., p. 127.
30. See Craig, op. cit., pp.117–22 and Showalter, op. cit., pp. 131–4.
31. Lloyd, op. cit., p. 262.
32. Howard, *The Franco-Prussian War*, p. 7.
33. Ibid., p. 35.
34. Ibid., p. 7n4.
35. Ibid., p. 118.
36. Henderson, 'The Training of Infantry for the Attack', pp. 344–5.
37. Henderson, 'Military Criticism', p. 146–7.
38. Lloyd, op. cit., p. 267.
39. See Howard, op. cit., pp. 93–112.
40. Ibid., p. 175.
41. Maude, *Notes on the Evolution of Infantry Tactics*, p. 73.
42. Balck, *Tactics* (1), p. 176.
43. Liebmann, 'Die deutschen Gefechtsvorschriften', pp. 457–8.
44. *Exerzier-Reglement für die Infanterie* (*ExRfd I*), para. II.13. Emphasis in original.
45. Ibid., II.30.
46. Ibid., II.69.
47. Ibid., II.19.
48. Ibid., II.20.
49. Ibid., II.14.
50. Ibid., II.79.
51. Ibid., II.80.
52. Ibid., II.82.
53. Ibid., I.132.
54. Ibid., II.82.
55. Ibid., II.71.
56. Ibid., II.84.
57. Holborn, 'Moltke and Schlieffen', p. 180.
58. See *ExRfdI* 1888, II.35, 54, 96, 103.
59. Ibid., II.35.

60. Ibid., II.101.
61. Ibid., II.54.
62. Ibid., II.121.
63. Ibid., II.16.
64. Ibid., II.21.
65. Ibid., II.54.
66. Walter (ed.), *Guns of the First World War*, p. 21.
67. Ibid., p. 23.
68. Liebmann, op. cit., pp. 457–8.
69. Ibid., pp.458–9.
70. Ibid., p. 460.
71. Ibid., pp. 459–60.
72. Borgert, 'Grundzüge der Landkriegführung', pp. 429–30.
73. Ibid., p. 435.
74. Ibid., p. 488.
75. Gudmundsson, *Stormtroop Tactics*, p. 8. Gudmundsson appears to have misinterpreted the regulations of 1888, believing that they sanctioned the use of close order tactics.
76. German General Staff, *The War in South Africa*, pp. 218–22.
77. Gudmundsson, op. cit., pp.20–1. Owing to his misinterpretation of the 1888 regulations, Gudmundsson believes this to have been a new development, rather than a reversion to those regulations.
78. Ibid., p. 26n10.
79. Liebmann, op. cit., p.460.
80. Ibid., p. 461.
81. The following discussion is based on ibid., pp.462–70.
82. *ExRfdI* 1906, para. 264, 336, 170, 357, 338a.
83. Ibid., para. 265.
84. Ibid., para. 342. The belief that close order was still possible may have been the result of a misreading of the Russo-Japanese War, in which a number of Japanese bayonet attacks had been successful. This was a consequence of the Russian Army being inculcated with the Dragomirov doctrine, based upon the shock action of narrow, deep formations. Its fire tactics, which still relied upon volley fire, were therefore inadequate. As in 1859 and 1864, the result was a reduction in the firepower of the defender sufficient to allow the use of assault tactics. Such circumstances were unlikely to occur in Europe. See Balck, *Tactics* (1), pp. 340–2.
85. *ExRfdI* 1906, para. 444.
86. Balck, op. cit. (1), p. 352.
87. Ibid. (1), pp. 174–6 and *ExRfdI* 1906, para. 336.
88. *ExRfdI* 1906, para. 324.
89. Borgert, op. cit., p. 431.
90. See *ExRfdI* 1906, para. 2, 144, 158, 251.
91. Borgert, op. cit., p. 486.
92. Ibid., pp. 487–8.
93. Balck, op. cit. (1), p. 50.
94. Ibid. (1), pp. 201–2.
95. *German Army Handbook* (April 1918), pp.9–11.
96. Showalter, 'Army and Society in Imperial Germany', p. 593.
97. Three years in the cavalry and horse artillery.
98. *Field Service Regulations of the German Army*, para. 1.
99. *ExRfdI*, para. 477.
100. Showalter, op. cit., p. 607.
101. PRO, WO 105/45, p. 6.
102. *German Army Handbook* 1918, p. 9.
103. Nash, *Imperial German Army Handbook, 1914–18*, p. 77.
104. *ExRfdI* 1906, para. 4.
105. Gudmundsson, op. cit., p. 18.
106. Henderson, op. cit., p. 161.

107. Bidwell and Graham, *Firepower*, p. 16.
108. Balck (1), p. 35, table.
109. Staff College, Camberley TDRC-6834, 'The Effectiveness of Reservists', p. 12.
110. PRO, WO 105/45, p. 5.
111. *German Army Handbook* 1918, pp. 25–6.
112. Sir A. Hunter, quoted by Amery, *The Problem of the Army*, p. 193n.
113. [Baker], *The German Army from Within*, pp. 69–70.
114. *German Army Handbook* 1918, p. 26.
115. [Baker], op. cit., p. 188.
116. For example Remarque, *All Quiet on the Western Front*, Picador, reprint, p. 56.
117. Showalter, op. cit., p. 602.
118. Ibid., p. 601.
119. Ibid., p. 602.
120. Ibid., p. 603.
121. [Baker], op. cit., p. 36.
122. Ibid., pp. 37–8.
123. *German Army Handbook* 1918, p. 23.
124. Ibid., p. 23.
125. Van Creveld, *Fighting Power*, pp. 132–3.
126. [Baker], op. cit., p. 85.
127. Henderson, op. cit., p. 161.
128. *ExRfdI* 1906, para. 4.
129. [Baker], op. cit., p. 142.
130. [Baker], op. cit., pp. 125–6.
131. Liddell Hart Centre, Edmonds papers, III/1, p. 4.
132. *German Army Handbook* 1918, p.11.
133. Rosinski, *The German Army*, pp. 101–3.
134. *German Army Handbook* 1918, p. 24.
135. Van Creveld, op. cit., p. 18.
136. Rosinski, op. cit., p. 102.
137. Van Creveld, op. cit., p. 19.
138. Liebmann, op. cit., p. 459.
139. *German Army Handbook* 1918, p. 54.
140. Balck, op. cit. (1), p. 273.
141. *German Army Handbook* 1918, p. 43, table.
142. Balck, op. cit. (1), p. 261n.
143. Showalter, op. cit., p. 591.
144. Bidwell, op. cit., p.22.
145. Ibid., p. 297n21.
146. Cron, *Geschichte des deutschen Heeres*, p. 116.
147. Macdonald, *1914*, pp. 160 and 162.
148. Edmonds, *The Official History, 1914*, Vol. 1, p. 159.
149. Ibid., p. 160.
150. Ibid., p. 173.
151. Ibid., p. 191.
152. Brigadier-General Robertson in Report of a Conference of General Staff Officers at the Staff College, 17 to 20 January 1910, p. 29.
153. Balck, op. cit. (1), p. 294.
154. Robertson, GSO Conference 1910, p. 29.
155. Balck, op. cit. (1), p. 295.
156. Ibid. (1), p. 269–70 and Major McMahon in GSO Conference 1910, p. 27.
157. This idea was first put forward by Wynne, 'Pattern for a Limited (Nuclear) War', pp. 489–91.
158. Ritter, *The Schlieffen Plan*, pp. 146–7.
159. Quoted in ibid., p. 51.
160. Ibid., pp. 173–4.
161. Ibid., p. 180–1.

162. *German Army Handbook* 1918, pp. 32 and 67–8.
163. Edmonds and Wynne, *The Official History, 1915* (1), p. 92; Wynne, *If Germany Attacks*, p. 28.
164. Edmonds, op. cit., p. 98n1.
165. Edmonds, op. cit., p. 100; Wynne, op. cit., p. 29.
166. See CDS 303: Experience Gained in the Winter Battle in Champagne, para. 4.
167. Gruss, 'Aufbau und Verwendung', p. 24.
168. Ibid., pp. 13–15.
169. Balck, op. cit. (1), p. 352.
170. For example, Bidwell, *Gunners at War*, p. 15; and Feeser, 'Infanterie-Geschütze', pp. 79–81.
171. Balck, op. cit. (2), p. 220 table.
172. Grenades were considered part of assault power, rather than of firepower, because their short range made them of use primarily in the assault, rather than in the preceding fire fight.
173. For example, Gudmundsson, pp. 33–4.
174. Bauer, *Der grosse Krieg*, pp. 87–8.
175. Ibid., p. 87.
176. Gruss, op. cit., p. 15.
177. See Bierman, 'Die Entwicklung der deutschen Minenwerferwaffe', pp. 482–4; and Reddemann, 'Die Totenkopf Pioniere', pp. 516–24.
178. Gruss, op. cit., pp. 15, 147–8 and 17.
179. Ibid., pp. 16–17.
180. Ibid., pp. 18–19.
181. Bauer, op. cit., p. 87.
182. Von Alten *et al.*, *Geschichte des Garde-Schützen-Bataillons 1914–1919*, p. 198.
183. Bidwell, op. cit., p. 22.
184. Von Alten, op. cit., p. 151.
185. Ibid., p. 125.
186. Bauer, op. cit., p. 87.
187. German General Staff, 'Die Entwicklung der deutschen Infanterie', p. 379.
188. Gruss, op. cit., p. 19.
189. Balck, *Tactics*, Vol. 2, p. 470.
190. Feeser, 'Infanterie-Geschütze', pp. 82–6.
191. *German Army Handbook* 1918, p. 105.
192. Gruss, op. cit., pp. 75–6.
193. Jünger, *The Storm of Steel*, p. 40.
194. SS 546: The 1916 Pattern Bomb-Thrower.
195. SS 153: Notes on the '08 German Maxim Gun.
196. SS 579: Extracts from the Experiences of the Sixth German Army.
197. Cron, *Deutschen Heeres*, p. 118.
198. Gudmundsson, op. cit., pp. 98–101.
199. German General Staff, 'Entwicklung der Infanterie', p. 380.
200. Bauer, op. cit., p. 88. Emphasis in original.
210. German General Staff, 'Entwicklung der Infanterie', p. 372.
202. SS 537: Recent Information Regarding the German Army, para. VI.B.8.
203. Nash, *German Infantry 1914–18*, p. 42.
204. Jünger, op. cit., p. 197.
205. Bull, 'German Grenades and Bombing Tactics (1)', p. 11.
206. Gruss, op. cit., pp. 73–4.
207. Jünger, p. 89.
208. SS 562: Manual of Position Warfare, p. 74.
209. Nash, *German Army Handbook*, pp. 90–1.
210. Ibid., p. 107.
211. Gruss, op. cit., p. 75.
212. Ibid., p. 80; Nagel, *Württembergische Sturmkompagnie*, p. 13.
213. Gruss, op. cit., p. 99.
214. Ibid., p. 43.
215. Ibid., p. 13.

## Chapter Four, pp. 94–123

1. Henderson, 'Military Criticism and Modern Tactics', pp. 108–64.
2. Ibid., pp. 117–18.
3. Henderson, 'The Training of Infantry for the Attack', pp. 344–5.
4. Henderson, 'Military Criticism', pp. 152–3.
5. Ibid., p. 119.
6. Ibid., p. 146.
7. Ibid., p. 146–7.
8. Ibid., p. 136–7.
9. Ibid., p. 163.
10. Ibid., p. 149.
11. Ibid., p. 152–3.
12. Ibid., p. 139–40.
13. Ibid., p. 130.
14. Ibid., p. 161.
15. Details from biographies in Travers, *The Killing Ground*, Appendix II, pp. 281–93.
16. Henderson, 'The Training of Infantry for the Attack', pp. 338–64.
17. Ibid., p. 344.
18. Ibid., p. 344.
19. See Henderson, 'Foreign Criticism', pp. 365–81.
20. Henderson, 'War'; and Henderson, 'The British Army', pp. 1–38 and pp. 382–434.
21. Sixsmith, *British Generalship in the Twentieth Century*, p. 37.
22. Henderson, 'British Army', pp. 410–11, emphasis added.
23. Sixsmith, op. cit., p. 37.
24. Quoted by Stone, 'The Anglo-Boer War', p. 117.
25. See Balck, *Tactics*, Vol. 1, pp. 459–63.
26. Career details from Henderson, *Science of War*, pp. xiii–xxxviii.
27. Report on a Conference of General Staff Officers (GSO) at the Staff College, 7 to 10 January, 1908, pp. 44–6.
28. GSO Conference, 18 to 21 January, 1909, pp. 9–12.
29. Ibid., p. 19.
30. *ExRfdI* (1906), para. 336; and see Balck op. cit., (1), pp. 174–7.
31. GSO Conference, 1909, p. 8.
32. Balck op. cit., (1), p. 374.
33. GSO Conference, 1909, p. 9.
34. Bidwell and Graham, *Firepower*, p. 27.
35. Edmonds, *The Official History, 1914* (2), p. 463n1.
36. GSO Conference, 1910, pp. 25–7.
37. Ibid., pp. 27–8.
38. Ibid., pp. 28, 30, 69–70.
39. GSO Conference, 1909, pp. 5 and 6.
40. GSO Conference, 1910, p. 31.
41. Ibid., p. 28.
42. Ibid., p. 32.
43. Bidwell and Graham, *Firepower*, pp. 49–50.
44. GSO Conference, 1911, pp. 65–6 and 72.
45. Ibid., pp. 66–7 and 74; and see Du Cane, 'The Cooperation of Field Artillery', pp. 97–113.
46. GSO Conference, 1914, pp. 76–7.
47. Travers, *Killing Ground*, p. 71.
48. Quoted by Pridham, *Superiority of Fire*, p. 56.
49. Ibid., pp. 56–7.
50. 'Infantry Training 1911', p. 89.
51. Edmonds and Wynne, *The Official History, 1915*, Vol. 1, pp. 366–7.
52. PRO: WO 95/231: First Army. No. 7 Mountain Battery RGA, August 1914–December 1915. War Diary, 10 March 1915; WO 95/327: Second Army Troops. Nos. 2 and 5 Mountain Batteries RGA, August 1914–November 1915. War Diary, 8 March 1915; WO

95/708: IV Corps, General Staff, March–April 1915. Memorandum on the Attack on Neuve Chapelle by First Army, Appendix C, 2.

53. PRO: WO 95/1707: 8th Division, 23rd Infantry Brigade, Brigade Headquarters, November 1914–May 1915. 8th Division Operations Order No. 12, 8 March 1915, para. 5.a–b.; 25th Brigade Operations Order No. 11, 9 March 1915, para. 6.a.; WO 95/708, Report of Operations of Mortar Section, 8th Division, 10–13 March 1915.
54. Edmonds, *Official History, 1915* (1), pp. 91–3.
55. 'The Other Side of the Hill, No. XVII', p. 35.
56. Edmonds, *Official History, 1915* (1), pp. 96–7; PRO: WO 95/708, Report of Operations of Mortar Section; WO/327, No. 5 Mountain Battery, War Diary, 10 March 1915.
57. Edmonds, op. cit., p. 92.
58. PRO: WO 95/327, No. 5 Mountain Battery, War Diary, 10 March 1915.
59. Edmonds, *Official History, 1915* (1), p. 98; Wynne, *If Germany Attacks*, p. 29.
60. Edmonds, *Official History, 1915* (1), p. 85n1.
61. See Wynne, 'The Chain of Command', pp. 23–37.
62. 'The Other Side of the Hill, 17', pp. 42–3.
63. PRO: WO 95/1628: 7th Division, General Staff, February–May 1915. 7th Division Operations Order No. 46, 8 March 1915, para. 6.
64. Quoted by Edmonds, *Official History: France and Belgium, 1915*, Vol. 2, p. 13.
65. Ibid., pp. 17–20.
66. Ibid., p. 14.
67. Ibid., pp. 20–1.
68. Ibid., p. 34.
69. PRO: WO 95/1672: 8th Division, General Staff, April–July 1915. 8th Division Operations Order No. 30, 5 May 1915, Appendix 13: Letter from Brigadier-General A. Holland, CRA 8th Division, to BGRA IV Corps.
70. Edmonds, *Official History, 1915* (2), pp. 10 and 31.
71. PRO: WO 95/1672, Report on Operations 9 and 10 May, 1915, 3.
72. PRO: WO 95/327, No. 5 Mountain Battery, War Diary, 9 May 1915.
73. PRO: WO 95/1683: 8th Division, Commander Royal Artillery, November 1914–December 1915. Special Instructions for 3-pounder Hotchkiss Detachment with Armoured Lorry, 7 May 1915.
74. PRO: WO 95/1628, 7th Division Operations Order No. 6, 5 May 1915, 2; and WO 95/709: IV Corps, General Staff, May 1915. IV Corps Operations Order No. 15, 3 May 1915, para. 4; and WO 95/1638: 7th Division, Commander Royal Artillery, September 1914–December 1915. 7th Division Operations Order No. 4, 4 May 1915, Special Instructions for the 7th Divisional and Attached Artillery, 5 May 1915.
75. Edmonds, *Official History, 1915* (2), p. 47.
76. Ibid., pp. 52–5.
77. Ibid., p. 59.
78. PRO: WO 95/1628, 7th Division Operations Order No. 11, 14 May 1915, para. 3.
79. Edmonds, *Official History, 1915* (2), pp. 150–2.
80. Ibid., pp. 174–5 and 165.
81. Ibid., p. 167.
82. Ibid., p. 175.
83. Ibid., p. 188.
84. Ibid., p. 299.
85. Bidwell, *Firepower*, p. 146.
86. SS 119: Preliminary Notes on the Tactical Lessons of the Recent Operations, July 1916, p. 2.
87. SS 135: Instructions for the Training of Divisions for Offensive Action, December 1916, p. 52.
88. PRO: WO 158/344, Memorandum on Trench to Trench Attack by a Battalion Commander in the Fifth Army, 31 October 1916, p. 11.
89. Wynne, *If Germany Attacks*, p. 52.
90. Edmonds, *Official History, 1915* (2), pp. 90–1.
91. PRO: WO 95/7008, IV Corps Operation Order No. 10, para. 5; and WO 95/1672, 8th

Division Operation Order No. 30.
92. Edmonds, *Official History, 1915* (2), p. 15.
93. Bidwell, op. cit., p. 124.
94. Simkins, *Kitchener's Army*, p. 282.
95. Edmonds, *Official History, 1915* (2), p. 89; and Simkins, op. cit., pp. 287–8.
96. Bidwell, op. cit., p. 124.
97. GSO Conference, 1910, p. 68.
98. Farndale, *The Royal Regiment of Artillery: Western Front 1914–18*, p. 341; and Farndale, *The Royal Regiment of Artillery: The Forgotten Fronts*, pp. 387, 394.
99. See PRO: WO 95/231, No. 7 Mountain Battery, War Diary; and WO 95/327, Nos. 2 and 5 Mountain Batteries, War Diaries.
100. Hogg and Thurston, *British Artillery Weapons*, p. 42.
101. Ibid., pp. 90–1.
102. Bidwell, op. cit., p. 194.
103. Edmonds, *Official History, 1915* (2), pp. 20–1.
104. Bidwell, op. cit., pp. 122–3; and Edmonds, *Official History, 1915* (2), p. 89n4.
105. *German Army Handbook*, p. 45.
106. Bidwell, op. cit., pp. 121, 127.
107. Bull, 'British Grenade Tactics', pp. 30 and 34.
108. Edmonds, *Official History, 1915* (2), pp. 193n3 and 89.
109. Bull, op. cit., pp. 34 and 30.
110. PRO: WO 158/182: First Army Report on the Action Fought at Neuve Chapelle, 10 March 1915, p. 3.
111. PRO: WO 95/708, Notes taken at Brigade Headquarters, 13 MMarch 1915, pp. 1, 3 and 5.
112. PRO: WO 158/344: Fifth Army: Notes and Lessons on 1916 Operations. Notes on Some Bombing Operations in the Reserve Army (8 October 1916).
113. For example, SS 135, p. 52.
114. Wright, 'Machine-Gun Tactics and Organisation', pp. 290–313.
115. Bidwell, op. cit., p. 124.
116. Wright, op. cit., p. 292.
117. Bidwell, op. cit., p. 123.
118. Coppard, *With a Machine-Gun to Cambrai*, p. 93.
119. Wright, op. cit., pp. 293–6.
120. Sixsmith, op. cit., p. 120.
121. Edmonds, *Official History, 1915* (2), pp. vii, ix.
122. Spiers, 'The Regular Army in 1914', p. 46.
123. Ibid., p.45, table 2.3.
124. Ibid., p. 44.
125. Amery, *The Problem of the Army*, p. 181.
126. Stone, op. cit., p. 12.
127. PRO: WO 105/45: Notes on Comparison of Military Standards of Efficiency, p. 6.
128. Amery, op. cit., p. 50.
129. Gooch, *The Plans of War*, pp. 34–5.
130. Amery, op. cit., p. 48.
131. Ibid., pp. 121, 188, 202–3, 250–1.
132. For example Spiers, op. cit., p. 56.
133. For example Winter, *Haig's Command*, p. 135; GSO Conference, 15 to 18 January, 1912, p. 12; and GSO Conference, 1909, p. 10.
134. Balck, op. cit., (1), p. 169.
135. TDRC-6834: The Effectiveness of Reservists, pp. 11–14.
136. Perry, *The Commonwealth Armies*, p. 6.
137. Beckett, 'The Territorial Force', pp. 128–9.
138. PRO: WO 105/47: Roberts Papers.
139. Balck, *Die Englische Armee im Felde*, pp. 15-18.
140. Perry, op. cit., p. 36.
141. IWM: Maxse papers, Box 5: Army Order (11 September 1914), pp. 18–20.
142. See also Winter, *Death's Men*, pp. 38–46.

143. Winter, *Haig's Command*, pp. 145–6.
144. Edmonds, *Official History, 1915* (1), p. 12n1.
145. Winter, *Haig's Command*, p. 149.
146. IWM: Maxse papers, Box 12, File 57: Report on Work Carried Out at the XVIII Corps School During the Summer Campaign, 1917.
147. Ibid., Box 11, File 55(1): XVIII Corps No. GS 82. Letter to Fifth Army (15 October 1917).
148. Ibid., Note by a Member of the Court of Enquiry [on Cambrai], para. 11 and 14.
149. Quoted by Winter, *Haig's Command*, pp. 146–7.
150. IWM: Maxse papers, Box 11, File 55(1): Court of Enquiry, para. 11.
151. Ibid., Box 12, File 58: Extracts from Report on One Week's Inspection in Second Army Area.
152. Ibid., Box 11, File 55(1): Court of Enquiry, para. 14.
153. Ibid., XVIII Corps to Divisional Commanders (30 January 1918).
154. Ibid., Court of Enquiry, para. 9.
155. Travers, *Killing Ground*, pp. 111–12.

## Chapter Five, pp. 124–57

1. Travers, *Killing Ground*, p. 86.
2. Ibid., pp. 92–3.
3. Ibid., p. 128.
4. Winter, *Haig's Command*, p. 50.
5. Travers, op. cit., p. 129.
6. Ibid., p. 129. Travers states that Haig and Joffre agreed that there would not be a separate wearing-out phase, but instead a 'straightforward preparatory attack'. Since some form of wearing out was still necessary, it may be assumed that the intention was not to abandon the idea of wearing out, but rather to merge it with the preparatory battle, designed to pin German reserves.
7. Winter, op. cit., pp. 50–1.
8. See also Farrar-Hockley, *The Somme*, p. 74.
9. Winter, op. cit., p. 49.
10. Ibid., p. 55.
11. Horne, *The Price of Glory*, p. 211.
12. Farrar-Hockley, op. cit., p. 69.
13. Ibid., p. 75.
14. Winter, op. cit., p. 52.
15. Travers, op. cit., p. 130.
16. Winter, op. cit., p. 58.
17. Edmonds, *Official History, 1916* (1), Appendix 8, The Somme. Plan for Offensive by the Fourth Army Submitted to GHQ 3 April 1916, para. 24.ii.
18. Ibid., Appendix 8, para. 32.
19. Ibid., Appendix 9, The Somme. GHQ Letters OAD 710 and 710/1 to General Sir H. Rawlinson, 12 April 1916, with Reference to the Fourth Army Plan, para. 3.
20. Ibid., Appendix 10, The Somme. Amended Plan Submitted by the Fourth Army to GHQ, 19 April 1916, para. 18.
21. Haig's preference for a shorter bombardment remained: ibid., Appendix 14, The Somme. GHQ Letter OAD 15 to General Sir H. Rawlinson, 20 June 1916, with Regard to Shortening the Bombardment, para. 3.
22. Ibid., Appendix 11, The Somme. GHQ Letter OAD 876 to General Sir H. Rawlinson, 16 May 1916, with Reference to the Fourth Army Plan, para. 3.
23. See ibid., Appendix 19, The Somme. Fourth Army Artillery Programme Preliminary Bombardment.
24. Edmonds, *Official History, 1916* (1), pp. 304–5.
25. Ibid., pp. 300–1.
26. Keegan, *The Face of Battle*, p. 238.
27. Edmonds, *Official History, 1916* (1), p. 302.

28. Middlebrook, *The First Day of the Somme*, p. 105.
29. Edmonds, *Official History, 1916* (1), p. 288.
30. Winter, op. cit., p. 60.
31. Bidwell and Graham, *Firepower*, p. 104.
32. Edmonds, *Official History, 1916* (1), p. 301.
33. Edmonds, *Official History, 1915* (2), p. 163.
34. Terraine, *White Heat*, p. 210.
35. Edmonds, *Official History, 1915* (2), p. 150.
36. Terraine, op. cit., p. 210.
37. Horne, op. cit., p. 51.
38. Ibid., p. 92.
39. Travers, op. cit., p. 138.
40. Edmonds, *Official History, 1916* (1), Appendix 10, para. 18.
41. Ibid., p. 299.
42. Van Creveld, *Command in War*, p. 160.
43. Edmonds, *Official History, 1916* (1), Appendix 11, para. 3.
44. Ibid., p. 258.
45. Keegan, pp. 212–13.
46. Wynne, *If Germany Attacks*, pp. 100–1.
47. Sixsmith, *British Generalship in the Twentieth Century*, p. 81.
48. Travers, op. cit., p. 161.
49. Keegan, op. cit., p. 238.
50. Terraine, op. cit., p. 210.
51. Edmonds, *Official History, 1916* (1), pp. 306–7.
52. Edmonds, *Official History, 1915* (2), p. 34, and PRO: WO 95/1672: 8th Division, General Staff, April–July 1915. 8th Division Operations Order No. 30, 5 May 1915, Appendix 13: Letter from Brigadier-General A. Holland, CRA 8th Division, to BGRA IV Corps.
53. Edmonds, *Official History, 1916* (1), Appendix 16, Preparatory Measures to be Taken by Armies and Corps Before Undertaking Offensive Operations on a Large Scale, with Appendices. Issued by the General Staff GHQ (OB 1207, 2 February 1916), para. 4.7.
54. Ibid., Appendix 11, para. 3.
55. Edmonds, *Official History, 1916* (1), p. 20.
56. Travers, op. cit., p. 140.
57. Ibid., p. 140.
58. Edmonds, *Official History, 1916* (1), p. 397.
59. Travers, op. cit., p. 145.
60. Wynne, op. cit., p. 103.
61. Edmonds, *Official History, 1916* (1), pp. 395–7.
62. Wynne, op. cit., pp. 107–11.
63. Ibid., p. 113.
64. Middlebrook, op. cit., p. 61.
65. Edmonds, *Official History, 1916* (1), p. 406n1.
66. Ibid., p. 395.
67. For order of battle see ibid., p. 503.
68. All details of *Activ* units in Nash, *Imperial German Army Handbook, 1914–18*.
69. *German Army Handbook* (April 1918), p. 32.
70. SS 394: Notes on . . . XIV Reserve Corps and 52nd Division (March 1916).
71. Details of deployments from von Stosch, *Somme-Nord. I. Teil: Die Brennpunkte der Schlacht im Juli 1916*, pp. 36–52.
72. Wynne, op. cit., p. 268.
73. Stosch, op. cit., p. 37.
74. Edmonds, *Official History, 1916* (1), Appendix 10, para. 18.
75. Wynne, op. cit., pp. 111–12.
76. Keegan, op. cit., pp. 239–40.
77. See also Samuels, 'Operation GOODWOOD', pp. 4–13.
78. SS 471: Essential Principles for the Defence of Positions as Laid Down in Instructions. Emphasis in original.

79. Miles, *Official History, 1916* (2), p. 27.
80. SS 490: The Principles of Trench Warfare.
81. SS 471, para. 3.
82. Ibid., para. 6.
83. Edmonds, *Official History, 1916* (1), p. 292. The pamphlet is reprinted as Appendix 18.
84. Travers, pp. 143–5.
85. The pamphlet is reprinted in Edmonds, *Official History, 1916* (1), Appendix 17.
86. 'Fourth Army Tactical Notes' (*Official History, 1916* (1), Appendix 18), para. 19; and SS 109, para. 6.
87. Sixsmith, *British Generalship*, p. 91.
88. Liddell Hart Centre, Edmonds papers, III/2, pp. 14–15.
89. IWM Maxse papers, Box 11, File 54: Letter from Adjutant-General, BEF, to Lieutenant-General Maxse (26 July 1918).
90. Travers, op. cit., p. 145.
91. 'Fourth Army Tactical Notes', para. 6.
92. Ibid., para. 12.
93. Middlebrook, *Somme*, p. 94.
94. GSO Conference, 17 to 20 January 1910, p. 27.
95. Edmonds, *Official History, 1916* (1), p. 313.
96. Middlebrook, op. cit., p. 96.
97. Edmonds, *Official History, 1916* (1), pp. 313–14.
98. Terraine, *The Smoke and the Fire*, pp. 143–7.
99. Brigadier S. Bidwell, *The Chindit War: The Campaign in Burma, 1944* (Hodder & Stoughton, London, 1979), p. 53, quoted by Terraine, *Smoke and Fire*, p. 146.
100. Balck, *Tactics*, Vol. 1, p. 363.
101. Edmonds, *Official History, 1916* (1), p. 400.
102. Ibid., p. 314.
103. Edmonds, *Official History, 1916* (1), Appendix 21, The Somme, 1st July. XIII Corps Plan of Operations, Appendix C, para. 2.
104. Ibid., p. 398.
105. Ibid., pp. 397–8.
106. Travers, op. cit., p. 143.
107. Edmonds, *Official History, 1916* (1), p. 400.
108. See ibid., pp. 400–2; Arthur and Munro (eds.), *The Seventeenth Highland Light Infantry*, pp. 40–2; Bond, *King's Own Yorkshire Light Infantry*, pp. 813–15; Chalmers, *A Saga of Scotland*, pp. 35–8; Oatts, *Proud Heritage*, pp. 268–70; Wylly, *The Border Regiment in the Great War*, pp. 83–5.
109. Middlebrook, op. cit., p. 130.
110. Stosch, *Somme-Nord*, p. 48.
111. See Edmonds, *Official History, 1916* (1), pp. 402–3; Barlow, *The Lancashire Fusiliers*, p. 61; Cooke, *Records of the 16th Northumberland Fusiliers*, pp. 43–5; Latter, *The Lancashire Fusiliers 1914–1918*, Vol. 1, pp. 131–4.
112. Cooke, *16th Northumberland Fusiliers*, p. 44.
113. Stosch, op. cit., pp. 46–7.
114. Cooke, op. cit., p. 45.
115. See Edmonds, *Official History, 1916* (1), pp. 403–6; Cunliffe, *The Royal Irish Fusiliers 1793–1950*, p. 307; Falls, *The 36th (Ulster) Division*, pp. 44–54; Fox, *The Royal Inniskilling Fusiliers in the World War*, pp. 67–9; Harris, *The Irish Regiments in the First World War*, p. 82; Orr, *The Road to the Somme*, pp. 165–72 and 178–80; 'The Other Side of the Hill, No. II: The German Defence During the Battle of the Somme', pp. 72–4; Middlebrook, *Somme*, p. 173–8.
116. Stosch, op. cit., pp. 36–7.
117. Ibid., p. 37.
118. Orr, *Road to the Somme*, p. 167.
119. Stosch, op. cit., p. 36.
120. See Keegan, *Face of Battle*, pp. 262–7.
121. Wynne, *If Germany Attacks*, p. 112.

122. Quoted by Keegan, op. cit., p. 264.
123. Keegan, op. cit., p. 266.
124. 'Fourth Army Tactical Notes', para. 67, 70–2.
125. Edmonds, *Official History, 1916* (1), pp. 409–11.
126. Ibid., p. 401.
127. Ibid., p. 406.
128. Edmonds, *Official History, 1916* (1), Appendix 21, para. 11.f.
129. Ibid., p. 399.
130. Keegan, op. cit., p. 267.
131. 'Fourth Army Tactical Notes', op. cit., para. 74–6.
132. Van Creveld, *Command in War*, p. 158.
133. Farrar-Hockley, *Somme*, p. 133.
134. Edmonds, *Official History, 1916* (1), p. 289n1.
135. Ibid., p. 406n2.
136. Ibid., pp. 406–7.
137. Ibid., p. 408.
138. Ibid., pp. 408, 410.
139. Edmonds, *Official History, 1915* (2), pp. 209–20.
140. Edmonds, *Official History, 1916* (1), p. 417.
141. OB 1782 (an official letter issued by Haig's CGS to the five British armies in France), para. 2.a. Emphasis in original.
142. For example Edmonds, *Official History, 1916* (1), p. 418.
143. SS 135: Training of Divisions for Offensive Action, p. 9.
144. Van Creveld, op. cit., p. 161.
145. Edmonds, *Official History, 1916* (1), pp. 408–16.
146. See Stosch, *Somme-Nord*, pp. 36–52; and Wurmb, *Das K. B. Reserve-Infanterie-Regiment Nr. 8*, pp. 66–73.
147. *German Army Handbook*, April 1918, p. 59. The company would have had about 30 automatic rifles.
148. Edmonds, *Official History, 1916* (1), p. 374.
149. Stosch, op. cit., p. 39.
150. Ibid., p. 40.
151. Edmonds, *Official History, 1916* (1), p. 419.
152. Ibid., p. 483.
153. Middlebrook, op. cit., p. 264.
154. Edmonds, *Official History, 1916* (1), p. 421n1.

## Chapter Six, pp. 158–97

1. Terraine, *White Heat*, pp. 210–11.
2. Terraine, *The Smoke and the Fire*, p. 119.
3. Wray, 'Standing Fast', p. 1.
4. Ludendorff, *My War Memories, 1914–18*, Vol. 1, p. 388.
5. Wynne, 'The Hindenburg Line', p. 211.
6. Wynne, *If Germany Attacks*, p. 61.
7. Miksche, *Blitzkreig*. p. 178.
8. *ExRfdI* 1888, para. II.85.
9. *ExRfdI* 1906, para. 397–416.
10. Ibid., para. 397.
11. Ibid., para. 400.
12. Ibid., para. 401.
13. Ibid., para. 444.
14. Ibid., para. 407.
15. Balck, *Tactics*, Vol. 1, p. 411.
16. *ExRfdI*, 1906, para. 408.
17. Ibid., para. 412.

18. Ibid., para. 406.
19. Balck, op. cit. (1), p. 421.
20. *ExRfdI*, 1906, para. 398.
21. Ibid., para. 409. Balck expressed this in the question, 'With how weak a force may I occupy the position and still obtain the frontal strength described in the regulations, and how strong can I make the general reserve so as to bring about a decision?' Balck, *Tactics*, (1) p. 411.
22. *ExRfdI*, 1906, para. 410.
23. Balck, op. cit. (1), p. 433.
24. *ExRfdI*, 1906, para. 402.
25. Liebmann, 'Die deutschen Gefechtsvorschriften', pp. 471–5.
26. Ibid., p. 473.
27. 'The Other Side of the Hill No. 17', pp. 32–5.
28. Ibid., p. 31.
29. Ibid., p. 35.
30. Ibid., pp. 37–8.
31. Ibid., pp. 39–40.
32. Wynne, 'Pattern for Limited (Nuclear) War: 1', p. 495.
33. 'Other Side of the Hill No. 17', pp. 43–4.
34. Ibid., p. 44.
35. Ibid., pp. 45–6.
36. Wynne, 'Pattern for Limited War: 1', p. 492.
37. Ibid., p. 494.
38. Edmonds, *Official History, 1915* (2), p. 15.
39. Ibid., p. 14.
40. Wynne, 'Pattern for Limited War: 1' p. 495.
41. Edmonds, *Official History, 1915* (2), p. 23n1.
42. Wynne, *If Germany Attacks*, pp. 60–2.
43. These were captured by the British and issued in translation in November 1915 as CDS 303: Experience Gained in the Winter Battle in Champagne from the Point of View of the Organisation of the Enemy's Lines of Defence; and CDS 304: Proposals for the Technical Methods to be Adopted in an Attempt to Break Through a Strongly Fortified Position.
44. CDS 303, para. 7, 8.
45. Ibid., para. 3.
46. Ibid., para. 8.
47. Ibid., para. 16.
48. Ibid., para. 10–13.
49. Ibid., para. 33.
50. Ibid., para. 10.
51. Ibid., para. 9.
52. Ibid., para. 11–12.
53. Ibid., para. 16–17.
54. Ibid., para. 23.
55. Ibid., para. 21.
56. Ibid., para. 20, 24.
57. Ibid., para. 4.
58. Ibid., para. 31.
59. Ibid., para. 25, 27.
60. Ibid., para. 29.
61. Wynne, *If Germany Attacks*, p. 19.
62. Edmonds, *Official History, 1915* (2), pp. 163–332.
63. Wynne, *If Germany Attacks*, p. 84.
64. Bauer, *Der grosse Kreig*, pp. 86–7.
65. Wynne, *If Germany Attacks*, pp. 84–5.
66. SS 471: Essential Principles for the Defence of Positions.
67. Bauer, op. cit., p. 86.
68. A translation of this document is given in Wynne, *If Germany Attacks*, pp. 98–9.
69. Ibid., pp. 85–8.

70. Ibid., p. 88.
71. 'Other Side of the Hill No. 17', pp. 34–5.
72. Wynne, *If Germany Attacks*, p. 89.
73. Quoted in ibid., p. 89.
74. See ibid., pp. 92–6.
75. CDS 303 and CDS 304.
76. SS 454: Experiences Gained From the September Offensives, by Below, GOC Second Army (5 November 1915), para. 2, 6. Although written by Second Army, Lossberg will have had an important part in the composition of this pamphlet.
77. SS 126: The Training and Employment of Bombers, pp. 87–8.
78. Wynne, *If Germany Attacks*, pp. 155 and 157.
79. Ibid., p. 97.
80. Edmonds, *Official History, 1916* (1), p. 316.
81. TDRC-5502: Ex. New Logic 1981, p. 10.
82. Wynne, *If Germany Attacks*, pp. 97–8.
83. Quoted by Miles, *Official History, 1916* (2), p. 27.
84. SS 490: The Principles of Trench Warfare, para. 13, 15, 18.
85. CDS 303, para. 3.
86. Wynne, *If Germany Attacks*, p. 103.
87. Ibid., p. 118.
88. Captured by the British and issued as SS 454.
89. SS 486: Extracts from 'Lessons Drawn from The Somme', para. 3.
90. Wynne, *If Germany Attacks*, p. 131. The report was translated by the British and issued as SS 553: Experience of the German First Army in the Somme Battle. Note that on 17 July 1916, the Second Army front was split and the northern section given to the new First Army, commanded by Below and Lossberg.
91. SS 553, para. 56, 58.
92. Ibid., para. 60–2.
93. Ibid., para 63. The final phase is taken from Wynne, *If Germany Attacks*, pp. 159–60, which expresses the meaning of the German more clearly.
94. SS 553, para. 16.
95. SS 494: German Formations Employed on the Somme, para. 4.
96. Ibid., para. 4.
97. Wynne, *If Germany Attacks*, p. 121.
98. SS 553, para. 52.
99. SS 486, para. 4.
100. SS 494, para. 2.
101. SS 485: Execution of Counterattacks, para. 4.
102. Ibid., para. 5.
103. Ibid., para. 2.
104. Ibid., para. 6–7.
105. SS 553, para. 68, 71.
106. SS 486, para. 4.
107. SS 553, para. 72.
108. Wynne, *If Germany Attacks*, pp. 112–13.
109. SS 485, para. 8.
110. Quoted in Wilson, 'Aggression, Initiative and Speed', p. 29.
111. Wynne, *If Germany Attacks*, p. 125.
112. SS 486, para. 3.
113. Wynne, *If Germany Attacks*, p. 125.
114. SS 553, para. 13.
115. Wynne, *If Germany Attacks*, p. 126.
116. SS 553, para. 11.
117. Ibid., para. 12.
118. Wynne, *If Germany Attacks*, p. 127.
119. SS 486, para. 8.
120. SS 553, para. 25–8 and SS 486, para. 8.

121. Edmonds, *Official History, 1916* (1), p. 497.
122. Miles, *Official History, 1916* (2), p. 553.
123. See Travers, *The Killing Ground*, pp. 217n7.
124. Wynne, *If Germany Attacks*, p. 131.
125. A. Horne, *The Price of Glory*, pp. 294–8.
126. Ibid., p. 302.
127. Bauer, *Der grosser Krieg*, p. 117.
128. Ibid., p. 58.
129. Horne, *Price of Glory*, p. 41.
130. Parkinson, *Tormented Warrior*, p. 21.
131. Wynne, 'Pattern for Limited War: 1', p. 496.
132. Ludendorff, *War Memories* (1) p. 145.
133. Ibid. (1), p. 271.
134. Ibid. (1), p. 273.
135. A translation of the second edition was issued by the British as SS 561: Manual of Position Warfare for All Arms: Part 8: The Principles of Command in the Defensive Battle in Position Warfare.
136. Bauer, op. cit., pp. 118–19.
137. Wynne, 'Hindenburg Line', p. 211.
138. A translation was issued by the British as SS 558. The third edition of 15 August 1917 was issued as SS 621: Manual of Position Warfare for All Arms: Part 1a: General Principles of the Construction of Field Positions (translated 12 December 1917).
139. Ludendorff, *War Memories* (1), p. 386–7.
140. SS 561: para. 6.
141. Ibid., para. 13.
142. SS 621, para. 7.
143. Wynne, 'Hindenburg Line', pp. 212, 217.
144. SS 621, para. 8.
145. Wynne, 'Hindenburg Line', p. 212.
146. SS 561, para. 19.a.
147. SS 621, para. 9.
148. SS 561, para. 19.b.
149. Ibid., para. 8.
150. SS 621, para. 11.
151. SS 561, para. 15.
152. SS 621, para. 4.
153. Ibid., para. 10.
154. SS 561, para. 15. Emphasis in original.
155. Edmonds, *Official History, 1917* (2), p. 44n1.
156. SS 561, para. 15. Emphasis in original.
157. Edmonds, *Official History, 1917* (2), p. 44n2.
158. SS 561, para. 16.
159. Ibid., para. 17.
160. Ibid., para. 7–10.
161. Ludendorff, op. cit. (1), pp. 387, 389.
162. Ibid. (1), p. 388.
163. von Moser, *Feldzugsaufzeichnungen*, pp. 1, 29, 34, 200, 206–26.
164. Ibid., pp. 245–6.
165. Ibid., pp. 247–8.
166. Ibid., pp. 248–50.
167. Ibid., pp. 253–5.
168. Ludendorff, op. cit. (1), p. 387.
169. Wynne, 'Hindenburg Line', p. 224.
170. SS 553.
171. Wynne, *If Germany Attacks*, pp. 161; Ludendorff, op. cit. (1) p. 387.
172. Wynne, 'The Development of the German Defensive Battle in 1917', pp. 17–18.
173. Wynne, *If Germany Attacks*, pp. 168–8.

174. Ibid., pp. 170–1, 173.
175. Ibid., pp. 173–8.
176. Ibid., pp. 180–2.
177. Ludendorff, op. cit. (2), pp. 420–1.
178. Ibid., p. 421.
179. For a valuable discussion of *Vollmacht* see Meyer, 'Operational Art and the German Command System in World War I', pp. 112–18.
180. Wynne, *If Germany Attacks*, p. 199–210.
181. Wynne, 'The Wotan Position', *Army Quarterly* 38 (2) (July 1939), p. 234.
182. Wynne, *If Germany Attacks*, p. 202.
183. Ibid., p. 202–14.
184. Ibid., p. 214.
185. Wynne, 'Wotan Position', pp. 243–5.
186. Wynne, 'The British Attack from Monchy-Le-Preux', pp. 248–64.
187. See Wynne, *If Germany Attacks*, pp. 226–54.
188. This was captured and a translation issued as SS 703: Manual of Position Warfare for All Arms.
189. SS 553, para. 63 and see Wynne, *If Germany Attacks*, p. 160.
190. Ludendorff, op. cit., (1), p. 387.
191. SS 703, pp. 3–5.
192. Wynne, *If Germany Attacks*, pp. 277–80.
193. Reproduced in ibid, pp. 332–40.
194. Wynne, 'German Defensive Battle: II', pp. 250–2.
195. Wynne, *If Germany Attacks*, p. 338.
196. Wynne, 'German Defensive Battle: II', pp. 253–5.
197. Ibid., pp. 255–6.
198. Wynne, *If Germany Attacks*, p. 304.
199. Ia/44122: German Principles of Elastic Defence, by Ludendorff.
200. Ludendorff, *War Memories* (2), p.489.
201. Wynne, 'German Defensive Battle: I', pp. 28–9.
202. Ludendorff, op. cit. (2), p. 490.
203. Wynne, 'German Defensive Battle: I', pp. 29–30.
204. Ludendorff, op. cit. (2), p. 488.
205. SS 710: New Defensive Tactics.
206. Ludendorff, op. cit. (2), p. 489.
207. Die Abwehr im Stellungskrieg, para. 10.
208. Wynne, *If Germany Attacks*, p. 315.

## Chapter Seven, pp. 198–229

1. Edmonds, *Official History, 1918* (1), p. 51.
2. Ibid., p. 35.
3. Ibid., p. 75.
4. Terraine, *To Win a War*, p. 37.
5. Edmonds, *Official History, 1918* (1), p. 15. Six French and five British divisions were sent to Italy in November 1917, reducing the totals to those given in the text.
6. Ibid., p. 37.
7. Ibid., p. 38.
8. Edmonds, *The Official History, 1916* (1), pp. 210–11.
9. Ibid., pp. 211–12.
10. Ibid., p. 38.
11. See CDS 303: Experience Gained in the Winter Battle in Champagne; CDS 304: Proposals for the Technical Methods to be Adopted in an Attempt to Break Through; and SS 454: Experiences Gained from the September Offensives.
12. Edmonds, *Official History, 1916* (1), p. 213.
13. Ibid., pp. 224–5.

14. Ibid., p. 214.
15. Ibid., pp. 215–16.
16. 'The Other Side of the Hill, No. VII', p. 67.
17. Ibid., pp. 69–72.
18. Ibid., pp. 73 and 75.
19. Edmonds, *Official History, 1916* (1), pp. 218–24 and 226n2.
20. For example, ibid., pp. 165–6.
21. Edmonds, *Official History, 1918* (1), p. 41n4.
22. Liddell Hart Centre, King's College London (KCL): Edmonds Papers, III/13, p. 9.
23. Travers, *The Killing Ground*, p. 288.
24. Edmonds, *Official History, 1918* (1), p. 289.
25. Travers, *Killing Ground*, p. 212.
26. Ibid., p. 285.
27. KCL: Edmonds Papers, III/12, p. 9.
28. Edmonds, *Official History, 1918* (1), p. 41n4.
29. KCL: Edmonds Papers, III/13, p. 9.
30. The British translated this as 'Manual of Position Warfare for All Arms'. While correct, this translation omits the sense that the regulations were being continually up-dated and inaccurately implies a unity of the various parts. These covered everything from mine warfare to the use of squadrons of fighter aircraft. The full list of the 16 parts is given in Ludendorff, *Urkunden der Obersten Heeresleitung*, p. 592.
31. GSO Conference, 12 to 15 January, 1914, lists the participants in order of seniority and places Edmonds above Jeudwine.
32. KCL: Edmonds Papers, III/13, pp. 9–10.
33. Issued as SS 621.
34. Wynne, 'The Development of the German Defensive Battle in 1917: I', p. 26.
35. Issued as SS 561.
36. Wynne, 'German Defensive Battle: II', p. 259n.
37. Edmonds, *Official History, 1918* (3), pp. vii–viii.
38. Winter, *Haig's Command*, p. 307.
39. Wynne, 'German Defensive Battle: III', p. 18.
40. Wynne, 'The Legacy', pp. 19–20.
41. See KCL: Edmonds Papers, III/13, p. 9; Edmonds, *Official History, 1918* (1), p. 41n4; and Wynne, 'Legacy', p. 20.
42. KCL: Edmonds Papers, III/13, p. 10.
43. Wynne, 'Legacy', p. 20.
44. Ibid.
45. Reprinted as Edmonds, *Official History, 1918* (1), Appendix 6.
46. Wynne, 'German Defensive Battle: III', p. 18.
47. GHQ Memorandum, para. 1.
48. Ibid., para. 2.a.
49. SS 561, para. 6.d.
50. SS 621, para. 6.
51. GHQ Memorandum, para. 2.b.
52. SS 561, para. 6.a.
53. GHQ Memorandum, para. 5.
54. Ibid., para. 2.c.
55. SS 561, para. 6.c. and SS 621, para. 2.
56. GHQ Memorandum, para. 2.d.
57. SS 561, para. 6.b.
58. GHQ Memorandum (*Official History, 1918* (1), Appendix 6), para. 3.
59. SS 561, para. 4.
60. GHQ Memorandum, para. 4.
61. SS 621, para. 8–10.
62. Ibid., para. 10.
63. Ibid., para. 8.
64. SS 561, para. 13.

65. SS 621, para. 8.
66. Ibid., para. 11.
67. Ibid., para. 9.
68. GHQ Memorandum, para. 6.
69. SS 561, para. 15–17.
70. SS 621, para. 8. This part of the doctrine was copied by the GHQ Memorandum in para. 4.
71. Edmonds, *Official History, 1918* (1), p. 41n4.
72. GSO Conference, 9 to 12 January 1911, pp. 15–19.
73. SS 561, para. 15. Emphasis in original.
74. Ibid., para. 16.
75. Ibid., para. 17.
76. GHQ Memorandum, para. 7.
77. Ibid., para. 8.
78. SS 621, para. 10.
79. GHQ Memorandum, para. 8.b.
80. Ibid., para. 8.e–f.
81. SS 621, para. 4.
82. Edmonds, *Official History, 1918* (1), pp. 257–8.
83. Swinton, *Eyewitness*, p. 157.
84. Edmonds, *Official History, 1918* (1), p. 258.
85. Wynne, 'Pattern for Limited (Nuclear) War: II', p. 41.
86. Travers, *Killing Ground*, p. 112.
87. Travers, 'A Particular Style of Command', p. 373.
88. Third Army Defence Scheme, Edmonds, *Official History, 1918* (1), Appendix 14.
89. VI Corps Defence Scheme, Edmonds, *Official History, 1918* (1), Appendix 15.
90. 18th Division Defence Scheme, Edmonds, *Official History, 1918* (1), Appendix 16.
91. SS 621, para. 8.
92. Edmonds, *Official History, 1918* (1), Sketch 14.
93. GHQ Memorandum, para. 4.
94. Edmonds, *Official History, 1918* (1), p. 123.
95. Ibid., p. 41n4.
96. Wynne, 'Pattern for Limited (Nuclear) War: II', p. 41.
97. Edmonds, *Official History, 1918* (1), p. 123.
98. Wynne, 'German Defensive Battle: III', p. 21.
99. 18th Division Defence Scheme, para. II.3–4.
100. Ibid., para. I.4.
101. VI Corps Defence Scheme, para. III.1.i.
102. Edmonds, *Official History, 1918* (1), p. 257.
103. GHQ Memorandum, para. 6.
104. Edmonds, *Official History, 1918* (1), p. 260.
105. 18th Division Defence Scheme, para. II.4.a.
106. Edmonds, *Official History, 1918* (1), p. 123.
107. Wynne, 'German Defensive Battle: III', p. 22n.
108. Edmonds, *Official History, 1918* (1), p. 257.
109. VI Corps Defence Scheme, para. II.3.b.
110. 18th Division Defence Scheme, para. II.4.g.
111. VI Corps Defence Scheme, para. III.1.ii.
112. Edmonds, *Official History, 1918* (1), p. 41n4.
113. Ibid., p. 124.
114. Wynne, 'German Defensive Battle: III', p. 21.
115. Edmonds, *Official History, 1918* (1), p. 256.
116. VI Corps Defence Scheme, para. III.1.iii.
117. Edmonds, *Official History, 1918* (1), p. 123n1.
118. Wynne, 'German Defensive Battle: III', p. 21.
119. Ibid., p. 21.
120. Edmonds, *Official History, 1918* (1), p. 258.

121. GHQ Memorandum, para. 10.
122. Ibid., para. 8.e.
123. VI Corps Defence Scheme, para. IV.1.
124. Edmonds, *Official History, 1918* (1), p. 116.
125. Wynne, 'German Defensive Battle: III', p. 21.
126. Ibid., p. 21n.
127. VI Corps Defence Scheme, para. II.4.
128. Ibid., para. IV.2.
129. Third Army Defence Scheme, para. III.3.
130. Wynne, 'Legacy', p. 24.
131. VI Corps Defence Scheme, para. I.1–2.
132. 18th Division Defence Scheme, para. I.a.2.
133. GHQ Memorandum, para. 4, 12.b.
134. 18th Division Defence Scheme, para. III.3.
135. Ibid., para. III.3.
136. Ibid., para. II.4.a.k.
137. Wynne, 'German Defensive Battle: I', p. 27.
138. Edmonds, *Official History, 1918* (1), p. 257.
139. Recent research suggests that restrictions were placed on manpower sent to France, but mainly by the CIGS, Robertson, and the War Office rather than by Lloyd George. Travers, *Killing Ground*, p. 221.
140. SS 561, para. 8.
141. Edmonds, *Official History, 1918* (1), p. 116n2.
142. The calculation is based on a ratio of two *Eingreif* divisions for every three front divisions, with deductions for impassable sectors of front. By October 1917, every German front division in a battle sector was given a complete *Eingreif* division. Wynne, 'German Defensive Battle III', p. 20n.
143. Edmonds, *Official History, 1918* (1), p. 116n2.
144. Ibid., p. 116n1.
145. Ibid., p. 55.
146. IWM: Maxse Papers, 69/53/11, File 54: the Infantry Section (Maxse, 27 May 1918), para. 3.
147. *Germany Army Handbook*, p. 44.
148. Cron, *Geschichte des deutschen Heeres*, p. 117.
149. Edmonds, *Official History, 1918* (1), p. 55.
150. Terraine, *The Smoke and the Fire*, p. 128, table F.
151. This was the number of French divisions on this sector at the end of 1917. Edmonds, *Official History, 1918* (1), p. 16.
152. Winter, *Haig's Command*, pp. 175–6.
153. Edmonds, *Official History, 1918* (1), p. 256.
154. Ibid., p. 99.
155. Ibid., p. 116n2.
156. Ibid., p. 99n1.
157. Ibid., pp. 125 and 256.
158. Fourteen entrenching battalions with 800 men each; 11 pioneer battalions with 600 men each; 11 engineer battalions with 400 men each; and 73 infantry battalions with 600 men each: a total of 66,000 men. Figures do not include divisions in reserve and allow for the use of men to hold defences and build other installations.
159. Edmonds, *Official History, 1918* (1).
160. Winter, *Haig's Command*, pp. 176–7.
161. Edmonds, *Official History, 1918* (1), p. 256.
162. SS 621, para. 11, 4.
163. Ludendorff, *My War Memories, 1914–1918*, Vol. 1, p. 387.
164. See Remarque, *All Quiet on the Western Front*.
165. Dolden, *Cannon Fodder*, p. 86.
166. Perry, *The Commonwealth Armies*, p. 20.
167. Dolden, op. cit., p. 149.

168. IWM: Maxse Papers, 69/53)12, File 58, Training 1918: Letter from DAAG to OCs Reinforcements (19 July 1918).
169. Mitchinson, 'The Reconstitution of 169 Brigade: July–October 1916'.
170. 'The 56th Division', p. 18.
171. Mitchinson, 'The "Transfer Controversy": Parliament and the London Regiment', p. 31.
172. IWM: Maxse Papers, 69/53/12, File 58, Training 1918: Paper on Training, Draft 4 (Maxse), para. 10.
173. Ibid., Letter from A. Ingram, GHQ, to Maxse (28 August 1918).
174. Terraine, *Smoke and Fire*, p. 125n2.
175. IWM: Maxse Papers, 69/53/12, File 58, Training 1918: Letter from A. Ingram, GHQ, to Maxse (28 August 1918).
176. Falls, *Official History, 1917* (1), p. 554.
177. Terraine, *Smoke and Fire*, p. 125n4.
178. See Samuels, *Doctrine and Dogma*, Chapter 6.
179. Harries-Jenkins, *The Army in Victorian Society*, p. 124.
180. Ibid., pp. 15–16.
181. Edmonds, *Official History, 1918* (1), p. 124.
182. Middlebrook, *The Kaiser's Battle*, p. 81.
183. 18th Division Defence Scheme Official History, 1918 (1), Appendix 16, para. III.1.e, II.3.
184. Edmonds, *Official History, 1918* (1), p. vii.
185. Quoted by Essame, *The Battle for Europe, 1918*, p. 34.

## Chapter Eight, pp. 230–69

1. Alfoldi, 'The Hutier Legend', p. 69.
2. Van Creveld, *Command in War*, p. 182.
3. Gough, *The Fifth Army*, p. 321.
4. Ibid., p. 326.
5. Edmonds, *Official History, 1918* (1), pp. vii–viii.
6. Travers, *The Killing Ground*, p. 231.
7. Terraine, *White Heat*, pp. 283–4.
8. Alfoldi, 'Hutier Legend', pp. 70 and 73.
9. For example German General Staff, 7th Department, 'Die Entwicklung der deutschen Infanterie', pp. 367–419.
10. *ExRfdI*, 1906, para. 446.
11. German General Staff, 'Entwicklung der deutschen Infanterie', p. 370.
12. Gudmundsson, *Stormtroop Tactics*, pp. 30–1; German General Staff, 'Entwicklung', p. 374.
13. German General Staff, 'Entwicklung', p. 375.
14. Gudmundsson, *Stormtroop Tactics*, p. 31.
15. CDS 304: Proposals for the Technical Methods to be Adopted in an Attempt to Break Through a Strongly Fortified Position.
16. Ibid., para. 1, 3.
17. Ibid., para. 6.
18. Ibid., para. 7, 14.
19. Ibid., para. 10.
20. Ibid., para. 13.a-b, d, 17.b.
21. Ibid., para. 16.
22. Ibid., para. 13.e, 8.
23. Terraine, *White Heat*, pp. 180–2.
24. Edmonds, *Official History: France and Belgium, 1916*, Vol. 1, p. 298.
25. Wallach, *The Dogma of the Battle of Annihilation*, p. 166.
26. Terraine, *White Heat*, pp. 182–3.
27. Meyer, 'Operational Art and the German Command System', pp. 296–7.
28. Bidwell and Graham, *Firepower*, p. 101.
29. Meyer, 'Operational Art', pp. 296–7.

30. Bruchmüller, quoted by ibid., p. 298.
31. Brooke, 'The Evolution of Artillery', p. 264.
32. Quoted by ibid., p. 265.
33. Bidwell, *Firepower*, p. 20.
34. Brooke, 'The Evolution of Artillery: Part IV', p. 377.
35. Bidwell, *Firepower*, p. 20.
36. Brooke, 'Evolution of Artillery: IV', p. 378; and Meyer, 'Operational Art', p. 298.
37. Brooke, 'Evolution of Artillery: IV', p. 378.
38. Meyer, 'Operational Art', p. 299.
39. Ibid., pp. 300–2.
40. Bidwell, *Firepower*, pp. 99–100.
41. Ibid., pp. 100–1.
42. Meyer, 'Operational Art', p. 301.
43. Edmonds, *Official History, 1916* (1), pp. 55–6.
44. Wynne, *If Germany Attacks*, p. 294.
45. Brooke, 'Evolution of Artillery: IV', p. 386.
46. Ibid., pp. 325–6.
47. Edmonds, 'Hutier's Rehearsal', p. 16.
48. Brooke, 'Evolution of Artillery: VII', p. 326.
49. Edmonds, 'Hutier's Rehearsal', pp. 17–18.
50. Simultaneous developments in the British Army culminated in the use of predicted fire to produce a brief but intense bombardment at the start of the battle of Cambrai, 20 November 1917.
51. Bauer, *Der grosse Krieg*, p. 87.
52. German General Staff, 'Entwicklung der deutschen Infanterie', p. 381.
53. Gruss, 'Aufbau und Verwendung der deutschen Sturmbataillone im Weltkrieg', p. 21.
54. Ibid., p. 27.
55. Ibid., pp. 150–1.
56. Ibid., pp. 33–4.
57. Ibid., p. 35.
58. Gudmundsson, *Stormtroop Tactics*, pp. 80–1.
59. Gruss, 'Sturmbataillone', p. 37.
60. Ibid., p. 40.
61. Ludendorff, *My War Memories, 1914–1918*, Vol. 1, p. 265.
62. Gruss, 'Sturmbataillone', p. 47. See Ia/38997: Programme of Instruction for Assault Troops.
63. Gruss, 'Sturmbataillone', pp. 48–51.
64. Ludendorff, *War Memories* (1), p. 273.
65. Gruss, 'Sturmbataillone', pp. 60–1 and 65–6.
66. Berktau, 'Sturmtruppen', p. 683.
67. Balck, *Entwicklung der Taktik im Weltkriege*, p. 66.
68. Ibid., pp. 117–18.
69. Ibid., p. 66.
70. Berktau, 'Sturmtruppen', p. 684.
71. Gruss, 'Sturmbataillone', p. 82.
72. Lupfer, 'The Dynamics of Doctrine: The Changes in German Tactical Doctrine During the First World War', p. 40.
73. Gruss, 'Sturmbataillone', pp. 43–5; gives the full text, p. 81.
74. Angriff im Stellungskrieg, title page.
75. Ibid., para. 2–9.
76. Ibid., para. 19–21.
77. Ibid., para. 12.
78. Ibid., para. 24–26.
79. Ibid., para. 28–29.
80. Ibid., para. 32–33.
81. Ibid., para. 35.
82. Ibid., para. 36.e, 47.

83. Ibid., para. 37.
84. Ibid., para. 40, 44.
85. Ibid., para. 53.
86. Ibid., para. 54.
87. Ibid., para. 60–1, 65.
88. Edmonds, *Official History, 1918* (1), p. 144.
89. Ibid., p. 106n1.
90. Ludendorff, op. cit. (2), p. 591.
91. 'Editorial', *Army Quarterly* 19 (2), pp. 238–41.
92. Edmonds, *Official History, 1918* (1), p. 95n3.
93. Ludendorff, op. cit. (2), p. 591.
94. Edmonds, *Official History, 1918* (1), p. 152.
95. See ibid., sketches 12 & 14.
96. Ludendorff, op. cit. (2), p. 585.
97. Middlebrook, *The Kaiser's Battle*, p. 43.
98. Ludendorff, op. cit. (2), p. 581.
99. Edmonds, *Official History, 1918* (1), pp. 142–3.
100. Jünger, *Storm of Steel*, pp. 240.
101. Middlebrook, op. cit., p. 62.
102. Ludendorff, op. cit. (2), p. 581.
103. Jünger, *Storm of Steel*, p. 240; Middlebrook, op. cit., p. 60.
104. Ludendorff, op. cit. (2), p. 581.
105. Sulzbach, *With the German Guns*, pp. 131–2.
106. Edmonds, *Official History, 1918* (1), pp. 161–263.
107. Ibid., p. 175.
108. Ibid., p. 200.
109. Middlebrook, *The First Day on the Somme*, pp. 320–2.
110. Middlebrook, *Kaiser's Battle*, pp. 390–1.
111. Edmonds, *Official History, 1918* (1), p. 153.
112. Middlebrook, *Kaiser's Battle*, p. 52.
113. Terraine, *White Heat*, pp. 210–11.
114. Meyer, 'Operational Art', pp. 329–30.
115. Edmonds, *Official History, 1918* (1), pp. 159–60 and sketch 13.
116. Ibid., p. 158n2.
117. Brooke, 'Evolution of Artillery: VII', p. 330.
118. Middlebrook, *Kaiser's Battle*, p. 148.
119. Edmonds, *Official History, 1918* (1), p. 159n1.
120. See Pitt, *1918: The Last Act*, pp. 75–8; Toland, *No Man's Land: The Story of 1918*, pp. 14–20; and Middlebrook, *Kaiser's Battle*, pp. 146–67.
121. Edmonds, *Official History, 1918* (1), p. 162.
122. For example Cunliffe, *The Royal Irish Fusiliers 1793–1950*, p. 347.
123. For example Fox, *The Royal Inniskilling Fusiliers in the World War*, p. 137; and Terraine, *To Win a War: 1918*, p. 60.
124. Edmonds, *Official History, 1918* (1), pp. 162–3.
125. For example Westropp, *The Manchester Regiment: A Record 1914–1918*, p. 49.
126. Gruss, 'Sturmbataillone', pp. 96–7.
127. Ibid., pp. 98–9.
128. Ibid., p. 99.
129. German General Staff, 'Entwicklung der deutschen Infanterie', p. 395.
130. See 'Alten Einsern', *Das K. B. 1. Infanterie-Regiment König*, p. 58; and Staubwasser, *Das K. B. 2. Infanterie-Regiment Kronprinz*, pp. 49–52.
131. Middlebrook, *Kaiser's Battle*, pp. 215 and 201; and Richter, *Das Danziger Infanterie-Regiment Nr. 128*, Vol. 1, pp. 354–5.
133. Seydel, *Das Grenadier-Regiment König Friedrich I*, pp. 320–3; and Middlebrook, *Kaiser's Battle*, p. 201.
134. Hoffmann, ed., *Infanterie-Regiment 463*, pp. 7–8.
135. Von Gottberg, *Dass Infanterie-Regiment Nr. 464 im Weltkriege*, pp. 159–66; and Fox, *Royal*

*Inniskilling Fusiliers*, p. 137.
136. Hoffmann, *Infanterie-Regiment 463*, pp. 184–9.
137. Fox, *Royal Inniskilling Fusiliers*, pp. 135 and 137.
138. See Gieraths, *Geschichte des Reserve-Infanterie-Regiments Nr. 210*, pp. 413–15; Fuhrmann *et al.*, *Königlich Preussisches Reserve-Infanterie-Regiment Nr. 211*, pp. 273–4; and Makoben, *Geschichte des Reserve-Infanterie-Regiments Nr. 212*, pp. 496–502.
139. Kendrick, *The Story of the Wiltshire Regiment*, p. 136.
140. Gieraths, *RIR 210*, p. 417.
141. Ia/47737: Divisional Order for the Attack, Nr. 1, para. 9.
142. See von Troilo, *Das 5. Westfalische Infanterie-Regiment Nr. 53*, pp. 96–7; Möller, *Paderborner Infanterie-Regiment (7. Lothring.) Nr. 158*, pp. 393–7; von Rudorff, *Das Fusilier-Regiment General Ludendorff (Niederrheinischen) Nr. 39*, pp. 168–9; Volckheim, *Die deutschen Kampfwagen im Weltkriege*, p. 27; and Schwerin, 'Das Sturmbataillon Rohr' in Heinrici, ed., *Das Ehrenbuch der deutschen Pioniere*, p. 561.
143. 'Incidents of the Great War (2): The 16th Battalion, The Manchester Regiment at the Battle of St Quentin, p. 129.
144. Ibid., pp. 126 and 129.
145. Edmonds, *Official History, 1918* (1), pp. 175–6.
146. Ibid., pp. 216 and 221.
147. Van Creveld, *Command in War*, p. 173.
148. Edmonds, *Official History, 1918* (1), p. 163; Falls, *The First Seven Battalions, The Royal Irish Rifles*, Vol. 2, p. 139; and Borrowes, *The 1st Battalion The Faugh-A-Ballaghs*, p. 110.
149. Seydel, *GrenRegt 5*, pp. 323–4; Richter, *IR 128*, pp. 356–7; Burrowes, *1st Faugh-A-Ballaghs*, pp. 110–11; Cunliffe, *Royal Irish Fusiliers*, pp. 347–8; and Edmonds, *Official History, 1918*, (1), p. 212.
150. See Richter, *IR 128*, pp. 355–6; Gruss, 'Sturmbataillone', p. 106; Edmonds, *Official History, 1918* (1), p. 176 (claims that the redoubt held out until 3.15 p.m.); and Middlebrook, *Kaiser's Battle*, p. 313.
151. See Falls, *Royal Irish Rifles*, pp. 139–40; Fox, *Royal Inniskilling Fusiliers*, pp. 137–8; Gottberg, *IR 464*, pp. 167–73; and Hoffmann, *IR 463*, pp. 189–95.
152. Middlebrook, *Kaiser's Battle*, p. 268.
153. See Westropp, *Manchester Regiment*, p. 135; Wylly, *The Green Howards*, pp. 103–4; Fuhrmann, *RIR 211*, pp. 275–6; Gieraths, *RIR 210*, pp. 415–17; and Makoben, *RIR 212*, pp. 501–3.
154. Rudorff, *FusRegt 39*, pp. 170–1.
155. E. Wyrall, *The King's Regiment (Liverpool), Vol. 3, 1917–1919*, p. 620.
156. Middlebrook, *Kaiser's Battle*, pp. 262–3.
157. See Troilo, *IR 53*, p. 97; Möller, *IR 158*, pp. 397–404; Rudorff, *FusRegt 39*, pp. 170–1; and Maurice, *The 16th Foot*, p. 202.
158. See Möller, *IR 158*, pp. 399–403; Rudorff, *FusRegt 39*, p. 171; 'Incidents of the Great War No. 2', pp. 126–30; Westropp, *Manchester Regiment*, pp. 46–53; and Middlebrook, *Kaiser's Battle*, pp. 263–6.
159. Westropp, *Manchester Regiment*, p. 53.
160. Middlebrook, *Kaiser's Battle*, p. 322.
161. Ibid., p. 311.
162. Ibid., p. 312.
163. Ibid., pp. 315–17 and 320–2.
164. Gough, *Fifth Army*, pp. 262–3.
165. Edmonds, *Official History, 1918* (1), pp. 166–7.
166. Ludendorff, *War Memories* (2), p. 598.
167. Middlebrook, *Kaiser's Battle*, p. 330.
168. Edmonds, *Official History, 1918* (1), p. 112.
169. Westropp, *Manchester Regiment*, p. 49.
170. German General Staff, 'Entwicklung der deutschen Infanterie', p. 395.
171. Van Creveld, *Command in War*, pp. 179–80.
172. Mullaly, *The South Lancashire Regiment*, p. 284; and Stanley, *The 89th Brigade*, p. 255–7.
173. Falls, *Royal Irish Rifles*, p. 140; and Fox, *Royal Inniskilling Fusiliers*, p. 138.
174. Winter, *Haig's Command*, pp. 178–9.

175. Third Army Defence Scheme (*Official History, 1918* (1), Appendix 14), part III.
176. See Principles of Defence on Fifth Army Front: GHQ Memorandum; and O.A.D. 761; GHQ Instructions to the GOC Fifth Army, reproduced in Edmonds, *Official History, 1918* (1) as Appendices 13 and 14.
177. Winter, *Haig's Command*, pp. 180–1.
178. Quoted by ibid., pp. 181 and 183.
179. Edmonds, *Official History, 1918* (1), pp. 258–9.
180. Ibid., p. 175.
181. Winter, *Haig's Command*, p. 182.
182. Keegan, *The Face of Battle*, p. 276.
183. Sheffield, 'British Military Police', p. 40.
184. Travers, *Killing Ground*, pp. 232–43.

## Conclusion, pp. 270–85

1. German General Staff, *The War in South Africa.*
2. Borgert, 'Grundzüge der Landkriegführung von Schlieffen bis Guderian', p. 430.
3. Collenberg, 'B-560: The Historical Section, OKH (1919–1945)'.
4. Liddell Hart Centre, Edmonds Papers, III/16, pp. 8–9.
5. See Borgert, 'Schlieffen bis Guderian', pp. 542–9; and Thompson, 'Notes on the German Post-War Training Regulations', pp. 352–7.
6. See 'The German Infantry Training Manual', pp. 320–4.
7. Terraine, *White Heat*, p. 286.
8. Quoted by Edmonds, *Official History, 1918* (2), p. 464.
9. Ludendorff, *My War Memories, 1914–18*, Vol. 2, p. 590.
10. Terraine, *To Win a War*, pp. 109 and 116.
11. Bidwell and Graham, *Firepower*, p. 136.
12. Terraine, *To Win a War*, p. 109.
13. Van Creveld, *Supplying War*, pp. 109–41.
14. Van Creveld, *Technology and War*, p. 176.
15. Macksey, *Guderian, Panzer General*, p. 37.
16. Guderian, *Panzer Leader* (Futura, London, 1974), p.21.
17. Borgert, 'Schlieffen bis Guderian', p. 576.
18. See Travers, 'The Evolution of British Strategy', pp. 173–200.
19. Winter, *Haig's Command*, p. 201.
20. Brooke, 'The Evolution of Artillery in the Great War, No. VIII', pp. 477–8.
21. Van Creveld, *Technology and War*, p. 178.
22. See Winter, *Haig's Command*, pp. 240–57 on the whole question of the *Official History*.
23. Ibid., pp. 243–4.
24. Ibid., p. 243.
25. Ibid., p. 352n12.
26. Report of the Committee on the Lessons of the Great War.
27. Liddell Hart, *Memoirs*, Vol. 1, p. 211.
28. For example, Kirke Report, p. 3.
29. Liddell Hart, *Memoirs* (1), pp. 211–12.
30. PRO: WO 32/3116: Kirke Reports: Memorandum from Colonel W. G. Lindsell for DSD to C1 (14 October 1932).
31. Kirke Report, p. 3.
32. Liddell Hart, *Memoirs* (1), p. 211.
33. Kirke Report, p. 5.
34. Liddell Hart Centre: Liddell Hart Papers, 11/1932/69.
35. Liddell Hart, *Memoirs* (1), p. 213.
36. GSO Conference, 9 to 11 January, 1933, pp. 5–8.
37. Ibid., pp. 9–10.
38. For example ibid., General Sir Charles Harington, pp. 22–3.
39. For example ibid., The Adjutant-General (General Sir Archibald Montgomery-

Massingberd) and Lieutenant-General Cameron, pp. 36, 41–2.

40. For example ibid., Lieutenant-General Sir Francis Gathorne-Hardy, pp. 31–2.
41. Notes on Certain Lessons of the Great War (War Office, 30 April 1934).
42. Kirke Report: Memorandum from C1 to AUS (12 January 1934).
43. Stone, 'The Anglo-Boer War and Military Reforms in the United Kingdom', p. 12.
44. Wallach, *The Dogma of Annihilation*, p. 3.

# Bibliography



## Archive Sources

### *Imperial War Museum (IWM)*

Laffargue, Captain, 153rd Infantry Regiment, *Impressions and Reflections of a French Company Commander Regarding the Attack* (HMSO, London, 1916).

Lieutenant-General Sir Ivor Maxse papers.

Army Printing and Stationery Service (SS Series):
SS 106: Notes on the Tactical Employment of Machine Guns and Lewis Guns (March 1916).
SS 109: Training of Divisions for Offensive Action (8 May 1916).
SS 113: Notes on the Attack. Impressions of a Battalion Commander (November 1915, trans. June 1916).
SS 119: Preliminary Notes on the Tactical Lessons of the Recent Operations (July 1916).
SS 126: The Training and Employment of Bombers (September 1916).
SS 135: Instructions for the Training of Divisions for Offensive Action (December 1916).
SS 144: The Normal Formation for the Attack (February 1917).
SS 153: Notes on the '08 German Maxim Gun (April 1917).
SS 155: Notes on Dealing with Hostile Machine Guns in an Advance (April 1917).
SS 161: Instructions for Battle (May 1917).

SS 185: Assault Training (September 1917).
SS 192: The Employment of Machine Guns: Part I Tactical (January 1918).
SS 201/3: Machine-Gun Notes (July 1918).
SS 210: The Division in Defence (May 1918).
SS 356 (January 1917): Handbook of the German Army in War.
SS 356 (April 1918) German Army Handbook.
SS 394: Notes on German Army Corps: XIV Reserve Corps and 52nd Division (March 1916).
SS 424: Notes on German Army Corps: IX Reserve Corps (May 1916).
SS 471: Essential Principles for the Defence of Positions as Laid Down in Instructions Issued by G.H.Q., German Second Army H.Q. (1 August 1915, trans. 1916).
SS 478: Experiences of the IV German Corps in the Battle for the Somme During July 1916 (22 August 1916, trans. 30 September 1916).
SS 490: The Principles of Trench Warfare as Laid Down in the XIV Reserve Corps (19 May 1916, trans. 13 October 1916).
SS 531: German Instructions for the Employment of Flame Projectors (12 December 1915, trans. 10 December 1916).
SS 537: Summary of Recent Information Regarding the German Army and its Methods (January 1917).
SS 546: The 1916 Pattern Bomb-Thrower ('Granaten-werfer '16') for Stick-Bomb ('Wurfgranate' 1915).
SS 548: Extracts from the German Official Textbook Regarding 'Minenwerfer' (15 November 1916, trans. March 1917).
SS 553: Experience of the German First Army in the Somme Battle 24 June to 26 November 1916, First Army H.Q. (30 January 1917, trans. 3 May 1917).
SS 561: Manual of Position Warfare for All Arms: Part 8: The Principles of Command in the Defensive Battle in Position Warfare (1 March 1917, trans. May 1917).
SS 562: Manual of Position Warfare for All Arms: Part 3: Weapons of Close Combat (1 January 1917, trans. 23 May 1917).
SS 567: Diagram Showing the Organisation of a Regimental Sector (captured June 1917, trans. 18 July 1917).
SS 579: Extracts from the Experiences of the Sixth German Army in the Employment of the '08/'15 Light Machine Gun (trans. 16 September 1917).
SS 703: Manual of Position Warfare for All Arms: Special Part: The Experience Gained During the English–French Offensive in the Spring of 1917 (10 June 1917, trans. 15 October 1917).
SS 710: New Defensive Tactics (trans. 14 November 1917).

### *Liddell Hart Centre for Military Archives, King's College London, Strand, London (KCL)*

Brigadier-General Sir James E. Edmonds papers.

Captain Sir Basil H. Liddell Hart papers.

Captain Graeme C. Wynne papers.

*Public Record Office, Kew (PRO)*

WO 32/3116: Kirke Report.
WO 33/179: System of Training of Staff Officers in Foreign Armies (1901).
WO 33/721: Tactical Notes (1915).
WO 33/725: Tactical Notes (1915).
WO 95/231: First Army. No. 7 Mountain Battery RGA, August 1914–December 1915.
WO 95/246: First Army Troops, No. 1 Motor Machine-Gun Battery, December 1914–March 1919.
WO 95/327: Second Army Troops, Nos. 2 and 5 Mountain Batteries RGA, August 1914–November 1915.
WO 95/708: IV Corps, General Staff, March–April 1915.
WO 95/709: IV Corps, General Staff, May 1915.
WO 95/1628: 7th Division, General Staff, February–May 1915.
WO 95/1638: 7th Division, Commander Royal Artillery, September 1914–December 1915.
WO 95/1651: 7th Division, 20th Infantry Brigade, Brigade Headquarters, May–August 1915.
WO 95/1660: 7th Division, 22nd Infantry Brigade, Brigade Headquarters, September 1914–August 1916.
WO 95/1672: 8th Division, General Staff, April–July 1915.
WO 95/1683: 8th Division, Commander Royal Artillery, November 1914–December 1915.
WO 95/1707: 8th Division, 23rd Infantry Brigade, Brigade Headquarters, November 1914–May 1915.
WO 95/2368: 32nd Division, General Staff, July 1916–February 1917.
WO 105/45: Notes on Comparison of Military Standards of Efficiency.
WO 105/47: Roberts Papers.
WO 106/46: Military Resources of Germany (18 January 1902).
WO 158/182: First Army Report on the Action Fought at Neuve Chapelle, 10 March 1915.
WO 158/288: Motor Machine Gun Batteries.
WO 158/344: Fifth Army: Notes and Lessons on 1916 Operations.
WO 158/374: Neuve Chapelle, IV Corps.

*Library, Staff College, Camberley*

BEF DOCUMENTS, FIRST WORLD WAR:
Ia/38997: Programme of Instruction for Assault Troops, by Captain Rohr, Assault Bn.
Ia/44122: German Principles of Elastic Defence, by Ludendorff (30 August 1917, trans. 20 January 1918).
Ia/47737: Divisional Order for the Attack, Nr. 1, by von Engelbrechten, 50th Inf. Div. (18 March 1918, trans. 28 March 1918).
O.B.1782: by Lieutenant-General Butler, Chief of the General Staff, Advanced GHQ (13 August 1916).

CENTRAL DISTRIBUTION SERVICE/ARMY PRINTING AND STATIONERY SERVICE (CDS/SS SERIES):

CDS 303: Experience Gained in the Winter Battle in Champagne from the Point of View of the Organisation of the Enemy's Lines of Defence and the Means of Combating an Attempt to Pierce Our Line, Third Army HQ (14 April 1915).

CDS 304: Proposals for the Technical Methods to be Adopted in an Attempt to Break Through a Strongly Fortified Position, Based on the Knowledge Acquired from the Errors which Appear to have been Committed by the French Army During the Winter Campaign in Champagne, Third Army HQ (14 April 1915).

SS 454: Experiences Gained from the September Offensives on the Fronts of the Sixth and Third Armies, by von Below, GOC Second Army (5 November 1915).

SS 485: Army Order Regarding the Execution of Counterattacks, by von Below, C-in-C First Army (23 August 1916, trans. 10 October 1916).

SS 486: Extracts from German Documents Dealing with 'Lessons Drawn from the Battle of the Somme' (11 October 1916).

SS 494: Extracts from the Reports of German Formations Employed on the Somme, 6th Bavarian Reserve Division (19 September 1916).

SS 621: Manual of Position Warfare for all Arms: Part Ia: General Principles of the Construction of Field Positions, 3rd edn (15 August 1917, trans. 12 December 1917).

Notes on Certain Lessons of the Great War (War Office) (30 April 1934).

GSO: Reports of Conferences of General Staff Officers at the Staff College (1908–14, 1927 and 1933).

Report of the Committee on the Lessons of the Great War (War Office) (October 1932).

## *Tactical Doctrine Retrieval Cell, Staff College, Camberley (TDRC)*

TDRC-3252: The Development of Artillery Tactics Since 1900. Colonel (retd) P. A. Lowe (October 1976).

TDRC-3977: Mobile Defence: The Pervasive Myth. A Historical Investigation. Colonel J. R. Alford, Defence Fellow, Department of War Studies, King's College, London, 1976–1977.

TDRC-5502: Ex New Logic 1981: A Counter-Attack Policy for 1 (Br) Corps. Major P. Howe.

TDRC-5760: Paralysis Warfare. Major-General P. D. Reid, Director Armoured Warfare Studies (September 1981).

TDRC-5889: Defence in the Land Battle. An Analysis of Defensive Methods and Means in Twentieth Century Land Warfare. Colonel M. G. C. Roberts, Defence Fellow, King's College, London University, 1974–75.

TDRC-6834: The Effectiveness of Reservists: A Historical Perspective: A Study for the Directorate of Battle Doctrine. E. R. Holmes, I. F. W. Beckett, R. d'A. Ryan and K. R. Simpson, Department of War Studies and International Affairs, RMA Sandhurst (July 1984). (Part of this paper is classified Confidential and was unavailable for research.)

TDRC-7028A: Tactical Doctrine: The Counter-Stroke. BAOR (31 August 1984).
TDRC-7498: Can any Lessons be Learnt from the German Offensives of March 21st 1918? Commandant's Paper 1985. Captain K. W. Kiddie.
TDRC-9051: Flanders 1917. Brigadier I. Mackay-Dick, Colonels D. Roberts and G. Bastiaans, HCSC 2 Case Study Presentation (January 1989).

## German Manuals

ExRfdI: Exerzier-Reglement für die Infanterie (1888).
German Field Exercise 1888. Part II: The Fight (trans. Captain W. H. Sawyer) (Stanford, London, 1888).
ExRfdI: Exerzier-Reglement für die Infanterie (1906).
Field Service Regulations (Felddienst Ordnung 1908) of the German Army (HMSO, London, 1908).
Der Angriff im Stellungskrieg (1 January 1918).
Allgemeines über Stellenbau, 5th edn (10 August 1918).
Die Abwehr im Stellungskrieg, 4th edn (20 September 1918).
Der Angriff im Stellungskrieg (amended to 25 June 1918).

## Published Sources

Note: In several cases the editions available to the author were reprints of works published by other publishers. It has not proved possible in all cases to identify the original publisher. Since page numbering may not be constant between the original and the reprint, all references in such cases are to the reprint.

ABBREVIATIONS

| | |
|---|---|
| *AQ* | *Army Quarterly* |
| *AR* | *Army Review* |
| *MI* | *Military Illustrated* |
| *MR* | *Military Review* |
| *RAJ* | *Royal Artillery Journal* |

### *Primary and Official Sources*

THE OFFICIAL HISTORY

*The Official History of the Great War: Military Operations: France and Belgium:*
*1914*, Vol. 1, Brigadier-General J. E. Edmonds (3rd edn, Macmillan, London, 1934).
*1914* (2), Edmonds (Macmillan, 1923).
*1915* (1), Edmonds and Captain G. C. Wynne (Macmillan, 1927).
*1915* (2), Edmonds (Macmillan, 1928).
*1916* (1), Edmonds (Macmillan, 1932).
*1916* (2), Captain W. Miles (Macmillan, 1938).

*1917* (1), Captain C. Falls (HMSO, London, 1940).
*1917* (2), Edmonds (HMSO, 1949).
*1918* (1), Edmonds (Macmillan, 1935).
*1918* (2), Edmonds (HMSO, 1937).
*1918* (3), Edmonds (HMSO, 1939).

*The Official History of the Great War: Military Operations: Gallipoli*, Vol. 2, Brigadier-General C. F. Aspinall-Oglander (Heinemann, London, 1932).

Altham, Major-General E. A., *The Principles of War* (Macmillan, London, 1914).
Amery, L. S. *The Problem of the Army* (London, 1903).
Ashurst, G. (R. Holmes, ed.), *My Bit. A Lancashire Fusilier at War 1914–1918* (Crowood, Marlborough, 1987).
[Baker, B. G.], *The German Army From Within by a British Officer Who Has Served in It* (Hodder & Stoughton, London, 1914).
Balck, Major [W.], *Taktik: Vol. 1, Einleitung und formale Taktik der Infanterie* (Eisenschmidt, Berlin, 1903).
—, Colonel, *Tactics*, 2 vols. (trans. First Lieutenant W. Krueger) (1911 and 1914, reprinted Greenwood, Westport, 1977).
—, Oberst, *Die Englische Armee im Felde* (Berlin, 1913).
—, Generaleutnant, *Entwicklung der Taktik im Weltkriege*, 2nd edn (Eisenschmidt, Berlin, 1922).
Bauer, Oberst [M.], *Der grosse Krieg in Feld und Heimat*, 3rd edn (Osiander, Tübingen, 1922).
Becke, Major A. F., *Order of Battle of Divisions*, 4 vols. (HMSO, London, 1935–1946).
Below, General H. von, 'Stosstrupp Lt.d.R. Wolter, Pi.K. 368', in P. Heinrici, ed., *Das Ehrenbuch der deutschen Pioniere* (Rolf, Berlin, 1931).
Berktau, Major, 'Sturmtruppen', in H. Franke, *Handbuch der neuzeitlichen Wehrwissenschaften*, vol. 2 (Grunter, Berlin, 1937).
Brooke, Brevet Lieutenant-Colonel A. F., 'The Evolution of Artillery in the Great War', a series of articles in *RAJ*:
I. *RAJ*, 51(8) (October 1924).
II. 'Factors Affecting the Evolution of Artillery', *RAJ* 51(6) (Jan. 1925).
III. 'The Evolution of Artillery Equipment', *RAJ* 52(1) (April 1925).
IV. 'The Evolution of Artillery Organisation and Command', *RAJ* 52(3) (Oct. 1925).
V. 'Evolution of Artillery Tactics (1)', *RAJ* 53(1) (April 1926).
VI. 'Evolution of Artillery Tactics (2)', *RAJ* 53(2) (July 1926).
VII. 'Evolution of Artillery Tactics (3)', *RAJ* 53(3) (Oct. 1926).
VIII. 'Artillery Lessons of the Great War', *RAJ* 53(4) (Jan. 1927).
Campbell, P. J., *In the Cannon's Mouth* (Hamish Hamilton, London, 1979).
Chapman, G., *A Passionate Prodigality*, new edn (Buchan & Enright, London, 1985).
Collenberg, Generalmajor L. Ruedt von, 'The Historical Section, OKH (1919–1945)' (B-560) (29 January 1946), in D. S. Detwiler, ed., *World War II German Military Studies*, Vol. 1 (Garland, New York, 1979).

Coppard, G., *With A Machine Gun To Cambrai* (Papermac, London, 1986).
'Das neue Exerzier-Reglement für die Infanterie', *Militär-Wochenblatt* Beiheft 7 (1906).
'The Development of the General Staff', *Army Review* 1(1) (July 1911).
*Die Armeen unserer Feinde* (Leipzig, 1914).
Dolden, A. S., *Cannon Fodder* (Blandford, Dorchester, 1980).
Du Cane, Brigadier-General J. P., 'The Cooperation of Field Artillery with Infantry in the Attack', *AR* 1 (1) (July 1911).
Editorial, 'British Tactical Doctrine', *Canadian Defence Quarterly* 15(4) (July 1938).
Edmonds, Brigadier-General J. E., General S. H. E. Franklyn, Brigadier C. N. Barclay and Major D. M. A. Wedderburn, 'Four Generations of Staff College Students – 1896 to 1952', *AQ* 65(1) (Oct. 1952).
Falkenhayn, General E. von, *General Headquarters 1914–1916 and its Critical Decisions* (Hutchinson, London, 1919).
Frederick Charles, Prince of Prussia, 'The Origins and Development of the Spirit of the Prussian Officer, its Manifestations and its Effect', (1860), reprinted in K. Demeter, *The German Officer Corps in State and Society: 1650–1945* (Weidenfeld & Nicolson, London, 1965), Appendix 1.
German General Staff, *The War in South Africa* (trans. Colonel W. H. H. Waters) (John Murray, London, 1904).
—, 7th Department, 'Die Entwicklung der deutschen Infanterie im Weltkriege (1914 bis 1918)', *Militärwissenschaftliche Rundschau*, 3 (1938).
'German Infantry Training Manual', *AQ* 32(2) (July 1936).
Godwin-Austen, Brevet-Major A. R., *The Staff and the Staff College* (Constable, London, 1927).
Gough, General H., *The Fifth Army* (Hodder & Stoughton, London, 1931).
Gough, Colonel J. E., 'Peace Training for Command', *AR* 1(2) (Oct. 1911).
Guderian, Generaloberst H., *Panzer Leader* (Futura, London, 1974).
Hamilton, General I. (Major A. Farrar-Hockley, ed.), *The Commander* (Hollis & Carter, London, 1957).
Henderson, Colonel G. F. R., 'Military Criticism and Modern Tactics', *United Services Magazine* (1891), reprinted in *The Science of War*.
—, 'The Training of Infantry for the Attack', *United Services Magazine* (1899), reprinted in *Science of War*.
—, 'Foreign Criticism', in 'My Experiences of the Boer War' (1901), reprinted in *Science of War*.
—, *Encyclopedia Brittanica* (1902), reprinted in *Science of War*.
—, 'The British Army' (1903), reprinted in *Science of War*.
—, *The Science of War* (Longmans Green, London, 1905).
Hindenburg, Marshal [P. von], *Out of My Life* (trans. F. A. Holt) (Cassell, London, 1920).
'Incidents of the Great War No. 2, The 16th Battalion, The Manchester Regiment, at the Battle of St Quentin, the 21st of March, 1918', *AQ* 8(1) (April 1924).
'Infantry Training 1911', *AR* 1(1) (July 1911).
'Infantryman', 'British Defence Doctrine, A Reply to Captain G. C. Wynne', *AQ* 36(1) (April 1938).
Jünger, E., *The Storm of Steel* (Chatto & Windus, London, 1929).

Kabisch, Generalleutnant E., *Michel: Die grosse Schlacht in Frankreich im Lenz 1918*, 7th edn (Schlegel, Berlin, 1935).

Kearsey, Lieutenant-Colonel A., *1915 Campaign in France. The Battles of Aubers Ridge, Festubert and Loos Considered in Relation to the Field Service Regulations* (Aldershot, n.d.).

Kiesling, Hauptmann H. von, *Operation Orders. A Technical Study*, 2nd edn (HMSO, London, 1910).

Kluck, Generaloberst A. von, *The March on Paris and the Battle of the Marne 1914* (Edward Arnold, London, 1920).

Liddell Hart, Captain B. H.,*The Memoirs of Captain Liddell Hart*, Vol. 1 (Cassell, London, 1965).

Liebmann, General der Infanterie, 'Die deutschen Gefechtsvorschriften von 1914 in der Feuerprobe des Krieges', *Militärwissenschaftliche Rundschau* 2(4) (1937).

Lloyd, E. M., *A Review of the History of Infantry* (1908, reprinted Greenwood, Westport, 1976).

Ludendorff, General E., *My War Memories, 1914–1918*, 2 vols. (Hutchinson, London, n.d.).

—, *Urkunden der Obersten Heeresleitung über ihre Tätigkeit, 1916–18* (Mittler, Berlin, 1920).

MacDougall, General P. L.,'Our System of Infantry Tactics: What is It?', *The Nineteenth Century* 17 (May 1885).

Martin, B., *Poor Bloody Infantry* (John Murray, London, 1987).

Maude, Colonel F. N., *Notes on the Evolution of Infantry Tactics* (Clowes, London, 1905).

Meiklejohn, Major M. F. M., 'Infantry Officers for War',*AR* 1(1) (1911).

Miksche, Major F. O., *Blitzkrieg*, 2nd edn (Faber & Faber, London, 1942).

'The Military System of Germany',*AR* 1(1) (July 1911).

Moser, General O. von., *Feldzugsautzeichnungen als Brigade–, Divisions-kommandeur und als kommandierender General, 1914–1918* (Belsersche, Stuttgart, 1920).

'The Other Side of the Hill', a series of articles published in the *Army Quarterly*:

1. 'The German Defence during the Battle of the Somme, July, 1916', *AQ* 7(2) (Jan. 1924).
2. 'The German Defence during the Battle of the Somme, July, 1916', *AQ* 8(1) (April 1924).
3. 'The Fight for Hill 70, 25th–26th of September, 1915', *AQ* 8(2) (July 1924).
4. 'Mametz Wood and Contalmaisons, 9th–10th of July, 1916', *AQ* 9(2) (January 1925).
5. 'The German Defence of Bernafay and Trones Woods, 2nd–14th of July, 1916', Part I, *AQ* 13(1) (Oct. 1926).
6. 'The German Defence of Bernafay . . .', Part II, *AQ* 13(2) (Jan. 1927).
7. 'The German Attack at Vimy Ridge, May 1916', *AQ* 17(1) (Oct. 1928).
8. 'Cambrai: The Action of the German 107th Division', *AQ* 20(2) (July 1930).
9. 'The Somme: 15th of September, 1916', *AQ* 26(2) (July 1930).

10. 'The Capture of Thiepval, 26th of September, 1916', *AQ* 27(2) (Jan. 1934).
11. 'In Front of Beaumont-Hamel, 13th of November, 1916', *AQ* 28(1) (April 1934).
12. 'The Night Attack at Landrecies, 25th of August, 1914', *AQ* 28(2) (July 1934).
13. 'The Fight for Zonnebeke, 26th of September, 1917', *AQ* 29(1) (Oct. 1934).
14. 'The Fight for Inverness Copse, 22nd–24th of August, 1917', *AQ* 29(2) (Jan. 1935).
15. 'The Battle of Vimy Ridge, 9th of April, 1917', *AQ* 33(1) (Oct. 1936).
16. 'Aubers Ridge, 9th of May, 1915', *AQ* 36(2) (July 1938).
17. 'Neuve Chapelle, 10th–12th March, 1915', *AQ* 37(1) (Oct. 1938).

Rohrbeck, Major, *Taktik: Ein Handbuch auf Grund der Erfahrungen des Weltkrieges* (Mittler, Berlin, 1919).

Rosinski, H. (G. A. Craig, ed.), *The German Army* (Pall Mall, London, 1966).

Schellendorff, General Bronsart von, *The Duties of the General Staff*, 3rd edn, revised by Colonel Meckel (trans. Lieutenant-Colonel W. A. H. Hare) (HMSO, London, 1895).

'Schlieffen's Tactical-Strategic Problems', *AQ* 38(1) (April 1939).

Schwarte, Generalleutnant M., *Die Militärischen Lehren des Grossen Krieges* (Mittler, Berlin, 1923).

Spohn, Colonel von, 'The Art of Command', *Jahrbücher für die deutsche Armee und Marine* (October 1907, reprinted Bates, Manchester, 1932).

Stallings, L., *The First World War: A Photographic History* (Daily Express, London, 1933).

Stosch, Oberstleutnant A. von, *Somme-Nord, I. Teil: Die Brennpünkte der Schlacht im Juli 1916* (Reichsarchiv, Schlachten des Weltkrieges, Vol. 20) (Mittler, Berlin, 1927).

Sulzbach, H., *With the German Guns* (Leo Cooper, London, 1973).

Swinton, Major-General E. D., *Eyewitness: Being Personal Reminiscences of Certain Phases of the Great War, Including the Genesis of the Tank* (Hodder & Stoughton, London, 1932).

Thompson, Major T., 'Notes on the German Post-War Training Regulations', *AQ* 8(1) (July 1924).

Volckheim, Major E., *Die deutschen Kampfwagen im Weltkriege* (Mittler, Berlin, 1937).

Wade, Major E. W. N., 'From Maxim to Vickers', *AQ* 28(1) (April 1934).

*Was bringen Feldienst-Ordnung und Manöver-Ordnung vom 22. März 1908 Neues?* (Mittler, Berlin, 1908).

Wheeler, Captain O., *The War Office: Past and Present* (Methuen, London, 1914).

Wilkinson, S., *The Brain of an Army. A Popular Account of the German General Staff* (Macmillan, London, 1890).

William, Crown Prince of Germany, *My War Experiences* (Hurst & Blackett, London, 1922).

Wright, Major R. M., 'Machine-Gun Tactics and Organisation', *AQ* 1(2) (Jan. 1921).

## *Unit and Formation Histories*

Alten, Hauptmann H. H. von, *et al.*, *Geschichte des Garde-Schützen-Bataillons 1914–1919* (Erinnerungsblätter deutscher Regimenter, Nr. 234) (Stalling, Berlin, 1928).

'Alten Einsern', *Das K. B. 1. Infanterie-Regiment König* (Erinnerungsblätter deutscher Regimenter, Bayerische Armee, Nr. 8) (Bayerische Kriegsarschiv, Munich, 1922).

Arthur, J. W. and I. S. Munro, eds, *The Seventeenth Highland Light Infantry (Glasgow Chamber of Commerce Battalion). Record of War Service 1914–1918* (Clark, Glasgow, 1920).

Atkinson, C. T., *The Seventh Division 1914–1918* (John Murray, London, 1927).

Barlow C. A. M., *The Lancashire Fusiliers. The Roll of Honour of the Salford Brigade (15th, 16th, 19th, 20th and 21st Lancashire Fusiliers)* (Sheratt & Hughes, London, 1919).

Biermann, 'Die Entwicklung der deutschen Minenwerferwaffe', in P. Heinrici, ed., *Das Ehrenbuch der deutschen Pioniere* (Rolf, Berlin, 1931).

Bond, Lieutenant-Colonel R. C., *History of the King's Own Yorkshire Light Infantry in the Great War 1914–1918*, Vol. 3 (London, 1929).

Boraston, Lieutenant-Colonel J. H. & Captain C. E. O. Bax, *The Eighth Division in War, 1914–1918* (Medici, London, 1926).

Brandis, Hauptmann C. von., *Die vom Douaumont. Das Ruppiner Regiment 24 im Weltkrieg* (Erinnerungsblätter deutscher Regimenter, Nr. 305) (Kolk, Berlin, 1930).

Buchan, J., *The History of the Royal Scots Fusiliers (1678–1918)* (Nelson, London, 1925).

Burrowes, Brigadier-General A. R., *The 1st Battalion The Faugh-A-Ballaghs in the Great War* (Gale & Polden, Aldershot, 1926).

Campbell, Captain G. L., *The Manchesters* (Picture Advertising, London, 1916).

Chalmers, T., *A Saga of Scotland. History of the 16th Battalion The Highland Light Infantry (City of Glasgow Regiment)* (McCallum, Glasgow, 1930).

—, *An Epic of Glasgow. History of the 15th Battalion The Highland Light Infantry (City of Glasgow Regiment)* (McCallum, Glasgow, 1934).

Commonwealth War Graves Commission, *The 7th Division in France and Flanders.*

—, *The 30th Division in France and Flanders.*

—, *The 32nd Division in France and Flanders.*

Cooke, Captain C. H., *Historical Records of the 16th (Service) Battalion Northumberland Fusiliers* (private, Newcastle-upon-Tyne, 1923).

Cunliffe, M., *The Royal Irish Fusiliers 1793–1950* (Oxford University Press, London, 1952).

Falls, Captain C., *The History of the 36th (Ulster) Division* (McCaw, Belfast, 1922).

—, *The History of the First Seven Battalions The Royal Irish Rifles in the Great War*, Vol. 2 (Gale & Polden, Aldershot, 1925).

Farndale, Brigadier M. B., 'The Royal Artillery in World War I', *Proceedings of the Royal Artillery Historical Society* (29 April 1976).

—, General, *History of the Royal Regiment of Artillery: Western Front 1914–18* (Royal Artillery Institution, London, 1986).

—, *History of the Royal Regiment of Artillery: The Forgotten Fronts and the Home Base 1914–18* (Royal Artillery Institution, London, 1988).

Feeser, Generalmajor F., 'Infanterie-Geschütze, Tank-Abwehr-Geschütze und Begleit-Batterien', in Oberstleutnant A. Benary, ed., *Das Ehrenbuch der Deutschen Feldartillerie* (Volk, Berlin, 1931).

'The 56th Division', *Stand To! The Journal of the Western Front Association* 31 (Spring 1991), 18.

Fox, F., *The Royal Inniskilling Fusiliers in the World War* (Constable, London, 1928).

Fuhrmann, Major H. *et al.*, *Königlich Preussiches Reserve-Infanterie-Regiment Nr. 211 im Weltkriege 1914–1918* (Deutsche Tat im Weltkrieg 1914/1918, Vol. 18) (Bernard & Graefe, Berlin, 1933).

Gieraths, G., *Geschichte des Reserve-Infanterie-Regiments Nr. 210* (Erinnerungsblätter deutscher Regimenter, Nr. 231) (Stalling, Berlin, 1928).

Gottber, Generalmajor D. von, *Das Infanterie-Regiment Nr. 464 im Weltkriege* (Prelle, Osnabrück, 1932).

Grosskopf, G., *Sturmbataillon Nr. 1 (einschl. bayer. Infanterie-Geschütz-Batterie Nr. 2) im Weltkrieg 19165/18* (Neumeyer, Landsberg, 1938).

Harris, H., *The Irish Regiments in the First World War* (Mercier, Cork, 1968).

Heinrici, P., ed., *Das Ehrenbuch der Deutschen Pioniere* (Rolf, Berlin, 1931).

Hoffmann, R., ed., *Infanterie-Regiment 463* (Leuver, Bremen, 1930).

Kendrick, Colonel, N. C. E., *The Story of the Wiltshire Regiment (Duke of Edinburgh's). The 62nd and 99th Foot (1756–1959)* (Gale & Polden, Aldershot, 1963).

Latter, Major-General J. C., *The History of the Lancashire Fusiliers 1914–1918*, Vol. 1 (Gale & Polden, Aldershot, 1949).

Makoben, Leutnant E., *Geschichte des Reserve-Infanterie-Regiments Nr. 212 im Weltkriege 1914–1918* (Erinnerungsblätter deutscher Regimenter, Nr. 352) Stalling, Berlin, 1933).

Maurice, Major-General F., *The 16th Foot. A History of The Bedfordshire and Hertfordshire Regiment* (Constable, London, 1931).

Möller, H., *Geschichte des Paderborner Infanterie-Regiment (7.Lothring.) Nr. 158* (Deutsche Tat im Weltkrieg 1914/1918, Nr. 32) (Bernard & Graefe, Berlin, 1939).

Mücke, Rittmeister K. von, *Das Grossherzöglich Badische Infanterie-Regiment Nr. 185* (Erinnerungsblatter deutscher Regimenter, Nr. 58) (Stalling, Berlin, 1922).

Mullaly, Colonel B. R., *The South Lancashire Regiment, The Prince of Wales's Volunteers* (White Swan, Bristol, 1955).

Nagel, L., *Württembergische Sturmkompagnie (Sturm-Btl 16) im grossen Krieg* (Körner, Stuttgart, 1930).

Oatts, Lieutenant-Colonel L. B., *Proud Heritage: The Story of the Highland Light Infantry*, Vol. 3 (Grant, London, 1961).

Orr, P., *The Road to the Somme: Men of the Ulster Division Tell Their Story* (Blackstaff, Belfast, 1987).

Reddemann, Mahor, 'Die Totenkopf Pioniere', in P. Heinrici, ed., *Das Ehrenbuch der deutschen Pioniere* (Rolf, Berlin, 1931), 516–24.

Richter, Oberleutnant W., *Das Danziger Infanterie-Regiment Nr. 128*, Vol. 1 (Aus Deutschlands grosser Zeit, Nr. 30) (Sporn, Zeulenrode-Thür, 1931).

Rudorff, Oberstleutnant F. von, *Das Fusilier-Regiment General Ludendorff (Niederrheinischen) Nr. 39 im Weltkriege 1914–1918* (Erinnerungsblätter deutscher Regimenter, Nr. 125) (Kühn, Berlin, 1925).

Seydel, Oberst A., *Das Grenadier-Regiment König Friedrich I (4. Ostpreussiches) Nr. 5 im Weltkriege* (Erinnerungsblätter deutscher Regimenter, Nr. 188) (Berlin, 1926).

Stanley, Brigadier-General F. C., *The History of the 89th Brigade 1914–1918* (Daily Post, Liverpool, 1919).

Staubwasser, Generalmajor O., *Das K. B. 2. Infanterie-Regiment Kronpirinz* (Erinnerungsblätter deutscher Regimenter, Bayerische Armee, Nr. 24) (Bayerische Kriegasarschiv, Munich, 1924).

Troilo, Oberstleutnant H. von., *Das 5. Westfälische Infanterie-Regiment Nr. 53 im Weltkrieg 1914–1919* (Erinnerungsblätter deutscher Regimenter, Nr. 109) (Stalling, Berlin, 1924).

Vischer, Oberst, *Das württembergische Infanterie-Regiment Nr. 180 im Weltkrieg 1914–1918* (Belsersche, Stuttgart 1921).

Ward, Major D., 'History of the 1st Battalion' in *History of the Dorsetshire Regiment, 1914–1919: part 1, The Regular Battalions* (Ling, Dorchester, 1932).

Westropp, Brigadier-General H. C. E., *Sixteenth, Seventeenth, Eighteenth, Nineteenth Battalions, The Manchester Regiment (First City Brigade) A Record 1914–1918* (Sheratt & Hughes, Manchester, 1923).

Whalley-Kelly, Captain H., *'Ich Dien'. The Prince of Wales's Volunteers (South Lancashire) 1914–1934* (Gale & Polden, Aldershot, 1935).

White, A. S., *A Bibliography of Regimental Histories of the British Army* (Society for Army Historical Research, London, 1965).

Wurmb, Major H. von, *Das K. B. Reserve-Infanterie-Regiment Nr. 8* (Erinnerungsblätter deutscher Regimenter, Bayerische Armee, Nr. 55) (Schick, Munich, 1929).

Wylly, Colonel H. C., *The Border Regiment in the Great War* (Gale & Polden, Aldershot, 1924).

—, *The Green Howards in the Great War 1914–1919* (Richmond, 1926).

Wyrall, E., *The History of the King's Regiment (Liverpool) 1914–1919: Vol. 3, 1917–1919* (Edward Arnold, London, 1935).

## *Secondary Sources*

Alfoldi, L. M., 'The Hutier Legend', *Parameters* 5 (1976).

Ascoli, D., *A Companion to the British Army, 1660–1983* (Book Club Associates, London, 1984).

Badsey, S., 'Mounted Combat in the Second Boer War', *Sandhurst Journal of Military Studies* 2 (1991).

Bailey, Major J. B. A., *Field Artillery and Firepower* (Military Press, Oxford, 1989).

Barnett, C., *The Swordbearers* (Eyre & Spottiswoode, London, 1963).

Baynes, J., *Morale: A Study of Men and Courage. The Second Scottish Rifles at the Battle of Neuve Chapelle, 1915* (Leo Cooper, London, 1967).

Beckett, I., 'The Nation in Arms, 1914–18', in I. F. W. Beckett and K. Simpson, *A Nation in Arms: A Social Study of the British Army in the First World War* (Manchester University Press, 1985).
—, 'The Territorial Force', in I. F. W. Beckett and K. Simpson, *A Nation in Arms*.
Bidwell, Brigadier S., *Gunners at War: A Tactical Study of the Royal Artillery in the Twentieth Century* (Arms & Armour, London, 1970).
—, and D. Graham, *Firepower, British Army Weapons and Theories of War, 1904–1945* (Allen & Unwin, London, 1982).
Bond, B., *The Victorian Army and the Staff College, 1854–1914* (Methuen, London, 1972).
Borgert, H-L., 'Grundzüge der Landkriegführung von Schlieffen bis Guderian', in Militärgeschichtliches Forschungsamt, ed., *Handbuch zur deutschen Militärgeschichte 1648–1939*, Vol. IX (Bernard & Graefe, Munich, 1979).
Bull, S., 'British Grenade Tactics, 1914–18', *MI* 7 (June–July 1987).
—, 'German Grenades and Bombing Tactics, 1914–18 (1)', *MI* 15 (October–November 1988).
—, 'German Grenades and Bombing Tactics, 1914–18 (2)', *MI* 16 (December–January 1988–89).
Chasseaud, P., *Trench Maps*, Vol. 1 (Mapbooks, Lewes, 1986).
Clark, A., *The Donkeys* (Hutchinson, London, 1961).
Craig, G. A., *The Battle of Königgrätz* (Weidenfeld & Nicolson, London, 1965).
—, *The Germans* (Pelican, London, 1984).
Cron, Oberstleutnant H., *Geschichte des Deutschen Heeres im Weltkriege 1914–1918* (Siegismund, Berlin, 1937).
Cushman, Lieutenant-General J. H., 'Challenge and Response at the Operational and Tactical Levels, 1914–45', in A. R. Millett and W. Murray, *Military Effectiveness: Vol. 3, The Second World War* (Allen & Unwin, Boston, 1988).
De Groot, G. J., *Douglas Haig, 1861–1928* (Unwin Hyman, London, 1988).
Dixon, N. F., *On the Psychology of Military Incompetence* (Futura, Aylesbury, 1979).
Dunn, Captain J. C., *The War the Infantry Knew 1914–1919* (Sphere, London, 1989).
Dupuy, Colonel T. N., *A Genius for War: The German Army and the General Staff, 1807–1945* (Macdonald & Jane's, London, 1977).
Elliott-Bateman, M., *Defeat in the East* (Oxford University Press, 1967).
—, S. S. Fitzgibbon and M. Samuels, 'Vocabulary: The Second Problem of Military Reform: Part 1 – Concepts', *Defense Analysis* (1990).
English, Lieutenant-Colonel J. A., *A Perspective on Infantry* (Praeger, New York, 1981).
Essame, H., *The Battle for Europe, 1918* (Batsford, London, 1972).
Falls, Captain C., *Caporetto 1917* (Weidenfeld & Nicolson, London, 1966).
Farrar-Hockley, A. H., *The Somme* (Pan, London, 1983).
Geyer, M., 'German Strategy in the Age of Machine Warfare, 1914–1945', in P. Paret, ed., *Makers of Modern Strategy* (Oxford University Press, 1986).
Goerlitz, W., *History of the German General Staff, 1657–1945* (trans. B. Battershaw) (Hollis & Carter, 1953).
Gooch, J., *The Plans of War: The General Staff and British Military Strategy c.1900–1916* (Routledge & Kegan Paul, London, 1974).

Goodspeed, D. J., *Ludendorff* (Hart-Davis, London, 1966).
Graham, D., 'Sans Doctrine: British Army Tactics in the First World War', in T. Travers and C. Archer, eds., *Men at War, Politics, Technology and Innovation in the Twentieth Century* (Precedent, Chicago, 1982).
Griffith, P., *Forward into Battle: Fighting Tactics from Waterloo to Vietnam* (Bird, Chichester, 1981).
Gruss, H., 'Aufbau und Verwendung der deutschen Sturmbataillone im Weltkrieg' (unpublished PhD. dissertation, Berlin University, 1939).
Gudmundsson, B. I., *Stormtroop Tactics: Innovation in the German Army, 1914–1918* (Praeger, New York, 1989).
Hamer, W. S.. *The British Army: Civil–Military Relations, 1885–1905* (Clarendon, Oxford, 1970).
Harries-Jenkins, G., *The Army in Victorian Society* (Routledge & Kegan Paul, London, 1977).
Herwig, H. H., 'The Dynamics of Necessity: German Military Policy during the First World War', in Millett and Murray, *Military Effectiveness: Vol. 1.*
Hogg, I. V. and L. F. Thurston, *British Artillery Weapons and Ammunition, 1914–1918* (Ian Allan, London, 1972).
Holborn, H., 'Moltke and Schlieffen: The Prussian–German School', in E. M. Earle, ed., *Makers of Modern Strategy* (Princeton University Press, 1943).
Holmes, R., *The Little Field-Marshal: Sir John French* (Jonathan Cape, London, 1981).
Horne, A., *The Fall of Paris* (Penguin, Harmondsworth, 1981).
—, *The Price of Glory: Verdun 1916* (Penguin, Harmondsworth, 1964).
House, Captain J. M., 'Towards Combined Arms Warfare: A Survey of 20th-Century Tactics, Doctrine, and Organisation', *Research Survey* 2 (Fort Leavenworth, August, 1984).
Howard, M., *The Franco-Prussian War, The German Invasion of France, 1870–1879* (Routledge, London, 1961).
Howard, M., 'Men against Fire: The Doctrine of the Offensive in 1914', in P. Paret, ed., *Makers of Modern Strategy* (Oxford University Press, 1986).
Hughes, C., 'The New Armies', in I. F. W. Beckett and K. Simpson, *A Nation in Arms: A Social Study of the British Army in the First World War* (Manchester University Press, 1985).
Hughes, D. J., 'Abuses of German Military History', *MR* (December 1986).
—, *The King's Finest: A Social and Bureaucratic Profile of Prussia's General Officers, 1870–1914* (Praeger, New York, 1987).
Keegan, J., *The Face of Battle* (Penguin, Harmondsworth, 1978).
—, *The Price of Admiralty: War at Sea from Man of War to Submarine* (Hutchinson, London, 1988).
Kennedy, P., 'Britain in the First World War', in A. R. Millett and W. Murray, eds., *Military Effectiveness: Vol. 1, The First World War* (Allen & Unwin, Boston, 1988).
Kitchen, M., *The German Officer Corps 1890–1914* (Oxford University Press, 1968).
Laffin, J., *British Butchers and Bunglers of World War One* (Alan Sutton, Gloucester, 1988).

Lind, W., *Maneuver War Handbook* (Colorado, 1985).
Lossow, Lieutenant-Colonel W. von, 'Mission-Type Tactics versus Order-Type Tactics', *MR* (June 1977).
Lupfer, Captain T. T., 'The Dynamics of Doctrine: The Changes in German Tactical Doctrine During the First World War', *Leavenworth Papers* 4 (Fort Leavenworth, Kansas, 1981).
Macdonald, L., *Somme* (Papermac, London, 1983).
—, *1914* (Penguin, Harmondsworth, 1989).
Macksey, K., *Guderian, Panzer General* (Macdonald & Jane's, London, 1974).
Matuschka, E. Graf von, 'Organisationsgeschichte des Heeres, 1890–1918', in Militärgeschichtliches Forschungsamt, ed., *Handbuch zur deutschen Militärgeschichte, 1648–1939*, Vol. V (Bernard & Graefe, Munich, 1968).
Messenger, C., *Trench Fighting 1914–18* (Ballantine, London, 1973).
Meyer, B. J., 'Operational Art and the German Command System in World War I', (unpublished PhD. dissertation, Ohio State University, 1988).
Middlebrook, M., *The Kaiser's Battle: 21 March 1918, The First Day of the German Spring Offensive* (Penguin, Harmondsworth, 1983).
—, *The First Day of the Somme, 1 July 1916* (Penguin, Harmondsworth, 1984).
Militärgeschichtliches Forschungsamt, ed., 'Die Generalstäbe in Deutschland 1871–1945', *Beiträge zur Militär- und Kriegsgeschichte* 3 (1962).
Millett, A. R., and W. Murray (eds), *Military Effectiveness Vol. 1: The First World War* (Allen & Unwin, Boston, 1988).
Millett, A. R., W. Murray and K. H. Watman, 'The Effectiveness of Military Organisations', in Millett and Murray, *Military Effectiveness: Vol. 1.*
Mitchinson, K. W., 'The Reconstitution of 169 Brigade: July–October 1916', *Stand To! The Journal of the Western Front Association* 29 (summer 1990).
—, 'The "Transfer Controversy": Parliament and the London Regiment', *Stand To! Journal of the Western Front Association* 33 (Winter 1991).
Model, H., *Der deutsche Generalstabsoffizier* (Bernard & Graefe, Frankfurt-am-Main, 1968).
Mountcastle, Lieutenant-Colonel J. W., 'On the Move: Command and Control of Armour Units in Combat', *MR* (Nov. 1985).
Nash, D., *German Infantry 1914–18* (Almark, London, 1971).
—, *Imperial German Army Handbook, 1914–18* (Ian Allan, London, 1980).
Ose, D., 'Der Auftrag: eine deutsche militärische Tradition', *Europäische Wehrkunde* 31 (6) (1982).
Otto, H., 'Enstehung und Wesen des Blitzkriegsstrategie des deutschen Imperialismus vor dem ersten Weltkrieg', *Zeitschrift für Militärgeschichte* 6 (1967).
Parkinson, R., *Tormented Warrior: Ludendorff and the Supreme Command* (Hodder & Stoughton, London, 1978).
Perry, F. W., *The Commonwealth Armies. Manpower and Organisation in Two World Wars* (Manchester University Press, 1988).
Pitt, B., *1918: The Last Act* (Papermac, London, 1984).
Pohlman, Oberst H., 'Die deutsche Infanterie-Division von 1870 bis 1945', *Feldgrau* 2 (1954).
Pollen, A., *The Great Gunnery Scandal: The Mystery of Jutland* (Collins, London, 1980).

Pridham, Major C. H. B., *Superiority of Fire: A Short History of Rifles and Machine Guns* (Hutchinson, London, 1945).

Regling, V., 'Grundzüge der militärischen Kriegführung zur Zeit des Absolutismus und im 19. Jahrhundert', in Militärgeschichtliches Forschungsamt, ed., *Handbuch zur deutschen Militärgeschichte 1648–1939*, Vol. IX (Bernard & Graefe, Munich, 1979).

Remarque, E. M. (trans. A. W. Wheen), *All Quiet on the Western Front* (1929, republished Picador, London, n.d.).

Ritter, G. (trans. A. and E. Wilson), *The Schlieffen Plan: Critique of a Myth* (Oswald Wolff, London, 1958).

Rothenberg, G. E., 'Moltke, Schlieffen, and the Doctrine of Strategic Envelopment', in P. Paret, ed., *Makers of Modern Strategy* (Oxford University Press, 1986).

Samuels, M., 'The Reality of Cannae', *Militärgeschichtliche Mitteilungen* 1/90 (1990).

—, 'Operation GOODWOOD: "The Caen Carve-up"', *British Army Review* 96 (Dec. 1990).

—, *Doctrine and Dogma: German and British Infantry Tactics in the First World War* (Greenwood, Westport, 1992).

Sheffield, G. D., 'British Military Police and their Battlefield Role, 1914–18', *Sandhurst Journal of Military Studies* 1 (1990).

Showalter, D., 'The Retaming of Bellona: Prussia and the Institutionalisation of the Napoleonic Legacy, 1815–1876', *Military Affairs* 44 (1980).

—, 'Army and Society in Imperial Germany: The Pains of Modernisation', *Journal of Contemporary History* 18 (1983).

—, *German Military History 1648–1982: A Critical Bibliography* (Garland, New York, 1984).

—, *Railroads and Rifles: Soldiers, Technology and the Unification of Germany* (Archon, Hamden, 1986).

—, 'Goltz and Bernhardi: The Institutionalisation of Originality in the Imperial German Army', *Defense Analysis* 3 (1987).

Simkins, P., *Kitchener's Army: The Raising of the New Armies 1914–16* (Manchester University Press, 1988).

Simpson, K., 'The Officers', in I. F. W. Beckett and K. Simpson (eds), *A Nation in Arms: A Social Study of the British Army in the First World War* (Manchester University Press, 1985).

Sixsmith, Major-General E. K. G., *British Generalship in the Twentieth Century* (Arms & Armour, London, 1970).

Speier, H., 'Ludendorff: The German Concept of Total War', in E. M. Earle (ed.), *Makers of Modern Strategy* (Princeton University Press, 1943).

Spiers, E. M., *Haldane: an Army Reformer* (Edinburgh University Press, 1980).

—, 'The Regular Army in 1914', in I. F. W. Beckett and K. Simpson (eds), *A Nation in Arms: A Social Study of the British Army in the First World War* (Manchester University Press, 1985).

Stone, J., 'The Anglo-Boer War and Military Reforms in the United Kingdom', in J. Stone and E. A. Schmidl, *The Boer War and Military Reforms* (University Press of America, London, 1988).

Terraine, J., *Douglas Haig: The Educated Soldier* (Hutchinson, London, 1963).
—, *The Smoke and the Fire: Myths and Anti-Myths of War, 1861–1945* (Book Club Associates, London, 1981).
—, *White Heat: The New Warfare 1914–18* (Sidgwick & Jackson, London, 1982).
—, *The First World War 1914–18* (Papermac, London, 1984).
—, *To Win a War: 1918, The Year of Victory* (Papermac, London, 1986).
Toland, J., *No Man's Land: The Story of 1918* (Methuen, London, 1982).
Travers, T. H. E., 'The Offensive and the Problem of Innovation in British Military Thought 1870–1915', *Journal of Contemporary History* 13 (1978).
—, 'Technology, Tactics, and Morale: Jean de Bloch, the Boer War and British Military Theory, 1900–1914', *Journal of Modern History* 51 (1979).
—, 'The Hidden Army: Structural Problems in the British Officer Corps, 1900–1918', *Journal of Contemporary History* 17 (1982).
—, 'Learning and Decision-Making on the Western Front, 1915–1916: The British Example', *Canadian Journal of History* 18 (1983).
—, *The Killing Ground: The British Army, The Western Front and The Emergence of Modern Warfare, 1900–1918* (Allen & Unwin, London, 1987).
—, 'A Particular Style of Command: Haig and GHQ, 1916–18', *Journal of Strategic Studies* 10 (1987).
—, 'The Evolution of British Strategy and Tactics on the Western Front in 1918: GHQ, Manpower, and Technology', *Journal of Military History* 54(2) (April 1990).
Van Creveld, M., *Supplying War: Logistics from Wallenstein to Patton* (Cambridge University Press, 1977).
—, *Fighting Power: German and U.S. Army Performance, 1939–1945* (Greenwood, Westport, 1982).
—, *Command in War* (Harvard University Press, Cambridge, 1985).
—, *Technology and War: From 1000 B.C. to the Present* (Free Press, New York, 1989).
Wallach, J. L., *The Dogma of Annihilation: The Theories of Clausewitz and Schlieffen and Their Impact on the German Conduct of Two World Wars* (Greenwood, Westport, 1986).
Walter, J. (ed.), *Guns of the First World War* (Greenhill, London, 1988).
Wilson, Lieutenant-Colonel H. R. G., 'Aggression, Initiative and Speed. The Case for the Revival of the Counterattack as a Basic Tactic', *British Army Review* 81 (Dec. 1985).
Winter, D., *Death's Men: Soldiers of the Great War* (Penguin, Harmondsworth, 1979).
—, *Haig's Command: A Reassessment* (Viking, Harmondsworth, 1991).
Wray, Major T. A., 'Standing Fast: German Defensive Doctrine on the Russian Front During World War II, Prewar to March 1943', *Research Survey* 5 (Fort Leavenworth, Kansas, 1986).
Wynne, Captain G. C., 'The Development of the German Defensive Battle in 1917, and its Influence on British Defensive Tactics'; Part I, *AQ* 34(1) (April 1937); Part II, 'The Counterattack Divisions', *AQ* 34(2) (July 1937); Part III, 'Field Service Regulation (1935)', *AQ* 35(1) (Oct. 1937).
—, 'The British Attack from Monchy-le-Preux on the 14th of April, 1917, and Commentary', *AQ* 35(2) (Jan. 1938).

—, 'The Chain of Command', *AQ* 36(1) (April 1938).
—, 'The Hindenburg Line', *AQ* 37(2) (Jan. 1939).
—, 'The Wotan Position', *AQ* 38(2) (July 1939).
—, 'The Legacy', *AQ* 39(1) (Oct. 1939).
—, 'Pattern for Limited (Nuclear) War: The Riddle of the Schlieffen Plan – Part 1', *Royal United Services Institute Journal* 102(4) (Nov. 1957).
—, 'Pattern for Limited (Nuclear) War: The Riddle of the Schlieffen Plan – Part 2', *Royal United Services Institute Journal* 103(1) (Feb. 1958).
—, 'Pattern for Limited (Nuclear) War: The Riddle of the Schlieffen Plan – Part 3', *Royal United Services Institute Journal* 103(2) (May 1958).
—, *If Germany Attacks: The Battle in Depth in the West* (1940, reprinted Greenwood, Westport, 1976).
Young, Lieutenant-Colonel F. W. (ed.), *The Story of the Staff College* (Camberley, 1958).

# Index

Printed in the USA/Agawam, MA
February 11, 2010

539695.095